1,001 Ingenious gardening Ideas

1,001 Ingenious gardening Ideas

New, Fun, and Fabulous Tips That Will Change the Way You Garden—Forever!

Deborah L. Martin, editor

Contributing Writers: Sally Jean Cunningham, George DeVault, Melanie DeVault, Erin Hynes, Tina James, Susan McClure, Sally Roth, Jo Ellen Meyers Sharp, and Sara Jane von Trapp

Rodale Press, Inc.
Emmaus, Pennsylvania

©1999 by Rodale Press, Inc.

Illustrations ©1999 by Elayne Sears

We're always happy to hear from you. For questions or comments concerning the editorial content of this book, please write to:

Rodale Press, Inc.
Book Readers' Service
33 East Minor Street
Emmaus, PA 18098

Look for other Rodale books wherever books are sold. Or call us at (800) 848-4735.
For more information about Rodale Press and the books and magazines we publish, visit our World Wide Web site at:
http://www.rodalepress.com

Editor: Deborah L. Martin

Contributing Editors: Karen Bolesta, Christine Bucks, and Karen Costello Soltys

Researcher: Heidi A. Stonehill

Cover and Interior Book Designer: Nancy Smola Biltcliff

Layout Designer: Susan P. Eugster

Cover and Interior Illustrator: Elayne Sears

Copy Editors: Christine Bucher, Erana Bumbardatore, and Stacey Ann Follin

Manufacturing Coordinator: Mark Krahforst

Indexer: Lina Burton

Editorial Assistance: Sarah S. Dunn, Susan L. Nickol, and Pamela R. Ruch

RODALE GARDEN BOOKS

Executive Editor: Ellen Phillips

Managing Editor: Fern Marshall Bradley

Associate Art Director: Patricia Field

Associate Copy Manager: Jennifer Hornsby

Studio Manager: Leslie M. Keefe

Production Manager: Robert V. Anderson Jr.

Manufacturing Manager: Mark Krahforst

Library of Congress Cataloging-in-Publication Data

    1,001 ingenious gardening ideas : new, fun, and fabulous tips that will change the way you garden—forever! / Deborah L. Martin, editor; contributing writers, Sally Jean Cunningham…[et al.].
        p.   cm.
    Includes bibliographical references and index.
    ISBN 0–87596–809–0 (hardcover : alk. paper)
    1. Gardening—Miscellanea. 2. Organic gardening—Miscellanea.
I. Martin, Deborah L. II. Cunningham, Sally Jean. III. Title: One thousand one ingenious gardening ideas IV. Title: One thousand and one ingenious gardening ideas
SB453 .A125 1999
635—dc21
                                      99–6038

Distributed in the book trade by St. Martin's Press

2 4 6 8 10 9 7 5 3 1   hardcover

Here at Rodale Press, we've been gardening organically for over 50 years—ever since my grandfather J. I. Rodale learned about composting and decided that healthy living starts with healthy soil. In 1940, J. I. started the Rodale Organic Farm to test his theories, and today, the nonprofit Rodale Institute Experimental Farm is still at the forefront of organic gardening and farming research. In 1942, J. I. founded *Organic Gardening* magazine to share his discoveries with gardeners everywhere. His son, my father, Robert Rodale, headed *Organic Gardening* until 1990, and today, the fourth generation of Rodales is growing up with the magazine. Over the years, we've shown millions of readers how to grow bountiful crops and beautiful flowers using nature's own techniques.

In this book, you'll find the latest organic methods and the best gardening advice. We know—because all our authors and editors are passionate about gardening! We feel strongly that our gardens should be safe for our children, pets, and the birds and butterflies that add beauty and delight to our lives and landscapes. Our gardens should provide us with fresh, flavorful vegetables, delightful herbs, and gorgeous flowers. And they should be a pleasure to work in as well as to view.

Sharing the secrets of safe, successful gardening is why we publish books. So come visit us at the Rodale Institute Experimental Farm, where you can tour the gardens every day—we're open year-round. And use this book to create your best garden ever.

Over the years, we've shown millions of readers how to grow bountiful crops and beautiful flowers using nature's own techniques.

Happy gardening!

Maria Rodale

Maria Rodale
Rodale Garden Books

CONTENTS
Contents

Nifty tools you can make, recycle, or reuse, including how to
turn a plastic milk jug into a cultivator, new uses for broken
tools, protecting your pants from your pruners, and three things
you can do with an old tire

What you need to know to make your own black gold—from what to
put in your pile and how to keep critters out, to creative compost bins,
a medley of mulch materials, super soil builders, and new uses for old
newspaper

Ingenious approaches to making mulch and supporting plants, clever
watering tricks, keeping row covers on, winter protection for roses,
and three neat ways to make garden pathways using broken dishes,
terra-cotta, or burlap

Harvest your earliest tomatoes ever, learn how to get a head start in
spring, turn everyday items into inexpensive cold frames, unlock the
secrets of a four-season harvest, and discover how to grow a great
garden under cover

Sow like a pro, and learn new ways to make sure every seed sprouts,
including presprouting secrets, transplanting tools, the best seed-starting
containers, lessons in lighting, and how to store all those extra seeds

Strange-but-true organic techniques for confounding critters—from
can't-fail companion planting combos and five ways to protect your
bulbs, to new life for old panty hose and creating a hindrance out of
human hair

Out in the Garden

How to Be an Ingenious Gardener

Gardening is about taking chances. Planting a garden is a gamble that the small, dry seeds and tiny plants you place in the soil will grow into something beautiful and productive. Being an *ingenious* gardener means doing things to improve your odds.

In this book, we've gathered more than 1,000 ingenious ideas from gardeners across the country and around the world who have found ways to tip the scales in favor of gardening success. Some of the ideas are remarkably simple, such as using the moistened tip of a toothpick to sow very small seeds. Others are full-scale systems that will let you garden year-round, no matter where your garden grows. But large or small, complex or simple, every tip in this book has passed this test: A real gardener has used it to make gardening easier, more successful, more productive, and more fun.

Browse for Inspiration

If you're already feeling ingenious, use this book as a springboard to reach new heights of gardening creativity. Browsing through the best ideas from hundreds of other clever gardeners and growers is a great way to cultivate your own gardening know-how. Check out the many "Homegrown Hints" for ideas that have spelled success for "regular" gardeners like Nancy Sutton of Washington State, who aerates her compost with recycled ski poles. You'll also see lots of great tips from commercial growers— people whose livelihoods depend on their gardening skills. Not surprisingly, the tricks that large-scale growers use often make sense in the home garden, too.

Go Straight to Solutions

You can also use this book to solve problems in your garden. We've arranged the ideas by subject so you can turn to the chapter that interests you and find tips that match your garden's needs. The book is divided into two parts: "Getting Ready to Garden," where you'll find chapters on such topics as soil care, composting, tools, and season extension, and "Out in the Garden," which includes chapters on specific kinds of gardening—vegetable, flower, herb, and more. If you're looking for ingenious ideas for a particular crop, turn to the chapter that covers that type of crop (for example, "Great Vegetable Gardens" or "Helpful Herb Gardening Hints"). Or, if you want ideas for a particular tool, technique, or plant, you can start with the index, where you're sure to pinpoint just the tips you need.

Within each chapter, we've called out certain kinds of ideas that we think you'll find especially useful. Watch for items with the "Problem Solver" logo—these are surefire solutions that other gardeners have proven effective. For example, container plants that dry out too quickly are a thing of the past when you add some compost to the soilless mix in each pot. "Timely Tips" are extra tidbits and twists that add to the great ideas you'll find on every page.

Most of all, have fun with all these ideas, from the amazing array of homegrown tools in Chapter 1 to the many ways to attract birds and butterflies in Chapter 12. Try them in your own gardens and landscapes, and use them as a way to stimulate your own ingenuity. A tip that you pass up on first glance may turn out—with a bit of tweaking—to be just what your garden needs. Gardening is an act of creativity, and every garden you grow will yield its own crop of ingenious ideas.

ingenious \in-ˈjēn-yəs\ *adj* **1 :** showing originality, resourcefulness, and brilliance of ideas or performance **2 :** distinguished by especial talent at inventing, discovering, or contriving

getting ready to
Garden

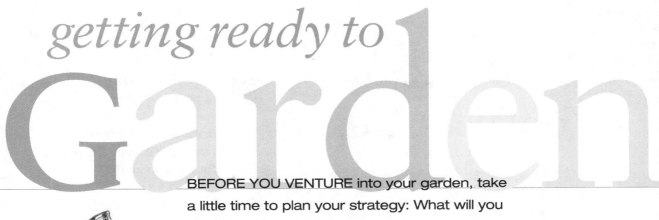

BEFORE YOU VENTURE into your garden, take a little time to plan your strategy: What will you do differently this year to get bigger yields, brighter flowers, and more fun from your garden? And how can you avoid any problems that have plagued your garden in the past? How will you stop weeds before they even start? What are some quick ways to boost soil fertility? How can you begin gardening earlier and make the growing season longer? What systems can you use to guarantee seed-starting success? Whether you're looking for a nifty tool to make planting a breeze, a simple technique to stretch the gardening season, or the latest ways to outsmart pests, in these chapters you'll find hundreds of garden-tested tips to help give your garden a great beginning.

terrific
Tools & Gadgets

What gardener isn't on the lookout for gizmos and gadgets that can make life in the garden easier? You'll find ideas in this chapter for tools you can make yourself and tools that can be improvised, scrounged, or recycled. You'll also discover new uses for traditional tools. There's no need to ever throw away a plastic soda bottle, bald tire, milk jug, or broken tool again! Breathe new life into these castoffs and others—turn them into handy implements that will make gardening a breeze.

Roll Out the Barrel

Big planters don't have to cost a fortune. "I use the rugged, dense plastic barrels you find at recycling centers," reveals Pennsylvania garden writer Duane Campbell. "They run about $20 and come in blue, black, and dark green."

Duane says the barrels are about 38 inches high and easy to cut with a jigsaw. "Just drill a small hole in the middle, stick the blade in, and roll the barrel as you cut."

Duane recommends 12-inch-tall planters, so after he cuts the barrel into two 19-inch-tall halves, he cuts a 7-inch band from the top of each to make his foot-tall planters.

He then uses the two 7-inch-tall hoops to create small raised beds in his perennial garden. Duane has discovered that if he fills the hoops with very loose soil mix, he can create the perfect drainage conditions that many rock garden and alpine plants require.

So for $20, Duane creates two handsome, durable plant containers plus the borders for two miniature raised beds. What a bargain!

Plants in Your Drawers

"When we remodeled our kitchen, I saved several of the old wooden drawers that were about 3 × 3 feet," recalls freelance garden writer Veronica Lorson Fowler of Ames, Iowa. "I drilled drainage holes in the bottoms and used them to start cuttings of 'Hicksii' Anglo-japanese yew (*Taxus × media* 'Hicksii')." Veronica adds that you can use drawers for rooting cuttings of just about anything, and she has even used them as indoor planters to grow lettuces in winter.

Mini-greenhouses

"I have discovered that the translucent, under-the-bed, plastic storage containers—the kind with snap-on lids—make excellent miniature greenhouses when turned upside down over seedling trays," says horticulturist Paul B. Barden of Corvallis, Oregon. "You can easily remove the plastic tray cover to allow air circulation on warm days, or leave it on when you have the seedling tray outdoors and need to keep your plants safe from marauding birds."

problem solver

MOBILE PLASTIC PLANT HOSPITAL

Use a plastic soda bottle to aid ailing plants. With a sharp knife, cut a 2-liter plastic soda bottle in half horizontally. The top half becomes a movable plant hospital for newly planted seedlings or plants that are suffering a bit. Just put the top over them to create a miniterrarium for them until they recover. As for the bottom half, cut drainage holes in it, then use it to raise seedlings. The bottoms of soda bottles also work well as flowerpots. Young children especially appreciate these, since the containers are clear and they can see the plant roots and can check that the soil is damp.

Anchored Milk Jugs

Covering cold-sensitive transplants with plastic milk jugs is a popular way of encouraging growth and preventing frost damage early in the season. New York home gardener Herb Mason offers this clever method for keeping those jugs in place. "I cut around the bottom of a jug on three sides, leaving a hinged flap. After I put the mini-greenhouse over young plants, I hold it in place by weighing down the flap with a mound of soil or a rock." Herb finds he can use these miniature greenhouses for two years before the plastic breaks down.

Herb says he sometimes cuts 1 to 1½ inches off the top of the jugs to make watering easier and allow more light to reach the transplants.

Keeping milk jug plant protectors in place is a snap when you turn the bottom of each jug into a flap for anchoring the cover.

Flap

Soda Bottle *Seedling* Nursery

Plastic 2-liter soda bottles make a good nursery for seedlings and transplants. Cut a 3-inch-wide flap in one side, starting at the bottleneck end and ending about 2 inches from the bottom. The flap gives you access for planting and watering and lets you adjust the humidity as your seedlings grow.

Then punch some drainage holes in the other side, and lay the bottle on its side with the flap facing up. Fill it about halfway with soil, then sow seeds in it. Try not to bend the flap back too much, so that it will stay closed and hold moisture in while the seeds germinate. When the plants get too big, you can either cut off the flap or move the plants to another container.

Placed on its side, a plastic soda bottle makes a nifty nursery for tender young plants. You can gradually increase the flap opening as your plants grow.

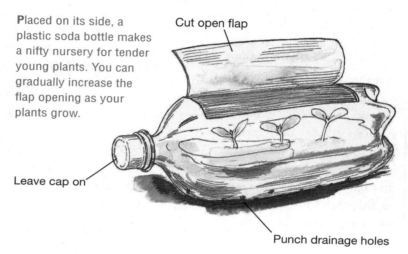

Cut open flap

Leave cap on

Punch drainage holes

Slick Mower *Trick* I

Moist grass clippings tend to clump and stick to the underside of lawn mowers. To keep them from clogging your mower, try this slick trick.

"Last fall, I noticed the paint on the underside of the mulching mower deck was peeling, and the roughness was letting the grass clippings build up badly," recalls botanist Kay Lancaster of the Northern Willamette Valley in Oregon.

"I wire-brushed the bottom of the mower and repainted it with slip plate, a graphite-based paint that farmers use to help grain slide out of a grain wagon easily. The clippings wash off the bottom of the mower easily now, and the buildup during mowing has been minimal."

According to Kay, slip plate is available at most farm stores and comes either as brush-on or spray paint. "It only comes in an ugly gray color, and it is electrically conductive. It sure seems to work for keeping gunk from building up on the mower deck."

Slick Mower Trick II

Here's another way to prevent grass clipping buildup on the underside of your lawn mower. Karen Bolesta, of Allentown, Pennsylvania, learned this trick from her father.

Periodically wax the underside of your lawn mower with automotive paste wax. If you begin to notice a bit of clumping or buildup, you'll know it's time to clean under the mower deck and apply a new coating of wax.

Heavy Crop? No Flop!

If you're tired of plant cages that flop under a heavy crop, here's the answer. "Concrete reinforcing wire makes the very best tomato cages," insists garden writer Duane Campbell of Towanda, Pennsylvania. "Those cages also work well for small vining veggies like malabar, spinach, minimelons, and cukes. They're especially nice for container-grown vining crops. And when stretched straight between two poles, a length of concrete reinforcing wire will support a major melon crop."

Duane adds that the wire cages are also great for tall but floppy flowers like delphiniums and dahlias. Cut a cage in half to make two shorter cages for peonies and other shorter perennials.

To cut the wire, Duane recommends using light bolt cutters, very heavy wire cutters, or "for the tool-impaired," a hacksaw. Take the same precautions you would when cutting any kind of fencing: Weigh it down so that it doesn't roll back up as you work with it (cinder blocks work well as weights), wear eye protection in case tiny clipped pieces go flying, and wear heavy work gloves so that you don't poke yourself with newly cut ends.

Timely tip

And what about maintaining the cages? Duane says, "After ten years or so, when the prongs break off the bottom, cut off the bottom circle of wire and you'll have all new prongs—although your cage will now be 6 inches shorter."

Reinforcing Wire Cages— A Real Plus

Pennsylvania garden writer Duane Campbell has another plant support solution made of concrete reinforcing wire.

"For totally floppy plants, like euphorbia, you can cut the wire into a fat plus-sign shape, and bend it into a cube with one open side," Duane explains. Set the cage over the plant, poking the open wire ends into the ground, and the cage will support both the sides and top of the plant.

Bend sides up to form a cage

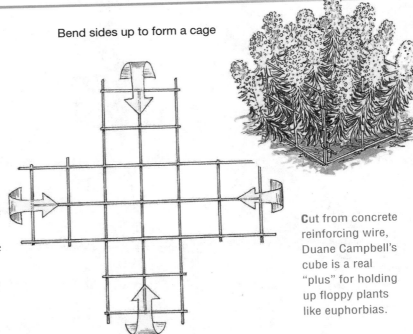

Cut from concrete reinforcing wire, Duane Campbell's cube is a real "plus" for holding up floppy plants like euphorbias.

Water *New Trees* with Ease

Watering new trees can be time-consuming, but with this submerged PVC pipe trick, you can save time and direct the water flow right where you want it—at the roots.

"Even though we get a fair amount of rain, getting trees established in our clay soil can be a challenge," admits Beverly Earls, Master Gardener from Memphis. "I've had success with using an 18-inch length of PVC pipe, in which we drilled ½-inch holes spaced about 1 inch apart. My husband then uses an auger attached to an electric drill to dig holes near the outer edge of the rootball of newly planted trees and shrubs (to avoid damaging the trunk or stem), and I push the pipe down into the soil beside the new tree."

Beverly notes that the top of the pipe should be level with the ground so you don't hit it with the lawnmower. Also, "If the ground is not level, put the pipe on the higher side so water runs toward the tree as you pour water into the pipe. This watering pipe method gets water to the roots of the tree slowly and works especially well on high ground where water runs off before it soaks into the soil."

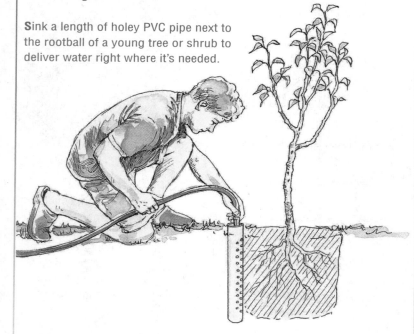

Sink a length of holey PVC pipe next to the rootball of a young tree or shrub to deliver water right where it's needed.

Garden *Groomer*

Combine two broken tools into one great homemade garden groomer.

"This is a bit prosaic, but handier than it sounds," insists Pennsylvania garden writer Duane Campbell. "When we moved into our home, there was a broken garden rake head in the garage. I fitted it with an 18-inch piece from the broken handle of another out-of-commission tool. It's perfect for grooming raised beds."

See Your **Dentist** Twice a Year

Put old toothbrushes to work when you sow seeds.

"Use the handle end of an old toothbrush as a dibble for making planting holes for medium-size and large seeds," suggests Sharon Gordon, of Ohio. "If you have several old toothbrushes, you can mark a different planting depth on each handle."

Timely tip

Once Sharon's seeds are sown, she uses the other end of the toothbrush to pull the soil over the seed, making this a double-duty tool.

Recycled Tire **Strawberry** Pot

For strawberries, Colin Wilson of Hull, England, suggests placing three tires on the ground to form a triangle. "Fill the center of each tire with potting soil. Then place three more tires on top of the others, but rotate them slightly away from the triangle below, so that pockets of soil show on the outside of the stack. Fill that layer with soil. Repeat with two or three more layers, then put strawberry plants in the pockets." Don't worry about the soil falling out of the tires that aren't in the first layer—the sidewalls are strong enough to hold the soil in place.

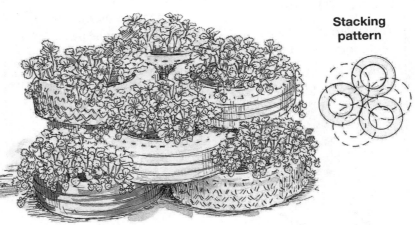

Stacking pattern

The next time you replace your tires, rotate them into a tiered strawberry planter. Or ask your local garage if they have tires to spare.

Clean *Protection* for Bulbs

An old washing machine drum offers perfect protection for your bulbs so burrowing animals can't devour them. "Our appliance repair technician gave me two old noncorroding, ceramic-coated, galvanized steel washing machine baskets—the agitator drums," recalls Nancy Lewis of Saint Helens, Oregon. Nancy sank one into the flowerbed, with the top flush with the ground, filled it with soil, then planted tulip bulbs in it. "No more rodent feasts!" Nancy says. "The washer drum prevents animals that use mole runs from digging into the bed from the sides."

Nancy uses the other basket as a planter in the greenhouse. It's filled with potting soil and planted with basil and 'Sun Gold' tomatoes. "The hole in the center of the drum, where the agitator used to be, makes an excellent support for the pole I tie the tomato plants to," Nancy says. "And the holes in the sides of the drum keep

Turn the drum from a washed-up washing machine into a below-ground planter to keep burrowing animals away from your bulbs.

the potting soil inside from getting too soggy."

Hold the Soap

Vickie Perrine of Curtice, Ohio, found this creative use for a broken hoe. "I hung the blade end of a broken hoe next to my hose, handle end up. It's a handy shelf for a bar of soap."

Depending on the length of the broken handle pieces, you can recycle them, too. A long section makes a sturdy stake. Or try George DeVault's tip below and sharpen one end to turn it into a dibble for making holes while standing.

When a tool breaks, there's bound to be another good use for it: Without its handle, a hoe blade makes a nifty outdoor soap holder.

Cast-Off Tools Become Handy Dibbles

When it comes to turning cast-off tools into handy dibbles, ingenious gardeners find that almost anything goes.

"I had one of those three-pronged cultivators that you hold in your hand for loosening the soil," recalls Audrey Bowman, a home gardener in Citrus Heights, California. "The weld on my cultivator broke, leaving only one prong, so now I use it to poke holes in the ground for seeds. It makes a nice round hole a bit larger than a pencil hole."

You could also convert an old set of screwdrivers, such as you might find at a garage sale, into dibbles for different seed sizes and planting depths.

problem solver

BROKEN-HANDLE DIBBLE

"You can pay $10 or more for a dibble from any of the garden catalogs, or you can make your own for free," observes garden writer George DeVault of Emmaus, Pennsylvania. "The dibble we use at Pheasant Hill Farm is simply a broken hoe handle. The handle broke at an angle, so it was easy to sharpen the broken end into a good point. Our dibble is about 20 inches long, so we can push it straight down into the soil while standing. It's just the ticket for making those nice, deep holes."

George suggests that a tool with a T-grip on top would make an even better dibble. "If you poke lots of holes all at once, remember that holding the rounded end of a dibble tends to cause blisters on the palm of your hand, so wear gloves."

Tired Potatoes *Grow Up*

Even if your garden space is limited, you can still have an abundant harvest of potatoes. The secret is to grow up, not out, by recycling used tires to make space-saving raised beds.

To grow potatoes in a small space, advises Colin Wilson of Hull, England, place a tire on the ground, fill it with good, loose potting soil, and plant a few seed potatoes. "When they begin to sprout," Colin instructs, "place another tire on top of the first one and fill it with soil. Each time you see potato sprouts pushing through, add another tire to the stack and fill it with soil. Continue until you run out of tires or the stack gets too high to be stable." When it's time to harvest, unstack the tires. Your yield depends on how tall your tire stack is, but Colin estimates that you should get five to six times more potatoes than you would if you planted them in the ground.

A stack of used tires filled with soil yields spud-growing success in a small space.

More Pointers for Tired Potatoes

Marg Millard of Nova Scotia adds these pointers for growing potatoes in tires:

➤ Set up the tires in full sun.

➤ Check the soil daily to see if you need to water. The black tires hold a lot of heat, so the soil dries out very quickly.

➤ Add soil gradually, up to about the top two sets of leaves on the sprouts. The buried portion of the stem will produce the potato tubers, and the stem above the soil line will produce more stem and leaves.

➤ If you cut off the smooth sidewalls—leaving just the tread part—the tires are lighter and easier to stack. Tear-down and harvest are a lot easier, as well.

Stop the Rust

Trying to keep rust and dirt off your clean tools? "Just give them a shot of nonstick cooking spray, such as Pam," recommends freelance garden writer Veronica Lorson Fowler of Ames, Iowa.

homegrown HINTS

THE PERFECT PLANTING GRID

If your efforts to eyeball the right spacing at planting time leave your garden looking lopsided, head to the garden with a section of concrete reinforcing wire. "Each square of the wire is 6 inches on a side," notes garden writer Duane Campbell of Towanda, Pennsylvania. "Four squares of wire make 1 square foot. So, for example, if you want to plant peppers at one plant per square foot, put one transplant at the intersection of four squares. Beans can be planted one seed per 6-inch square. Onions can go two per 6-inch square, in opposite corners."

The squares also provide a frame of reference that helps you broadcast seeds more easily. For instance, instead of scattering carrot seeds over a large garden bed, you'll get more evenly spaced results if you broadcast them over the smaller, 6-inch areas one at a time. You'll still have to thin the seedlings, but you're less likely to have clumps of carrots in some spots and bare patches in others.

There's no reason to leave your grid in place once your garden has been planted. You can simply lift this spacing tool off the garden plot and store it in your shed, garage, or basement until next year.

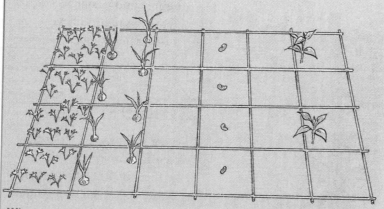

When you use a planting grid made from concrete reinforcing wire, it's easy to space seeds and transplants evenly.

Nimble Fingers and Clean Nails

If you can't stand garden gloves but don't like grubby fingernails either, take a tip from Mary Weaver of Knoxville, Tennessee.

"My favorite garden tool of late is a pair of disposable latex gloves, which I use as weeding gloves," says Mary. "It's nearly impossible for me to hand-weed in fabric or leather gloves (I can't feel the weeds), but these things are as good as bare hands—with the added advantage of preventing the perennial mud under the nails."

According to Mary, the most economical place to find these gloves is in the paint section of home-improvement centers. "And, if you don't puncture them while you're weeding," she adds, "you can even wash and reuse them, to really get your money's worth."

Timely tip

Mary adds that once a latex glove is shot, you can still get some use out of it. She cuts off the fingers and uses them to tie vines to trellises.

problem SOLVer

POISON IVY PATROL

Here's another great use for latex gloves—the heavy-duty dishwashing kind—from gardener Deb Martin of Allentown, Pennsylvania. The next time you spy a bit of poison ivy growing in your yard or garden, slip on an extra-large pair of dishwashing gloves (the longer they are, the more protection they give to your arms), and pull the poison ivy, roots and all, out of the ground. Place the plants in a plastic grocery bag, tie the handles closed, and toss them in the trash can. Toss the gloves out, too, so that you don't get the oil on anything else. Avoiding a bad case of poison ivy is well worth the price of the disposable gloves.

"To get the most out of a pair of gloves, I wait for a cool, cloudy day in early summer, then I patrol the whole yard, pulling out every piece of poison ivy I see," Deb says.

Tidy Tote

"I keep a 1-gallon plastic container in my garden cart to hold bits of broken glass, old plant labels, and other trash that shows up in the garden," says gardener and freelance garden writer Veronica Lorson Fowler of Ames, Iowa.

"I keep another container by my compost heap to collect old plant labels, plant ties, Legos, and other non-decomposing surprises."

Flat Shade for *Baby* Plants

Here's an easy way to keep young transplants from wilting while they adapt to the outdoors. "I use an ordinary, empty plastic plant flat with drainage holes, turned upside down, as temporary shade when I'm putting out new transplants," explains California home gardener Karen Winters. "I just prop the flat up on a few upside-down pots. It provides filtered light while the little plants are adjusting to the sunlight."

Besides clay or plastic pots, you can also use bricks, large yogurt containers filled with soil, or anything else that is heavy enough to stay put and high enough to elevate the flat over the plants. To keep the flat from blowing off, weigh it down with a small rock on each end.

A propped-up seed flat makes a great awning to shade young transplants on sunny days.

homegrown HINTS

TRÉS TRAY

If you like to bottom-water seedlings that you start indoors, you'll need a supply of sturdy, waterproof containers with low sides to set the pots or soil blocks in. Lee Lawton, of Over the Rainbow Farm in Junction City, Oregon, offers two inexpensive alternatives to specialized plant trays—Styrofoam meat trays and cafeteria trays.

"The butcher at your favorite grocery store is usually willing to give you a good deal on meat trays. You can wash and reuse them if you're careful with them. An even better choice is cafeteria trays, which are available, new or used, at many restaurant supply stores." Lee says, "I've purchased them for as little as three for $2. They last forever and are just perfect for the job!"

Measuring Tools

Here's a way to keep a measuring device handy when you work in the garden. "Use a permanent marker to calibrate the handles of your commonly used garden tools, such as a hoe or spade, in feet and inches," says Ada Davis of West Fork, Arkansas. Then, instead of running for a tape measure, you can easily measure the length of a bed, the distance between rows or plants, or the width you want your garden path to be.

Diapers for Baby Plants

Tired of constantly watering young plants? Diaper them instead. "I want to water my seedlings only every four days, because the growing shed is not in the house, and in winter I don't care to run out back every day," explains Amy O'Donnell of Alexandria, Virginia. "So I 'borrowed' a newborn-size diaper from my neighbor. I laid it in the bottom of the tray liner under my 12 × 24-inch flats, with the plastic side down. I placed the seed pots on top. Twice a week, I pull one pot out and pour water in. The diaper soaks up the water and spreads it through the tray to all the pots."

Turn a disposable diaper into a quick capillary mat that keeps seedlings moist without daily watering.

Strawberry Basket Cover-Ups

Strawberry baskets can provide a bit of shade for tender new transplants. "If the weather is quite warm in late spring and early summer," says Sue Murphy, greenhouse manager of the Utah State University/ Utah Botanical Garden in Ogden, Utah. "I use up-ended plastic mesh strawberry containers over some of the new plants to give them a bit of shade for a few days."

Sue adds that she pushes twigs through the sides of the baskets and into the ground to keep them from blowing away.

Jug-Handle **Cultivator**

A cut-up plastic milk jug works as a shallow cultivator. "Cut a triangular shape from the handle side of the jug, leaving enough plastic to provide a good stiff edge," says Annetta Green of Longwood, Florida. "Make it long enough to get a little of the bottom curve. With the handle still attached, it works as a small hoe for those little weeds that get in between plants." In a pinch, it also doubles as a funnel or as a small shovel or scraper for planting.

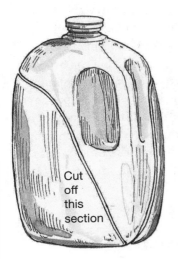

Cut off this section

Cut a triangular chunk that includes the handle from a sturdy plastic jug, and you'll have one handy—and free—cultivator.

Timely tip

Since you're cutting so much of the milk jug away when you use Annetta's cultivator idea, don't let the scraps go to waste. Use the remaining portion of the jug as a cloche to protect young transplants while letting in light and keeping plants moist.

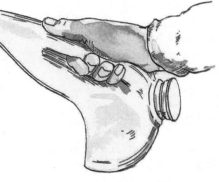

homegrown HINTS

JUG INSULATORS FOR PLANTS

Opaque plastic jugs filled with water can help protect your plants from an ill-timed hard freeze.

"Use a dark-colored jug, like those for laundry detergent or antifreeze," advises Phil Uecker, a certified organic producer in Covington, Texas. "Dark jugs work better than clear milk jugs because they absorb heat. I put three filled jugs around a seedling or small transplant and four around a larger plant. Throw a blanket over them and you're good down to 24°F or so."

Phil says this method of frost protection lets him get tomatoes and peppers out a full month before the last frost date.

Army-Issue **Digger**

When a spade is too big and a trowel is too small, try an entrenching tool. Garden writer Duane Campbell says, "This infantry tool is a small folding shovel available at Army surplus stores or sporting goods stores that sell camping supplies. It's larger than a trowel and smaller than a spade—perfect for raised beds or crowded perennial borders."

homegrown HINTS

GARDEN ART DOES DOUBLE DUTY

Your old dishes can find a new life as useful garden art. "My daughter begged slightly imperfect pieces of glazed pottery from a neighborhood potter who was going to throw them out," recalls garden writer Erin Hynes of Chapel Hill, North Carolina. "She brought home teapots, mugs, and a pitcher that look fine, with just a chip or crack here and there."

When Erin's daughter got tired of her pottery treasures, Erin snatched them up to use in the garden, where she arranged them to look like a hastily abandoned Mad Hatter's tea party.

You can do the same thing with old chipped dishes, ceramic ware, and other treasures gathered from garage sales and flea markets.

Bricks Prevent Plant *Heaving*

To keep iris rhizomes and the roots of other perennials from heaving out of the soil during the winter's freeze-thaw cycles, try this heavy idea from Ginny Prins of British Columbia.

"I put a rock or brick on top of each newly planted iris before freeze-up," says Ginny. "Then I remove the bricks after the spring thaw, since iris rhizomes need to bake in the sun. It really works!"

Hanger Pins

Clothes hangers make inexpensive—or free—garden pins. "Use wire clippers to cut the curved tips and the corners off wire hangers," suggests Ada Davis of West Fork, Arkansas. "Use the sections as earth staples to hold down the bottom of temporary fencing or to secure soaker hoses."

If you run out of curves, you can use other parts of hangers to make more staples, but you'll have to bend them into shape yourself.

Cut corners and curved tips off wire hangers, and use the resulting pins to hold down hoses or row covers.

Protect Your Pants from Your *Pruners*

That old eyeglasses case can save you from poking holes in your pants. "Protect your pruners and your pants by using an eyeglasses case— the style where you slip the glasses in from one end— as a holder for the pruners," recommends Terry Klokeid of Amblewood Farm on SaltSpring Island, British Columbia. The padded eyeglasses case can protect your pants pocket from a folding pruning saw, too.

The *Tootsie* Temperature Test, Part I

Put your best foot forward when checking the temperature of your soil. If you can't wait to get out in the garden each spring and you're anxious to walk barefoot and feel the soil between your toes, this tootsie temperature test may be great for you to try.

"I tend to use my feet to see if the soil is warm enough for planting, because I can never find my thermometer," explains Natalie McNair-Huff, an organic gardener in Tacoma, Washington.

"I walk barefoot on the edge of my garden plot to test the soil temperature. If my feet start to hurt from the cold, I know the soil is 40°F or colder, and it's too early to plant anything. If I can walk a short distance without my feet hurting, but it's still not really comfortable, I know the soil is close to 50°F. If the soil feels 'mud-between-your-toes' great, I know it's nearing 60°F, and it's warm enough for transplants."

Your feet may be more or less sensitive than Natalie's, so you may want to "calibrate" your feet the first time by comparing your "feet" reading with one taken with a soil thermometer.

And, of course, you'll want to walk just along the edge, like Natalie does, so you don't compact your garden soil too much.

The *Tootsie* Temperature Test, Part II

Amy LeBlanc of Whitehill Farm in East Wilton, Maine, is another gardener who likes to use her bare feet to determine when it's time to plant her vegetables.

"I wait until I feel it's 'no pain,' but still chilly, to plant the peas and spinach," says Amy. "The no-chill point is safe for most transplants, like onions, cabbages, and broccoli."

Amy adds that, "The 'warm-as-toast' feeling is a requirement for planting beans and pole beans and transplanting tender seedlings like tomatoes, peppers, and eggplants."

problem solver

BLADE PROTECTOR

If you or your neighbor are having vinyl siding installed, save any scraps of the finishing strip. "The finishing strip is a long, narrow piece of siding material that is folded over so that the last sheet of siding can be slipped in and held tightly," explains Terry Klokeid of Amblewood Farm on SaltSpring Island, British Columbia.

"The finishing strip will grip any narrow blade that is slid into it, and it's easy to pull the blade out again. I use finishing strip to protect blades on garden tools, such as pruning saws, knives, and hoes, and other tools such as drywall saws and drawknives. Just cut the strip to the appropriate length for your tool," says Terry.

If you're cutting a small amount of the siding, you can get away with using a pair of craft scissors. If you happen to own tin snips, they'll work even better.

Mini *blinds* Make Mini *markers*

"I use an old miniblind, cut up into little pieces, to mark plants," says Pat Kolb of Phoenix, Arizona. "Write on it with a permanent marker, or with a pencil if you want to reuse it. You can even poke a hole in the miniblind and tie it to a larger plant."

Stirring Plant Labels

Veronica Lorson Fowler, of Ames, Iowa, advises, "Those paint stirrers that they give you at the hardware store make good plant labels. I always grab a handful!"

Depressing Plant Markers

"Use tongue depressors as plant markers," says Cyndi Lauderdale, horticulture agent with the North Carolina Cooperative Extension Service. "Depending on how many you need, they are cheap, or free from your doctor. You can also get them at craft stores." To identify a plant, write on the depressors with an indelible marker.

homegrown HINTS

MEAT TRAYS MARK THE SPOT

"I put those wimpy Styrofoam meat trays to use in my greenhouse," says Amy LeBlanc of Whitehill Farm, East Wilton, Maine. "I use a paper cutter to nip off the curved edges and cut the trays into strips. I cut the strips into slim triangles for plant markers. A medium-point ballpoint pen will write on them just fine and leave an impression in the foam, as well. I sell 3,000 to 4,000 heirloom tomato and pepper seedlings every spring, all with meat tray tags."

Laminated *Labels*

Home gardener Karen Helfert of Rockville, Maryland, offers some advice on an easy, inexpensive way to make long-lasting, waterproof plant labels.

"To make long-lived plant tags, buy plastic laminating sheets, not adhesive shelf paper. Print the plant information on squares of paper. Remove the protective layer from one laminating sheet, lay it sticky side up, and arrange the paper squares so that you leave approximately ½ to ¾ inch of space on the sides and bottom and at least 1 inch on the top. Generous spacing is better than too close."

Karen says to then apply a second laminating sheet, sticky side down, sandwiching the paper squares between the two sheets.

"Cut out the individual labels and use a paper hole puncher to make a hole about ½ inch from the top of each label," says Karen.

Use a twist tie to hang the label from the plant. Or fasten the label to a metal stake that you stick in the pot or into the ground.

Timely tip

Since the laminated labels are coated on both sides, you can make the labels double-sided by writing information on both sides of the paper. Make your labels more useful by including the plant name on one side and the care information on the other.

Clay Pot
Plant Pokes

Here's another clever idea for do-it-yourself plant labels. "I use broken clay pot shards as plant markers," says Candy Sheagley, a gardener in Brookston, Indiana.

"I write the plant name in indelible marker. For a personalized tuck-in gift tag, I paint the shards with fancy flowers or another garden theme."

problem SOLVer

RECYCLED CANS CAN'T MISS

Nancy Sutton, a home gardener from Federal Way, Washington, recycles soda cans to label her plants. To make long-lasting, nonfading plant tags, use craft scissors to cut the sides out of aluminum soda pop cans, then cut them to the desired size, says Nancy.

"Fold over one corner to make it double thick for strength, then punch a hole through the doubled corner with a paper hole puncher. Write on the tags firmly with a ballpoint pen to engrave the name. Then use thin wire to loosely attach the tag to a branch, or use 16- to 18-gauge wire to stick the tag into the ground. The labels should stay put and be readable forever," Nancy says.

Bucket Seats

If you tire of crouching and stooping while working in the garden, try this tip from Floridian Annetta Green, a home gardener. "In our garden, we use old 5-gallon buckets to sit on while weeding. We use outdoor materials glue to attach a small cushion or foam padding to the lid to make the seat comfy. If the work needs a closer look, you can lie across the cushioned lid and have two hands free.

"What's more, you can keep tools in the bucket—small scissors, a plastic sieve from a beach set, and more conventional garden tools—so they're handy as you walk through the garden and see a plant or weed that needs attention."

Annetta adds that you can also attach the cushion with Velcro, which makes the cushion easy to remove and launder. "Use some self-stick Velcro for the plastic lid and the sew-on type for the cushion."

Lots of gardeners use 5-gallon buckets in the garden—for carrying compost, weeding, and more. Make yours more useful—and more comfy—by adding a cushion and turning it into a portable weeding seat.

Funnel-*to*-Furrow Pipeline

Make a handy seed-planting tube so you won't have to stoop or bend to sow your seeds. "Use duct tape to attach a funnel to a 1-inch-wide length of PVC pipe," says Sharon Gordon of Ohio. (Choose a length of pipe that is comfortable for your height.)

"Then, open a furrow with a hoe, position the pipe over the furrow, and drop in the seed. Cover the furrow with a hoe after planting all the seeds in the row."

Planting Hole **Plunger**

Here's another back-saving device to use at planting time from Yvonne Savio, gardening education coordinator for the Los Angeles County Cooperative Extension Service.

"To punch planting holes for seeds like corn and beans without bending, place a rubber washer around a length of dowel at the correct planting depth," says Yvonne. "Move the washer up or down the dowel to adjust for different seed depths."

No-Turn *Compost* Tools, Part I

"The best and cheapest all-purpose compost tool is a 3- to 4-foot length of ½- or ⅝-inch rebar, the metal rod used in reinforced concrete," recommends Don Boekelheide, who coordinates and teaches community composting classes in Charlotte, North Carolina.

Don says that rebar cut to this length is usually available at large home-improvement centers, hardware stores, or lumberyards, and it generally costs less than a dollar.

"Rebar is perfect for poking through your compost to improve aeration. It's strong enough to open a passage—even in a new heap full of tough leaves or straw—creating a hole for adding kitchen scraps deep in the pile. By putting scraps in the center of the compost, you'll avoid any insect and critter problems."

Don adds that rebar offers another plus for composters. "As a bonus, the rod heats up, providing a low-cost 'thermometer' to show whether your pile is heating in the middle."

problem SOLVer
FREE PLANTING TUBES ARE HIDING IN YOUR HOME

Kay Lancaster, an Oregon gardener, recommends planting seeds through a tube, especially if you suffer from arthritis. Here are some of her suggestions for back-saving items you may find around the house or shed that will work great for planting larger seeds.

"Rummage around in the scrap pile to see if you can find a 3- or 4-foot piece of PVC pipe, electrical conduit, or skinny, lightweight pipe of some sort. Those of you with golfers in the family, see if your golfer uses the plastic tubes that keep the handles of the clubs from banging together in the bag." Kay also recommends the cardboard roll from gift-wrap tubes or a plastic shower curtain rod cover as planting tube ideas.

"Trace the planting line with a hoe or dibble, then walk along the line, dropping your seeds down the tube. Cover with a hoe or your foot after you're done planting."

homegrown HINTS

SKI POLE COMPOST POKER

Nancy Sutton, of Washington State, has her own method for making lightweight compost pokers. "I use old ski poles. They're usually aluminum, lightweight, smooth, and sharply pointed," says Nancy. "I remove the basket, and now I have an invaluable tool to aerate my compost, which is in a recycled plastic, perforated bin. I don't have to turn the bin because I can easily plunge the pole to the bottom and then rotate the top, make a circle as large as I can manage, and repeat this at various locations in the pile."

To remove the basket from the ski pole, you may need a hacksaw or a pair of pliers, depending on whether the basket is made of metal or plastic.

No-Turn *Compost* Tools, Part II

To go along with his rebar poker, Don Boekelheide also uses a tool he calls a hole enlarger and scraps poker.

1. Cut off one end of a 4-foot length of 2 × 4 at a 45-degree angle.

2. Drill a 1-inch hole 6 inches from the other end.

3. Put a 12-inch length of ¾-inch pipe through the hole as a handle.

"I open a hole in the compost with the rebar, then use the 2 × 4 tool to enlarge the hole," Don explains. "The pipe handle gives great leverage." Don adds kitchen scraps deep in the center of the pile, where hot microbial activity makes short work of everything, even citrus peels. "The 2 × 4 is great for ramrodding the scraps into the pile and covering them with material to avoid pests and smells."

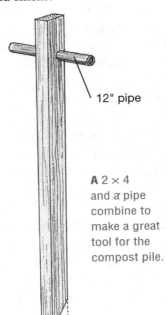

12" pipe

A 2 × 4 and a pipe combine to make a great tool for the compost pile.

Totally Tubular Seed Planting

If bending to plant seeds bothers your back, try this tidy tip from Donna Warren of Tennessee. "Because of a back condition, I try to garden without crouching," Donna says. "So I plant with a vacuum cleaner tube."

Donna drops the seeds through the vacuum cleaner tube into prepared soil, spacing the seeds according to the directions printed on the seed packet.

"I use the handle of a rake to push the seed to the right depth. If it's a new bed where soil still crusts, I funnel some compost on top of the seed, again using the vacuum cleaner tube. Then I tamp the soil in place with the business end of the rake to firm it."

homegrown HINTS

NO BIRDS ALLOWED!

Birds enjoy the vegetable garden just as much as humans do. But birds don't always wait for the veggies to mature. They just help themselves the minute they spy those tender seedlings. "Use plastic mesh baskets that cherry tomatoes or strawberries are sold in to protect newly sprouted seedlings such as corn, cucumbers, melons, and squash from birds," recommends Yvonne Savio, gardening education coordinator for the Los Angeles County Cooperative Extension Service.

"By the time the seedlings are tall enough to reach through the tops of the baskets, it's safe to remove them because the plants are no longer as tender and delectable as the birds prefer." The baskets also provide a temporary barrier against nibbling rabbits and voles.

Handle Pads *Pad* Hands

If the wooden handles on your rakes, wheelbarrow, and other garden implements are giving you blisters, head to the bike shop. "I've discovered that the thick, spongy, tube-shaped cushions bicycle shops sell for handlebars protect my hands from the wear and tear of wooden handles," reports garden writer Erin Hynes of Chapel Hill, North Carolina. "They can be a bit tricky to slip on. I find it helps to lubricate the handle and the inside of the tube with petroleum jelly or liquid dish soap."

Durable Plant Ties

Many people who suffer from respiratory problems use canisters of supplemental oxygen to aid in breathing. The tubing that connects to the oxygen canisters can also help in the garden. Susan Sam, a home gardener in El Reno, Oklahoma, has found that oxygen tubing—which must be changed fairly often—makes wonderful plant ties. "I have used it for everything from small trees to tomatoes to tall flowers, to even an emergency gate latch. It's soft and has never damaged anything that I have used it on."

Umbrella Cloche

Broken umbrella? "Take off the fabric, cover the metal frame with floating row cover—or the cover of your choice—and you have a cloche," points out Stephanie Ferguson of Indianapolis, Indiana. "When you don't need it for your plants, you can call it into duty as a handy gadget for keeping flies off food at a picnic."

Tomato Cages That Won't *Blow Away*

"In my part of West Texas, it isn't uncommon to experience wind gusts of 70 to 80 miles per hour during thunderstorms," says Debi Stewart of Abilene, Texas.

To keep her tomato cages from becoming airborne, Debi uses scraps of PVC pipe to anchor them. She hammers three pipes into the ground around the tomato cages, which are 6 feet tall, about 4 feet in diameter, and made of concrete reinforcing wire or other heavy fencing material. Then she lashes the cages, near the bottom, to the poles, using twine or wire.

Pick *This*, Part I

Create a lightweight fruit picker with PVC pipe. "Choose pipe wide enough for the fruit you want to harvest to fit through," suggests Pat Kolb of Phoenix. "Cut a notch in one end of the pipe to hook the fruit. When you snag the fruit from the tree, it rolls through the pipe into your basket. PVC by its nature is pretty lightweight, especially when compared to many commercial fruit pickers."

You can make your own lightweight fruit-picking tool with notched PVC piping.

Pick *This*, Part II

"To make a citrus fruit picker," says Michelle Doll, an organic home gardener in Tampa, Florida, "use long handles left over from brooms and other old or broken tools. Put a couple of nails, fairly close together, sideways through one end."

To harvest the fruit, simply put the nails on each side of the stem, and twist the handle to pick the fruit without damaging the skin, allowing it to drop into your basket.

A broom handle and a couple of nails make a handy and inexpensive citrus fruit picker.

Electric *Currants*

The right tool for the job of harvesting berries comes from an unlikely source. "As an electronics constructor, I have a small pair of wire cutters that comes with a gadget that holds the cut piece of wire so that it doesn't fall into the equipment or fly into your eye," explains Alan Pemberton of Sheffield, England. "I have found them invaluable for harvesting my black currants. I can snip off strings of currants one-handed and then transfer the fruit, still clinging to the cutter, to my collecting vessel, leaving my other hand free to manipulate branches or hold the vessel."

Check your local hardware store for wire-grabbing wire cutters, and try them on anything with a small stem, such as grapes or currant tomatoes. They're even handy for cutting hard-to-reach flowers.

Sunflower Seed **Scraper**

"To separate sunflower seeds from the flower head," suggests Pat Kolb of Phoenix, "scrape the head across an old washboard."

Reinforced Recycled *Harvest* Basket

Recycle your leftover grocery bags into a durable, leak-proof harvest basket. "Simply start with three paper grocery bags and two plastic grocery bags that fit

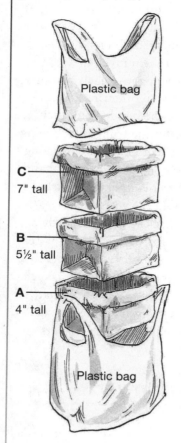

C —
7" tall

B —
5½" tall

A —
4" tall

Plastic bag

If you have a stack of grocery bags waiting to be recycled, put them to work in the garden instead as a durable harvest basket.

the paper bags," says Sharon Gordon of Ohio.

1. Fold a 1½-inch cuff in the top of one of the paper bags (Bag A).

2. Continue making 1½-inch folds until the bag is about 4 inches high.

3. Repeat for the second bag (Bag B), but make one less fold so that it's about 1½ inches taller than Bag A.

4. Repeat for Bag C, making one less fold than for Bag B.

5. Place Bag B into Bag A so that the top of Bag A's cuff is just touching the bottom of Bag B's cuff. Staple the bags together through Bag A's cuff.

6. Place Bag C into Bag B, and staple the bags together through Bag B's cuff.

7. Line Bag C with a plastic grocery bag.

8. Place the four-bag unit inside a plastic grocery bag with handles.

"The paper bags give the basket shape and stability, and the plastic bags keep it dry," Sharon explains.

Water Tube Makes Posting *Easier*

Now you don't have to mangle the tops of posts when you hammer them into the ground. "I soldered a female hose connection on the end of a 6-foot piece of ½-inch hard-wall copper tubing," says Jim Oberschelp of Minden, Nevada. "I attach the hose, turn on the water, and push the tubing into the ground where I want to place my pole. The pole then goes into the ground very easily."

Jim notes that this works for other projects, such as deep root watering of trees. He's even used it to blow debris out of his shop vacuum hose.

Quick Tool *Cleanup*

"I keep a bucket of gravel and coarse sand soaked with lin-seed oil near my tools," says Sally Anne Sadler of the Cooperative Extension Service in Seattle. "I dunk my tools, shovel, spade, and forks in it to scrape off rust and to oil them." Sally Anne also uses the linseed oil to season or protect her tools' handles.

Nifty Sifter

"Remove the seat from an old, metal, straight-legged kitchen chair to make a compost sifter," says Bonnie Knesek of Sparks, Oklahoma. "Make a sturdy wire mesh box, or a box from old boards with a wire mesh bottom. Attach the box where you would normally screw in the seat. Dump compost into the box and work it through the sifter."

Transform an old dinette chair or stool into a compost sifter with legs. You don't have to hold the sifter as you work, and it's easily moved to wherever you want to use the finished compost.

A *Soffit* Touch

Use scraps of vinyl soffit covering to make durable plant collars. "Because vinyl soffit material is perforated with many small holes, it lets air circulate around plants," says Terry Klokeid of Amblewood Farm on SaltSpring Island, British Columbia. "You can easily bend a scrap of soffit material into a circle about 4 to 6 inches around, and one side clips into the other, making a nice cylindrical plant collar."

Use plant collars on seedlings to keep birds, rabbits, and other critters away. As with vinyl siding, vinyl soffit material is extremely durable. And you can usually get scraps from a builder for free.

Garden *Forks* and *Knives*

Think twice before selling those old fondue forks at your next garage sale. "They come in handy for grilling or roasting marshmallows, but mainly I use them as digging forks out in the yard," says Laura McKenzie of Springville, Alabama. "Since they are skinny and small, they can reach the weeds right next to your plants. They also prick out lettuce seedlings when thinning.

"Another tool I couldn't do without is an old paring knife. I sharpened it and use it to dig out clumps of grass and other weeds that are really rooty."

Polish Up Those Handles

To keep from losing or misplacing your hand weeder, paint the handle bright orange or red. And, rather than buy paint when you only need a small amount for this purpose, use some old red nail polish. This is a job children really love. Let them mix all your old bright colors together, do their nails—however messily—and color the tool handles at the same time. Materials needed: one or more children, old red nail polish, and one bottle of nail polish remover for the remainder of their hands, your yard furniture, and your deck.

problem SOLVER

SELF-SUPPORTING WHEELBARROW

"Make your wheelbarrow support its own load by adding wheels to the rear legs," says Yvonne Savio, gardening education coordinator for the Los Angeles County Cooperative Extension Service.

Yvonne anchors a bar to each leg with a U-bolt. Then she attaches two small wheels to the ends of the bar with a bolt and washer on both the outside and inside of the wheel. The smaller the wheels, the less the rear of the wheelbarrow is raised.

"The wheels enable you to push without lifting the wheelbarrow, making heavy loads much easier to move with less strain."

"Waterfall" Planter

"We took an old wheelbarrow and tossed it on its side. Then we mounded up soil in it and let some spill out in front of the wheelbarrow," says C. J. England of Jonjea Acres Family Farm in Hope, Idaho. "We planted flowers in it that are low to the ground and will bloom blue, such as petunias and ageratum, to make it look like it's spilling out 'water'!"

Anything Goes

Wondering what to do with an old wheelbarrow? "If it's deep enough, use it as a planter. If it's not, it's a birdbath. Upside down, it can be a home for a toad," says Stephanie Ferguson of Indianapolis.

Flat Transporter

Anne Warren of Sudoa Farm, Notch Hill, British Columbia, recycles old wheelbarrows. "I pick up broken wheelbarrows at the dump to fix and rebuild. Last year I was able to make a flat-decked wheelbarrow from bits I'd scrounged," says Anne. "It is excellent for transporting flats from the greenhouse to the garden."

Salad to Go

"Plant a salad garden in a wheelbarrow. Lettuces and radishes look quaint, and they can be conveniently located near the door. Be sure to drill holes in the bottom for drainage," suggests Vera Smith of Rusk, Texas.

Vinyl Siding Scraps

Terry Klokeid of Amblewood Farm, SaltSpring Island, British Columbia, has lots of uses for light-colored vinyl siding scraps. Cut them into a variety of dimensions to make:

➤ plant markers for the garden

➤ seedling markers for flats

➤ large signs to install on posts in larger plots

➤ plant labels for the sides of homemade wooden planters

➤ relatively tall markers to place in the ground when laying out spacing for larger plants and perennials

➤ small labels that travel with small batches of seeds as they move from harvest to drying to storage

➤ dividers in flats, to keep seedling roots from becoming intertwined

"The best tool for cutting vinyl is aviation snips, which are widely sold in hardware stores," says Terry.

Timely tip

Empty plastic diaper-wipe containers are just the right size for storing seed packets.

Garden *Glove* Trap

"Create a glove trap by attaching a mousetrap to the door of your potting shed or wall near an entrance to the garden," suggests Yvonne Savio, gardening education coordinator for the Los Angeles County Cooperative Extension Service. "The gloves are accessible and will dry quickly."

Cardboard Box Raised **Beds**

A cardboard box can serve as a one-season raised bed. "To make a potato planter, fold both top and bottom flaps of a large box to the inside so that they are flush against the inner walls of the box," suggests Ada Davis of West Fork, Arkansas. "Bury the bottom edge of the box about 6 inches below ground level so that it won't blow away, then plant potatoes as usual." At the end of the season, toss the box on your compost pile to decompose.

Ada also suggests using small cardboard boxes as biodegradable planters. "But make sure the soil goes up to the top edges so that the box won't wick away moisture."

Garden Tool **Hang** Ups

Trying to organize all those tools cluttering the garage? "Hang an old garden rake and use the tines to hang smaller garden tools," suggests Sally Anne Sadler of Washington State University Cooperative Extension, King County.

More Garden Tool *Hang Ups*

If you have an old dish draining rack, you have an instant shed organizer. "Cut the drainer in half lengthwise with wire cutters," instructs Stephanie Ferguson of Indianapolis. "Form the newly cut wires into hooks. Then mount the drainer on the garage or shed wall and hang tools from it." If you hang the drainer with the cut side up, it forms a basket that will hold gloves, seed packets, and other nonhanging items.

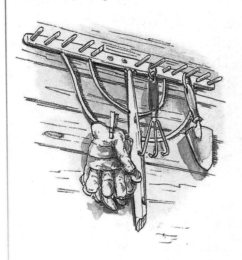

A garden rake with a broken handle (*left*), or a discarded wire dish rack cut in half (*right*) can both gain new life as hangers for tools. Two nails tapped into the shed or garage wall is all you need to hang these items—then you have space to hang gloves, trowels, cultivators, pruners, and more.

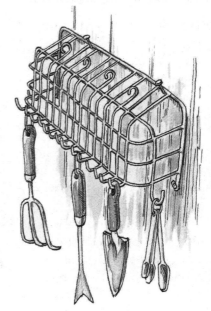

Tissue Box Seed **Organizer**

Organize your seed packets with empty tissue boxes. "Cut four diagonal slits in the top of an empty cardboard tissue box from the opening to each corner," explains Sharon Gordon of Ohio. "Fold each of the four wings to the inside, and staple each wing twice to the body of the box, near the ends of each flap. File seed packages in alphabetical order by type and variety. If you have a lot of seeds, use a different box for each type of plant, such as vegetables, herbs, and flowers."

To keep seeds moisture-free, Sharon recommends placing several of these cardboard seed boxes in a large, sealed plastic container.

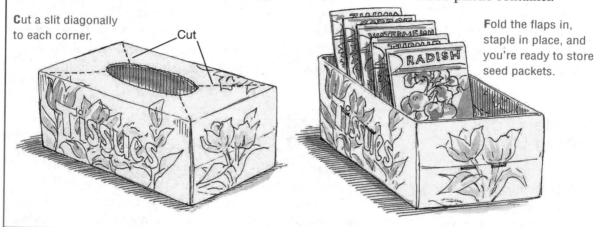

Cut a slit diagonally to each corner. — Cut

Fold the flaps in, staple in place, and you're ready to store seed packets.

Catnip Protector

Cats destroying your catnip patch? "Set an old dish drainer over the planting of catnip to keep the cats from pulling the snack out of the ground by the roots," advises Natalie McNair-Huff of Tacoma, Washington. "They can still rub on it and prune it as it grows through the wires, but they won't be able to kill it." And don't worry about appearances—the bushy catnip will quickly grow large enough to hide the drainer.

Kitty can still enjoy the catnip as it grows through a dish drainer, but she won't be able to yank it out of the ground.

Seed Storage Units

If photography is one of your hobbies, it can benefit your gardening habit, too. "Most good gardeners take pictures and have plenty of 35-mm film containers laying around," says Bill Stockman, owner of Spider Web Gardens in Center Tuftonboro, New Hampshire. "These containers make excellent units to store seed." They're airtight and opaque, so seeds won't lose their freshness.

"Use peel-off stickers to label the containers so that you'll remember what's in them," suggests Bill.

Built-In *Hand* Cushions

"I wrap the handles of some of my tools with moleskin," says gardener Bambi Cantrell of Jacksonville, North Carolina. "It makes them more comfortable to hold and makes the wooden handle less likely to cause a blister."

Just make sure that you don't let the tools get wet, because moleskin will absorb the water and can even come unstuck, so you'd have to replace it.

Sheer Substitute for Row Covers

Sheer curtains can go from window covers to row covers to extend your growing season. "It's quite easy to buy secondhand, gauzy sheer curtains at garage sales. I've bought them for as little as a dime!" reveals gardener Eileen Anderson of Little Rock, Arkansas.

"Plenty of light seems to go through, and all sorts of plants profit from them. I use them over lettuce to moderate the temperature. The sheer curtains keep them warmer in the winter and cooler when it starts to get warm. And I couldn't grow tomatoes without using the curtains as protection from the birds. I imagine they would be good protection from cabbage moths, too."

To support the sheer row covers over summer crops, Eileen uses tomato cages that she makes herself from fencing material.

"I make tomato cages out of 4-foot fencing that I buy in a roll at a farmer's supply store. I simply trim the fencing in pieces to make cylinders that are about 18 inches in diameter, and fasten them together with wire. I use these cages for tomatoes and beans in the summer, and a group of them will support the sheers beautifully."

Eileen uses the same cages in the winter, but she lays them on their sides to protect her lettuce crop. "I can lay two or three cages in my lettuce patch and cover them with the sheers. The sheers let water through, and they'll even support snow with no sagging."

Eileen's secret to achieving no-sag sheers is to anchor the cages to the ground with clothes hanger garden pins (see page 14 for directions on making these). Then she attaches the sheers to the cages with clothespins.

Timely tip

Eileen has devised a way to use her sheer covers in raised beds, too. She stacks four bricks on the timbers and then lays a 4 × 6-foot chain-link fence gate on top of them. Eileen then covers the whole thing with a sheer curtain.

"I use this row cover system for spring lettuce, and the lettuce seems to love it. I even had a bunny living under there for a while—the lettuce was so prolific that there was plenty for both of us!"

homegrown HINTS

THE ALMIGHTY STICK

"I call my favorite—and darn near only—gardening tool the almighty stick," says Lee Flier of Atlanta, Georgia. "It's just a branch from a tree, about 1¼ inches thick, waist to chest high, forked at one end, and sharpened to a very blunt point on the other."

Lee uses the sharpened end as a digging stick for planting. "Assuming you have good soil and are doing no-till and deep mulch, all you need is the almighty stick to twist into the soil. Then mulch a little and make a hole, drop the seed in, and use the stick to brush a bit of soil back over the seed. The stick is also useful if you mulch with newspaper layers. Just make sure the newspaper is wet, and the stick will poke right through."

Lee has other uses for her almighty stick, too. She uses the forked end to move squash vines out of the way in order to harvest the beans off a "three sisters" bed of corn, beans, and squash so that she doesn't step on them. Other uses? How about harvesting fruit off of trees and aerating the compost pile? As Lee sums it up, "It's a great little invention!"

Bookcase Bed

Don't throw out that old bookcase, even if it is a little wobbly. "Take the back off and use it as a frame for a small raised bed," suggests home gardener Ada Davis of West Fork, Arkansas.

You can leave the shelves in as row dividers—or you can take them out, leaving just the outer frame to enclose your bed.

Kid's Stuff

Here are two garden-related recycling ideas for parents. "Diaper-wipe containers work as drainage trays. Each one holds two small pots really well," says Deborah Turton, a gardening columnist in Gaithersburg, Maryland.

"And save empty formula cans for scooping or storing dry stuff like birdseed or bonemeal."

Shocking Stop

When you use an electrical tool or lighting in the garden, you often need to use an extension cord. But you could be setting yourself up for a shock if you don't take a few precautions.

"Use a coffee can and two plastic lids to protect the connection of two outdoor extension cords from the weather," recommends Yvonne Savio, gardening education coordinator for the Los Angeles County Cooperative Extension Service. Here's Yvonne's method:

1. Remove the metal bottom from the can.

2. Slit each plastic lid from one edge to the center, and enlarge a center hole in each lid to be slightly smaller in diameter than the cord.

3. Slide the can over the end of one cord, connect the cords, center the connection in the can, and slip on the plastic lids.

Yvonne advises, "Keep the slits pointed downward to allow drainage, in case of condensation."

problem SOLVEr

PRYING ROOTBOUND PLANTS FREE

Have you ever tried to get a large rootbound plant out of an 18-inch pot? "The pressure of the roots makes it almost impossible without breaking the pot," says garden writer Duane Campbell of Towanda, Pennsylvania.

"I use a soil auger—the $5 kind designed to fit a ⅜-inch drill—to drill several holes through the soil right up against the side of the pot," says Duane. The result is a double benefit. "It relieves the pressure and root prunes the plant at the same time."

By using Duane's method, you spare the pot and give the plant a better start once it's planted in the ground. Be sure to wear eye protection while you're working with the drill.

Claw Your Way through *Clay*

If you have hard clay soil and just the thought of planting bulbs gives you blisters, try this idea from Edie Carlson of Saint Thomas, Ontario.

"I use a garden claw to dig holes for bulbs," says Edie. "Even in hard clay, I can dig a hole that is big enough for some bonemeal, good soil, and the bulb."

Spare Hands

Here's a helping hand for gardeners who have arthritis or who have lost strength in their hands or fingers. "Try to find hand tools with longer handles, or replace short handles with longer ones," recommends Nancy Anderson of the North Carolina Cooperative Extension Service in Fayetteville. "You may have to purchase a longer handle than you need and cut it to size. (I cut mine 8 to 10 inches long.) Then use Velcro to make a strap to attach the tool to your forearm. The idea is for the arm to do the work and not the hand."

Follow these steps to add a strap to your hand tools.

1. Cut a 12-inch strip of both the hook and loop sections of the Velcro.

2. Lay the smooth side of the hook section against the loops of the other piece of Velcro. Sew them together with a ¼-inch seam across one short end.

3. Sew another seam about an inch or so from the first seam. This will form a loop that you can slip over your tool handle. So make sure you leave enough room to fit the tool into the loop.

4. Slip the handle of the tool through the loop and wrap the Velcro around your arm, adjusting the straps so that they fit snugly.

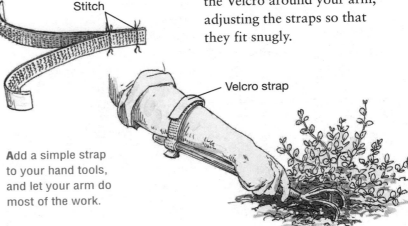

Stitch

Velcro strap

Add a simple strap to your hand tools, and let your arm do most of the work.

Yo-Hoe Tool Grabs Weeds

Here's a creative homemade gadget for up-close weeding. "My husband made me a tool we call a yo-hoe," reports Kim Cook of Prince Edward Island. "He cut a piece of scrap metal to form a triangle that's about 3 inches long and 1½ inches wide at the widest. He welded the end to a steel rod a little thinner than a pencil and attached the rod to

This homemade weeding tool makes use of an old hammer handle. Since the inside of the blade that's welded to the handle is sharp, pull it toward you to grab and slice weeds.

Old hammer handle

Steel rod

Scrap metal

an old hammer handle. The steel rod sticks out of the handle about 4 inches. The tool is shaped like a 7, and the inside edge of the blade is sharpened. I drag it toward

me, and since the inside blade edge and the rod part of the handle form an angle, they trap the weeds, making it easier for the blade to slice through them."

homegrown HINTS

COMPUTER COVER DOUBLES AS COLD FRAME

"The ancient IBM Display Writers and similar machines from the early days of office computers had huge hoods to muffle the sound of the printers," says John Boston of Tulsa, Oklahoma. "They're natural cold frames! These covers are about 3 feet square, taller in the back than front, with a hinged Plexiglas cover and a layer of foam insulation inside. IBM was even so kind as to include an electric fan on one side for ventilating your plants on warm days. You can plug in the fan when needed, or do as I did and hook up an inexpensive thermostat to regulate the ventilation."

If you can find a company that still has these old clunkers around in storage, you can probably have one for free. Who knows—they may even pay you to haul the unused hood away!

By turning one of these old printer covers into a cold frame, you not only save money but you also recycle obsolete computer equipment that would otherwise have ended up in a landfill.

That Phone Wire Is Busy

Old telephone wire need not head to the landfill, according to master scrounger Terry Klokeid of Amblewood Farm on Salt-Spring Island, British Columbia. "If new telephone lines are being installed or upgraded in your neighborhood, you have an excellent source of wire for tying plants up and repairing stuff.

"If you get your mitts on the old wire, you can re-purpose it. Use it instead of string or anything else you may have to buy to tie up plants or to bundle wooden stakes together for storage."

Kindling
Splitting Support

"To make the job of splitting kindling for firewood easier, I have built a stabilizing gadget," explains Terry Klokeid of Amblewood Farm on SaltSpring Island, British Columbia. "It looks vaguely like a football goal post with a wooden base under it. The plywood base is about 24 × 9 inches. I attached two 2 × 4 posts near one edge of the base, using two screws per post through the underside of the plywood. Then I stretched a deflated bicycle inner tube taut between the posts."

Before attaching the inner tube to the posts, you can slip one or two metal rings over the tubing, to slide along the tubing to tighten it around the firewood and hold the wood secure. Any kind of ring large enough to slip over the tubing and strong enough to hold against pressure will do. Split rings, like those on key chains, are a good choice.

Then place the tube at a height that's about two-thirds the length of kindling you want. Finally, attach the tubing to the upright posts by screwing small pieces of plywood to the posts.

How do you use this contraption? Terry replies, "I insert a small piece of firewood between the two bands, rest it solidly on the plywood base, and split it into the desired thin bits of kindling. It's much safer than holding the wood in one hand and whaling away on the wood with an ax in your other hand. I find I can set two, three, or sometimes four pieces of wood in the stabilizer and process them all at once. This is a real timesaving gadget, not to mention a finger-saving one as well."

A homemade vise is nice for holding wood while you cut it into kindling. Attach two 2 × 4s to a plywood base, then slip a deflated bicycle inner tube over the 2 × 4s. You can use a key ring or two to cinch the tube snug against the wood.

clever

Compost Tips

It's been said before, but it really is true—it all starts with the soil. From scrounging on trash day to using up what you have on hand, learn how to enhance your soil and your yields with these ingenious composting tips. Gardeners from around the country share their best secrets, short-cuts, and solutions for improving the soil you have. You'll also find clever ways and places to compost—right down to how to disguise that active compost heap in the backyard!

Trash-Day *Sleuths* and Sunday **Night** Scouts

Almost everybody knows that adding organic matter is the way to improve any kind of soil, but *finding* enough organic matter isn't always easy. Here's an easy solution—use everybody else's throwaways! Trash or garbage day often yields bundled-up brush, piled leaves, newspapers, and even pots full of "used" soil. You'll also see lots of unwanted grass clippings set out after the weekend's mowing is done. Collect these, too, as long as you're sure they haven't been coated with pesticides and weed killers.

Post-Halloween *Treasures*

Another excellent time to scour your town for free compost and soil-building material is the week after Halloween. Lots of people decorate with bales of straw and corn stalks, and many of them gather leaves in those bright orange pumpkin-face bags. So be prepared to hit the brakes when you see curb-side orange!

How to Become a **Rake**

Sally Cunningham, author of *Great Garden Companions*, needs lots of organic material, so she uses this ingenious technique to gather free leaves: "When I'm driving around in fall or spring, I often see wonderful piles of pine needles or leaves. The problem is, my rake is at home." But Sally always has garbage bags under the seat, so she developed her "human rake" technique.

Place a large trash bag facing a pile of leaves. If there's a curb, the bag goes beneath the edge of the curb. Facing the leaf pile yourself, put one foot on each side of the bag to hold the mouth of the bag open. Wait until no cars are coming by, since this looks ridiculous—or worse—from behind. Then bend from the hips and scoop with your arms, pushing all the leaves between your feet right into the bag. Sally adds, "It's one great waist exercise, too!"

Always carry trash bags in your car, and you'll be ready to gather up a wealth of curbside lawn waste for composting.

Under-the-Sheets **Composting**

This tip earned writer Sally Cunningham some teasing over her years of teaching organic soil building. It's not about sleeping late or dreaming of compost. But it *is* an easy way to improve soil.

Whenever you cover the soil with black plastic sheets—a really good mulching and weed-killing material—use the opportunity to get lots of coarse organic material under it. Just stuff shredded newspaper, chopped leaves, grass clippings, weeds, and unfinished compost *right under the sheets!* The stuffing can be 4 to 6 inches thick, and it will be well decomposed by the end of the season.

This technique even protects the soil when you step on the plastic. "It feels spongy, and if you peek under it, you will be amazed at the earthworms enjoying it, too!" says Sally.

Timely tip

Gathering grass? Be sure to keep layers of grass clippings less than 4 inches deep when mulching or composting with it. Grass is mostly water, so a deep pile becomes oxygen-deprived, or anaerobic, very quickly—and when that happens, it really smells!

homegrown HINTS

HELP OTHERS HELP YOU

Believe it or not, many homeowners rake up leaves or grass without a thought of composting or mulching, and they work hard to pick up the piles and put them into open containers or trash bags to go out to the curb.

So why wouldn't they gladly put the stuff into your containers? Just watch for a raking-gathering project in progress, stop by, and offer to leave your garbage bags, cans, or baskets for them to fill. People are glad to have the "trash" gone so quickly and especially appreciate it if you do the hauling. In addition, you'll be saving them the cost of all those trash bags and teaching them a lesson about recycling right on the spot. Maybe next year they will be composting their own yard waste.

Chicken Wire *Keeps* Critters at **Bay**

If you're trench composting, you shouldn't have a problem with animals digging up what you've buried if you avoid meat, bones, and fats. Even the most fragrant fruit and vegetable scraps will not attract scavengers when buried under 8 inches of soil!

However, if dogs do like to dig in your trenches, use a roll of chicken wire to cover your buried treasure, rolling it out over one hole at a time. The roll moves along gradually, so it also marks where you buried something last.

Trench composting is easy and trouble-free when you protect your trench with chicken wire.

Can't Compost? Use Trenches

If you have a small yard and no place to compost, you may find that trench composting is the best way to use your food scraps to add nutrients to your soil. How do you do trench composting? Just dig a hole in your garden every day, about 8 inches deep, and bury the kitchen scraps. If you start along one side of a garden row, you'll actually be side-dressing or fertilizing nearby vegetables as well as boosting soil texture and fertility for next season.

Wet Soil? Plant in *Compost*

Paul Kranz, a Master Gardener and environmental engineer in Amherst, New York, has heavy clay soil, which never dries out in time to plant spring peas and onions. He recommends, "Overlay the untilled soil with a 6-inch raised bed of compost." Paul gets his compost from the town compost facility. "Plant peas, lettuce seeds, or onion sets right in the compost for an early start. They grow great!"

The *Acid* Test

If you don't have time for a soil pH test, which is always a wise idea before starting a garden, nature may give you clues to the acidity or alkalinity of your soil. Check the weeds that sprout up in your gardens. If you find many of one type of the weeds or wild plants below, or a mix of several species from one of the lists, you'll have a a good indication of the general soil pH.

Plants that indicate acid (low pH) soil: Canada mayflower (*Maianthemum canadense*), star grass (*Hypoxis hirsuta*), wood anemones (*Anemone quinquefolia*), frost weed (*Helianthemum canadense*), rhododendrons, blackberries, or blueberries.

Plants that indicate alkaline (high pH) soil: Lady fern (*Athyrium filix-femina*) and most other ferns, Jack-in-the-pulpit, bloodroot (*Sanguinaria canadensis*), wild geranium (*Geranium maculatum*), poison ivy, enchanter's nightshade (*Circaea quadrisulcata*), figwort (*Scrophularia marilandica*), sweet cicely (*Myrrhis odorata*), goosegrass or catchweed bedstraw (*Gallium aparine*), and goldenrod.

Do the *Soil Ribbon* Test

Joanne Gruttadaurio, soil professor *extraordinaire,* has taught thousands of Master Gardeners and Cornell University students this down and dirty way to determine whether soil is clay or sand. Grab a lump of your soil and form it into a patty. Start flattening it out by pressing with your thumb against the soil, pressing toward your fingers. Squeeze a ribbon of soil out over your index finger, easing it along with your thumb. If you can form a ribbon that holds together for an inch or two, you have clay soil. If it fails to hold together in a ribbon and falls off in loose particles, it is sandy soil.

A simple squeeze of the soil though your fingers will reveal your soil's texture.

Once you recognize your soil type, you can plan your garden and select plants. You may want to grow vegetables, perennials, or a mix of landscape plants, but keep in mind that it's easier to work with the soil you have rather than to change it significantly. If your soil is one extreme or the other—either clay or sand—you can start improving the soil with organic matter, the most effective cure in either situation.

problem solver THE FIRST SPRING CUTTING

The first lawn mowing of spring usually provides long, thick clippings, making it the one time it's worthwhile to rake the clippings rather than to let them decompose in place. Here are two good uses for an abundance of grass clippings: Spread them around the vegetables and flowers at least 2 inches thick as a short-term mulch. Or use them for quick-start compost. Alternate 4-inch layers of grass clippings with 4-inch layers of dry leaves or shredded newspaper. Your compost will be really cooking in a matter of days.

Bedsprings in the Spring *Beds!*

"My father always dragged bedsprings behind the small riding tractor to remove rocks from a clay tennis court, and it gave me this great idea for helping my garden dry faster in the spring," says Marge Vogel in Eden, New York.

"When the soil is drying in the spring but is too wet for walking or tilling, drag an old bedspring (child-size is easiest) over your raised beds. You don't need a tractor, but you do need two people. Each one walks on the paths on oppo-site sides of the garden beds, pulling the spring along by ropes. It breaks up the soil crust and stirs up any mulch you left on the garden, yet it's not so heavy as to damage soil structure. And one pass is all it takes. Of course, you can also rake the surface lightly to accomplish this, but that's a *lot* of work in a big garden!"

To use this technique, look for the old-fashioned open-coil bedsprings. You may find them at a curbside in the country, in dumps or junkyards, in basements or attics of old homes—or even under a mattress!

Put an old bedspring to work in the garden, where the wire coils can loosen the top crust of soil and drag out any rocks that have risen to the surface over the winter.

homegrown HINTS

OLD NEWSPAPERS, NEW BEDS

Joanne Tanner, a Master Gardener in Orchard Park, New York, says, "In late summer or early fall, I lay several sheets of newspaper right over the lawn where I want to make a new planting bed. On top of this, I put a couple of inches of compost (finished or not) topped with a few inches of shredded leaves. I finish it off with a covering of landscape fabric."

Sally Cunningham, author of *Great Garden Companions*, echoes this idea. "If your back is like mine, double-digging a new bed is out of the question." Sally suggests piling any organic matter you have on the newspaper, such as brush, manure, straw, leaves, or grass clippings. "Make each layer no thicker than 4 inches, and use the coarsest materials on the bottom." Sally says she's used this method to build beds anywhere from 8 inches to a few feet high. Sally finishes her layers off with compost for an early spring planting.

Build **Down**, Not Just *Up*

Peg Giermek, Master Gardener and owner of Nature Calls Landscaping in Erie County, New York, tries to convince her customers of the importance of building the soil before adding landscape plants. Not everybody wants to see a raised bed in the landscape, so she devised a method to build the soil while serving customer tastes.

"When installing a garden in an area of extremely poor soil, it's possible to do more than just raise the bed and amend. Dig a good 2 to 3 feet down into the soil and remove it. (Add the poor soil to a compost pile, where active microorganisms will bring it back to life.) Rebuild your garden by layering compost, peat moss, good-quality topsoil, and composted manure. Repeat the layering, making each layer a few inches thick. Continue layering until the garden has been raised above ground level as high as is practical in your situation."

The bed will sink a few inches in the first year, so take that into account as you layer.

Timely tip

With Peg's method of garden building, it's also very easy to incorporate small hills or berms into any size garden. Just start below ground, and keep building up on one side as desired.

Berms are a great asset for certain plantings. For example, plant tulips, daffodils, or other early-spring blooming bulbs on the far side of a hill or berm (from the viewing area), and plant irises in front of them. Tulips and daffodils will emerge first in the spring, followed by irises, which will hide the waning bulb foliage. Or, plant your bulbs on the north-facing side of your berm to delay their bloom a bit later than normal.

Yesterday's News

One of the great underused—but widely available—soil amendments is newspaper, according to Rochelle Smith, Master Gardener and owner of EarthCare, Inc., a landscape firm in Buffalo, New York. She encourages homeowners to work with an organic lawn and landscape program, and adding newspaper to the soil helps.

Rochelle uses at least six to eight sheets of newspaper under a layer of mulch. Newspaper blocks weeds, and earthworms love it. And earthworms provide valuable nitrogen, potassium, and phosphorus—three essential plant nutrients—all in a form that's readily available to your plants.

You put something free (the paper) into this processing plant (the worms), and out comes fertilizer! For faster action than the worms can provide, shred some newspaper into 1-inch strips and turn it into the soil, or spread it on the soil surface under mulch.

What *Becomes* of Peat?

A landscaper's daughter, Michele Diegelman of Buffalo learned from her dad that leftover peat moss does some great decomposing right in the bag. She put the bags in the basement in the fall and let them sit. In spring, after the peat had decomposed some more, she cut slits in the bags and added organic matter like grass clippings and compost. Then she planted spreading flowers in the bags. Voilà: instant container gardens!

homegrown HINTS

VOLUNTEER VINES

While she has never planted a pumpkin in compost on purpose, Nancy Smith, a compost teacher from East Aurora, New York, admits she does grow at least one pumpkin and a gourd or squash on the compost pile every summer. "Just watch for volunteers from the pumpkins you tossed in after Halloween, and pick the best plant!" Of course, you may not be sure exactly what is coming up, but that's part of the fun. And don't be surprised if the pumpkin grown in the compost turns out to be the biggest pumpkin in the garden.

Bury the Rusty Rake

Jean Seibert of East Aurora, New York, remembers the first composter she ever knew—her dad, Harry Harper. Jean says, "Dad would return home on trash day with the worst-looking rusty hoes and rakes."

Jean thought the find looked rather dubious. But he stuck the rusty tools upright in his compost, with the tool ends buried. When it came time to turn the pile, all he had to do was twist the tools up and out.

"And a second benefit," says Jean, "was the satisfaction that man took in never wasting anything!"

Wiggle-and-Pull Aeration

Most composting instructions tell you to put all the larger sticks and coarse brush on the bottom, but Sally Cunningham, author of *Great Garden Companions,* suggests saving the longest sticks for this use: As you build a compost pile, put long sticks (up to 2 inches in diameter) across the pile, every foot or so, with their ends sticking out. After you have a tall pile and the initial heat buildup slows down, you can wiggle the sticks to turn and aerate the compost. Or, use a wiggle-and-pull technique to remove the sticks and introduce some new air spaces.

Hiding Compost in the Hedgerow

OK, maybe you don't have an actual hedgerow, but even a cluster of shrubs will do. You can hide a compost pile behind or among trees or shrubs. Some people don't hide compost in these shady areas because they think that a pile needs sunlight—but it doesn't! The heat comes from *inside* the pile during decomposition, and shaded compost can be just as hot as that kept in full sun. Shaded compost can take longer to dry out, though, so keep a tarp handy to limit the rainfall on compost under the trees.

Don't Compost Those Leaves

Master Gardener Fran Evans, from Hamburg, New York, has found a better way to cope with fallen leaves. "Don't compost the leaves!" says Fran. "Instead, shred and bag them in the fall and hold them until summer. Then mulch the vegetable garden with them. Till them in the soil after the crops are harvested, and you'll create great humus for the following year."

Peas and Beans **Succeed**

Not only do climbing peas and beans grow beautifully up the sides of a compost pile, they also cover it for a long season with succession planting. Plant the peas as soon as you can poke a finger into cold soil. Later, beans replace them, and a fall crop of peas completes the cycle. Scarlet runner beans, planted every third plant, add a bright red-orange glow to the whole display.

Climbing peas and beans cover up compost with their flowering vines, and they also provide you with a summer's bounty of good eating.

Cover Compost with *Glory*

Morning glories are happy to climb up the sides of a chicken-wire compost bin, or one made of fencing or boards. If the sides aren't rough enough to provide places for the vines to cling, simply tie strings to the top of the bin, and attach them to the soil with pins to provide vertical trellises. Your pile will be a blaze of heavenly blue, white, red, purple, pink, or crimson from summer until frost makes its appearance.

Flower Boxes *on* **Top**

Some great gardening friends were traveling to a gardening conference, and one of the subjects of conversation was how to beautify a compost pile. Nobody remembers who thought it up first, but the gardeners, Marty, Mary, Sally, and Jean, now have the prettiest compost bins in New York State!

Try their creative idea: Make compost bins with the pallets laid sideways, so the closed end is up and the open ends are on the sides. Then use flower boxes on top, loaded with trailing vines like licorice plants. They really beautify the business end of composting.

One gardener used wallpaper-soaking trays, which are just about the same length as a pallet, for the flower boxes. Plant trailing annuals like 'Pink Wave' petunias, and enjoy the view.

Flower boxes filled with trailing plants dress up a compost bin made from wooden shipping pallets.

Compost *Needs* a Chimney

Compost needs air to enable the microorganisms to do their job. You can always turn the pile, but that's hard work! Here are a few clever ways to get air into your compost pile with a minimum of labor.

PVC chimney: One way to get air into your compost pile is to provide a central "chimney," or a column of air that gets down into the center of the pile, to keep those microorganisms going. Poke a PVC or metal pipe with air holes right into the center of the compost pile.

Cinder-block chimney: Another method is to stack about four or five cinder blocks in the center of a 4-foot pile with the holes lined up vertically. When

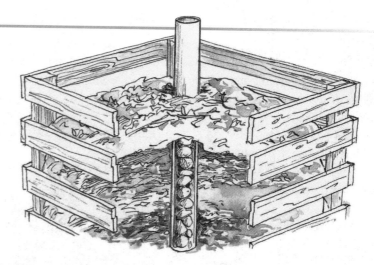

This cardboard compost chimney will decompose, leaving a stack of rocks—and air space—in the center of the pile, which is exactly what it needs. Best of all, there's no need to turn the pile.

you stack them, place some stones on top of each layer of cinder blocks to let air in from the sides.

Cardboard chimney: One gardener made a great chimney out of 4-inch cardboard tubing left over from a

construction project. He then filled it with rocks. Yes, the cardboard decomposed in that hot compost heat—but by that time, the rocks were all lined up in a tall pile and provided lots of air space in the middle of the compost.

problem SOLVER

FEED THE TOMATOES

In the great race for the neighborhood's first and largest tomato of the season, a compost pile can give you an edge. Just make a tall compost pile, at least 4 × 4 feet, and enclose it with the kind of wire mesh sold for tomato cages. ("Hog wire" will also do.) Plant tomatoes just outside the wire, and gently tie them right against the wire. Pluck off the lower leaves facing

the pile. New roots will reach right into that rich compost where the leaves were plucked, and the tomatoes will be deliriously happy. And you don't have to wait until the compost pile is completed before planting the tomatoes. You can add to the pile all summer long, providing the tomatoes with a constant source of nutrition and helping them produce lots of fruit.

homegrown HINTS

THE HANDY COVER

Gardeners are the best scroungers, and smart ones see the potential for free tarps and covers from lots of sources. Possible free covers for the compost pile include: tarps that come with barbecue grills or lawn mowers, lawn furniture "overcoats," children's pool covers, painter's tarps, discarded shower curtains, and cast-off rugs, just for starters.

It is a good idea to have a tarp or cover that's 2 to 3 feet bigger than your compost pile so that the tarp can drape over the sides. Cover compost before a rain if the compost is already wet enough, or after a rain if you want to keep the moisture in. Adapt your cover-uncover routine, depending upon how much moisture you want to let in.

Strawberry Tower **Compost**

If you want a strawberry tower without paying the catalog price, make it with compost. As Sally Cunningham, author of *Great Garden Companions,* says, "You'll save the cost of fertilizer, too!"

1. First, make a chicken-wire cylinder, 4 to 5 feet high with at least a 2-foot diameter, and fill it with compost ingredients like yard waste, kitchen scraps, and manure—as raw and "hot" as you want. Finish with a 4-inch layer of soil, and then plant strawberries on top.

2. Enclose the cylinder with another circle of wire about 1 foot shorter and 9 inches larger in diameter than the center column. Fill that circle with more "raw" ingredients on the bottom and 4 inches of soil on the top. Plant another circle of strawberries.

3. Make as many outer circles as you want, each one about 1 foot lower than the previous one. But,

A chicken wire and compost strawberry tower can keep producing for years. Refresh it by adding soil or compost any time you replace an old strawberry plant with a young runner.

be sure you plan how to reach the center for picking later on! One suggestion is to break the circle, making the outer rings C-shaped rather than full circles. Use a footstool to reach the higher rings.

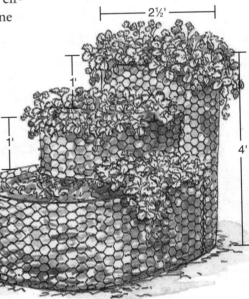

Surrounded by Sunflowers

A good place for building a compost pile is a back corner of the garden. It's convenient for adding in spent plants, leaves, and other garden debris, as well as for using the finished product.

To conceal active compost and still have it nearby, use tall plants like sunflowers. A double circle of sunflowers or hollyhocks or a combination of these with cosmos or tall nicotiana will hide the composting work in progress and provide a lovely focal point to enhance your garden's beauty.

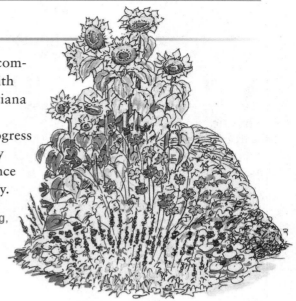

An arc of quick-growing, tall annual flowers is just the ticket for camouflaging an active compost pile.

Straw Planters Turned Compost

Nancy Ondra, nursery owner and garden writer, teaches this easy method for using straw bales as planters now and compost later. Place bales of straw wherever you'd like a raised bed or wherever you wish to grow vine crops but have soil that's too hard or nutrient-poor. Use a trowel or bulb planter to open up "pockets" on top of the bale, spacing them wherever you want to plant a vegetable or flower. Put compost into the pocket, and plant directly into it.

Poke holes in straw bales, fill them with compost, and plant vining flowers or vegetables. The bale makes a raised bed for a season, then decomposes to nourish next year's crops.

Nancy says, "You'll be surprised at how quickly the straw inside the bales begins to decompose, providing nutrients to the plant roots." She adds that this method is especially effective with vine crops like squash or melons. The vines will take up less space in your garden because they'll naturally trail down the sides of the bales. "They're also easy to water this way," she adds.

"By the end of the season, your straw will be nearly half composted. You can spread it in place and plant into it next season, or use it to activate a new compost pile. It will be full of hungry microorganisms and very valuable wherever you use it."

Compost Starters **for** **Cheap**—or *Free*

There's no need for you to buy compost starters to get those decomposing microorganisms going. Master composters know that manure, soil, and compost are loaded with them and will be happy to start a new batch for you! (For optimum production, just spread an inch or so of the material every 4 to 6 inches in your pile.)

Master Gardener John Holnbeck, from Colden, New York, says this, "If you are just starting out and the earthy elements are scarce, buy alfalfa meal from the feed store. It's cheaper than at the garden center, and it's the same stuff. It's high in nitrogen and gets things heated up quickly." Rabbit and horse feeds are made of alfalfa.

By the way, for city folks who don't have a feed store nearby, some cat box fillers are made of alfalfa meal. Won't the cat be surprised to see *clean* litter tossed out! (By the way, never put *used* cat litter on your compost pile, to avoid the possible spread of disease organisms.)

problem SOLVer GET SOME LIFE IN YOUR CONTAINERS

Compost can add some much-needed life to container gardens, too—it's not just for traditional garden beds.

Some container-planting teachers tell you to use soilless mix (without synthetic fertilizers blended in) or potting soil in container plants because it is purer and you avoid soil "critters" that might cause problems in a contained situation. However, many potting soils are very light, and container plantings end up easily tipped over, or they dry out quickly. Also, organic gardeners tend to think that every soil should have some life in it, and soilless mixes surely need something.

Compost is the best answer. Use your choice of potting soil, but mix in compost (worms and all!). Compost improves the medium's texture and water-holding ability and delivers a gradual supply of nutrients, not to mention the valuable worm castings. Container plants with compost added literally spill over with beautiful flowers and lush foliage.

Give **Worms** What They **Want**

Penny McDowell, a Master Gardener and home landscaper in East Aurora, New York, says, "I find that worms are like kids. They like fruit better than vegetables. So I make sure that some fruit is mixed in with the kitchen scraps." And for even faster worm composting, run food scraps through your blender before feeding the worms. They'll turn blended scraps into rich compost in a mere three months!

Slow *May Be* Even Better

A study by Bob Kozlowski, of the Homes and Grounds Department at Cornell University, showed that compost made the slow way—without ever achieving real heat—was actually more nutrient-rich than compost that heated up and processed quickly. So, if you think your compost is a failure because it doesn't get hot, resist the temptation to heat it up. It may take longer, but in the end, it will be that much more valuable.

Creative Composting

Ingenious gardeners make compost bins out of many things, including snow fence, cinder block, pallets, window screens, and all kinds of fencing. Here are some of the more creative bin ideas.

Dog kennels: Some great compost bins resulted when one family took apart a series of dog boarding kennels. They were made of steel mesh framed in wood, and the doors (4 × 4 feet) and sides (4 × 6 feet) formed generous compost-bin rectangles, tied together with wire. Best of all, the front was already a door, complete with a hinge and a latch for easy access.

The last leaf collection: When it became too cold to build new compost piles, a gardener near Buffalo continued to build anyway. He simply gathered the late fall bags

A compost bin can double as a storage site for tools or stakes. Add a wrought-iron shepherd's crook and brighten your bin with a hanging basket or two.

of leaves from the curbs around town and heaped them in a 4-foot circle around a low compost pile. The bags provided some heat, the contents decomposed slightly, and the center of the circle provided an unfrozen compost pile for accepting kitchen scraps all winter.

Double-duty pallets: Lots of gardeners make compost bins from pallets, but the pallets are usually positioned with the end boards horizontal and the open ends facing sideways. Instead, try placing them with the end boards in a vertical position and the open sides up. It's the perfect place to store garden stakes, long-handled tools, or row-cover hoops.

"Almost" Counts in Composting

A former Extension Agent and professional cut flower grower, Roxanne McCoy of Lilies of the Field in West Falls, New York, used to teach composting. She often joked with her class about the slides that show happy composters (neatly dressed, too) pushing fine, finished compost through a sieve.

"Fine compost, actually strained through a sieve!" said Roxanne. "Who can wait that long?"

In reality, most composting experts use their compost a lot sooner than the ready-to-strain stage. If there are still a few pieces of eggshell, grape-fruit rind, or sticks showing, that's okay. Just use the finer parts and keep the big chunks to add to a new pile. These chunks are loaded with hungry microorganisms that will immediately go to work helping to break down the pile. If the chunks don't bother you, use the compost as is—chunks and all. Just turn the bigger pieces under a couple inches of soil, where they'll add important nutrients to your beds as they continue to decompose.

Build It Where **You** Want It

Many gardeners have reported variations on this idea—build the compost heap (or place the tumbler or portable bin) right where you want a new bed. If you do this in late summer or fall, and the compost is deep enough to become an active pile for a couple of months, you can use most of it in spring. Just dump or spread the compost around the former pile, and keep the unfinished material to move right along with the container for a new start somewhere else.

Kitchen-Door **Compost**

It can become a daunting task to lug food waste to the outer limits of your property— especially in bad weather. If you like to cook, consider keeping the compost right by the kitchen door near the garbage cans, where you're more likely to use it every day.

Keeping the compost near the kitchen door doesn't mean you'll have to look at the unsightly pile, however. Several types of commercial bins and tumblers are attractive and respectable looking. You can also mask your cans and compost with fencing, flowering vines such as clematis, moonvine, and morning glory, or perennials such as columbine, daylilies, and purple coneflower. Not only will you have a convenient compost pile, you'll have a pretty flowerbed, to boot!

Timely tip

Always keep some straw or leaves near the compost. Then, when you do make the trek to the compost bin with your food scraps, you can cover the food layers every time you add them.

problem solver   FOOD SCRAPS ANONYMOUS

One deterrent to composting year-round is that people want the kitchen garbage out of sight as quickly as possible. But avid composters have devised all sorts of ways for holding food waste until it's time to take it out for composting. Here are just a few.

Containers on the counter: Cookie jars, decorative pots, large pitchers, an unused bread box, or a canister set all make great countertop containers for food scraps. If the container is airtight, it won't have a smell until you open it; but dump frequently since the anaerobic conditions make a powerful odor! If you poke holes in the containers for ventilation, you can simply dump them as needed.

Containers near the door: Some people camouflage the compost-in-waiting by putting it in bags or milk cartons and stashing these in wicker bins, decorated milk cans, large tins, or even an umbrella stand!

And outside, waiting for the final trip: Try stashing compostables in a pretty mailbox, an old milk box, or a window box or flower planter that is not in use during winter. Once the material is frozen, there is no odor and no hurry to bury it; just wait for some temperate days and add a whole compost layer at once. If you have really wet compost ingredients, add shredded newspaper with every addition to absorb some of the moisture.

How Much Compost?

Many gardening books recommend adding soil amendments in *pounds* per 100 square feet. Agricultural advisories even suggest *pounds or tons per acre!* Well, home gardeners don't usually have a scale around to measure pounds of compost (not to mention tons), so try the bushel basket rule of thumb. It's a lot more practical.

Try to make enough compost to spread 2 or 3 bushels per 100 square feet of your garden every year. (If you have a scale, that's about 1 to 1½ pounds per square foot.) Depending on your compost's texture, this amount should give you enough to spread compost an inch or more deep over the soil surface. Make sure to spread it before planting.

But just how much compost is in a pile, anyway? Here's another way to estimate how much compost you're creating. A 4 × 4 × 4-foot pile (64 cubic feet) should give you enough to spread over a 40 × 50-foot (or 2,000-square-foot) garden.

If all this math seems too complicated, don't worry. Just keep adding to that compost pile. After all, you can *never* have too much compost!

Start Compost on a **Tarp**

You don't need a fancy compost bin to start composting. You can start a compost pile on top of a tarp. Simply poke a few small drainage holes in it and start piling materials on! Some folks leave the compost for a few months, then pull out the tarp with a lot of the finished bottom layer on it. (You can also lift off the top two-thirds of the pile and pull out the bottom.)

Or, you can pull out the tarp earlier in the composting cycle, in about three weeks, to simulate a first turning. Just pull out the bottom stuff and put it back on top of the pile.

Start **Early** by Waiting *Longer*

Most gardeners know that you need people and machines kept off the soil so that soil texture, or *tilth,* isn't destroyed—especially when it is wet. But spring fever can make an eager gardener forget all that. To force yourself to put away the tiller or shovel for a while, remember this: If you really want an early start in the garden, *wait longer!*

Working wet soil—soil that still clumps in your hand when you squeeze it—causes it to form hard clods that do not dry out nearly as quickly as untouched soil. (The clay particles form a powder that combines with moisture and forms a rocklike texture.) The root hairs of transplants actually take longer to start growing in soil in this condition, compared to unpulverized soil. As a result, plants can take two to three weeks *longer* to start growing.

So what *can* you do when spring fever hits and it's too wet to work the soil? Fern Bradley, managing editor of Rodale Garden Books, recommends jumping in the car and visiting a nearby garden center. "Reward yourself for your self-control by buying one new exciting plant that you can plant when the soil is ready to till."

Portable **Pens** for **Manure** Makers

Many gardeners know the benefits of raising geese, chickens, and ducks for the organic fertilizer they produce. These barnyard fowl are also valuable as pest-control agents. But, admittedly, these animals don't always eat just what you'd like when you'd like it, and they need to be kept *out* of the garden when some plants are in the seedling or fruiting stage.

The solution? Make a lightweight, portable duck pen (about 4 × 5 feet) out of chicken wire and a ½ × ½-inch wood frame. Two people can easily move it whenever you want your helpers to patrol for pests or fertilize new territory.

Direct from the **Bunny**

Gathering compost materials tends to involve a lot of hauling. So plan ahead for ways to ease the burden. Marge Vogel, of Eden, New York, does. Marge keeps pet rabbits, which produce great fertilizer. The rabbit cages have floors that are half wood and half ½-inch mesh (large enough for rabbit droppings to fall through). On cage cleaning days, Marge sweeps the droppings from the solid sections right onto the open mesh to fall out. Underneath each cage she uses a child's wagon that is exactly the width of the cage.

For a great timesaving way to gather rabbit droppings for the compost, park a child's wagon beneath the pen.

After a cage cleaning, her child (the one who wanted the bunny) pulls the wagon to the compost pile.

---

homegrown HINTS

MULCH THAT MANURE

All kinds of manure make wonderful soil amendments and fertilizer, yet many gardeners are afraid to use it because it can be full of weed seeds (especially horse manure, which is the kind most readily available). The single answer from thousands of gardeners: If you use manure, plan on mulch! Generally a 3-inch mulch of leaves, grass clippings, straw, compost, or a combination will suffice to block weeds. In a landscape planting, wood chips also work well. The few weeds that do pop through will be weak and poorly attached to the soil, so they'll be easy to pull. And, since mulch is so good for plants— from trees to tomatoes—the garden will benefit twofold, from manure and mulch.

Old Tire *Worm* Bin

If you love the idea of *vermiculture*, but don't want a bin full of wriggly worms taking up residence in your house, try this creative idea from Brian Geary, Master Gardener in Erie County, New York, and owner of Northern Lights Landscape. He encourages homeowners to landscape with nature in the backyard as well as right by the kitchen door. Brian says, "Recycle rubber tires and make the perfect worm bin!"

To make your own steel-belted worm bin, stack the tires five or six deep, filling the rim of each with shredded newspaper. Then, in the bottom of the "bin," start layering shredded paper, kitchen scraps, and some starter worms (red wrigglers). Keep adding indoor and outdoor organic matter as you go, and the worms will just keep reproducing and making compost. Actually, worm castings are the *diamonds* in the "black gold" department!

Don't try making the worm compost bin without using the tires, though. They're much more than just a container. They also provide ideal insulation for cold climates. If the worms are cold, they move toward the center of the tires, and when it is warm, they climb higher and toward the outside. A filled-up tire bin should let red wrigglers survive through most winters, even the harsh ones Brian faces in Buffalo, New York.

Old tires offer perfect outdoor shelter for worms. They keep the worms warm in the winter so you don't have to house them under your kitchen sink!

problem SOLVER

WHAT WOOD CHIPS STEAL, COMPOST RETURNS

Wood chip mulches are a great weed barrier, and they last a long time so you don't have to replace them often. But wood chips can tie up soil nitrogen. So what's a savvy gardener to do?

Compost solves the problem. It gives soil microbes a rich source of nutrients as they work on digesting the wood chips, so the microbes don't have to raid all the nitrogen that's present in your soil while they do their work. Just spread a layer of compost on the soil you want to mulch before you put down those nitrogen-stealing wood chips. In a landscape planting, this combo gives you and your plants the advantages of both mulch and compost.

Hooked on Caffeine

If you work in an office building, take advantage of something that usually gets dumped in the trash—coffee grounds. Find out where the coffeemakers are in your building, and leave a 3-pound covered tin marked "Used Grounds." Then make the rounds routinely and take home all that potential black gold. (You don't have to separate the coffee grounds from the paper filter. You can dump the grounds, filter and all, right into your compost pile, because the filter will decompose, too.)

Ellen Phillips, executive editor of Rodale Garden Books, collects the coffee grounds at her building every day. "I started collecting coffee grounds in the winter when I was adding lots of wood ashes to my compost pile," says Ellen. "Ashes are alkaline, and since coffee grounds are slightly acidic, I thought they would help neutralize the pile. Earthworms love coffee grounds, and of course they smell good, too. And I get a special bonus since I work at Rodale Press—our coffee grounds are organic!"

Pepper the Compost

Homeowners often worry that animals will be attracted to compost piles, especially in urban situations. As an extension educator, Sally Cunningham has learned to explain that if you bury food scraps at least 8 inches deep into the pile, there should be no odor or attraction for animals. And of course, use *no* meat scraps, bones, or fats!

However, a city dweller who refuses to give up composting in spite of neighborhood varmints recommends some extra insurance. Sprinkle pepper on the food layers every time you add them. The odor, taste, and sneeze-effect are all just too much—even for a rat!

Spring Fever? Turn Up the Heat!

Get a jump on spring planting by heating up your soil. It's easy if you have room for a raised bed and have access to fresh horse manure (other kinds work, too). Build a bed of manure and top it with 2 to 4 inches of soil or finished compost, then plant into the top and water normally. The composting manure will produce heat and get your plants growing even when air temperatures are low. Once you've harvested your crops, you can add the manure and soil into your permanent beds or return them to the compost pile. Next spring, repeat the process.

homegrown HINTS

USE MANURE TO WARM SOIL SAFELY

To take advantage of the heat that fresh manure gives off as it composts, try this simple cardboard box trick.

Put the manure in cardboard boxes, and line them up or stack them around your raised beds. The heat may help the soil warm up in spring or fall, and when the manure matures and cools off, it is convenient for spreading. Even the cardboard boxes will be easy to open and lay flat to help block out weeds.

A *Home-Garden* Compost **Spreader**

Compost can be hard to spread evenly because it is heavy when damp, hard to dig with a shovel, and not very crumbly. This is especially true if you use it before it's fully decomposed. So why not steal an idea from farmers: Use a spreader.

With a little ingenuity—and an old wheelbarrow—you can build a garden-size spreader that helps you put an even layer of compost on your garden.

Here's how to make it:

1. Look for an old wheelbarrow at the local dump or at a garage sale. Or maybe you already own one.

2. Use a saw with a metal-cutting blade to carefully cut a window at the end of the wheelbarrow. Make the cuts right where the sides meet the bottom of the wheelbarrow. The opening should be 2½ to 3 inches wide and run from side to side at the front end of the wheelbarrow (the end over the wheel and opposite the handles).

3. Carefully bend the cut edges toward the outside of the wheelbarrow so that you don't cut yourself on them when you use the compost spreader.

Here's how to use it: This tool works best if you pull the wheelbarrow, rather than push it, and shake it from side to side as you go. The opening should be wide enough to drop clumps of compost or even amounts of manure or leaves as you pull it along. If your load is too clumpy to slide out easily, get a friend to act as the "spreader." Your friend can use a push broom or garden rake to shove the compost or manure out the opening as you move along.

Cut an opening in the front of an old wheelbarrow and it becomes a garden-size spreader. Just pull the wheelbarrow along your garden's rows, shaking it from side to side.

Never Renovate Without It!

If you are going to take on the work of renovating a perennial bed, don't do so without compost! Follow these basic steps for a renovated and rejuvenated bed.

1. Lift the plant.

2. Divide.

3. Work some compost into the planting hole.

4. Replant.

Once you've finished the digging and dividing, you may think you're finished, but you're not! You can also give a boost to the rest of the plants. Just dig a 6-inch-deep hole on either side of every plant, and fill them with compost.

Turn *a Slope* into a **Lush** Garden

If your property slopes, you don't have to give up on having a beautiful garden. Take a tip from Sally Cunningham, author of *Great Garden Companions*. She's successfully amended her soil on a long slope and has had wonderful results from her garden.

"I have a garden on a long sloping hill, and I've often wished I had started it higher up the hill for better drainage. So year by year I'm moving the garden up the hill and making better soil at the same time."

Every year during spring cleanup, Sally makes a new 3-foot-wide by 3-foot-deep compost pile along the length of her garden on the slope above it. She uses leaves, sticks, perennial debris, some manure, and the clippings she collects from the first few lawn mowings. "Some might just call it a raised bed, but I find some warm composting going on, too, when I use the manure or grass—enough to call it compost."

Sally leaves the compost— which is really the future bed—at the back of the garden all season, occasionally giving it a stir or working in some kitchen scraps. It is soon hidden by tall flowers or tomatoes. Meanwhile, if nutrients run out of it, they flow downward, into the garden. According to Sally, "It tends to settle all year so that by next spring I have 3 more feet of great garden to plant in. Over ten years I have moved that garden 30 feet up that hill!"

problem SOLVer

KEEP SIDE-DRESSING WHERE IT BELONGS

Most crops benefit from a side-dressing of compost about a month after planting. But compost is so valuable that it's a shame to see it run off into the garden path or away from the root zone if a spring rain comes just after you have spread it.

Prevent nutrient runoff by using a pointed hoe first. Drag the hoe beside the plants, about 4 inches from their centers, or far enough that you aren't hilling up soil on the plant stem, making a little trench along the row. Don't make the trenches more than 2 inches deep, and look to be sure you are not disturbing new roots. Then sprinkle your compost along the trench, and it will do its work where you want it—even if it pours that day.

creative

Garden Care

You've planted the garden, the seeds are sprouting, and the excitement is just beginning! To make caring for all of your beds, borders, and container gardens easier and more fun, here are dozens of ideas from creative gardeners just like you. From innovative ways for making garden walkways and inexpensive, clever ideas for supporting growing plants to new methods for winterizing delicate roses and the best watering techniques, taking care of the gardens you've so lovingly created has never been easier.

Passive-Aggressive **Stump** Removal

Getting rid of a tree stump doesn't have to be back-breaking work, claims Kay Lancaster of Hillsboro, Oregon. As Kay attests, using her method may take quite a while longer, but your back will love it!

"What I do is bore as many deep holes into the stump as I can," explains Kay. "Then I add a mixture of dilute fertilizer and ground-up rotting wood, preferably from the same species as the tree I've removed."

Next, Kay packs the mixture into the holes well and covers the stump with plastic or melted paraffin to hold moisture.

The result? In a couple of years, Kay can usually kick the stump apart and remove the pieces.

Kay adds, "If you have a really rotten piece of wood to inoculate the stump with and an old blender that you no longer use for food preparation, put the wood in the blender with plenty of water and mix it up. Then dribble the mixture into the holes."

Containing Invasive Plants

If you happen to love a plant that has a reputation for being invasive, you don't have to be afraid to grow it. You just need to take the appropriate precautions.

"To stop invasive plants—and here in Mexico we have many—plant them in a pot sunk in the ground," instructs Wendy Holdaway of Mexico City, Mexico. "The roots grow out the holes in the bottom, but they don't seem to send out suckers the way they do when planted directly in the ground."

For really big plants such as bamboo, Wendy suggests cutting the bottom out of a 4- or 5-gallon plastic container and burying it to surround the plant's roots. "It's not totally effective," she adds, "but it goes a long way toward controlling the spreading."

Terra-Cotta Walkways

"After I bought my house, I discovered a bunch of broken terra-cotta pots and tan cement drainpipes at the far end of the backyard," says garden writer Erin Hynes of Chapel Hill, North Carolina. "I broke them into chunks and laid them in the garden as short walkways.

"The smallest pieces I used are about 4 inches square, and some chunks are as big as 10 × 6 inches."

Make sure you turn all the pieces so that any sharp edges are safely embedded in the soil.

When you use recycled items, adding a pathway is quick, easy, and inexpensive. A mosaic path made from pieces of broken pots and drainage tiles lets you turn trash into treasure.

Bury Weeds under a Burlap Pathway

"We line our vegetable garden paths with burlap coffee bags salvaged from a local roaster. We fold the bags in half and slightly overlap the ends to form a continuous path of burlap," says Natalie McNair-Huff, an organic gardener in Tacoma, Washington.

Natalie says she pins the bags in place with homemade staples made from old wire hangers (see page 14).

"Now the weeds will have to make it through four layers of burlap. And because the bags decompose, we don't have to remove them."

Award-Winning Path

There are plenty of unusual items that can make great garden stepping stones, says Stephanie Ferguson of Indianapolis, Indiana. You just need to think creatively. "My husband plays racquetball pretty well and wins lots of award plaques. Since he doesn't care to hang them up, I'm going to make garden stepping stones out of them."

Broken Dishes Stepping Stones

"Use broken dishes and concrete to make really cool stepping stones," says Karen Macomber, a home gardener in Cohocton, New York.

For molds, she uses old clothes boxes because she can simply peel off the box and compost it after the stepping stones have hardened. She pours the concrete mix into the mold, lets it set a little, then presses pieces of broken pottery on top to simulate a stained-glass effect.

Karen adds that you can pour concrete into any shape container. "You can even use old pie tins or cake pans. Simply let the concrete set somewhat, then turn it out onto a flat surface and decorate. Or, you can make a form on the ground with sand and pour the concrete directly where you want it to go." The leftover sand around the edges simply washes away.

Create customized stepping stones when you press broken dishes into partially set concrete. You can use cardboard boxes, old cake pans, or other cast-off containers to shape the concrete.

Variation for a **No-Dig** Garden

Newspaper is the standard base for gardeners preparing their no-dig garden beds, but cardboard is the material of choice for Godfrey Pearlson, a home gardener in Baltimore, Maryland.

"My garden is big and I've had much better luck using flattened cardboard boxes—which you can easily get for free from grocery stores," Godfrey says. "Flattened cardboard boxes cover larger areas than newspaper, they last longer, and they don't blow away while you're laying out the garden."

Extra! Extra! Wet Paper Stays Put!

Here's the answer for anyone who has struggled to put down newspaper mulch on a breezy day. "When laying down newspaper for weed control, fill a bucket with water to dip the paper in before placing it on the ground," says Dominique Herman of Bound Brook, New Jersey.

The wet paper will stay in place as you spread straw, wood chips, or whatever you plan to put on top of the newspaper. Dominique adds, "I fill a 5-gallon bucket and dip in whole sections of the newspaper—probably 10 to 12 sheets, or roughly ½ inch—to cover each area of the garden."

Slow Strawberry Pot *Evaporation*

"Paint the inside of clay strawberry jars with pot paint (available at garden centers) to keep water evaporation to a minimum," recommends Pat Kolb of Phoenix. "Some strawberry jars already have this coating when you purchase them, but some don't."

Perennial **Swap**

You can get plenty of perennials without a trip to the garden center—and without the expense.

"My twice yearly event called the 'Perennial Swap' is my favorite ingenious gardening effort," says Mimi Luther of Portland, Oregon. "I inherited a well-maintained garden overflowing with beautiful perennials. But I wanted to put in some other plantings and simply had no space. So, I invited all my friends and neighbors to the first Perennial Swap.

"For this spring and autumn event, everyone digs up some of their plantings and brings them to trade and share." Mimi made room for some additions to her garden, shared some lovely old species, and saved a bundle.

If you host or attend a plant swap, remember these guidelines: Don't swap plants that have disease or insect problems or that come from beds that have serious weed problems. Also, if you're swapping something that's a rapid spreader or that self-sows prolifically, warn the recipient so she can plant it with due caution.

Tree-Slice Garden Path

"Tree slices cut from a log provide handy stepping stones for deep flowerbeds, and they're quite attractive," says home gardener Mary Leunissen of Guelph, Ontario. "You can cut them as thick as you want with a chain saw or a carpenter's saw. Mine are about 2 inches thick."

Don't worry about the wooden stepping stones decaying rapidly from moisture and mulch. Mary assures, "I cut my slices three years ago and they still look good, even though they get a fair amount of moisture dumped on them." Mary adds that her tree slices have saved more than one plant, too, since they are large enough to work from "without the usual balancing act and resultant squashed plants!"

Log slices make a sturdy path that lets you step lightly through your garden.

problem SOLVER

SOD SOLUTION

When you dig out sod to make a new garden, you can compost it or use it to patch bare spots in your lawn. But if you have a lot, you can use it to build a living fence, like home gardener Tanya Huff of Ontario is doing.

"We're building a sod wall at the north end of our orchard," says Tanya. "It's about 20 feet long, 3 feet wide, and will, in time, be about 4 feet high. It's roughly based on a 17th century sod wall we saw at Culloden, Scotland."

To create the wall, Tanya lays the sod like haybales on a wagon—alternating lengthwise and crosswise pieces, and being careful to keep cut edges from aligning to prevent gaps. According to Tanya, "Grass needs very little encouragement to grow. I cut sod in spring and fall when the ground is moist and rain is frequent enough so the sod quickly roots into lower layers."

Winter Protection for Roses, **Part I**

Here's a quick way to get roses ready for the onset of cold weather. "I recycle 1-gallon (or larger) plastic pots that perennials are sold in, and use them as collars for my roses in the winter," explains home gardener Mary Leunissen of Guelph, Ontario.

"I use a utility knife to cut out the bottom and up one side so that they open up, like the letter C. I place two wrapped around each other and the rose bush, then fill them with mulched leaves and compost."

Snap a pair of modified large plastic pots around a rose bush, and you have a sturdy wall to hold insulating mulch or compost in place.

Leaf-Sucking Vacuum

Why rake when you can vacuum? "I take my trusty (and now rusty) shop vac outside and vacuum up the leaves," confesses Diana Pederson, editor of *The Enabling Gardener*, of Lansing, Michigan. "It's much faster than raking."

Although vacuuming is quick and easy, Diana offers a few cautions. "Watch that you don't vacuum up too big a wad of wet leaves—they stuff up the hose. Also, be sure to dry out the vacuum container afterward, or you'll wind up with a rusty one like I have!"

A **Big** Box of Leaves

You don't have to wrestle with stuffing raked leaves into garbage bags. Della Kapocius of Grand Forks, North Dakota, has an easier solution. "Rake your leaves into a large cardboard box laid on its side. It's much easier than using leaf bags, especially if you're trying to do the cleanup alone."

Della suggests asking your grocer for the large boxes that toiletpaper comes in. "They hold a lot of leaves, but even when they're full, they aren't too heavy to drag across the yard."

On-the-Fly Tree Protection

Young trees can be virtual magnets to rodents looking for something to eat, so they need to be protected.

"When you don't have a tree guard handy," says Ada Davis of West Fork, Arkansas, "wind small sections of bird or deer netting loosely around the bottom of young trees as a temporary mouse, vole, and rabbit barrier."

Try wrapping the tree with aluminum foil first, then follow up with the netting to ensure that no one can get his nose through the netting for a tasty tree-bark treat.

Winter Protection for Roses, **Part II**

Here's a method for protecting tender rose bushes and fertilizing them at the same time. "For winterizing, rose cones have drawbacks (such as moisture buildup inside), so I find that it's better to mound the bushes," explains home gardener Colette Tremblay of Québec.

"To hold the mounding material, instead of using the small, flimsy rose collars found in the stores, I make my own out of chicken wire." Colette recommends a 4 × 3-foot piece of wire, folded in half so it measures 48 × 18 inches. She ties the chicken wire into a circle with wire or twine to make a generous-sized collar— 18 inches high and 15 inches in diameter—which can hold a lot of insulating material.

You can fill the collar with leaves, straw, or soil, but Colette prefers to use compost or well-rotted manure. "When added late in the fall when the ground is at least partially frozen, compost doesn't promote untimely growth, and next spring, when you remove the collars, you can rake the compost or manure over the bed and lightly work it in. *Voilà!* Most of the fertilizing is done for the season."

Colette adds, "When I use a fine-textured insulating material such as screened compost, I line the inside of the chicken wire with newspaper first, to prevent the compost from falling through the chicken-wire holes."

Photographic Memory

Don't trust your memory of what blooms when in your garden? "Take photographs of your flowerbeds every week or so while they are blooming," recommends Sharon Gordon of Ohio. "The photos make it easier to plan future plantings by showing what blooms at the same time."

To keep your photos organized, label them and put them in a photo album or garden journal, and keep them with your perennial and seed catalogs for easy winter browsing and planning.

problem SOLVer   JUNK MAIL MULCH

At last, a use for all that junk mail. "For the past two years I have shredded my junk mail with a very inexpensive home paper shredder, saved it, and then used it as mulch on our garden," says horticulture specialist Jeanne Schwaller of Jefferson City, Missouri. "It works just great."

Jeanne puts an in-line drip system next to the plants, then adds about a 4- to 6-inch layer of shredded junk mail. Then she sets the timer on the drip system to keep the plants moist beneath the mulch. Jeanne recommends wetting the paper with a hose first to keep it from blowing away.

According to Jeanne, she's only had to spend about ten minutes a week pulling weeds since spreading the junk mail mulch on her garden. But, she adds, "The most therapeutic part of this is spreading the junk mail and knowing it actually did some good."

In the late fall, Jeanne tills the decomposed paper into the garden where, she reports, it has somewhat improved her clay soil.

homegrown HINTS

HOMEMADE WATERING CANS

If you don't want to go to the expense or bother of installing drip irrigation, try this simple "watering can" system from Dr. Jeanne Schwaller, a horticulture specialist in Jefferson City, Missouri.

Use a 6- or 8-penny nail to punch holes in the bottom of 5-pound coffee cans or institutional-size vegetable cans. "The bottom of the can will look similar to a sprinkler head, but with fewer holes," says Jeanne. Set one can by each plant, and fill the cans with water. This trick makes short work of watering and soaks the soil deeply and efficiently, like drip irrigation does, without washing the soil away from your plants' roots. Refill the cans as needed.

Slow Drip Fertilizer

"For deep watering and fertilization, I cut the top off a 2-liter bottle, drill small holes in the bottom, fill it three-quarters full with compost, and bury it between plants," says home gardener Kim Barwick, of Hoffman Estates, Illinois. "When I water, I fill the bottles with water, which releases a weak compost tea deep into the root zone."

Soda Pop Irrigation

"When I transplant my tomatoes, I also plant a plastic 2-liter bottle with the bottom cut off and a hole drilled in the cap. I stick the capped end in the soil where the roots will grow—about 4 to 6 inches deep—and put a bottle about 12 inches from each side of the plant," says Mike McLain of Leroy, Alabama. Then all Mike has to do is fill the soda bottles with water about twice a week, instead of watering the plants daily.

Mike says that the size of the hole you drill in the cap can vary for different locations and conditions. "In my sandy loam soil, a 1/16-inch hole works fine, but you may need a larger hole if you have clay soil. I usually cut the bottoms off the bottles with my band saw, but I have also cut some with a utility knife. I find that soda bottles with a longer, V-shaped neck and bigger neck ring stay in place the best."

Take a break from daily watering with this practical soda bottle watering system. Your garden will enjoy the benefits of a steady supply of water while you tend to other garden tasks.

Boiled Eggs Aren't Just for Breakfast Anymore

"My grandmother taught me to use the water eggs are boiled in for watering plants, because it makes plants healthy and strong," says C. J. England of Hope, Idaho. "I've gotten in the habit of keeping all discarded eggshells in an odor-proof half-gallon container. When the container is about three-quarters full, I boil the eggshells and use the water on houseplants and in the garden. I've also had very good results using this water on seedlings. My grandmother used it to start plant cuttings, too."

Getting to the Roots

To encourage deep roots on sprawling or climbing vegetables—especially cucumbers, squash, and tomatoes—try this clever watering trick.

Yvonne Savio, Common Ground Gardening program manager for University of California Cooperative Extension in Los Angeles County, recommends burying a 5-gallon nursery container at the center of a planting hill, to within 3 inches of its rim, for a noncollapsible watering-and-fertilizing hole. "Plant seeds or seedlings in a slight depression just beyond the rim, and fill the depression with water to get the plants settled. Early in the season, each time you water the circle surrounding the container, also fill the container so water will seep out the bottom holes." By the time really hot weather comes, the plant roots will be deep enough that you can just fill the container when you water—you won't have to water from above. Your vegetable plants will appreciate the extra big drinks. And you'll love being able to just plunk the hose into the bucket.

For a midseason feeding, Yvonne recommends adding a shovelful of compost to the container. That way, you give your plants a dose of compost tea every time you fill the container with water.

Keep Moisture In

If you need to go out of town on business, you don't have to worry about your plants in clay pots drying out while you're away. According to Kathleen Weber of Upper Darby, Pennsylvania, you can simply wrap the clay pots with aluminum foil. "It keeps the clay pots damper for a longer period of time, so less watering is needed."

problem solver

RECYCLE YOUR COOKING WATER

Cooking dinner can use a surprising amount of water, and with a little advance planning, you can save that water and put it to good use. "Use the water from steaming vegetables, cooled down, of course, to water your potted plants," suggests Connie Gardner, assistant manager of Horsford's Nursery in Charlotte, Vermont. Just keep a plastic bucket on hand in your kitchen. Then when you're done steaming the veggies, pour the water into the bucket instead of down the drain. When dinner is done, the nutrient-filled water will be cool, and you can make the rounds of your houseplants or outdoor containers.

When to *Water*

Instead of guessing when it's time to water or using some fancy tool to check the moisture level of the soil, use a device that's always handy: your fingers. Stick them into the soil until they're completely covered, and feel for moisture. If they come up dry, it's time to turn on the sprinkler or get out the watering can.

PVC Pipeline *to the* Roots

While lots of gardeners have clever ways to water with soda bottles, you don't have to drink a lot of soda pop to create a watering system. Try this PVC pipeline tip from Natalie McNair-Huff, of Tacoma, Washington.

"Before you plant, bury all but the top of an 8- to 10-inch-long, 3-inch-diameter PVC pipe. Use one pipe for each plant. Then plant your tomatoes, peppers, or whatever beside the pipes. When the plants need deep watering, simply pour the water into the pipe."

You can use either perforated or regular PVC for this technique.

2-Liter **Irrigation** *Variation*

Here's another variation of the soda bottle watering system, from Laura Archbald of Clover, South Carolina.

Use a 2-liter soda bottle with the cap on, and punch about 8 to 12 holes in the top third of the empty bottle with a nail or awl. Turn the bottle upside down, and cut a hole about ½ inch from the bottom that is large enough for a garden hose to fit into. (Laura reports that she used to just cut off the bottom of the bottle, but she found that the water evaporated too quickly and the bottle would fill with debris, which would block the holes.)

Laura recommends burying about two-thirds of the bottle, capped end down, in the middle of a melon hill. "It also works great next to tomatoes. You can fill it with water once or twice a week, or use a watering can to fill it with a dilute fish-emulsion and seaweed combination," says Laura.

This twist on the soda bottle drip irrigation system leaves the bottom intact to reduce evaporation. Cut a hole that is just large enough for your hose to fit into, and you can make sure most of the water reaches your plants' roots.

Timely tip

Laura says that soda bottles last a few years, so here are her ideas for storing them between growing seasons. "The bottles clean up pretty well with the hose. Once they're clean and dry, you can hang them in the garage or basement and use them to store large seeds, bulbs, onion sets, and the like by stringing the bottles on a rope (tie the rope around the neck of each bottle). Or pull old panty hose or knee-high stockings over the bottles, knot them, and hang them by the knot.

Liquid *Life-Support* for Tomatoes

Kim Barwick, who gardens in Hoffman Estates, Illinois, shares her inexpensive method for making a funnel irrigation system for caged tomatoes. "This system encourages deep rooting," says Kim.

To make the funnel, drill a ¼-inch hole in the cap of an empty 2-liter soda bottle. Cut a 3-foot length of ¼-inch tubing, and push the end of the tubing into the hole, making sure it fits tightly.

Kim then cuts the bottom off the bottle and punches two small holes about 1 inch above the cut on opposite sides of the bottle. "Run a wire through the holes and use it to hang the inverted bottle on the tomato cage."

To complete the system, bury a 1- to 2-foot-long section of PVC pipe, at least 1¼ inches in diameter, at an angle about 1½ feet below the plant, so the end sticks out above the soil. Place the loose end of the ¼-inch tubing into the pipe. When you fill the bottle with water, it slowly drips into the PVC pipe, which channels the water directly to the roots.

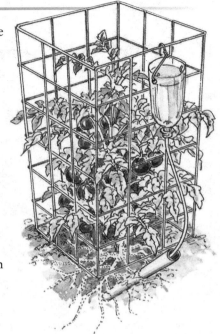

"Fill it and forget it" is all you have to do with this soda bottle watering system that sends a steady supply of water right to your tomato plant's roots. Water from the bottle "funnel" drips gradually into a pipe pushed into the soil, encouraging the plant to produce deep, healthy roots.

problem SOLVER

PUT WATER EXACTLY WHERE YOU WANT IT

"There is no better watering tool than a battery filler," claims Pennsylvania garden writer Duane Campbell. "It looks like a turkey baster, but it is a bit bigger and sturdier. It's available for a few dollars from hardware or auto supply stores, and it puts exactly the amount of water exactly where you want it. No more mopping up water from the windowsills and floor when the spout overshoots."

With bushy plants, where the stream from a watering can spout runs off the leaves, you can slip the battery filler through the leaves and squirt the water right onto the soil. According to Duane, "The stream is gentle enough to water seedling flats, and you can control it to a drop at a time if you want. For very small pots, you can give them half an ounce at a time if needed. Best of all, one full squeeze gives you the same amount of water every time."

Duane adds, "When you go away for a few days and leave your houseplants' care to a brown-thumb neighbor, you can leave instructions to give this plant one squeeze, that one two, and so on."

homegrown HINTS

ICE YOUR HOUSEPLANTS

"I use ice cubes to water my houseplants because they don't run through the pot as fast as water does," says Gary Pierce, assistant agriculture extension agent in Smithville, North Carolina.

Gary recommends covering as much of the soil mix in the pot with ice as possible, being careful not to put the ice on the stem or leaves. "The ice doesn't freeze the roots, because the water has to be at least 33°F before it will flow into the soil. And, as the water makes contact with the soil particles, it gains heat. But if ice touches the stems or leaves, the plants can be damaged."

Since ice takes up more volume than water, Gary adds that overwatering is rarely a problem. As the ice cubes melt, they slowly release water. So there's plenty of time for the mix to absorb the water and become saturated, even if it's a mix that's rich in peat, which tends to shed water. Gary finds he only has to give his plants the ice treatment once or twice a week.

Weatherproof Rain Barrel

Toni Hawryluk of Seattle shares an idea for an inexpensive rain barrel that won't decay like the wooden ones.

"I found 45-gallon plastic drums at a discount store for just $15—and they live forever! I had a handyman attach a faucet near the bottom to control drainage, and then I put the drum on a rack under a downspout so my watering can fits under the faucet."

In addition to filling her watering can from her plastic rain barrel, Toni says, "I can also attach a garden hose to the faucet and dribble away."

$1 Rain Barrels

Grocery stores, bakeries, and restaurants are all good places to look for large plastic pails with handles and lids, which make perfect rain barrels in your garden. Food items such as flour and sugar are delivered in these pails, and you can often get them free—or at least cheap, in an array of sizes.

Gardener June Dean of Narragansett, Rhode Island, reports that she bought several of these pails for $1 each, and she uses them to both haul mulch and collect rainwater.

"They hold 40 pounds of mulch or 22 gallons of water. When not in use, these pails get tucked away out of sight. But when it rains, I take off their lids and capture the rainwater to pamper some of my plants that do better with rainwater than they do with chlorinated water from the tap."

Hanging Basket Oasis

Mary Yontz of Goshen, Indiana, shares this idea for preventing hanging baskets from drying out so quickly. "Put oasis or florist foam—the green stuff florists use in flower arrangements—into hanging baskets. It holds water longer so you don't have to water as often. I use about a 3-inch cube in the center of 8- to 10-inch pots, surrounded by potting soil."

Protecting Plants from Pets

Sometimes pets just don't respect garden boundaries. Here's a clever idea for a garden fence that looks nice while keeping dogs at bay.

"As I am owned by two Welsh Corgis who feel that they have a right to prowl through the garden at will, I have to work at keeping them off the newly emerging crowns of my perennials and herbs in the early spring," says Sue Murphy of Ogden, Utah. "What I came up with is cheap and easy."

Sue saves the prunings from a weeping mulberry and cuts them into 2½-foot sections. She uses the sections to edge her beds, pushing the ends into the soil and intertwining and overlapping them enough to eliminate Corgi-size holes.

Sue says, "This fence has worked very well and usually this looks so good that I leave it in for the growing season as a rustic edging to my walkways and borders. In the fall, I simply remove the twigs and then shred them."

In case you're wondering, Sue says no twig-ends have ever self-rooted.

If you don't happen to have a weeping mulberry, you can achieve the same effect in your garden using trimmings from trees such as weeping cherry, weeping willow, or any tree or shrub with flexible young branches, such as a forsythia.

Create a rustic fence or border for your garden with prunings of flexible branches. It's a great-looking solution for keeping dogs—and humans—on the path and out of the garden beds.

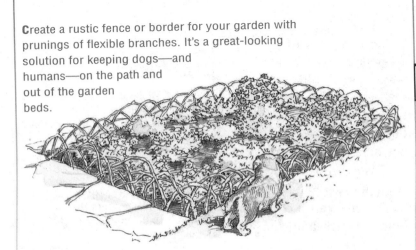

Temporary Bagging

If you receive bareroot perennials from a catalog before you have time to plant them, or if it's just too early to put them in the ground, here's a good solution for storing them until the time is right for planting.

Karen Helfert of Rockville, Maryland, reports that she stores bareroot hostas and peonies in freezer bags. "I put soil and the plants into plastic freezer bags, one plant per bag." To store them, put them in a plastic box and water them. Karen suggests leaving the bags open to prevent molding. You can store them inside, then move them to a porch as the weather warms, before finally transplanting them outside.

Timely tip

If you buy the freezer bags that have an area for labeling the contents, it's easy to record what type of plant is in each bag. And consider using the new ventilated zipper-top vegetable storage bags. That way you don't have to keep the bag open, and air can still circulate.

problem SOLVer

MOLESKIN TO THE RESCUE

"When I'm going to do a lot of raking or heavy digging, I put a piece of adhesive-backed moleskin over the blister-prone area of my hand before putting on my gloves. Then I just peel it off when I'm done working," says Bambi Cantrell, of Jacksonville, North Carolina.

Bambi recommends using the moleskin on gardening tools, too, to cushion their handles.

Soothing Treatment *for* Gardener's Hands

Linda Pek of Vienna, Austria, swears by this healing hand treatment after a long day in the garden.

"After you come in from gardening all day with your hands all rough and red, scrub your hands to get rid of all the dirt, then slather them all over with lots of your favorite hand cream. Afterward, put on rubber gloves, and hand wash all the dirty dishes that your family deposited in the sink while you were outside. Be sure to use really hot water. There's something about doing it with very hot water that causes the hand cream to penetrate skin really well!"

Handy Drinks **Revive** Parched Gardeners

Freeze ahead for a supply of cold, refreshing drinking water to sip during those hot, tiring summer afternoons in the garden, suggests garden writer Barbara Ellis, author of *Taylor's Guide to Growing ‿h America's Favorite*

Barbara saves 12- and 16-ounce plastic juice and water bottles, fills them three-quarters full of water, and freezes them. When she heads out to the garden, she tosses one in her garden cart.

"Just when I'm really starting to get hot, there's enough melted water in the bottle to quench my thirst," Barbara says.

Rice Remedy for Gardening **Aches** and **Pains**

Sometimes gardening is better for the soul than it is for the body. But there are ways to remedy aching muscles and other symptoms of garden over-indulgence.

Here's how Laura McKenzie of Springville, Alabama, handles gardening aches and pains. "I fill a bleached, clean sock—a thick sports sock—with rice, knot the top of it, and stick it in the freezer for treating garden-sore muscles. The rice conforms to the aching joint or limb better than ice or even a bag of frozen peas, and the soft sock is comfortable next to the skin," says Laura.

Timely tip

Laura says a sockful of rice is great for warm relief, too. "If you heat the sock in the microwave—with a cup of water next to it to be safe—it works as a heating pad. It even soothes bug bites." A word of caution with the microwave: Don't overheat the rice. Since you are heating it in a sock and not water, it can burn if it is cooked too long.

Easy Pruning Cleanup

"When you prune, first place a tarpaulin on the ground near your work space," recommends Peg Baseden, a Delaware Master Gardener. "Throw all the trimmings on it, and you can easily pull them to your compost pile."

Look for old bedspreads at yard sales to use as tarps. They're cheap and sturdy—and large enough to hold lots of trimmings.

Garden **Hose** Fencing

"You can make inexpensive fencing to define small garden plots, such as those in community gardens," says Peg Baseden, a Delaware Master Gardener. "If you're planning to discard a garden hose and old broom handles or similar wood, use the broom handles for posts and string the old hose between them."

Peg says to attach the hose near the top of the posts by tying it on with twine or tacking it on with nails. "It keeps people out of the plots and looks 'gardeny'."

Secure Tunnels

Tunnels covered with plastic sheeting are a great way to protect plants at the start and end of the growing season, but keeping the plastic from blowing off the arch supports can be a challenge. Stephanie Ferguson of Indianapolis has found a way that works for her raised box beds. "I have *finally* achieved success with tunnels!" she exclaims. Here's Stephanie's winning method.

Stephanie uses two sizes of PVC pipe to hold the plastic row covers in place over her arched tunnels—one about 2 inches in diameter and a second that is almost small enough to fit inside the 2-inch pipe. In addition to the PVC pipes, you'll need nuts and bolts for anchoring the plastic.

1. Cut each pipe in half lengthwise and nest the pipe with the smaller diameter inside the larger pipe, like two spoons nested together.

2. Drill holes along the length of each nesting pair of PVC pipes, about every 8 to 12 inches.

3. Separate the pipes, put the plastic between them, and nest them back together.

4. Secure the pipes together by putting bolts through the holes and fastening nuts on the bolts.

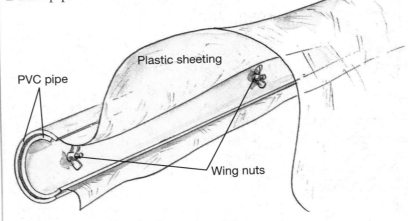

Hold plastic sheeting or floating row covers securely in place with nesting PVC pipe anchors. No more blowing away or tearing apart!

Anchoring Plastic Covers

"The nailing-strip edge of vinyl siding, which is quite strong because it is folded over a couple of times in manufacture, is commonly cut away around windows and doors in long strips during installation on a house," notes Terry Klokeid of Amblewood Farm on SaltSpring Island, British Columbia. "These long strips are great for attaching plastic over cold frames, rabbit hutches, and the like.

"The folded part gives the material some rigidity and holds the plastic sheeting down well, yet it's possible to attach the nailing strip to the wood frame of the structure with short screws. You don't need nails, which can pop out, or long screws, which make big holes and are hard to remove. Simply drill a small pilot hole through the vinyl, where it's one layer thick."

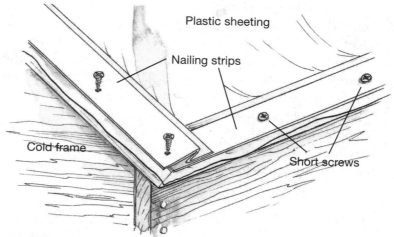

If you can get your hands on leftover vinyl siding nailing strips, either from your own home-improvement stash or a construction site in the neighborhood, they make a sturdy yet easy way to attach plastic sheeting to cold frames.

homegrown HINTS

EASY ANCHORS FOR TUNNEL HOOPS

Here's an easy way to anchor large plant tunnels. Find metal pipes narrower in diameter than the PVC you'll be using for the hoops. For example, use ½-inch-diameter metal piping for ¾-inch-diameter flexible PVC. "Cut the metal pipe into 2-foot lengths, and pound them about 1 foot into the ground, 18 to 24 inches apart within a row," explains Ginny Prins of Victoria, British Columbia.

Next, gather flexible PVC piping for the hoops. To frame [your] hoop house, "just slip your PVC over the metal pipes and [h]ave the beginnings of a hoop greenhouse," Ginny says.

Snow Shovel Does *Double Duty*

"In the fall we wait until all the leaves are down, then my husband pushes them into a big pile with a plastic snow shovel," says Sue Blyth of Ottawa, Canada. "Because the snow shovel is plastic, the edge isn't sharp, so it just slides over the lawn or pavement and scoops everything in its path, including the acorns."

J-Channeling
Plastic Covers

Another type of vinyl-siding scrap can keep rigid plastic panels from blowing off cold frames and other structures, says Terry Klokeid of Amblewood Farm on SaltSpring Island, British Columbia.

"You can use scraps of J-channel from vinyl siding to support lightweight plastic or wood panels," says Terry. "If you use a rigid cover over a cold frame, then just a few bits of J-channel, strategically placed at the corners, will hold

it firmly even in the wind."

Simply screw short lengths of the J-channel at the corners (or along the entire side if you prefer) on both of the sloping sides of the cold frame, and slide the cover in so it's sandwiched between the two Js.

The J-channel used to hold vinyl siding in place also works in the garden. Attached to a cold frame, it lets you slip a cover in or out.

Another piece of J-channel or a piece of scrap wood may be required on the lower edge of the frame to prevent the cover from sliding out.

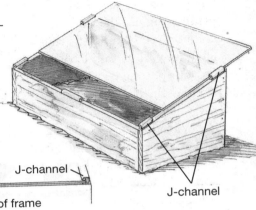

Top view   Plastic cover   J-channel

Back edge of frame

J-channel

Weighted
Row Covers

Here's an easy method for keeping row covers from blowing off of your garden. "If you need more weights than you have heavy rocks,

fill some plastic gallon jugs nearly full with water," suggests Sharon Gordon, a bio-intensive gardener in Ohio. "Put the caps back on and use the jugs to weight the edge of the cover."

Save those plastic gallon jugs from milk, water, or juice, and fill them with water to use as weights to keep your row covers in place. When it's time to remove the row covers, you can use the weights to water your plants.

The *Light* Timing

Even if you don't have a timer for your indoor plant light setup, there's an easy way to make sure your seedlings consistently get 18 hours of strong light per day. Just make turning the lights on and off part of your daily routine, as Deborah Turton of Gaithersburg, Maryland, does. "I plug my lights in around dinnertime, leave them on all night, and unplug them around lunchtime," says Deborah. "This lets the seedlings have about 18 hours of intense light."

Get the *Upper Hand* on *Hanging Baskets*

Here's the answer if you've ever struggled to make a hanging basket where the plants hang out the sides and bottom. Instead of struggling to work with the basket on your potting bench, try hanging the basket at about chest height.

"When planting a hanging basket that will contain plants that will hang out of the bottom or sides, use a stepladder and broom or rake to create a convenient place to hang the basket," advises Della Kapocius of Grand Forks, North Dakota. "Open the stepladder and place the broom or rake handle across the roller-tray shelf and the opposite ladder rung. Hang your basket from the handle, and your basket will be positioned just right."

Planting the sides and bottom of a hanging basket can be tricky when it's resting on a table. Hang your basket from a broom handle slipped through the tray and top rung of a ladder, and plant all around your basket with ease.

problem solver

BUYING TIME FOR PERENNIALS

"When dividing perennials, I always pot up the divisions, using that pile of black gallon-size nursery containers I have carefully accumulated out in the garage," says gardener and garden writer Duane Campbell of Towanda, Pennsylvania.

Duane says that he gives some potted perennials to friends and sells others at his spring yard sale. Even those divisions he plans to replant in the garden get potted first. That gives Duane a few days to consider their new location rather than making a snap decision.

Duane also likes to keep at least one division in the pot for a season to see how it does. "Some of my best patio container plants are perennials that took well to container growing. Mums get divided every year and always produce more divisions than I can possibly use. But potted in gallon containers, they can grow strong and lush in an out-of-the-way spot (but near enough for the hose to reach them). Then in fall, when the annuals falter, I have dozens of mums ready to plop in their places and keep the garden looking great."

More Space for *Hanging* Plants

If you have a fenced-in yard, you can turn that fence into a display area for hanging baskets with the addition of some inexpensive garden lattice. Lyn Belisle, a home gardener from San Antonio, did just that.

"I nailed a 2-foot-wide strip of lattice horizontally onto the 2 × 2 that runs along the top of my fence like a cap board," says Lyn. (She let a little of the lattice board hang over the back of the fence for balance.) To hang baskets, lay a bamboo pole across the top of the lattice, then slip the hanging baskets up through the holes in the lattice and hook them over the bamboo.

"It's strong and sturdy, and I can move the plants around without any trouble just by repositioning the bamboo pole," says Lyn. And here's the real reason Lyn thought of this idea in the first place—she wanted to keep her cat from jumping over the fence. So if you know a curious cat that you'd like to keep in—or out—of your yard, try Lyn's hanging plant rack idea.

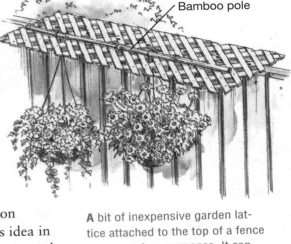

Bamboo pole

A bit of inexpensive garden lattice attached to the top of a fence can serve two purposes. It can give you a great place to display hanging baskets, which will brighten your garden. And it can keep your cat—or the neighbor's cat—from vaulting over the fence to areas where it doesn't belong.

homegrown HINTS

THE FINE ART OF SIFTING

If you have rocky soil or a supply of compost that needs to be sifted, Terry and Libby Klokeid of Amblewood Farm on SaltSpring Island, British Columbia, recommend sifting in two or more stages rather than just one, because it's easier. "We have had to sift rocks from all our garden soil, because our property has never been cultivated before."

Terry says they built a series of seven sifters, each measuring about 2 × 3 feet, with successively finer mesh, from chicken wire to window screen. Terry says, "We call the chicken wire sifter a 7 and the window screen a 1." Sift into a box, crate, or wheelbarrow, then repeat the process.

Terry adds, "We can customize what we do—for beds that will hold small-seeded plants such as carrots, the soil goes through a few siftings, using sifters 7, 5, and 3 or 2. Since crops like tomatoes don't mind a few sticks or rocks, we use larger sizes of mesh for sifting compost for those beds."

homegrown HINTS

PERFECT PEONY SUPPORT

Every gardener who loves the lush springtime blooms of peonies knows how tough it can be to keep them standing—especially after a spring shower. You can buy peony supports, but sometimes they are not enough to keep your peonies upright and beautiful.

"For beds of peony plants that are too big for those standard metal peony support rings," reports home gardener Edie Carlson of Saint Thomas, Ontario, "I use the 12-inch-tall lattice used for topping fences that you can buy at home-improvement or hardware centers. I simply construct a small fence that goes around the whole peony bed."

Lawn Edging Is **Child's** Play

For a tidy lawn edging that's easy enough for your kids to install, try this idea from Kathryn Marsh of County Dublin, Ireland.

"I keep a pile for all those irritating too-small-to-use stones that come up in the garden," says Kathryn. "Every so often the children have an entertaining hour or two arranging them in a 1-foot-wide band along a stretch of lawn edge, just below soil height. Then we sweep a mixture of sand and cement into the stones, and the kids go over it with the watering can."

The result of this "child's play" is a decorative lawn edging you can mow across, a good barrier to stop the grass from running into the borders, and happy kids. "And you will never need to neaten the lawn edge again."

Kathryn cautions that it is important to make the stone edging low enough so that the lawn mower blades won't hit it. One way to do this is to strip off the sod and put the layer of stones down on the soil underneath. Or you can simply have your helpers place the stones in a band on the soil at the existing edge between lawn and garden bed.

Stake Protection

"Cut a slice in old racquetballs or tennis balls that have lost their bounce, and slip the balls over the top of low stakes," recommends Susan Schoneweis, extension coordinator for Home/Environmental Horticulture at the University of Nebraska–Lincoln. That way, if someone trips and falls on a stake, they'll be less likely to injure themselves. If you don't have racquetballs or tennis balls, you can also use wads of old nylon hose and secure them with duct tape to the stakes, but it's a lot more work.

Be a **Cheap-Stakes** Winner

Don't find yourself short on stakes when plants flop. When freelance garden writer Veronica Lorson Fowler, of Ames, Iowa, did a remodeling project in her house, she saved pieces of quarter-round wooden molding that was used as trim along the floor. "The molding pieces make great plant stakes," Veronica says. "And whenever a tall tool, like a rake or broom, breaks, I always saw it off. Again, great staking material."

Wrap Up for Winter

"To help keep potted perennials from freezing, I line the insides of the pot with bubble wrap before planting," says home gardener Debra Schaefer, of Pittsboro, Indiana. "This allows me to leave marginally hardy plants outside and enables less-hardy ones to survive in the garage." But don't line the bottoms of pots, so water can still drain out of them.

Houseplant Insurance

"When you buy a new house-plant, always root a cutting as soon as possible and give it to a friend," quips garden writer Duane Campbell of Towanda, Pennsylvania. "That way, when yours dies, you'll know where to go to replace it."

Six-Pack Plant Supports

For staking perennials that die back each winter—specifically those with dense leaves at the top and stalky undergrowth, such as peonies—save the plastic six-pack rings from your soda or juice cans. Dawn Alleman, an extension agent from Norfolk, Virginia, says, "As the plants sprout in the spring, drop the intact plastic ring over the emerging shoots. As the shoots grow through the rings and raise them up, the rings support the plant so that it won't flop over with heavy buds and blooms."

Dawn suggests using several six-pack rings to support larger plants, and she reminds gardeners to be sure to put on the rings when the plants are just emerging. "As with any grow-through staking, if you wait too long, the stems will leaf out and you'll have to bend the plant into the holes."

Instead of recycling the plastic rings from six-packs, reuse them as support for emerging peonies. As the foliage grows, the plastic holders won't be visible, and they'll help prevent the heavy blossoms from drooping.

Downspout Solution, **Part I**

"I planted Corsican mint (*Mentha requienii*) where my downspouts meet the grass," says home gardener Liz Bonfiglio of North Hills, Pennsylvania. "I don't use the weed wacker often, and the mint keeps the grass in check and adds a delightful mint scent when I mow the edges."

Liz adds that you can also use woolly thyme (*Thymus pseudolanuginosus*) instead of mint or grass, but only if your downspout area isn't consistently wet or soggy.

Downspout Solution, **Part II**

"I put pieces of broken clay pots under my downspouts to keep soil from washing into the yard or onto the sidewalk," says Candy Sheagley, an Advanced Master Gardener in Brookston, Indiana.

A *Means* of *Support*

Don't throw away that torn, bent, or broken umbrella. Take the cloth off the frame and use it to stake bush-type peas, which lean instead of climb.

"Stick the handle of a fully opened umbrella in the ground so that the spokes are about 5 to 6 inches above the ground," instructs Pat Lenzo of Boston, Georgia, editor and publisher of the *Home-steader's Connection*. "Plant peas below each spoke, and as they grow, the tendrils will grasp the spokes for support."

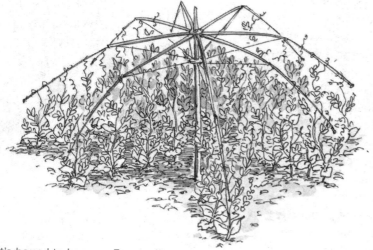

It's bound to happen. Eventually your umbrella tears or bends, and you need to replace it. But save the old one and remove the fabric. The metal frame is just the right size for supporting bush-style peas.

Clothespin Tension Line

"Tie twine through the springs of two clothespins, and clamp them to a stake on each side of a cucumber, pea, or other reluctant climbing vine to create a trellis," suggests Yvonne Savio, gardening education coordinator for the Los Angeles County Cooperative Extension Service. "The clothespins allow you to move or adjust the tension on the twine easily, without a lot of untying and retying knots that are hidden in the plant foliage."

Yvonne adds that you can use her twine and clothespin method in conjunction with trellis netting, too. She says that adding the twine over the trellis "helps tie in straggling and unruly growth that doesn't attach itself to the netting."

Poultry Netting to the *Rescue*

Poultry netting, also called chicken fencing or chicken wire, is easy to hang as a trellis support for lightweight vines. You can attach it to the side of a garden shed or to the edge of a porch roof with a staple gun or by hanging it on small nails.

"I use it to support morning glories and loofahs. I grow them where they provide shade for a west-facing window," explains home gardener Vera Smith of Rusk, Texas.

Timely tip

Vera has other ingenious uses for poultry netting. "I also use poultry netting as a type of bulletin board; I hang it on the shed wall and use clothespins to hang seed packages and garden plans. And I use it in a dark area to hang herbs to dry."

Low-Cost, *Flexible* Arbor

For an inexpensive arbor for climbing plants, consider a panel of cattle fencing. Gardener Vera Smith of Rusk, Texas, says she finds that it makes a great arbor.

"The panel is 16 feet long and 4½ feet high—and it's flexible. You can bend it into an arch and grow climbing plants on each side. The fencing bends to form an arch that is tall enough for adults to walk through."

Vera explains that to install her arbor, she simply bent the fencing and butted the ends next to the wooden sides of her raised garden beds to make an archway over the path area. She says that the tension of the wire keeps the flexed panel upright, and the raised beds anchor the arch at its base. "We like it because it provides a shady sitting spot out in the garden."

If you like Vera's arbor but don't have raised beds in the right position to hold it in place, anchor your fence-panel arbor with tent stakes instead. Make sure to wear gloves to protect your hands from rough edges or wire ends.

Updated **Bean-Pole** Teepee

Here's an improved version of the classic bean-pole teepee. "To make an hourglass bean teepee, pound three or more stakes into the ground several feet apart in a triangle or circle (so that they cross at their centers), and tie them together at the center," says Sharon Gordon of Ohio.

Sharon says that the beans will grow away from each other once they cross the center of the pole, making the beans easier to see and harvest.

"I use 6-foot stakes. Although 8-foot stakes would work well too, you'd need a ladder to stand on for pounding the stakes into the ground."

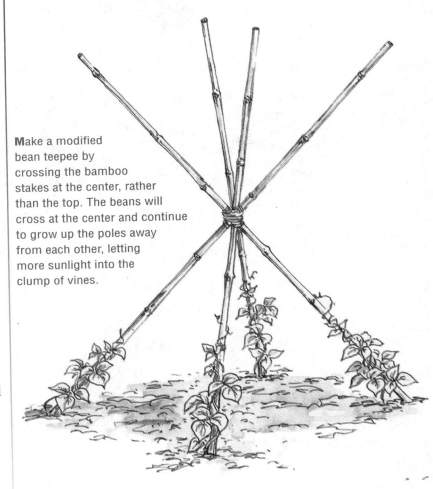

Make a modified bean teepee by crossing the bamboo stakes at the center, rather than the top. The beans will cross at the center and continue to grow up the poles away from each other, letting more sunlight into the clump of vines.

Bicycle Wheel Rims *Find New Life* as Plant Supports

If you have some old bicycle wheel rims laying about the garage or basement, give them new life as supports for climbing beans and peas. That's what Shona Lamoureaux of Christchurch, New Zealand, did. You need two rims for each unit you want to make, and according to Shona, each unit can support about 25 plants.

Just because your old bicycle is ready for the junkyard doesn't mean it's not good for something! Save the old wheel rims and use them to train climbing peas. All you need is some string and a wooden stake, and you can make this clever round trellis.

Here's Shona's technique:

1. Remove all the spokes from two rims.

2. Use a cross of wood or pipe to divide the center of one rim into four sections. You can nail the wood in place through the spoke holes.

3. Next, find a pole that's slightly taller than the height that your beans or peas will grow. (You'll push about one-third of the pole into the ground to make it sturdy.) So if your peas grow to 6 feet tall, you'll need an 8-foot pole. Nail the pole to the center of the cross so that it's perpendicular to the plane of the rim. If you use a metal pole (which won't rot in the ground), you'll need to drill a hole to attach it to the wooden crosspieces.

4. Put one rim on the ground, and push the pole with the other rim attached to its top into the soil in the center of the rim on the ground. Connect the top and bottom rims by stringing twine through the spoke holes, then secure the bottom rim to the ground with tent pegs or ground staples. (See page 14 for information on making your own staples.)

5. You're ready to plant!

"Plant beans or peas around the bottom rim, and they will climb up the string," says Shona. "I usually plant a tomato plant or some sort of herb or flower in the center of the rings, too, to take advantage of the space."

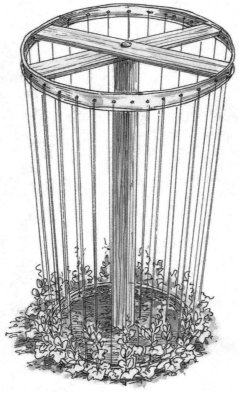

snazzy
Season Stretchers

Few things gladden a gardener's heart as much as picking the first ripe tomato in the neighborhood or surprising friends with a garden-fresh dinner in midwinter. Finding methods for overcoming whatever adverse conditions come your way is what season extension is all about. Whether your garden goal is to gather the earliest harvest ever or to stretch your fall crops into winter and then into spring, you'll find lots of great tips to guide you and tools to help you. Get ideas from market gardeners and home gardeners who have figured out their own clever ways to outsmart the elements.

Mobile Gardens *Extend* the Seasons

"Container growing is the ultimate season extender, since the container can be placed wherever conditions are suitable," says Mac Cheever. Mac has to contend with subzero temperatures during much of the winter in his Zone 4 market garden in Milton, Wisconsin.

You can move potted garden plants anywhere when frost threatens—even into your house, Mac says. "Plants such as hot peppers generally survive winter in the house fairly well and take right off the next year like they never quit," he explains. "Both early and late production are enhanced, and you have the added benefit of red, ripe peppers outside the usual season."

Hanging baskets make nifty season stretchers, too. Many flowers and vegetables will grow quite nicely in them, and their hanging height can raise them above low spots where frost settles. "Hanging containers give you the option of concentrating them in an area that may be more easily covered during early frosts than a conventional garden is," adds Mac.

Four-Season
Harvest Secrets

Eliot Coleman, author of *The New Organic Grower* and *Four-Season Harvest*, says there are basically just three secrets to his year-round garden production in Harborside, Maine:

1. Proper variety selection.

2. Carefully timed planting.

3. Simple season extenders.

Eliot plants only the most cold-hardy varieties. As the days grow shorter in fall, he makes successive plantings every few days inside his un-heated hoop houses. He then covers the beds with spun-bonded row covers.

Don't forget to water during the winter, Eliot ad-vises. By keeping it moist, you can increase the minimum temperature by 4°F under the spunbonded covers.

Plant cold-hardy varieties in a hoop house, cover the beds with row cover, and you can enjoy fresh produce year-round.

problem solver

SUCCESS STARTS WITH SEED SELECTION

It's no surprise that Robert L. Johnston Jr. cites variety selection as the number one secret of success in extending the season. The founder and chairman of Johnny's Selected Seeds in Albion, Maine, knows that enjoying garden-fresh vegetables be-yond the "normal" growing season starts with the seeds you sow.

"Grow really hardy varieties, and be sure to plant them so they mature at the right time of year," Rob says. "Then just leave them in the garden." As an example, he mentions one of his own favorite season-stretching vegetables, 'Roulette' cabbage.

"It's an English-type winter cabbage that may be harvested from the field all winter in New Jersey (Zone 6). It's like a big brus-sels sprout." Rob says the thin, slightly crin-kled leaves of 'Roulette' are tops in taste for adding to salad or stir-fry, or for making coleslaw.

"In severe gardening climates, you can mulch 'Roulette' with leaves or straw to allow air circulation while protecting it from direct hits from frost," Rob explains. "It's too cold to do that in Maine," he adds, "but we have some in my root cellar here, and it stores well."

Don't *Fight* to Grow **Fussy** Crops

Instead of fighting to grow plants that are fussy about day length, temperature, or moisture, find substitutes that are more forgiving of the elements, recommends Milton, Wisconsin, market gardener Mac Cheever.

"I grow 'Stonehead' cabbage because the compact heads resist the splitting that can be caused by an early, hot summer following a cool, wet spring," says Mac. "Most cabbages keep quite well right in the ground. This year's 'Stonehead' cabbage was planted in April, and it still looked good before Christmas.

"Likewise, I substitute Swiss chard for lettuce and spinach," Mac adds. "It's incredibly cold-hardy in my Zone 4 garden, doesn't bolt, and makes it through the hot days of summer quite nicely when either one of the other two would fry. I also don't have to plant successive crops, which saves time and cultivation efforts, and helps to extend my enjoyment of the gardening season, as well as the length of the season itself."

homegrown HINTS

PICK THE RIGHT PLANTS

Engineer and inventor Buckminster Fuller's advice was, "Don't fight forces, use them." So Maine market gardener Eliot Coleman, author of *Four-Season Harvest,* asks himself which plants actually like cold. His list of favorites includes mache (corn salad), claytonia (miner's lettuce), and oriental greens such as mizuna and tatsoi.

"They not only like our growing conditions, but were designed to grow in them," says Eliot. "Sow tatsoi in September and, man, it is so happy in winter!"

But you'll get this enthusiastic response only if you plant early enough that your plants become established before the days get too short, Eliot cautions. "Where we are in coastal Maine we have less than ten hours of daylight from November 7 through February 7. Anything you plant during that time will just sit there."

Turn Up the Heat!

"The most ingenious thing we do to extend the season is live in the maritime Pacific Northwest," jokes Bob Gregson. Bob and his wife, Bonnie, are market gardeners who have little trouble raising most crops on Vashon Island in Puget Sound, Washington. But even in this mild climate, there are some crops that benefit from season extenders.

"Melons, tomatoes, and other heat-loving plants don't like the cool nights here, so we have to do everything we can to protect them," Bob says. "We harden off the plants well and try to get them out as early as we can."

The Gregsons transplant their sturdy seedlings into beds warmed by a layer of 6-mil clear plastic mulch and cover them with row cover.

The result is success: six kinds of canteloupes and three or four watermelon cultivars in a climate not meant for these heat lovers. Bob adds that he and Bonnie grow only small, short-season melon cultivars, like 'Earligold'.

Build a Big Box of *Extra-Early* Greens

If you have an unheated greenhouse and want to grow plants like lettuce that are only somewhat cold-hardy, take a tip from market gardener Elizabeth Henderson of Newark, New York.

"I built a wooden box cold frame in my greenhouse, and I transplant small lettuces into it in fall. They sit through winter, and in February they get going without my heating the greenhouse at all," says Elizabeth. Her planting box measures 5 × 10 feet. It's 2 feet deep and it's nearly filled with garden soil.

Elizabeth says she moves the lettuce into the cold frame in her double-poly hoop house (a hoop-shaped greenhouse covered with two layers of polyethylene) during the first week in October, when the plants are no more than 2 inches tall. She also transplants small collard plants (full-grown collards just go to seed), tatsoi, Chinese cabbage, and spinach into her homemade cold frame.

"The half-grown plants are the ones that really seem to overwinter well," she explains. "Then, in February, they really take off!"

Maintenance is a snap. "If it gets really, really cold, I just throw a tarp over the bed. Other than that, I don't do anything to protect the plants," Elizabeth says. "There is just one catch: In March, we start heat in the greenhouse for our newly planted seedlings. And as soon as they get heat, these overwintered plants get covered with aphids."

The solution to this problem is simple: Make sure to use up all your overwintered crops of greens before you turn up the heat in your greenhouse for starting seedlings.

A cold frame makes it easy to grow extra-early greens in an unheated hoop house.

A **Warm Spot** in *Early* Spring

To give his young plants a head start on Minnesota's short growing season, gardener Jim Tjepkema uses a heating cable to warm his 60 × 28-inch cold frame. The 33-foot-long cable is mounted on plywood and strung back and forth across the bottom of the frame beneath a layer of sand. A piece of hardware cloth on top of the sand provides a sturdy resting place for plants in pots or trays, Jim explains. He keeps the heating cable's thermostat set at 71°F.

"I take the cover off the frame on sunny days when I won't be at home to adjust the ventilation. I use a stick to hold it partway open on mild, sunny days if it gets too hot in the frame," Jim says. A thermometer in the frame lets him keep an eye on the temperature. "I close the frame at night, and on very cold nights, I cover it with old blankets. I have had good luck with a variety of plants for three years now."

Jim adds that it's important to follow the manufacturer's instructions when installing heating cables and similar items in a cold frame, to avoid the risk of fire and to make sure you keep your plants warm, but don't cook them.

Timely tip

If you're like Jim and can't always be around to uncover your heated cold frame on sunny days, consider putting a high-tech helper to work. A thermostatically controlled automatic vent opener, available from mail-order greenhouse- and garden-supply businesses, can be set to raise and lower the cover of your cold frame, depending on the temperature inside the frame.

problem SOLVer

NEW PLASTICS SOFTEN THE SUN

West Point may not teach anything about organic gardening, but Michael Contratto says his West Point education in mechanical engineering has helped turn him into a better gardener.

When Mike began sharing a neighbor's greenhouse, it didn't take him long to figure out why it was overheating during the day. "We were getting too much light and cooking everything," says Mike, who gardens in Zone 5 in Chillicothe, Illinois. "I had to put up a shade cloth on the inside in order to keep the vegetables from cooking by late March and early April. It got up to 100°F in there!"

The shade cloth was only temporary. To make the greenhouse more manageable, Mike replaced its Plexiglas covering with double-pane, extruded plastic sheets. He says the new covering is very strong and flexible, and it diffuses sunlight much better than Plexiglas. The dead-air space between the two layers of plastic provides more heat-holding insulation at night and helps keep the temperature from soaring during the day. As a result, Mike says, "We harvest lettuce a month before anyone else can even think about it. It's so easy to walk out the back door and grab either a whole plant or just a couple of leaves."

Dig That *Crazy* Greenhouse!

All of the old gardening books advise digging pit greenhouses—it's a reliable and economical greenhouse design. So Keith Crotz decided to try it one summer in his Chillicothe, Illinois, garden. He and his neighbor Mike Contratto grabbed their spades and hand-dug a pit that measures 12 × 4 feet and extends a full 4 feet below ground. To make the greenhouse beds, they mounded 6 to 8 inches of topsoil on each side of the pit and added liberal amounts of compost to the beds themselves. Over the pit, they built a shallow A-shaped frame of 2 × 4s on a 2 × 12-inch foundation, and they covered it with ⅛-inch Plexiglas.

"As long as the outside temperature doesn't go below 10°F , nothing freezes in the

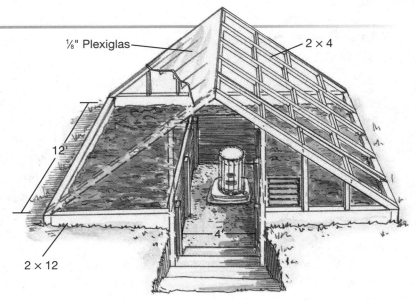

⅛" Plexiglas   2 × 4   12'   2 × 12   4'

With a kerosene heater to warm it on winter's coldest days, an easy-to-build pit greenhouse provides good growing space all year long.

pit," says Keith. "When it gets really cold, I put a kerosene heater on low inside, and everything is just fine."

Keith uses his greenhouse to get a jump-start on spring and to stretch the growing season. "I use the pit greenhouse to start all of my flowers and vegetables," he says. "I start the peppers on a heat mat. Lettuce grows in there all winter in 6 to 8 inches of topsoil and compost on both sides of the pit.

"That's not all," Keith adds. "We overwinter Mike's bonsai collection in there!"

Fabric for a **Tougher** Tunnel

It's safe to say that a lot of gardening ingenuity has come from gardeners' desire for homegrown tomatoes. Binda Colebrook, author of *Winter Gardening in the Maritime Northwest*, uses tunnels to coax yields from heat lovers such as tomatoes. Her success lies in the material she uses to cover her tunnels.

Instead of polyethylene, Binda uses Fabrene, a translucent spun greenhouse fabric (see "Resources" on page 317 for product information).

"I use this for my summer tunnels, too," Binda says, "because with our cold, damp summer season, you just can't grow tomatoes and peppers without it."

Enjoy Your Garlic Twice

Nearly everyone who grows hardneck garlic cuts off the seedheads when they start emerging and coiling like snakes in June. Trimming off the flowerstalk down to where it emerges from between the leaves directs more of the plant's energy into the bulb and results in larger bulbs later in the summer. But what the heck do you do with all of those seed tops?

If you cut them early, before they have curled twice and become too hard and fibrous, you can eat them. "They're absolutely delicious!" says Emmaus, Pennsylvania, garlic grower George DeVault. "Our customers chop them up in salads and sauces or use them to add great garlic taste to stir-fry dishes. My favorite technique, though, is to pickle the tops in vinegar so that you can munch on garden-fresh garlic greens throughout the year."

Wear gloves when you cut the seedheads, notes George, because the seed stems contain the same aromatic juices as garlic bulbs. Store seedheads in a sealed plastic bag in your refrigerator, where they'll keep for about four weeks.

Storing Heat

To extend the growing season, "I spray 2-liter soda bottles with flat black paint and fill them with water," says Kim Barwick of Hoffman Estates, Illinois. "I use them in my cold frame in early spring, at the base of my tomato and pepper plants. They absorb heat during the day, then release it at night."

Gardening Undercover

"I'm a person who likes to bring fresh food into the house from the garden for just as long as I can," says Judy Dornstreich, a home gardener in Perkasie, Pennsylvania. To produce a continuous supply of zesty winter salads for her family of six, Judy depends on an unheated, plastic-covered hoop house.

"Select well-prepared ground that has had a lot of attention, compost, and manure. The site should be slightly raised so that there is good drainage," she advises. "We have made some slightly raised beds that are mulched with straw. That makes the hoop house extremely pleasant to work in." Judy waits until well into fall to cover the hoop-house framework with clear plastic. "If you cover it up after a rain, you probably won't have to water under the hoop house at all because the moisture doesn't evaporate that much."

Choose the crops for your undercover garden with care, Judy suggests. "Don't try to re-create summer," she warns. "Forget about tomatoes." Instead, try to extend spring and fall. "Plant cut-and-come-again lettuces, arugula, curly cress, mache—a variety of stuff—so you can cut a variety for your salads." Judy adds that Swiss chard, onion sets, lemon thyme, tarragon, sorrel, and even rosemary all overwinter nicely inside a hoop house. "They'll be ready for spring harvest a month earlier than normal."

Timely tip

While many herbs will thrive through the winter under the cover of an unheated hoop house, it's not for everything. "Don't try basil," Judy cautions. "It will just sit there and get white flies."

Straw, the Low-Tech Season *Extender*

All it takes is a good, thick layer of straw mulch over cold-hardy vegetables, and the soup's on well into winter in market gardener Melanie DeVault's Emmaus, Pennsylvania, kitchen.

Melanie recommends growing some good winter keepers in proximity to the house so that finding them under a cover of snow is easier and quicker. Her standard soup includes a mix of carrots, leeks, kale, turnips, parsley, and other herbs (and, of course, homegrown potatoes and onions taken from storage on the cool side of the basement).

"A quick trip to the garden and a little broth make a wonderful treat in January," Melanie says. "In half an hour you have a hearty, tasty meal."

Jill Jesiolowski Cebenko, senior editor at *Organic Gardening* magazine and fellow Pennsylvania gardener, agrees. "I have people over for dinner in winter and just go out to the garden to round up some parsnips and beets. Guests are both surprised and delighted," Jill says. "Using straw is a simple, low-tech season extender. You don't need a cold frame or anything."

Soup's on in no time when you grow an assortment of tasty winter vegetables.

Winter Mulch *without* Spring Work

Layers of heavy mulch can safely carry hardy plants through winter. But removing all that mulch can also create a lot of extra work in spring, when you already have too much to do in the garden. Here's a way to protect your plants without a lot of work.

"If you mulch perennial or biennial plants to protect them over winter, invert plastic flowerpots over them before dumping the mulch," says Bob Wildfong, a gardener in Kitchener, Ontario, who works with Seeds of Diversity Canada. "It makes it a lot easier to free them from the mulch in spring."

Keep a variety of different-size pots on hand. That way you'll be able to match the size of the pot to the size of the plant—and the pot won't end up crushing your plants.

Timely tip

Avoid using clay or terra-cotta pots for under-the-mulch protection, advises Bob. Both clay and terra-cotta absorb moisture, causing the pots to crack and break when they freeze.

Treasure in the Trash

"The best cold frame I have is made from a salvaged skylight. It's slanted and bubble-like, with two layers of Plexiglas," says Jill Jesiolowski Cebenko, a senior editor at *Organic Gardening* magazine. "All I had to do was build a rectangular wooden frame as the base to support the skylight. Now my lettuces, spinach, tatsoi, and mizuna stay cozy all winter. Keep an eye out for treasures in the trash pile!"

Avoiding the Crunch

Like many gardeners, John Boston of Tulsa, Oklahoma, uses clear 2-liter soda bottles with the bottoms cut off to protect seedlings early in the season. But his soda bottles also serve another purpose. "On very cold nights," John says, "I bury the entire bottle under a foot of straw to insulate the plants. The bottle then prevents the mulch from crushing the seedlings."

If you don't have straw on hand, try covering the plants with a blanket for insulation.

Custom Cart Cradles Clumsy Covers

Floating row covers, plastic row tunnels, and other crop protectors are great, but many come on such big rolls that they're nearly impossible for one person to handle. Andy Lee, Virginia gardener and author of *Backyard Market Gardening,* solved that problem by turning his homemade garden cart into a roll carrier. He bolted a 72-inch-long, 1-inch-square metal bar to the handlebars behind the cart box. He inserts a round rod of the same length into the cardboard tube holding the row cover and hangs it with wire from the support rod.

"All you have to do is move the cart into position at the end of the bed," Andy says. "Take the loose end of the material and walk to the other end of the bed. The roll of plastic or Reemay hanging down from the handlebars has plenty of clearance, yet it is low enough to the ground that a little breeze won't disrupt the laying procedure."

Timely tip

"Early morning and late afternoon are usually the calmest periods of the day," Andy notes. "Don't try to lay out protective covers if there is more than just a light wind—unless you want to go parasailing in the garden!"

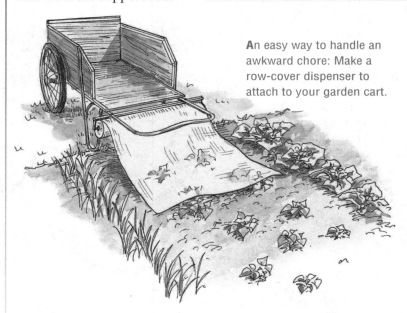

An easy way to handle an awkward chore: Make a row-cover dispenser to attach to your garden cart.

homegrown HINTS

YOU'LL FALL FOR FALL PEAS

As a third-generation Pennsylvania Dutch farmer, Bob Hofstetter admits he can be a little set in his ways. Bob follows the tradition that says the best time to plant peas is around St. Patrick's Day (March 17). Never mind that gardening friends have been tempting him for years with fresh-picked peas in fall.

"Well, I finally tried late planting this year, and it worked beautifully!" exclaims Bob, who manages the Rodale family gardens at the original *Organic Gardening* Experimental Farm near Emmaus, Pennsylvania. "I planted 'Sugar Daddy' snap peas on July 28. The plants weren't quite as tall in fall as in spring, but I had good yields of crisp, sweet peas."

Roll Out
the Barrels

Not beer barrels, but the big blue plastic barrels that come packed with pickles, vinegar, and other food products make great temporary cloches, says Emmaus, Pennsylvania, market gardener George DeVault. "I buy them every time I see some for sale along the roadside or outside an institutional food purveyor. The biggest ones are almost the size of 55-gallon drums.

"Cut them in half lengthwise, and there is no end to the neat things you can do with them. I use them to keep frost off tender seedlings in spring and as a sort of cold frame to keep carrots and other root crops well into winter."

To split a barrel, you don't have to measure or mark anything. Take a saber saw and follow the seam all the way around. Just be careful not to saw off the handle on the top—it comes in handy when you're moving the barrel halves around.

Saw blue plastic food barrels in half and you'll have a handy holder/washtub for your harvest. The halves make quick cloches, too, when frost threatens.

Saber saw

Seam

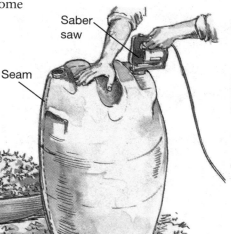

Timely tip

George's barrel halves also are handy at harvesttime. Each holds a couple of bushels of carrots, beets, or broccoli. Round bottoms make them easy to drag out of the garden by the handle. "Flop a garden hose inside, and they become instant hydro-coolers and great washtubs for freshly harvested vegetables," says George.

For Flowers Forever **Plant Early**—And *Late*

So many people call Lynn Byczynski the "Flower Farmer" that she used that nickname as the title of her book on raising and selling organic cut flowers. Here are two favorite season-extending tips from the Flower Farmer of Lawrence, Kansas:

1. "In fall, direct-seed anything that would normally self-sow in your garden, and the plants will be up and ready to go in spring just as soon as the temperature is right," Lynn says. Her fall-sowing list includes bachelor's button, larkspur, and agrostemma (corn cockle).

2. Start other flowers from seed, then grow transplants under hoops. "It's a little trickier because you never know just how cold it's going to get," Lynn warns. "If it's not much below 28°F under the row cover, you can safely use Reemay. It will warm up the plants during the day."

Lynn also lays down drip irrigation tape and black paper mulch at planting.

Drip tape extends under mulch

Paper mulch

Flower gardeners use vegetable-growing tools and techniques to get a big jump on the season. Lynn Byczynski's transplants flourish under covered hoops with paper mulch to block the weeds and drip tape to keep things moist.

Without the mulch, she says, weeds will grow faster than your flowers.

She recommends growing transplants of annual statice (*Limonium sinuatum*), pink poker (*Limonium suworowii*), snapdragons, bishop's weed (*Ammi majus*), lisianthus (*Eustoma grandiflorum*), and annual clary sage (*Salvia viridis*) under hoops. The plants need to be well rooted and hardened off thoroughly before you set them out.

To harden-off the plants, set them outside (in a protected area) for a little while each day for a week, gradually increasing their outdoor time.

Timely tip

Don't stop your season stretching with early plantings, Lynn adds. A lot of flowers can be planted up to the middle of summer. "You can plant cosmos, zinnias, and sunflowers as late as 50 days before the first hard frost of the season," Lynn says. "A mistake a lot of people make is thinking that they have to plant everything at once in spring, and then they're done."

Lynn's advice for successful season-long flower gardening is simple: "Plant before you're supposed to be able to and long past the time you're supposed to be finished." You'll be rewarded with a steady supply of color to enjoy both in your garden and as cut flowers.

Fall Blueberries—
Without the Birds!

Frank Pollock tried everything to keep birds out of his blueberries. But nothing worked—not scare-eye balloons, not cheesecloth, not even shotgun-launched noise-makers. The birds just kept coming back for more of his early and midseason berries.

But by the time his late-season berries were ready to pick in September, it was a different story. There just weren't that many birds hanging around Frank's berry patch in Pennsylvania's Pocono Mountains.

Plant late-season 'Elliott' blueberries for lots of fall fruit minus the birds.

"'Elliott' is the latest blooming and most prolific blueberry there is," Frank recommends. "It's the only one I plant now. That's the easiest and best way I know to extend the growing season for blueberries."

problem SOLVer   SAVE SOME SPUDS FOR SUMMER PLANTING

David Ronniger offers some unusual varieties in his seed potato catalog (Ronniger's Seed and Potato Company). He also offers some unusual—and practical—season-extending advice for organic gardeners: Try summer potato planting. "Planting in the summer can be successful throughout the Mid-Atlantic, the southern Midwest, and into the Deep South—in fact, wherever fall is long and mild," David reports.

The best reason to plant this late (up to July 15) is to avoid the Colorado potato beetle. Reportedly, the beetle becomes less active by August, giving the plants (and the gardener) greater freedom from pests. Other advantages include easier soil preparation, quick emergence, ideal growing conditions, better keeping quality, and freshly dug new potatoes well into fall.

But just try to find seed potatoes in July. ("Potatoes?" laughed the clerk at a garden center in Pennsylvania. "Why, we've been sold out of seed potatoes since May 4!")

So include a few short-season (60-day) to midseason (80-day) varieties in your spring seed potato order, and keep them refrigerated until summer planting time rolls around. Or resist the temptation to eat all of your early spring potatoes. Save enough to plant a season-extending second crop in summer.

Pepper Protection— *By the Peck*

"I had 900 extra hot pepper plants and planted them close together everywhere, including between cucumber rows," says Milton, Wisconsin, market gardener Mac Cheever. "A surprising side effect of this surplus was a good deal of shelter later in the season. Although frost knocked the tops back, the bottoms were still fairly well protected by the cucumber leaves, and I harvested peppers for a few more weeks."

homegrown HINTS

DOUBLE COVERS KEEP GREENS GROWING

Sometimes, when fall nights start to turn chilly, an extra blanket on the bed is all it takes to keep you cozy without firing up the furnace. Likewise, using two layers of floating row cover instead of one is all Pennsylvania gardener Jill Jesiolowski Cebenko does to keep harvesting tasty greens such as spinach and lettuce well into the fall.

"A double layer of Reemay keeps my spinach and lettuce going much later in the fall," says Jill, a senior editor at *Organic Gardening* magazine. "It also keeps the plants in good shape through our milder winters for early spring harvest," she adds. "Using this method is very easy, too— just two layers of row cover lying right on top of the plants, anchored with rocks, boards, or what-have-you."

Put **Row Covers** in Their Place

Virginia gardener Andy Lee has found the perfect tool for firmly anchoring the edges of season extenders. His method works for both plastic mulch and floating row covers.

Using twine stretched between two stakes as a guide, Andy runs his wheel hoe— equipped with a furrower or moldboard—down each side of the bed. He keeps the vertical edge next to the bed, throwing soil to the right.

Next Andy unrolls the row cover and anchors the edges into the furrow by backfilling with soil he just turned over. Just be sure that the cover floats on the bed and is not too tight, he advises.

If you're applying row cover over a bed that already has plastic mulch, Andy recommends installing the cover at least 1 inch away from the plastic so that you don't pull up the plastic when you remove the cover in a few weeks.

A wheel hoe, available from farm-supply stores and mail-order tool companies, makes it easy to anchor row covers with a ridge of soil.

homegrown HINTS

OATS AID WINTER SPINACH

A carpet of oats helps organic market gardener Richard de Wilde get his spinach crop through the winter in Viroqua, Wisconsin. "The first week of September, we plant spinach just the way we plant it any other time of year," Richard says. The spinach comes up in about a week.

After the spinach is up, Richard broadcasts "a pretty heavy amount of oats" around the spinach, and then he cultivates it, so the cultivator covers up most of the oat seeds. "What I end up with going into winter is a growing carpet of oats all around the spinach," he explains. The oats winter-kill, providing a natural mulch that helps protect the spinach during winter.

"Most spinach varieties, especially some of the old savoyed ones, have consistently overwintered here for the past seven to eight years," Richard notes, adding that this spinach is the first crop he harvests in the spring. "The quality is far superior to anything planted in the spring or summer," he says. "It has a very thick leaf and is dark green and sweet. It's somewhat like spinach harvested late in the fall.

"The challenge," Richard adds, "is keeping the deer out of the spinach in the winter. They've been known to go through a foot of snow to get at it."

It's *in the* Bag

Plastic garbage bags can give your tomatoes an early boost. "I cut the end off a clear garbage bag to create a tube, and I slide the tube over my tomatoes cages in the early spring, securing the open top to the cage," says Kim Barwick of Hoffman Estates, Illinois. "It creates a warm, humid environment for young tomato and pepper plants— on a 50°F day, the temperature inside is about 80 to 85°F. With the top open, you don't have to worry about cooking your plants. On cold nights, you can slide a whole bag over the top."

A **Tomato** That *Waits* for You

Anyone who has ever gone on vacation for a week or two in August almost dreads returning to the garden—and all of those overripe tomatoes.

But what can you do? "Plant a tomato that will ripen on the plant—and then will just sit there for three to four weeks," recommends Robert L. Johnston Jr., chairman of Johnny's Selected Seeds in Albion, Maine.

There really is such a tomato, Rob explains. "It's not a so-called long-keeper, which contains a gene that actually prevents fruit from ripening on the plant. Rather, it's a tomato with a long shelf life—and good taste! And its name is 'Daniela'."

"If the fruit is allowed to get dead ripe on the plant, it is delicious," Rob says. "Before we put this variety in our catalog, we sampled it with gardeners throughout the country. I guarantee you it will keep for a good three weeks on the plant."

'Daniela' matures in 77 days and is resistant to verticillium and fusarium wilt and tobacco mosaic virus.

Nature's Freezer *Sweetens* Spinach

"My husband, Bill Warner, and I grow spinach all winter without any heat in hoop houses—in southern Wisconsin (Zone 4)," says market gardener Judy Hageman. "We plant in September and harvest all winter."

The only real problem with this method, she says, is cold, cloudy days when the temperature outside stays right at 10°F. You can't harvest the spinach when it's frozen, but Judy doesn't let that hinder her.

To thaw the spinach before she picks it, Judy puts a small hoop-shaped plastic cover over the spinach inside the hoop house. This raises the temperature enough to let her gather unfrozen spinach. Judy says the freezing doesn't harm the crop—if anything, it improves it, because it increases the spinach's sugar level. "The spinach tastes just like candy after it freezes and thaws!"

This method not only lets Judy extend her spinach season, it also helps her beat the winter blues by allowing her to garden when the snow is flying and the temperature is dipping below 0°F.

Tunnel *Your Way to* Early Tomatoes

Warming the soil with black plastic mulch is the first step organic market gardener Richard de Wilde takes toward producing an early crop of tomatoes in Viroqua, Wisconsin. Then, once the plants are in place, he explains, "We put cages over them immediately. These 'cages' are really tunnels made from sections of the wire that is used to reinforce concrete. The tunnels serve as a support for the Reemay that we put over them." Richard cuts the reinforcing wire to form half-circles, 10 to 11 squares wide. He leaves 3-inch legs on each edge to poke into the ground to anchor the tunnels.

"We lay the tunnels almost end-to-end, leaving just space enough to walk through at the end of every other one," says Richard. He adds that he is relying more and more on low-cost, low-tech season extenders to stretch production in his market garden.

"We keep the tomatoes covered for three to four weeks, until it's 90°F in there or the tomatoes are bursting out of the tunnels." Later in the season, Richard plants tomatoes in bare ground. Then, as summer wears on, he stretches his tomato production in the other direction: "We actually mulch to cool the ground, to slow the tomatoes down so that we have a longer tomato harvesting season."

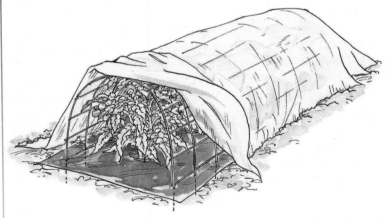

Combine simple season extenders like black plastic mulch and tunnels covered with floating row cover to enjoy extra-early tomatoes this summer, even in chilly northern regions.

Sleepover at Camp Kale

Whenever Arctic air breaks out of Canada and hurricane-force winds cause temperatures to plummet in the normally mild foothills of Washington's Cascade Mountains, Binda Colebrook runs for her trusty old sleeping bag. A bunch of old sleeping bags, actually. She keeps them stashed in a shed near her garden.

"I throw them over the kale and spinach cold frames, then I cover the sleeping bags with plastic so they don't get all wet," Binda explains. She takes advantage of the falling temperature to anchor everything in place: "I pour water over the plastic so that the water freezes and the covers won't blow off."

problem SOLVEr   SWEET POTATOES IN VERMONT!

Even in a mild winter, the temperature in central Vermont dips to -20°F for at least a few days. It gets so cold up there that winter weather kills an average of about half the blackberries every year—and blackberries are pretty tough.

But that doesn't stop Alan LePage. "We grow the marginal to the near-impossible," he says matter-of-factly. His favorite crop is sweet potatoes!

"We think we can grow almost any kind of sweet potato here," says Alan, who lives in Barre, Vermont. "We have never had a crop failure, and we've always had decent yields. We buy sweet potato plants (from Fred's Plant Farm in Tennessee)—we don't grow them. We want to receive them between May 15 and 20."

Alan tucks his sweet potato plants into raised beds that have been warmed for a few weeks with a covering of IRT (infrared transmitting) mulch, also called wave-length selective mulch. IRT mulch warms the soil more quickly than black plastic by allowing near-infrared light to pass through while blocking the visible light that weed seeds need in order to sprout.

Frost protection is also critical. "There are threats of light frost into June," Alan says, "but we ignore those with row covers." To keep the frost off his tender sweet potatoes, Alan blankets them with Agrofabric Pro 17 row cover. This covering stays in place all season, until harvesting begins around September 1. In addition to keeping his sweet potatoes toasty, using row covers all season eliminates insect pests, Alan notes.

Alan says his favorite sweet potato variety is 'Vardaman'. "It doesn't need to be cured, and it resists splitting—a big problem in the North when we have periods of cold, rainy weather followed by hot spells," he explains.

sensational

Seed-Starting Secrets

What gardener doesn't live for the morning when that first seedling pops through the moist soil? And what gardener hasn't been disappointed by a seed that never sprouted? Use these ingenious tips for storing and organizing your seeds, germinating even the teeniest seeds, and taking care of those seedlings once they've sprouted. With foolproof ideas from the experts, you'll be presprouting, soil blocking, and transplanting before you can say, "Hand me a dibble."

Proper Seed Storage **Saves $$$**

Everyone wonders whether that forgotten packet of seeds from a couple of years ago is still worth planting. Bob Wildfong, who works with Seeds of Diversity Canada, in Ontario, says a little care with seed storage not only can give gardeners peace of mind but can also save them lots of money because they won't have to buy new seeds each year. The key, Bob says, is to store seeds in conditions opposite those needed for germination. Since seeds need warmth and moisture to germinate, cold and dryness are your tickets to successful storage. You can use the same package of seeds for several years if you store them correctly, he says.

To keep seeds cold and dry, store them in your refrigerator. Bob recommends placing seeds in paper envelopes inside a glass jar. (Add another envelope of silica gel or powdered milk to absorb moisture.) Seal the jar, then put it in the refrigerator. The seeds will remain viable for about twice as long as if they were stored at room temperature.

Try Coffee Filters for **Presprouting**

If you aren't sure whether your old seeds are still good, try presprouting to see if they will germinate. Every spring, *Organic Gardening* Senior Editor Jill Jesiolowski Cebenko presprouts larger seeds by moistening unbleached #2 coffee filters and evenly spacing the seeds in the moistened filters. "Place one or two coffee filters upright in an old yogurt container with a clear lid to hold the moisture in," she says. When (and if) the seeds germinate, Jill says you'll see a bulge in the coffee filter and you'll know the seeds are still viable.

Using the clear lid and the envelope-shaped filter makes it easy to check on the sprouting process, too. Check the seeds daily, and as soon as you see that a seed has sprouted, carefully remove the sprout with your fingers or tweezers, and plant it.

This presprouting method is a great space- and money-saver too. You don't waste space in a six-pack cell due to nongermination and you don't waste seed by oversowing directly into six-packs, Jill adds.

Presprout on *Top* of the Fridge

Bud Glendening says he presprouts most of his seeds on top of the refrigerator, placing the seed on damp paper towels in small plastic bags. "It's how I started sprouting seeds, and I really haven't found anything better," says Bud, the owner of Fox Hollow Seed Co. in McGrann, Pennsylvania. "I check them twice a day."

The top of the refrigerator provides just the right amount of warmth without getting too hot. Even pepper seeds like it. And it's a lot more cost-effective than using hot mats, Bud adds.

You need to keep a close eye on seeds you're presprouting, Bud says. You don't want to let them dry out from the warmth of the fridge or let them grow too long inside a plastic bag. As soon as seeds sprout, you need to get them out of the bag and into moist planting medium. Otherwise, their new roots may grow into the paper towel, making them likely to break off when you plant the seedlings.

Timely tip

Most seeds need a warm environment to germinate. But once they germinate, let them keep their cool, says Nancy Bubel, author *of The New Seed-Starter's Handbook.* "If you keep seedlings in a cool room, they won't lose as much moisture to transpiration."

To presprout seeds, put them on top of the refrigerator. Put the seeds on damp paper towels inside plastic bags—that way they won't dry out too quickly.

Organize Packets by Planting Time

Market gardener Cass Peterson has devised a simple bag-and-tub system to keep her seeds separated and easy to find. Cass puts seed packets in sealable plastic bags that are labeled with the month of planting. She keeps the bags in lidded plastic tubs in the walk-in cooler so the right seeds are on hand when the greenhouse planting schedule shows that it's time to plant.

Cass says that she can't afford to forget a scheduled planting of arugula for her restaurant clients or sunflowers for the mixed bouquets that her farm, Flickerville Mountain Farm and Groundhog Ranch, in Warfordsburg, Pennsylvania, offers at farmer's markets. She needs to have seeds ready to go at a moment's notice. This system works so well for Cass that she suggests that home gardeners use the same system on a smaller scale.

The key is to organize your seed packets by putting vegetable and flower seeds in separate containers, labeling the containers by planting date, and keeping the sealed tub in the back of the refrigerator, a cool basement, or an unheated closet. When the calendar says it's planting day, just grab the right container and plant away!

If you're storing several kinds of seeds but no large quantities, you could even adapt Cass's system for use with a three-ring binder. Tuck your seed packets into the zippered plastic pockets that fit into a binder, then label and date each one with the proper planting time.

Double Duo Aids Pea Germination

"You can cut pea seed germination time in half by taking two important measures," says *Organic Gardening* Senior Editor Jill Jesiolowski Cebenko. "Presoak all pea seeds and be faithful about inoculant," she says.

"These big seeds need a lot of moisture to puff up," Jill explains, and sometimes this can take a while in the garden. At the proper planting time, she wraps the seeds in a damp paper towel, sticks the towel in a plastic bag, and lets it sit for one to two days. "Then I pop them in a furrow in the garden with a sprinkling of inoculant," she says.

Legume inoculants, available through many seed catalogs and local garden centers, are dry, natural peat-based cultures of beneficial bacteria used to treat legume seed before planting. They're completely organic. The inoculant encourages formation of high-nitrogen nodules on plant roots for richer soil, bigger plants, and higher yields, explains the catalog from Johnny's Selected Seeds in Albion, Maine.

problem solver

SOAK STUBBORN SEEDS

When starting flowers from seed, keep in mind that some seeds (morning glories, asparagus fern, and lupines, for example) have a very hard seed coat and take days—or even weeks—to germinate. To help germination along, try soaking seeds in hot tap water for 12 to 24 hours before planting, says Bill Stockman, owner of Spider Web Gardens in Center Tuftonboro, New Hampshire.

homegrown HINTS

FOOLING GLOBE ARTICHOKE SEED

If you ever want to grow globe artichokes and get them to set artichokes the first year, you can fool the seed, says Wanda Boop of Briar Patch Organic Farms in Mifflinburg, Pennsylvania. (Most globe varieties are biennial and produce artichokes in the second year if you can successfully overwinter them.)

"Fool the seed by placing it in the freezer in December and keeping it there until about February," says Wanda. This tricks the seed into "thinking" it's been through the cold season, and it will set flowers the first year, she says. Then, in February, soak the seed for 24 hours, and plant in trays. Set the seedlings outside when all danger of frost is past.

Tiny Helpers for Tiny Seeds

Planting seeds, especially those small seeds, can be a tricky business. So an expert gardener says she always keeps a good, old-fashioned pair of tweezers nearby for those times when she's planting teeny, tiny seeds. For thinning, she snips off extra seedlings with narrow-bladed scissors to avoid disturbing the roots of the seedlings she wants to keep.

Freeze Seeds for Better Germination

Some perennial and northern wildflower seeds need a period of deep cold before they'll germinate, but you can "fool" seeds like this by freezing them! The cold requirement is nature's way of telling the seeds when it's safe to sprout; winter freezing and spring thawing change the chemistry in the seeds, allowing them to sprout only in springtime. Gardener Bob Wildfong of Kitchener, Ontario, says you can simulate a winter freeze indoors by literally freezing your seeds.

"In the late fall or early winter, sow your perennial or wildflower seeds in a sealable plastic container, half full of vermiculite," he says. If the seeds are small, just sprinkle them on top of the vermiculite. Add enough water to saturate the vermiculite, and let the seeds soak for at least 24 hours. Once the seeds have absorbed some water, put the lid on the container and place the container in the freezer.

Leave the container in the freezer for at least two months (some seeds require up to three months of freezing). Once your simulated winter freeze is over, take the lid off the container and put it in a bright, warm place. You can cover the top of the container with plastic wrap to keep the vermiculite from drying out, Bob says. Some wildflowers germinate in a week, while others take up to four weeks. Be patient and keep the vermiculite damp, but don't soak it, he advises. You should soon see sprouts.

Timely tip

Nancy Bubel, author of *The New Seed-Starters Handbook*, says it's important to work with Mother Nature when starting plants outdoors. "Don't plant seeds outdoors after early September," she cautions. "Otherwise, they may not harden-off enough to endure harsh winter conditions."

Presprouting and **Plastic** Provide Early Corn

Getting corn to germinate in cold soil is an age-old problem, but Dan Tawczynski of Great Barrington, Massachusetts, has found a method that helps corn seed survive and thrive despite a chill. He presprouts early corn to get past that germination hurdle, and then plants the presprouted seed in beds prepared with black plastic mulch. The seed is set in holes in the black plastic at the proper planting intervals.

Dan germinates the seed by putting a little potting soil in a plastic flat (the kind that holds a half-dozen six-pack containers) to maintain moisture, and then filling the flat with corn. The trick is to plant seeds as soon as tiny white sprouts appear. It usually takes two days for the seeds to sprout. Three days can be too long.

"In Massachusetts, I've planted the presprouted seed on April 12, and it didn't freeze. We've had corn by the end of June," he says. The plastic protects the seed through most frosts. There can be danger of frost to the plant once it grows above the plastic; early corn is worth the risk.

Make a Simple **Seedling** Sprinkler

Remember the old sprinkler bottles that moms used to sprinkle clothes before ironing? Even though you can't buy them anymore, you can make a suitable substitute to water tender seedlings or seeds that haven't sprouted yet. "Take a good-size plastic bottle with a fair-size lid, like a big Cremora bottle, and poke about five holes in the lid with an awl," says Kris Johnson of Williston, Ohio. (A Cremora bottle is the size of a 1-quart bottle and has a wide-mouth lid that measures about 3 inches across.) She fills the bottle with water and compost tea or fish fertilizer and sprinkles her seed flats. "Presto! Watering seed flats is so much easier with a sprinkler bottle," she says.

Squirt Small Seeds

Instead of taking the time to plant tiny seeds individually, mix them in a gel solution, and squirt them down the plant row. "Mix one package of plain gelatin with 1 tablespoon of warm water, and stir until it's dissolved," instructs Pat Kolb of Phoenix. She adds water sparingly until the mixture is thick enough so that tiny seeds don't sink and thin enough so that the mixture flows evenly through a pull-top detergent bottle. Pat says you may need to experiment with the number of seeds in the solution in order to get a nice even flow of seeds when you "plant" your rows.

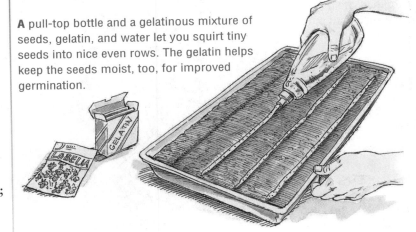

A pull-top bottle and a gelatinous mixture of seeds, gelatin, and water let you squirt tiny seeds into nice even rows. The gelatin helps keep the seeds moist, too, for improved germination.

problem SOLVer

DOCTORED PLASTIC FORK IS TOPS

Take a plastic fork and remove the outer tines to make the best little seedling transplanting tool, says Kathy Moen, garden manager at Seed Savers Exchange, whose 170-acre headquarters in Decorah, Iowa, is a living museum of historic seed varieties.

The remaining prongs of the modified fork are close together so that you can dig under a seedling's tiny roots. Just lift up for easy transplanting.

Toothpick *Tricks*

Tiny flower and vegetable seeds can be real rascals when you try to plant them. Want an ingenious solution? Try using a plain old toothpick for planting tiny seeds, says Lawrence, Kansas, market gardener Lynn Byczynski, author of *The Flower Farmer*. Start by emptying the seed packet into a small bowl, then "just wet the end of a toothpick and use it to pick up a dry seed," Lynn explains. When you touch the seed to moist soil, it's attracted to the wetter soil surface and almost plants itself. And the process makes quick work of seed planting in the springtime. "You can get really fast with a toothpick!" says Lynn.

To quickly plant small seeds, wet the end of a toothpick, touch the toothpick to a seed, then deposit the seed onto moist soil.

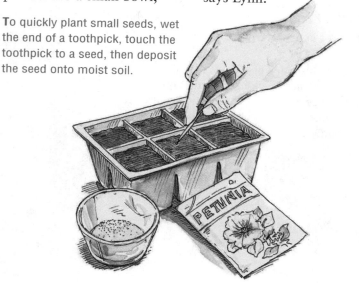

Grits Make Small Seeds *"Sow"* Easy

Sometimes seeds are so small that they're nearly impossible to sow evenly without spreading them too thickly. When Martha Daughdrill and her husband, Paul Benton, ran into trouble with using tiny seeds in a mechanical seeder at their Newburg Vegetable Farm in Maryland, Paul found a solution—in his breakfast cereal!

No matter how they set their seeder, the fine seeds came through the holes too fast. So Paul looked at the seeds and at the grits in the cupboard—and got an idea. He mixed dry grits with the seeds to thin them, and it worked beautifully. "He got a better stand with the small-seeded plants," Martha says, "and he almost never has to eat grits for breakfast!"

Timely tip

If you don't use a mechanical seeder, mix some grits with small seeds for hand sowing, too. The results will be the same (but you may have to eat more grits). Mixing small seeds with sand is another way to thin them out for more even sowing, and the sand makes it easy to see where you've sown.

Cut a *Yardstick* Down to Size

When sowing vegetable or flower seeds into seed flats, forget unpredictable broadcasting. Lay out tidy rows for the seed by using an old yardstick. Cut the yardstick into two pieces, one the length of the flat and the other the width of the flat, to mark rows in your flats in either direction, advises Cass Peterson of Flickerville Mountain Farm and Groundhog Ranch in Warfordsburg, Pennsylvania. The yardstick lengths make uniform, evenly spaced rows, and the seeding goes quickly.

Just spread moistened soil mix in a flat, and level it off. Take either of the yardstick lengths and use it to mark indentations about 1 inch apart, either across the width of the flat for short rows or down the length of the flat for longer rows. You can adjust the depth according to the seeds you're using, indenting rows slightly deeper for normal-size seeds or barely denting the surface for small seeds such as petunia that won't be covered with soil mix after planting. It's a quick and easy method for keeping seed rows neat.

Cut an old yardstick into pieces that match the dimensions of your seed flats to create a simple tool that speeds seed sowing.

Planting Boards **Save Time**

Kathy Moen, garden manager for Seed Savers Exchange in Decorah, Iowa, says one of her favorite tools is a planting board that marks planting holes for individual cell packs. A planting board is just a flat piece of wood cut to the size you need with a handle fastened on the back, and ½-inch-diameter dowels glued on the front. Wood or carpenter's glue is ideal for this project. You can cut the board to the size of a four-pack, for instance, and position four dowels so that they leave a shallow hole in the center of each cell in the pack. Or you can cut the board to the size of a larger container, such as a 32-cell, with 32 dowels glued to the board.

To use the board, turn the board dowel side down, line up the dowels with the center of the cell packs, and press the dowels into the soil to create planting holes.

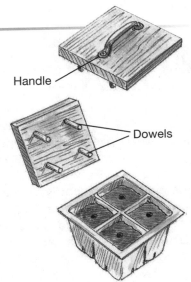

Handle

Dowels

Save time when planting into cell packs by making a planting board to mark planting holes.

Garlic Planting in *No Time*

Pennsylvania market gardener George DeVault uses a garden-size planting board when he plants garlic cloves outdoors. He cut old 1-inch square tomato stakes and screwed them together to create a rectangular frame. His planting board measures 8 × 30 inches. Instead of dowel dibbles, he spaced long drywall screws on the two 30-inch sides at 5-inch intervals, the ideal spacing for garlic. He says the idea was adapted from *Growing Great Garlic* by Ron L. Engelland.

To use the board, press the drywall screws into the soil to create planting holes. George says the system not only makes planting go extremely fast, but it also ensures planting at a constant depth. After dropping the garlic clove root end down into the hole, cover it with soil, and firmly press it down.

George says many market gardeners use similar planting-board devices when transplanting lettuce, fennel, and other crops outdoors in spring.

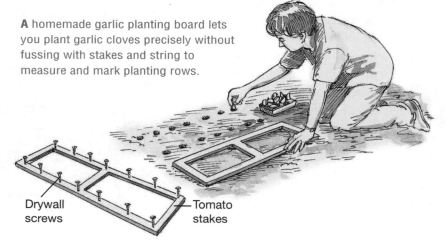

A homemade garlic planting board lets you plant garlic cloves precisely without fussing with stakes and string to measure and mark planting rows.

Drywall screws

Tomato stakes

problem **solver**

MINIBLIND MARKERS

Cut old plastic, nonlead miniblinds into short lengths and use them as plant markers when starting seeds in six-packs or flats, advises Teena Bailey of Red Cat Farm, Germansville, Pennsylvania. "They're flexible, durable, and easily cleaned. They take pencil or markers perfectly," she says. And that's not all! As the seedlings grow into garden-ready transplants, she cuts the miniblinds into longer sections and uses them as markers right in the garden. (If you're unsure whether your miniblinds contain lead, you can buy an inexpensive lead testing kit at your local hardware store.)

Cass Peterson also uses old venetian blinds at her farm, Flickerville Mountain Farm and Groundhog Ranch, in Warfordsburg, Pennsylvania. She likes them because they're flexible and can be cut to lengths that are tall enough to spot in the field. Cass uses permanent markers to write plant names on the blinds. She's found that permanent marker ink doesn't fade on the blinds the way it does on wooden markers. At Flickerville Mountain Farm, they staple the blinds onto tomato stakes for extra durability. Cass says she reuses the plant markers by using liquid abrasive to take off the old plant names.

Just a *Little* Clip

Nancy Bubel of Wellsville, Pennsylvania, says there's nothing like an old pair of nail clippers for scarifying, or scratching, a seed coat to hasten germination. "They work really well to cut a hard seed like lupine," she says.

Take **Note!**

Market gardener George DeVault of Emmaus, Pennsylvania, is a firm believer in using a seeder. It makes planting for the home or market gardener go quickly and efficiently. But with all of the seed plates and seed sizes, sometimes it's hard to find just the right plate—especially when you're in a real rush to get seed planted.

For example, George's seeder has two pea plates— one for large peas and one for smaller. So what's what? George experiments the first year, then writes the cultivar name in permanent marker right on the plastic plate. Then he knows: 'Sugar Ann' snap peas take the small pea plate. Next year, when he's in a hurry to beat the weather, the information is right at hand.

homegrown HINTS

BE SURE TO SOAK YOUR SEED FLATS

"There's nothing like a good bottom soak for seed flats," says Bob Hofstetter, manager of the Rodale family gardens near Emmaus, Pennsylvania. Once you've filled the flat with moistened potting mix and planted the seed, just place the flat in tepid water about two-thirds the depth of the flat, he advises. This can be done in a sink or plastic-lined box or in any container that holds water. Make sure the soil is thoroughly wet before taking the flat out.

"There is no such thing as saying water every three days," he says. "The bottom line is never let it dry out. Normally in greenhouse conditions, the seeds will germinate while the soil is still moist from the first bottom soaking." However, Bob says he does resoak if the soil looks as if it's drying out. If just the top of the soil is dry, he'll mist the flat to replace any lost moisture. Bob says that bottom-watering is especially great for fine seed that can't cope with top-watering.

Bob says the key to success is to be sure that your potting mix is damp right at the start. He cautions that if the potting soil is very dry or if you're using a soilless mix, bottom-watering alone won't work, and you'll need to supplement with top-watering.

Go for the *Big* Roots

The trick to getting the best results from home-started seedlings is to choose the seedlings with the biggest root systems when you transplant. The length of the stem and size of the leaves isn't as important as hearty roots. "Throw out weak plants with few roots. They won't do well anyway," says Judy Dornstreich of Perkasie, Pennsylvania. Transplanting only those seedlings with strong root systems will be more time- and cost-efficient in the long run, because the plants will establish themselves more quickly and need less coddling.

Buffer the Heat

If you start seeds in flats on top of heating mats, you may need to raise the flat a bit to help diffuse the heat. Ellen Ogden, of The Cook's Garden in Londonderry, Vermont, raises her flats by putting a screen, a brick, or a plastic tray across the rack that extends over the mat. She says you need to take care not to let the plants get overheated.

Ellen uses commercial heating mats with temperature controls and usually keeps them at 68°F. "The home models are usually set at 72°F, and that's too hot for most plants," she says. Sometimes she stacks her flats so that the heat lovers get the most heat, but she makes sure all the flats get the warmth they need without being over-cooked. She loves heating mats because they "give germination an added boost." They're especially useful if you want to pretest the quality of old seed, Ellen says. The mats speed germination so you can quickly tell whether the seed is still viable.

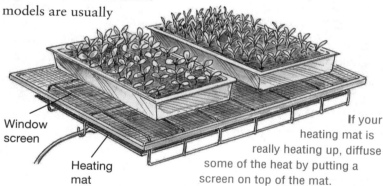

Window screen

Heating mat

If your heating mat is really heating up, diffuse some of the heat by putting a screen on top of the mat.

Self-Sowing Seeds

"I have kale and corn salad that sow themselves," says Binda Colebrook, a longtime organic gardener in Everson, Washington. She just lets a certain percentage of her Russian red and Siberian kale and corn salad plants go to seed before she uproots the plants. When the time comes to sow those crops, she clears a bed, rakes it, waters it, and the right species just pops up. If you're a sloppy harvester, she says, this process happens all by itself.

Seedlings *Love* Space Blankets

Commonly called a "space blanket," that shiny silver piece of Mylar found at camping stores is great for starting seedlings, says Bruce Butterfield, research director at the National Gardening Association in Burlington, Vermont. He spreads the Mylar blanket on the shelf under his plant lights and then sets seedling trays on it. He then pulls up each end of the blanket and tapes it to the outside cover of one of the fluorescent lights. "It not only concentrates the light," he attests, "but it also does a good job of holding in the heat."

Kitchen Utensils to the **Rescue**

If you find you have a lot of runoff when you water seedlings, try reaching into your kitchen drawer for a solution. "I use a turkey baster to direct the water right where I want it," says Esther Czekalski of Lancaster, Massachusetts. The seedlings get a steady water flow right where they need it—at the roots.

homegrown HINTS

COOL OFF YOUR HEAT MATS

If your heat mat tends to get too hot and doesn't have a temperature regulator, put the heat mat on a timer and set it so that it shuts off at night, says Bud Glendening of Fox Hollow Seed Company in McGrann, Pennsylvania. Or, he suggests, put it where it catches a draft—someplace where the air keeps moving so that it varies the heat level, like near a door that's opened frequently or near where you walk around and stir up air currents.

"The key is to mimic nature as much as possible," he says, "by creating 'daytime' heat and 'nighttime' cooling."

Do the *Seed Flat* Switch

If you rotate your flats under Gro-Lights but find that you're always crunched for space, follow Hal Seagraves's space-saving rotation system: Hal set up extra shelves with Gro-Lights across from the table, and once a day, he switches the seed flats under the lights with the seed flats on the shelves. He keeps the lights on all the time so the area stays warm and bright, and the plants love it. The arrangement works well for two reasons—the plants get both "rest time" on the shelf and bright, warm light for germination.

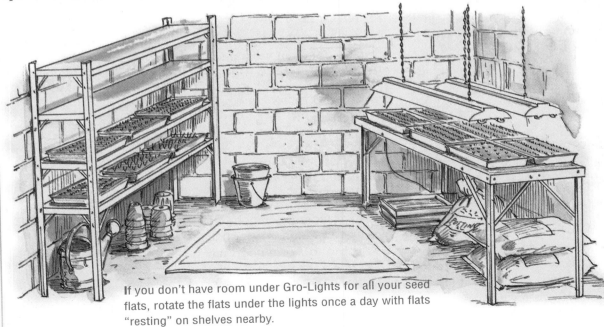

If you don't have room under Gro-Lights for all your seed flats, rotate the flats under the lights once a day with flats "resting" on shelves nearby.

Give Seedlings a **Bonemeal** Boost

Jill Jesiolowski Cebenko, *Organic Gardening* senior editor, says she noticed some of her tomato seedlings suffering from phosphorus deficiency (which gives the undersides of the leaves a telltale purplish tinge). Once she started adding a tablespoon of bonemeal to each gallon of the soil mix that she uses to pot up the transplants, the problem quickly disappeared.

"This is just enough bonemeal to solve the problem and give the plants a healthy green color," she says. "The little guys are in such a small space and the root system grows so fast, you have to give them a little something extra to ensure success."

Plastic Holds Up *for Years*

Many gardeners use paper cups or other makeshift containers to start seeds, but market gardener Lynn Byczynski of Lawrence, Kansas, thinks it makes more sense to invest in durable, easy-to-use plastic flats and inserts with clear plastic dome lids. "The plastic stuff holds up a long time—if you keep it out of the sunlight and take care of it," she says. "And that includes washing and disinfecting the trays after use."

Lynn, who's the author and editor of the *Growing for Market* newsletter, says she has had some of her trays for more than ten years and that they were well worth the investment.

Soak Parsley and Celery Seed

"Have trouble germinating parsley and celery seed?" asks Wanda Boop of Briar Patch Organic Farms in Mifflinburg, Pennsylvania. Soak the seeds for 24 hours before planting them in the garden or seed trays, she advises. "You will be amazed at the germination—almost 100 percent!"

Leeks **Love** Special Treatment

Broadcast leek seeds in a flat, cover with soil, and let them grow for a month so you can give them full protection during that delicate stage, says Pennsylvania gardener Judy Dornstreich. She says it takes leeks so long to germinate and grow that weeds would take over if you sowed the leeks outdoors. "We take the little leeks directly from the flat and plant them outside," she adds. Setting a larger leek in weed-free ground gives it a head start. The little leeks look like blades of grass, are easier to see at this size, and are less likely to be uprooted when you pull weeds, says Judy.

problem **solver**

SPHAGNUM STOPS DAMPING-OFF

Have a problem with damping-off? Cass Peterson of Flickerville Mountain Farm and Groundhog Ranch, in Warfordsburg, Pennsylvania, says that she sprinkles a fine layer of milled sphagnum moss over the top of a seed flat after seeding. "This helps keep the surface soil dry and keeps moisture away from the stems," she says. Cass recommends the moss for zinnias or any other seedlings that are susceptible to damping-off.

Fan Those Transplants

Use a small fan to circulate air around transplants that are under Gro-Lights, advises Bruce Butterfield, of the National Gardening Association. "It starts to harden them off and helps them fight danger by toughening them up a bit for when they're moved outside," he explains. It gives the transplants a taste of the outdoors and is good for both vegetable and flower seedlings, he adds. And the added air circulation helps prevent damping-off in the tender young transplants.

Fans can help preharden and toughen up transplants by giving them a taste of the outdoors—while they're still indoors.

Think Twice Before You Hill

Most seed packets offer the option of planting cucumbers, melons, squash, and pumpkins in "hills," but Bob Wildfong, of Seeds of Diversity Canada, Ontario, says most gardeners will have better results if they plant these crops directly into a garden bed. The theory behind the "hill is better" practice, says Bob, is that hilled soil warms up faster in the spring and causes the seeds to sprout earlier.

The down side is that the hill of soil also dries out faster in the summer, reducing fruit-set considerably, he explains. The method originated in Northern Europe, where spring is cooler and summers are wetter than in the United States. Settlers brought this trick with them, but in this part of the world, flatter is better.

Keep Watch for Slow-Start Seedlings

Pepper and leek seeds don't all germinate at once, so keep the seed-starting medium moist for a week or two after you've transplanted the seedlings that have already popped up, advises Kitchener, Ontario, gardener Bob Wildfong. "Keep watching because there are more on the way," he adds. Giving the seeds a little more time to germinate not only means more seedlings but also means less time spent germinating additional seeds.

Bob starts his pepper and leek seeds early by thickly sowing them in a small container of damp vermiculite. "When they sprout (two to three weeks for peppers, two to four weeks for the leeks), you should loosen the vermiculite with your fingers, gently pull the seedlings out, and transplant them into individual containers of potting soil," he explains. Even though you have to be quite careful transplanting most seedlings, peppers and leeks are tough enough to survive any beginner's fingers because they have very thick, sturdy roots, explains Bob.

Room to Grow

Mac Cheever of Milton, Wisconsin, starts seeds of warm-season vegetables in flats indoors early in the spring, then transplants them into 1-gallon nursery pots (you know, those black containers that almost everyone has left over from nursery plants). The larger pots afford the seedlings more room to grow if the outside weather isn't suitable for transplanting at the recommended time, Mac explains. When they're finally planted outdoors, the plants grow quickly because of their large, strong root systems.

In Wisconsin, Mac says he starts plants in early April and transplants them into the larger containers in early May, hoping to plant outdoors in late May or early June, depending on the weather. This works extremely well for tomatoes, peppers, cucumbers, pumpkins, squash, and gourds. "It gives you the added bonus of waiting for suitable weather without losing any growth," he says. "A well-established root system will take right off as soon as it is in the ground."

Or, Mac suggests that you may want to leave some of the plants in the large containers for the patio or porch. Remember to provide enough nutrition during the growing season for container plants, he says. You may want to use organic compost, liquid seaweed or kelp, or fish emulsion to promote healthy growth.

If you often play a waiting game with unpredictable spring weather, transplant seedlings into large, 1-gallon containers right from the flats. The bigger containers allow plants more room to grow if the weather is still too cold when the recommended planting time arrives.

Shade *Saves* Summer Lettuce

If you have trouble getting lettuce to germinate in hot summer soils, let your other garden plants lend a hand, recommends Wanda Boop of Briar Patch Organic Farms in Mifflinburg, Pennsylvania. "Sow your lettuce seed in the shade of taller plants, such as corn or peppers, and cover them with a quarter inch of soil and a board to keep them cool initially," she says. The secret to middle-of-the-summer lettuce is to keep the soil cool—the taller plants and the board work together to keep the soil from becoming too hot. As soon as the seeds germinate, remove the board, and water them generously. The shade of the taller plants will keep the lettuce roots cool and will help prevent the plants from bolting (setting seed).

Keep lettuce cool in hot summer soils by planting it in the shade of taller plants like corn or peppers.

Blocking Is **Best**

"I love soil blocks!" declares Eliot Coleman, author *of The New Organic Grower* and *Four-Season Harvest*. "I still think they are the simplest of all container systems because there is no container. There is no expense other than the soil," says the Harborside, Maine, market gardener. For those of you unfamiliar with soil blocks, they are simply blocks made out of lightly compressed potting soil, pressed out by a form (available in many seed catalogs). The block serves as both container and growing medium for a transplant seedling, Eliot explains. The only trick to successful soil blocking is finding the right soil block mix.

Eliot says that soil block mixes aren't available commercially in the United States (they're widely available in Europe, where soil blocking is more popular). So Eliot makes his own blocking mix using soil, compost, peat, and sand, along with smaller quantities of lime, bloodmeal, colloidal phosphate, and greensand.

Stamped-out soil blocks make a perfect "containerless" container for starting seeds. They don't restrict root growth, so transplants take root as soon as they're planted in the garden.

Most importantly, he says, you need a very good quality peat—Eliot uses ProMix—that will give your soil block body.

Soil blocks have two important advantages over peat pots, says Eliot. For one thing, you don't have to worry about whether the transplant roots will grow through the peat pot once you've planted it in the garden. Also, there's no danger of moisture being wicked away from the roots, as there is when the edges of a peat pot stick up above soil level in the garden. Soil blocks don't restrict roots in any way, which means that transplants take root immediately, he says.

Soil Block Problems? **Lighten Up!**

The secret to successful soil blocking is in the soil used in the blocking mix, says Jerome Gust of Sparta, Wisconsin. Jerome makes his soil blocking mix of equal parts soil, compost, and peat moss, then adds dashes of greensand, bloodmeal, and lime.

"People try soil blocking and don't like it because they do not get good root growth," he says. "In most cases it's because they have a heavy clay soil that tends to pack, making it harder for roots to grow. Even when you're adding peat moss or sand, heavier soil still tends to pack," says Jerome, "so your best bet is to keep adding sand to loosen it up."

Hand-y Helpers

When making soil block mix, keep a box of latex gloves handy to protect your hands. The ingredients for soil block mix are often abrasive and can roughen up tender skin. And one of the staples of soil block mix—peat moss—may contain bacteria that can be harmful if you have cuts on your hands.

The *Right* Lights

A high-intensity sodium halide light is as much a part of raising transplants as the plants themselves for Michael Contratto. Once he transplants seedlings from trays into cell-type containers, Michael, who gardens in Chillicothe, Illinois, moves the trays under a 240-watt sodium halide light. "It provides better light and generates a lot of heat. I can put an awful lot more seedlings under one sodium halide light than I can under a fluorescent light because fluorescents have to be so close to the seeds," he says. Suspended 5 feet from the floor, his sodium halide light illuminates a 6 × 6-foot area—enough room for eight flats.

The two drawbacks to sodium halide lights are minor. First, the humidity in the area won't stay as high because of the heat that the bulb generates. Second, the initial investment for a sodium halide bulb is high. Each bulb costs about $70 and lasts about two years. In the long run, says Michael, it's actually cheaper to buy one sodium halide bulb than to replace all of those fluorescent tubes. The base unit for the sodium halide light also costs about $300, "a one-time investment," he says. Michael says he also gets his money's worth out of the sodium halide unit by using it to overwinter his collection of tropical bonsai.

Timely tip

Michael has a comprehensive system for seed starting before the sodium halide bulb even comes into play. "The last two years, I've started vegetable seeds in rows in trays and then transplanted into containers, rather than simply starting everything in containers. I have much better control," he says. He waters from underneath, keeping the moisture level up, and he hangs overhead fluorescent lights about 1 inch above the seeds, using eight 40-watt lights and alternating warm and cool white tubes.

Humidity Helper

A good way to increase humidity around potted seedlings is to set a couple of seedling pots in a larger pot of pebbles, says Nancy Bubel, author of *The New Seed-Starter's Handbook*. She stresses that the pebbles should be fingernail size and that there should be just a small amount of water in the pebble container—enough to create humid conditions, but not enough to touch the bottom of the pots. "You don't want potted seedlings in standing water all of the time because the roots will rot. I learned the hard way," she confesses.

Increase humidity around potted seedlings by setting the pots in a container of pebbles, then half submerging the pebbles in a little water.

Greenhouse *within* a Greenhouse

For proper germination, some seeds just like it *hot!* That's why Emmaus, Pennsylvania, market gardener Melanie DeVault built a miniature greenhouse inside her greenhouse. Melanie's miniature greenhouse measures 5 × 4 feet and is built around a wooden potting bench. Making your own miniature greenhouse is as easy as 1, 2, 3.

1. For uprights, cut two 2 × 4s into two 18-inch lengths each. Using screws or nails, attach one upright to each corner of a wooden potting bench.

2. Lay thermostatically controlled heating pads on the bench.

3. Drape a sheet of heavy clear plastic over the entire potting bench and uprights to form a tent over heat-loving seedlings. Do not attach the plastic permanently because you may want to raise the sides for ventilation. Just tuck the ends in here and there when you need to keep the heat in. On really sunny days, remove the plastic so the seedlings don't overheat.

You don't really need a greenhouse to make a mini-greenhouse. The same type of structure will work just fine on a table inside your house, barn, shed, or basement, providing you turn up the heat and place plant growth lights under the cover, says Melanie.

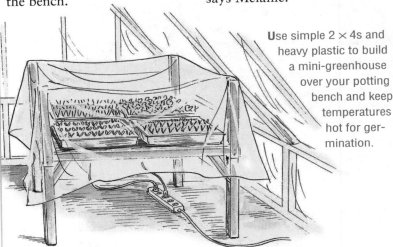

Use simple 2 × 4s and heavy plastic to build a mini-greenhouse over your potting bench and keep temperatures hot for germination.

Plant Nursery in a **Pot**

When rooting cuttings, Juanita Mitchell of Hunt, Texas, makes a clay pot nursery to keep the cuttings moist. She uses two clay pots, one twice the size of the other. She places a cork in the bottom hole of the smaller pot and fills the pot with water. She fills the bottom of the larger pot with potting soil, then places the water-filled smaller pot on top of the soil. Then Juanita adds soil to fill the space between the two pots, and places her cuttings in this loose soil. The water in the smaller pot provides moisture for the cuttings while they root, and the moist soil allows easy removal for transplanting.

Outdoor Solutions Work *Indoors,* Too

If you have trouble keeping seedling flats moist indoors, turn to an outdoor solution—floating row covers! These lightweight coverings let air circulate, admit light, and keep the humidity high for germination. Simply recycle a scrap of row covering from the garden, and lay it on top of the flat.

Mini-Greenhouse *Saves* on Heat

Heating an entire greenhouse can get awfully expensive. To keep costs manageable when germinating seeds, Tony Ricci, a market gardener in Pennsylvania, built a mini-greenhouse for seed starting right inside his larger greenhouse. He fashioned the miniature structure out of an existing greenhouse bench, metal conduit, conduit clamps, furring strips, and clear plastic, and you can do the same in your basement or shed. Just follow these steps.

1. Using a pipe bender (available at hardware stores or rental centers), bend two lengths of metal conduit into semicircular hoops. Fasten each end to the greenhouse bench with conduit clamps to create an arch.

2. Using conduit clamps, fasten a furring strip to the top of each arch to create supports for the plastic.

3. Drape the clear plastic over the furring strips, allowing enough length on each side to reach the top of the greenhouse bench. Using a staple gun, staple a furring strip to the cut edges of the plastic on two opposite sides of the bench; this allows you to roll up the plastic for ventilation.

4. To provide heat, place an electric space heater and thermostatically controlled germination mats inside the mini-greenhouse.

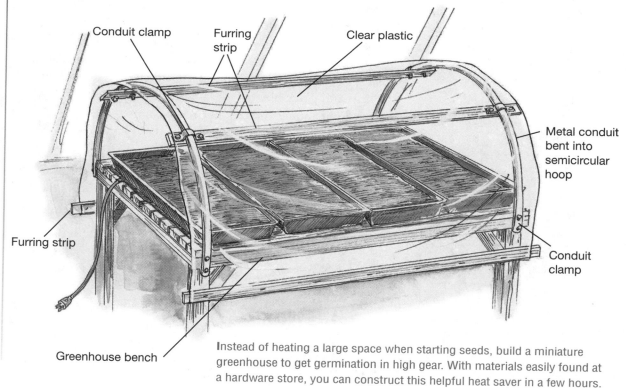

Instead of heating a large space when starting seeds, build a miniature greenhouse to get germination in high gear. With materials easily found at a hardware store, you can construct this helpful heat saver in a few hours.

smart

Solutions to Garden Problems

Most gardeners are nature lovers—except when "nature" gets the best of their garden! When it comes to controlling garden pests, diseases, and weeds, there isn't one best answer. But clever gardeners have devised all sorts of ways to discourage, trick, and repel animal pests, harmful insects, tenacious weeds, and plant diseases. From maintaining a natural habitat for wild animals to knowing which crops will keep pests away from your vegetables, you'll find dozens of solutions for keeping your plants healthy and your garden weed-free.

Know the Signs

Lots of animal-control methods work well—but only if they are directed at the right target! Save money, time, and frustration by correctly identifying the animal causing the problem. Nature centers, Cooperative Extensions, Soil and Water Conservation offices, and libraries are places that can teach you to identify animal tracks and signs. Here are two clues to get you started.

What ate the plants? Look at the place where the plant was nipped off. If the cut is smooth and slanted and just a few inches from the ground, it's probably a rabbit's work. (The distance above "ground" will vary if there is deep snow.) But if the tears are ragged—especially 3 to 4 feet above ground—they are most likely from grazing deer.

Who ripped up the lawn? Moles are one of nature's most maligned creatures, and often falsely accused! If you see open tunnels, you have meadow mice, or voles—not moles! The mole tunnels are under the soil surface—some are right under the surface and others are farther underground.

Who's Wearing the *Lamp Shade?*

Sometimes dogs, cats, or kids (or even chickens or wild animals) knock down your flowers. Wind is even worse about damaging delicate flower stems and can flatten a promising stand of annuals or perennials just when they begin to fill out nicely.

To prevent flowers from being flattened, "try using old lamp shades," says Penny McDowell, a Buffalo Master Gardener. Penny suggests looking for lamp shades at garage sales or at the curb in the trash. Then take off the fabric and place the shades over the plants that are at risk of being scratched at, laid on, walked on, or blown over.

"Once the flowers grow and fill out around the shade, you won't even know the frame is there," Penny points out. "Then they function as great plant supports!"

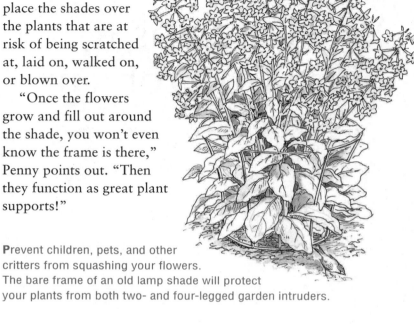

Prevent children, pets, and other critters from squashing your flowers. The bare frame of an old lamp shade will protect your plants from both two- and four-legged garden intruders.

Let **Dogs** Mark *Your* Territory

While the presence of dogs is generally a deterrent to wildlife in the yard, a more specific "product" helps to ward off rabbits, raccoons, squirrels, and other creatures. Get your dogs to mark their territory around the perimeter of your garden. Sally Cunningham, author of *Great Garden Companions,* has lots of wildlife around her country property, and lots of pets, too. Yet she has gardens that aren't eaten. According to Sally, the dogs and cats can help.

"Start a good habit by walking your dog on a leash right around your garden— outside the beds. If you take the dog straight from the house to that area, she is more likely to mark the territory with urine, and it will become a habit." (Be careful that the habit starts where you will continue to want dogs to go— maybe behind the garden or between the garden and the field or fence.)

Timely tip

Sally says that the routine walk around the garden has two other benefits, too. "First, dogs get the idea that this is their area to patrol, and they very likely will watch it more diligently during the growing season. So when the rabbits get interested, the dog is quicker to scare them away.

"Second, when you are training your dog using a choke collar, give a tug and say 'No, no!' in a firm voice that shows you mean business when she pulls to go *into* the garden. Even dogs can be trained to stay off the soil!"

homegrown HINTS

RED PEPPER PRODUCT BREAKTHROUGHS

While red pepper sprays have been used as home remedies to solve many garden pest problems, they do present a problem of their own—they wash off easily. Try one of the new products that combines ground-up hot red pepper sauce with *wax*, and the essence of hot pepper will last longer. Studies have shown that red pepper often discourages rabbits, chipmunks, and squirrels, and it's an effective insect repellent and miticide, too. You can use the products on houseplants, where studies have shown they are as effective as insecticidal soaps and better than traditional pesticides. Some of the hot pepper wax products, such as Hot Pepper Wax, are labeled as safe for use on vegetable plants, too. Call (888) NOPESTS for more information on this hot new option in gardening pest control.

Ferrets Are This Gardener's Best Friend

An unusual pet is the answer to critter problems for Master Gardener Penny McDowell of Buffalo. Penny lives in the country, where many creatures could be attracted to her vegetables, flowers, and shrubs. She also tends the flowerbeds for many landscape customers. Her answer to pest control? Ferrets!

"If you have problems with mice, moles, rabbits, or rats," says Penny, "get a ferret—or make friends with the owner of one." Why? Penny uses wood shavings for her ferrets' litter and then sprinkles their used litter in the vegetable bed and among the flowers.

Penny says that litter from male ferrets works better than litter from females. And she adds, "If I plan to sprinkle ferret litter on the lawn (especially to deter mice, who know the smell of an enemy!), I use clay litter. This worked in the yards of 12 different customers, but I do have some mole tunnels left in a couple of beds. At the very least, the litter and shavings add manure and make great soil texture."

Red Pepper— Too **Hot** to **Handle** or Munch!

"I tried growing some really hot chili peppers for my family's favorite chili sauce recipe," offers Sally Cunningham, author and extension educator, "but they were too hot for the sauce and *way* too hot to work with." But because they grew prolifically, she had to think of something to do with them.

Wearing gloves, Sally strung her peppers on strings for decoration. But she ended up using them outdoors. "I put the chili pepper strings around the trunks of the crabapples. I nailed one end of the string to the ground and wound the string like a candy cane right up to the lowest branch. The rabbits and mice didn't nibble on the tender trunks as they had in other years."

Timely tip

To keep the essence of pepper fresh as the winter wears on, Sally suggests squeezing the peppers (remember to wear those gloves) occasionally after a rain or snowfall and, later in the season, tying an extra string of peppers that has been stored inside around the tree.

homegrown HINTS

TAKE ADVANTAGE OF KITTY'S SENSES

When it comes to protecting their spring plantings from kitty's digging, some gardeners take advantage of cats' sensitive olfactory systems. Effective products for keeping cats away include onion sprays, a sprinkling of chopped onions or chives, and anything strongly perfumed, including the scented inserts from catalogs and magazines.

Cats and Chicken Wire Don't Mix

When you plant flower seeds or small plants in the spring, keep a roll of chicken wire handy, says Marge Vogel of Eden, New York.

"Cats don't like to step on anything coarse, so just unroll some chicken wire, and spread it out flat, at least around the outside of the beds," Marge suggests. "Cats won't walk over it to get to the inner areas. It's those soft, just-tilled beds they like to dig in, so once the plants get going or you mulch the beds, the cats will look elsewhere. Then you can take up the chicken wire."

Chicken wire is an easy solution to keeping cats—both the neighbor's and yours—off your flowerbeds, or even away from your birdbath. While garden plants and warm soil or mulch may be tempting to cats, they won't walk on the coarse wire to get to those delights.

Developing Good Personal Habits— for the Cat!

Cats are creatures of habit, and they're very fastidious, so appeal to their better natures when you set up your spring planting beds or vegetable garden. Here's one easy trick you can try. Put out some clean litter in a prepared section of soil that is removed from the garden. You might even put some droppings there to reinforce the hint. Show Kitty the area, and it most likely will become the "powder room."

Gutter Guard Bulb Protection

Planting bulbs under a flat layer of wire mesh or chicken wire is often recommended. The wire mesh protects the bulbs from hungry rodents, but it can also trap the young plants as they grow. Pulling up the wire can tear their young leaves and buds.

A better bulb-protecting solution is gutter guard. It's lightweight and has a more closely woven mesh so the emerging leaves of bulbs or small plants can push it up but won't get stuck in it.

Static-free Deer Repellent

If deer are a problem in your landscape, tie antistatic strips or strips of dryer sheets to your shrubs every few feet. These strongly perfumed white strips that go in the clothes dryer to prevent static and scent the clothes work just as well to repel deer, according to naturalists Beth and David Buckley of Ashford Hollow, New York. The Buckleys have studied a herd of deer for about 30 years, so they're aware of the landscape damage deer can do.

"We have rhododendrons, which are deer's absolute favorite, lining our driveway," says Beth. "And we have a herd of over 100 deer out there, but they won't touch the rhododendrons." An extra advantage with dryer sheets is that periodic rains revive the scent from the dryer strips, at least a few times, so that they only need replacing every couple of months.

No Corn *without* Roughage

Well-meaning folks often put out corn for hungry deer. While that's a good source of protein, deer also need *browse* material—roughage in the form of twigs and branches. If they can't get it in the field or woods, they'll get it from suburban landscapes. As David Buckley explains, "If you give them corn, they'll be drawn in toward your home and will want the *browse* material to go with it—your shrubs! So don't feed them unless you can provide the protein in the corn *and* the brush for browsing."

So how can you take care of the deer? The best thing you can do for deer is to leave some natural habitat, says this deer expert. The second best thing is to provide brush piles

Instead of attracting deer to dine on your shrubbery by offering them corn and other food, give them a brush pile. The brush supplies what they need to nibble far away from your beloved azaleas.

wherever you can. Walk your property in midwinter, and cut down scrub saplings and crowded young trees, sumac, or whatever you can spare. Make large piles with the coarsest logs on the bottom to provide shelter for pheasants, turkeys, and other small animals. The leaf buds and branch tips that would have been out of reach to deer now make great munching. Deer need this supplemental food most in late winter (February or March), when food is scarcest.

homegrown HINTS

DEER ME

Bill Stockman, owner of Spider Web Gardens in Center Tuftonboro, New Hampshire, recommends draping aluminum foil spread with peanut butter over a single strand of electric fence in order to deter deer. He says, "Deer love peanut butter, and when they put their noses on the highly conductive foil—zap!—they aren't too happy about it."

Glads for Deer

Minnesota farmer Callie Frye says her neighbor gave her this idea for keeping deer out of the garden. Plant gladiolus in thick rows (about 1½ to 2 feet wide) along the edges of the garden, because deer don't like the tall stalks hitting them around the legs as they amble toward the beans. "It works in my neighbor's beautiful garden," Callie adds. "The blooms from the gladiolus also attract bees, and I have never seen tomatoes like his."

Plant a crop of gladiolus as a deer barrier. Deer won't eat them, and they don't like to walk through them to get to their favorite crops.

Deer *Won't Walk* on the Carpet

Master Gardener Flo Zack has no trouble with deer in her garden, even though she has gardened for several decades in Elma, New York, where a herd of deer live in the wild area right behind her house. Her secret? Carpets!

For years, Flo has picked up discarded carpet wherever she finds it—both used rugs placed along the curb for trash pickup and discarded remnants from new installations. She lays the carpet on the ground around the outside of her garden in a path 4 to 6 feet wide. And amazingly, deer won't put a foot on it. "They're suspicious of the texture," says Flo, "and won't take the chance of walking on it."

If you're concerned that when it snows in winter, the deer will just walk on the snow to get at the remaining perennials, shrubs, and fruit trees—don't worry. Flo explains, "By the time the snow is deep, the deer have developed their browsing and travel patterns, so they don't even walk on the snow that covers the carpets."

problem solver

BOARDS HELP KEEP DOGS ON THE PATH

In *Great Garden Companions*, author Sally Cunningham reports success with garden paths that keep foot traffic—including dogs—off the soil. "Most creatures take the path of least resistance," says Sally, "and dogs are smart enough to do that too. In fact, my older dogs would rather not get their feet damp or dirty. So I provide wide boards or even cardboard as garden paths. If the path points even partly in the direction they are going, the dogs will use the paths."

Sally's dogs will even stick with a path that curves! Sally explains that she made a mixed perennial/shrub border with a curving path that leads from deck to barn. "Even in a hurry, the dogs (or children) run on the path rather than through the planting, which is a really good thing!"

CDs Scare Birds and Stop Bugs

The out-of-date music or computer CDs your family no longer uses can find new life controlling pests in your garden or greenhouse.

"To discourage birds pecking fruit before I can vest it," explains Nancy Lewis of Saint Helens, Oregon, "I tie old CDs into the cherry and peach trees and string them above blueberry bushes and strawberries. They work as well as the bird-scare tape, but are 'free'."

Nancy uses CDs with yellow labels in the greenhouse to trap flying insects. "I spread

The shiny, reflective quality of CDs makes them scary objects to birds. Hang CDs with string from fruit tree branches to ward off would-be scavengers.

a film of oil over the yellow side and insert the CD into the slightly split end of a straight stick inserted upright in a pot."

Dogs Will Be *Dogs!*

When Sally Cunningham, author of *Great Garden Companions*, asked her dog trainer how to "break" dogs of digging in the garden, she learned that some dogs have the instinct to dig, and we should not try to fight it. Instead, the trainer suggested giving the young dogs an appropriate place to dig, and establishing the habit early of digging in that place only.

During the planting season, dig up a soft area by the garden, and play with your dog and his favorite chew toy or a scented rawhide bone. Then bury the toy in the soil while he's watching, and leave. He will delight in digging it up and bringing it to you. And next time he will be more likely to use that "best hiding place" rather than your recently tilled garden.

Timely tip

Just in case the dog you're trying to train is the independent type, lay out some chicken wire over new beds for a while, as added insurance against digging.

Baby Your Bulbs

When you find bulbs that have been dug up, it is usually squirrels who are guilty, although mice and chipmunks might have had a role in the mischief.

Sprinkle baby powder around bulb plantings to deter squirrels. They don't like the texture or odor. Plus, it lets you be a super sleuth—you'll know they were there from the footprints.

Season Your Bulbs with Onion

Many people report red pepper, black pepper, and onion juice (one of these or a combination) as their favorite repellent for keeping rodents away from their bulbs. You can sprinkle the bulbs well with these products before planting them, and follow up by sprinkling the soil surface liberally, as well.

Sally Cunningham, author of *Great Garden Companions*, says she keeps a cheese grater in the garden tool bucket to use to grind onion juice on any new planting. "I never throw away soft onions; I just put on a mask and grate them onto the plants!"

Bag Bulbs in Mesh

Nylon stockings or panty hose are too closely woven to let roots grow through, but when mesh stockings were "in," a stylish gardener reported a great use for her torn stockings. Make little bags for bulbs; the roots can grow down, the top can grow up, and the animals can't get at them. (Be sure the weave is open enough to let tops emerge.) You can even put several bulbs in a long stocking, tying a knot between bulbs to keep them separate.

Look for mesh or fishnet stockings at your local thrift store. They provide protection for your bulbs from hungry squirrels, yet they still offer enough room for roots and plants to grow through.

Soda Bottle Transplant Collars

To discourage squirrels from digging up new transplants, Eleanor Rodini of Madison, Wisconsin, makes protective collars for her plants. She cuts soda bottles crosswise into 3-inch-wide rings. She places the rings around the stem of each new transplant, pushing the edge of the plastic into the ground just enough to hold it firmly in place. For a larger plant, she cuts the ring open to place it around the stem to prevent damaging the plant.

Eleanor says that squirrels sometimes scratch around the edges of the plastic rings, but they don't dig up the new transplants. "After a week or so, the squirrels lose interest in the site, and I remove the plastic ring and use it again."

Timely tip

Even if squirrels aren't a concern where you live, you may still find this soda bottle ring idea a valuable one. The rings also keep cutworms, slugs, and other undesirables from getting to plant stems.

homegrown HINTS

SOLID GROUNDCOVER BLOCKS SQUIRRELS

Some groundcovers are really tough to penetrate, so little animals may not bother fighting through them to dig up the bulbs. What to plant to protect your bulbs? Try sedums, creeping phlox, and sweet woodruff.

Although squirrels find the groundcovers too dense to bother with, most spring bulbs can break through. As an added benefit, you can create many attractive groundcover and bulb combinations.

Squirrel-Proof Bird Feeder

Syl Wargo, a Master Gardener in Kenmore, New York, offers a unique design for a bird feeder that truly is squirrel-proof. After attending Master Gardener conferences all over the country, Syl found no other bird feeder quite like it: "It works 100 percent of the time," he says. And other gardeners he's talked to report a similar level of satisfaction.

To make your own squirrel-proof bird feeder, you'll need a 2-foot square of sheet metal, a 1¼-inch-wide galvanized pipe that is at least 8 feet long and threaded at one end, a large nail, and a drill. Make or buy a bird feeder, and attach it to the end of the galvanized pipe. Screw a thread-o-let to the threaded end of the

pole, then attach that to the bottom of the bird feeder.

Bury 2 feet of the pole in the ground, making sure that you place the feeder far away from the house and trees so that squirrels can't jump on top of the feeder from these outposts.

Drill a hole about halfway up the pole, and stick the nail through it. Cut a 2-foot diameter circle out of the sheet metal, as shown. Make a cut into the center of the circle, and cut away a smaller, center circle that will fit the pole loosely. Wrap the sheet metal circle around the pole so that it rests on the nail. The fit should be loose, so if a cunning squirrel should find some way to climb the pole or jump onto the shield, the metal cone will move and not support the squirrel's weight.

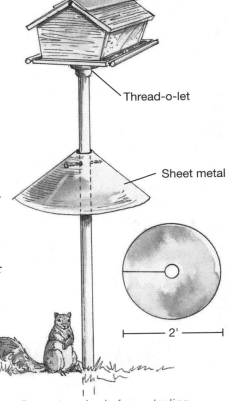

Thread-o-let

Sheet metal

⊢———— 2' ————⊣

Prevent squirrels from stealing your birdseed and encourage them to move to another neighborhood with this squirrel-proof bird feeder.

The *Hairy* Wreath

If a decorative grapevine wreath becomes too ragged for over the mantel or on the front door, you can recycle it in the garden to help keep away rabbits and other animals. The wreaths are perfect receptacles for holding dog hair. Just brush your dog and poke the tufts or clumps of hair into the spaces in the wreath. Hang the wreath so that its lowest point is about 9 inches above the ground. And don't worry about the weather. Whenever it rains, the wet-dog smell gets even stronger. In this case, the doggier it smells, the better!

The next time you need to brush Fido, don't dismay. The loose fur is a great rabbit repellent for your garden. Tuck the fur into a grapevine wreath and hang it near bunny's favorite snack food.

Braiding the Dog Hair

Here's another way to use dog hair to keep rodents out of the garden. Braid it with baling twine into a rope. Then drape the ropes around low garden fences. For added protection, drill holes through motel-type soap bars and dangle them on the dog hair braided ropes. Between the scent of the soap and the dog, critters will avoid your garden.

Twist dog hair into a twine rope to hang in the garden. Add a few bars of scented soap, and rodents won't want to dine in your vegetable garden.

Timely tip

Human hair works as an animal pest repellent, too! Just like dog hair, human hair says "Danger!" However, most human hair doesn't clump the way dog hair does. So gather the hair from your brush, local salon, beauty college, or barbershop, and put it in mesh bags or nylon stockings. Then hang your hair sachets anywhere around the border of the garden you want to protect. Hair is good in your compost pile, too, and it's also reported to have slug-repelling properties.

homegrown HINTS

IF YOU PLANT LETTUCE, THEY WILL COME

One smart Connecticut gardener reported "making a deal" with her garden-nibbling neighborhood rabbits. She took advantage of rabbits' timid natures—and their love of lettuce—and planted a lettuce border around the vegetable garden on the side where rabbits approach from the fields. Then she left a space between the lettuce and the larger garden and planted onions—not a rabbit favorite—in the first few feet of the main garden. Naturally, the rabbits ate what they found first, and they left the onions and everything else alone.

The Bean *Alternative*

Beans are a bunny favorite, but they're also a nitrogen-fixing, soil-improving cover crop. So improve your soil while you offer the bunnies something good to eat—which will keep them away from the rest of your crops.

Plant a 6-foot swath of beans on the side (or sides) of your garden toward the edge of your property. The rabbits will eat some of the plants, but most of them will survive just fine. And it's the roots you want for improving the soil, anyway. You may still get to pick a few beans, and you'll surely have your valuable bean plants to turn under and improve your soil.

Make the First Taste *a Bad One*

Fran Evans, a Master Gardener in Hamburg, New York, says that rabbits don't persist if their first bites of a crop are unnatural-tasting or bitter. He explains, "Rabbits generally begin eating at the end of a row of beans or peas. Dusting the first 2 to 3 feet with some bad-tasting dust or spray will discourage the little pests since one or two bites are enough to make them quit." In addition to red or black pepper and garlic/onion/chive sprays, try dusting your vegetables with talcum powder. Or flavor your garden with an organic commercial repellent mixture labeled for rabbits. (Be sure it's safe for use on edibles first.)

Flo's **Bunny Prevention** Trick

Master Gardener Flo Zack from Elma, New York, has used rotted hay for many years to keep rabbits from eating her beans, lettuce, strawberries, and other bunny favorites.

Flo buys the hay a year ahead of when she'll use it and leaves it outside to rot. The following year she mulches her vegetable garden with it.

Flow says that mulching one side of each row is enough. "Rabbits just don't like the smell of rotted hay. In fact, one time, I nearly stepped on a rabbit in the garden nibbling at some weeds, yet the strawberries with the rotted hay mulch weren't even touched."

Let **Rabbits** Eat *Weeds!*

Not everybody thinks rabbits are a problem. After all, as one study of Missouri cottontails reported, they do eat dandelions, knotweed, ragweed, crabgrass, and even poison ivy—often as a preference over garden vegetables. So leave the area around your garden unweeded to give rabbits the dietary weeds they love.

problem SOLVer

CREATE A MOLE HEAVEN

If you know you have a resident mole, you might try this trick, suggested by a real nature lover with a large yard. Give the mole a more appealing section of the yard, and it may just leave your preferred garden area intact. One way is to select a damp section of the yard and cover it with huge black plastic sheets or tarpaulins from late winter through spring. Mr. Mole will surely love the dark, moist soil that is so soft and easy to tunnel through. Of course, the covering will also kill the turf and weeds in that area, so it may also serve to prepare a place where you can plant wildflowers or wetland plants later in the season. And, if you patrol the rest of the yard and gardens with a cat and stamp down any unacceptable tunnels you spot, your mole "heaven" might keep Mr. Mole right where you want him.

Keep Them in Alfalfa

"I know farmers have real problems with woodchucks," admits Sally Cunningham, "but when I see one sitting complacently on his haunches, surveying his kingdom, I can't imagine that anybody would want to shoot one!"

Sally, the author of *Great Garden Companions*, tried this solution for woodchucks, with good results. She planted a 25 × 4-foot strip of alfalfa at the back of her mowed lawn area. She left about 150 feet between the alfalfa and the vegetable beds. Since woodchucks would rather not cross a large open area where dogs and other predators can find them, they stayed right around the alfalfa the whole season, where Sally says they looked fat and happy. "I think the alfalfa made the difference. Giving them what they want worked."

Woodchucks Sent *Packing*

To outsmart wily woodchucks, try using dried blood to drive them out of their homes. Woodchucks are one of the peskiest inhabitants of the garden and lawn. They'll steal your vegetables, nibble your flowers, and make holes in your lawn or garden. But there's one thing that woodchucks hate, according to Shelia Brackley, perennial production and sales assistant at Bigelow Nurseries, Inc., in Northboro, Massachusetts. "For easy woodchuck removal, dump ⅓ cup dried blood fertilizer in his hole, and he won't go home," Shelia says. With luck, he'll move right out of your yard. Dried blood is available at most garden centers.

Give a woodchuck its own alfalfa bed—away from your garden—and it just might leave your vegetables alone.

A *Time* to Sow, A Time *to Weed*

If you have problems with weeds (and what gardener doesn't?), remember that timing can make a difference. "It's best to pull weeds before they go to seed," says University of Georgia Extension weed scientist Greg Mac-Donald. "But if seedheads have already formed, weed *early* in the day. The moisture that's present in early morning can keep the seedheads from shattering and dropping seeds in the garden."

If you plan to weed during early morning when moisture is present, do it with care. Greg cautions, "My father always said never to walk in the garden very early in the morning or after a rain, because disease is easily transmitted by spreading dew or rain droplets from plant to plant."

Lettuce As a Spring *Weed Blocker*

Block spring weeds between your cabbage plants by sowing fast-growing leafy crops like lettuce between the cabbages. As soon as you transplant broccoli and other cabbage family crops into your spring garden (usually a few weeks before the last spring frost in your area), toss a thick sowing of seeds of lettuce, spinach, or other leafy greens around the transplants. Lettuce grows quickly, likes shade, and blocks most of the weeds. Don't let the lettuce

Prevent early weeds from taking hold while you wait for your broccoli or cabbages to grow. Instead of using traditional mulch, plant lettuce between the rows. It will block weeds and you can harvest it for crisp spring salads.

weed barrier go to waste. Thin the lettuce or greens as they grow, and use the thinnings for tender salads.

Have a Gardening *Night* Party!

You've heard of garden parties and gardening days, but a "gardening night party"?

According to some research studies, tilling at night prevents many weeds from germinating. Certain weeds need light in order to germinate, and just those few post-tilling hours of being exposed to air without light renders the seeds unproductive.

A gardener near Ithaca, New York, says his farming family declared a nighttime tilling and planting party in late spring, when the soil was warm enough to work. They rigged up dim lights on the tiller, walked ahead of it to pick up rocks, and—at least in theory—left a lot of disappointed and unfulfilled weed seeds turned up behind them.

The nighttime tilling scene was part magical and part comical, and best of all, one the family will never forget! While some weeds are sure to germinate even when the tilling is done in the dark of night, at least this family believes the weed count was way down. Plus, it's cooler working at night, and the party was certainly a lot of fun!

problem SOLVer

TAP INTO SOIL NUTRIENTS

Dandelions, with their long, thick taproots, can capture nutrients from several feet below the surface of the soil. By composting dandelions, you can put those nutrients back into the soil surface. The trick is to let the rootstocks dry out before you compost your dandelions. Toss the pulled dandelions off to the side to dry in the sun for a couple of days. After they've dried and shriveled, you can toss them in the compost heap. Also, be sure to cut off the heads if they are even approaching the flower-to-seed stage!

Flame Weeder Recommendation

"We used a flame weeder last summer for the first time in our ¼-acre organic garden and found it to be worth its 30-pound weight," reports Amy LeBlanc, of Whitehill Farm in East Wilton, Maine. "I have a bad back, and it has been my savior."

While Amy found the flame weeder worked well on very small weeds, out of concern for insects and tiny animals that live on the soil surface, she used it mostly on weeds that had reached 2 to 4 inches tall. She found that regular flaming sets weeds back so they had far less impact on crops and never had the chance to flower and reseed. "The best thing about the flame weeder is

that it is fast," Amy says.

"When you get the rhythm of your swing going, you can move right along and see the results only an hour or so later," she explains.

Amy recommends making another pass over the weeds a few days later to ensure you've gotten them all. She adds, "Our flame weeder has a special extra widget that is essentially a pilot light, which allows us to stop flaming for a moment then continue without having to completely stop and relight it. It's a great feature—and one that any serious gardener would appreciate!"

You can find flame weeders at some specialty garden centers and farm stores as well as through farm and garden catalogs.

Cardboard for Weed-Free Paths

Who has time to weed a path, when there are more important things to do in the garden? Whether your path is made of gravel, wood chips, flagstone, or sawdust, it is easy to prevent even the peskiest of weeds from working their way through. How? Use cardboard!

You can get cardboard free from the grocery store. A double thickness of cardboard box material will kill any weeds underneath it, and it lasts a long time.

One thickness of cardboard will work, but persistent weeds like quackgrass will find any cracks between the pieces. So "insure" the project by using a double layer of corrugated cardboard in your pathways.

Timely tip

Cardboard can be a little slippery as a walking surface, so use it as the bottom layer of the path. Start the path in a shallow trench, a couple of inches lower than the planting bed level. Put 2 to 3 inches of your chosen path material on top of the cardboard, and the sliding will be minimal.

homegrown HINTS

FIGHT WEEDS—AND WATER WOES—WITH WEEDS

"Broad-leaved weeds—and I mean *really* broad-leaved weeds—make a great mid-summer mulch," reports Allentown, Pennsylvania, gardener Deb Martin.

"I had a couple of common burdock plants (*Arctium minus*) growing in my yard, and they were starting to bloom," Deb explains. "I wanted to get them out of there before they started spreading seeds everywhere." Deb used a pair of loppers to fell the 4-foot-tall weeds, then dragged them to the driveway to wilt in the sun.

"I cut the largest leaves off the burdock—they were easily a foot wide and 1 to 2 feet long—and laid them on the moist soil around some newly planted bee balm." The leaves covered the soil, then Deb dressed them up with about an inch of compost.

"I was away on vacation during a week when there was no rain, and my plants survived just fine," Deb says. "The burdock leaves really helped keep things moist. And they'll give my perennials a little nutrient boost as they decay."

Queen-Anne's-Lace—A Welcome Weed

Some gardeners select weeds for the garden on purpose! Sally Cunningham, author of *Great Garden Companions*, recommends allowing certain "weeds" such as Queen-Anne's-lace to volunteer around the garden.

"The trick," says Sally, "is to recognize these plants when they are tiny and to choose right then which ones you want in which location." Queen-Anne's-lace is desirable around the garden because of the many beneficial wasps and flies it attracts. Tachinids and several types of tiny parasitoid wasps flock to it because the nectar is so readily available. And it provides food for swallowtail butterfly caterpillars.

But, it's easy to weed the babies out along with ragweed and other unwelcome weed seedlings. And, Queen-Anne's-lace has a taproot, so it isn't easy to transplant. Sally recommends getting to know this welcome weed by its seedlings and letting it stay in some parts of your garden.

But keep it away from the carrots, she cautions. Queen-Anne's-lace can carry aster yellows, a disease that affects carrots, asters, and mums. So keep this weed where beneficial insects can enjoy it, but make sure it benefits your garden—or pull it.

Learn to recognize seedlings of "beneficial" weeds such as Queen-Anne's-lace. As long as it's not growing in a bad spot, this is one weed that's pretty enough to keep, and it attracts and feeds beneficial insects, too.

Salad "Dressing" in the Flowerbeds

Most perennials start small in spring, and some arrive late—at least late enough to give weeds a good head start!

Try planting lettuce, spinach, or mesclun (mixed salad greens) all around the young perennials. They will block weeds, and you can pull them up and eat them by the time the perennials are ready to fill out the space.

Or, if you are planning to put tender annuals among the perennials, the lettuce will be done and ready to bolt (set seed) just about when the soil is warm enough to plant the annuals!

Desirable Weeds— Good for You and Your Garden

Some weeds are actually good for your garden. These desirable "weeds" are plants that attract beneficial insects. They include wild daisies, dandelions, dead nettle (stinging nettle), goldenrod, common sorrel, tansy, and even lamb's-quarters. If you let them share some of your garden space, they can help reduce insect problems on your "real" garden plants. And while you're at it, try harvesting edible weeds such as lamb's-quarters (*Chenopodium album*) and chickweed (*Stellaria media*). When young, they make a tasty salad.

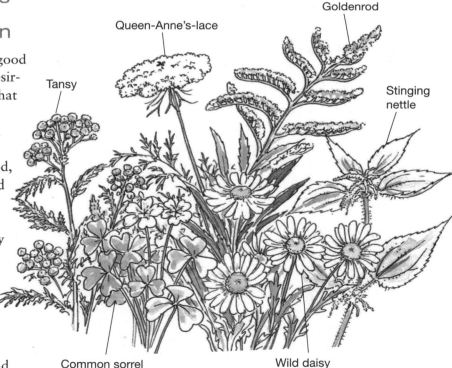

Some weeds get an undeserved bad rap. The weeds shown here all help your garden by providing food and shelter for beneficial insects that can help keep pest populations in check.

Tea **and** Botany

An elderly English gardener who had lived many years in a small town in New Jersey, commented, "I just don't understand why some Americans pay so much for those nasty herbicides just for weeds in the sidewalk! It's so easy to take care of them!"

Her solution? Every Sunday after church she prepared her tea and boiled a bit of extra water. While the tea steeped she took the boiling pot of water out to the sidewalk in front of the house and poured it along the cracks. "Once a week with boiling water is quite enough," she said.

Acid Test

Maintaining your brick or flagstone path doesn't need to be a time-consuming chore. A new, organic, acetic acid-based product from ECOVAL will destroy various common weeds in just hours.

Nature's Glory Fast Acting Weed and Grass Killer will kill the top growth of both annual and perennial weeds. Allentown, Pennsylvania, gardener Deb Martin decided to try it on the poison ivy in her yard. She reports that it burned the leaves but did not kill the plant. However, the spray also fell on some weedy violets nearby and took care of those invasive plants completely. Because the spray is nonselective, it's best to use it where it won't damage crops or ornamentals.

Deb says, "This product really does a number on weeds growing in driveway and sidewalk cracks. And I can use it without having to worry that it may harm my children if they play near where I spray."

For another equally effective and fast-acting weed killer, try dousing the offending plants with straight vinegar (use 3 percent acidity, if it's available). Vinegar has a drastic effect and can acidify the soil to the point where plants will not grow. Ordinary table salt, poured onto the soil and watered in, also will kill roots and make the soil uninhabitable. Be aware, however, that both vinegar and salt are more permanent methods, are nonselective, and can effectively sterilize the soil for months.

Save Beneficials by **Mowing** Just Half

Cover crops like rye, buckwheat, and clover build your soil and supply a place for beneficial insects to live and breed. But when you mow or turn under a crop, you kill or disrupt the beneficial insects. So how can you save the beneficials?

No matter what your "cover and mow" or "cover and turn" routine, do it in halves. Till or mow down the *right* side of every row the first time and down the *left* side two weeks later. Although you can't save every beneficial insect, this method lets you maintain a permanent habitat and some good hiding places for the population to grow in at every stage of the insects' development.

Timely tip

In the case of paths, one garden designer suggests that the main garden paths should be wide ones, planted in clover, which is an ideal draw for beneficial insects and bees. She recommends making the paths twice as wide as the lawn mower, which makes it easy to mow down half a path every two weeks.

A **New Use** for *The Wall Street Journal*

Rochelle Smith, a landscape designer and diagnostician in Grand Island, New York, is always looking for ways to provide customers with solutions to landscape problems at a reasonable cost. Rochelle writes, "I use the same weed barrier in all of my landscape installations—*The Wall Street Journal*." While lots of landscapers use newspaper, Rochelle explains, "I prefer not to use the small inserts, since they take more time. My favorite is *The Wall Street Journal* because of its large, thick sections, and no inserts!

"Newspaper is especially useful in low-maintenance groundcover plantings where the plants need to be spaced for healthy development and where hand-weeding would increase the maintenance of the site." It works wonders—even on light slopes. To use newspaper in a landscape installation, Rochelle first prepares the soil thoroughly; then she installs the hardscape (paths, and so on) and plants the large trees and shrubs. Then it's time to put down the newspaper.

Rochelle says the goal is to have a cohesive layer of newspaper between the soil and the top mulch. To use her method, spread the newspaper in large open sections, six to eight sheets thick, with plenty of overlap between each section. Before planting, wet the paper with a light spray from the hose, and place a thin layer of mulch all over.

To complete the bed, punch through the paper with a trowel to plant small perennials, groundcover plants, and bulbs. (You do need to break the weed barrier for bulbs, because the paper does not let them push through.) Finish with 2 to 3 inches of mulch. The garden will look neat and tidy, while the mulch will both provide an effective insulator for plants and enhance the weed-controlling properties of the newspaper.

Timely tip

Rochelle and others have learned the hard way that laying newspaper can be difficult if you try to do too much at once—especially if the wind picks up! She suggests laying out small areas at a time—perhaps no more than 10 × 10-foot spaces, wetting the paper as you go.

Trip Up the Thrips

Many summer-flowering bulbs, such as freesia and gladiolas, are very susceptible to flower thrips, tiny insects that deform buds and ruin blooms. Bill Stockman, owner of Spider Web Gardens in Center Tuftonboro, New Hampshire, has discovered an easy way to protect these bulbs: Soak them in a dip of 1 gallon of warm water mixed with 2½ tablespoons of Lysol.

Bill says, "Let the bulbs sit at least 12 hours, then plant them straight from the dip. At bloom time later in the season, there will be no thrips!"

Tomato Hornworms Take Up *Tobacco*!

Fran Evans is a Master Gardener who has eliminated tomato hornworms from his Hamburg, New York, garden. Fran says, "Plant one or two tobacco plants with the tomatoes. Hornworms prefer the tobacco plants and are easy to pick off the tobacco and destroy." Fran says this method can keep your garden hornworm-free for two to three years.

Insects—Are They *Pests* or *Friends*?

Insects are blamed for a lot of gardening disappointments, but most of the time the problem is really the growing conditions the gardener has provided. So before you kill an insect, make sure it's really the culprit you think it is. In many cases, the insect you see is a beneficial one, there to help you with the real pest. (Or at the very least, an innocent insect just passing by.)

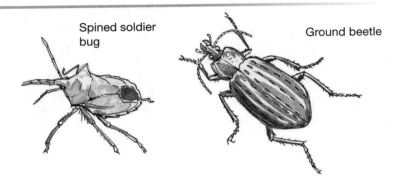

Get to know the good guys in your garden. Spined soldier bugs eat many kinds of caterpillars, plus Mexican bean beetle and Colorado potato beetle larvae. Ground beetles gobble up slugs, snails, cutworms, and many other pests.

Experts tell us that 95 to 99 percent of the insects in our yards and gardens are beneficial or harmless. So, make sure you've got a bad guy before you squish!

Use Growing-Degree Days to *Bypass* Pests

The time that certain insects or plants emerge is different from region to region. Nature doesn't use a calendar. Instead, insect and plant development are governed by signals from nature—especially the light and heat that have accumulated during the season.

So how can you plan for the onset of particular garden pests, such as Japanese beetles, forest tent caterpillars, and gypsy moth larvae? There is a formula, used to measure that accumulated heat, called growing-degree days (GDDs). This formula is the key to intelligent pest management. For instance, there is no point in taking any steps toward pest control if the pests aren't there yet. And they're only there when nature's signal tells them that it's time.

You can get charts of GDDs for insect and plant behaviors from your local Cooperative Extension or other educational sources, and the charts are good tools to have. Ask your local extension or weather station for the current GDDs, and then check the chart to anticipate insect emergence.

Slug Lite

"On night slug patrols, you usually need three hands—one to hold the flashlight, one to scoop up the slugs, and one to hold the slug container," notes Sharon Gordon of Ohio.

To make slug collection a two-handed operation, Sharon suggests buying a headlight from a camping or backpacking store. When you wear the headlight, the light will point wherever you look, leaving your hands free for scooping up slimy slugs and other pests that feed at night. A headlight will also help you gather greens after dark.

homegrown HINTS

TIME YOUR PLANTING AROUND INSECT LIFE CYCLES

Once you know when insect pests are likely to arrive (see the growing-degree days tip on page 127), make sure their favorite plants are not what you just planted! Here are some smart garden timing tips for better pest management.

Cabbage loopers: Plant cabbage early (about four to five weeks before the last frost), and harvest by late spring—before the cabbage loopers have emerged to begin chewing.

Corn borers: If you plant corn two weeks after the last frost date, you may just be able to avoid these pests.

Potato leafhoppers: These insects come on strong in July, so plant your potatoes as soon as possible in spring, and try to harvest them all by late July.

Carrot maggots: These pests are the worst when you plant early to get those first sweet carrots. Instead, wait until after June 1 in the North (or until early summer) to plant your carrots.

Of course, timing isn't everything, and there are other reasons to plant a crop early or late. But if a certain pest is your primary problem, look at the pest's timing to see if there are ways to avoid the problem.

Row Covers
Add a Few Ounces of **Prevention**

The old "ounce of prevention" adage is surely correct when it comes to using row covers (polyethylene fabric) to prevent many insect pests on crops. However, row covers often blow away in spring breezes, and they sometimes tear when you try to tack them down with boards, rocks, or pins.

Instead of leaving the fabric loose, try this idea from Sally Cunningham, author and organic gardener from East Aurora, New York. Staple the outside edges (on the long sides) to long ½ × ½-inch wooden strips, like the ones used for interior trim or moldings. "I find 6- or 8-foot lengths are the longest lengths that are still manageable," says Sally. "They give the tunnels structure, prevent blowing, and hug the ground."

If there are gaps or uneven ground, Sally recommends mounding a little soil over them. You can still use tunnel hoops if you want an elevated

Inexpensive molding stapled to the edges of row covers keeps the covers in place during prime insect time. When pests are no longer a problem, wrap up the covers and store them for next year.

tunnel. When it is time to remove the row covers, just wrap the cloth around your wood strips until next season.

Turn Torn Row Covers into *Plant Hoods*

If your row covers are torn repeatedly over a few years of use, cut the sections that are salvageable into squares, which you can fashion into little bags for individual plant covers. If you're handy with a sewing machine, fold the squares in half and sew down each side. Or, you can try the easy way—use clothespins!

Then you can place the individual bags, or hoods, over vulnerable plants in any part of the garden—from an eggplant hiding from the flea beetles to a newly planted hill of squash.

Salvage old, torn row covers by turning them into individual plant covers. You don't even have to sew! Simply pin the fabric edges together over the plants with pinch-type clothespins. Be sure to bury the bottom edges of the bags to prevent pests from finding their way into the bags.

Ants in Hot Water

Gerry Rising is a nature columnist for the *Buffalo Evening News* and a Master Gardener, as well. While ants aren't a serious problem in Buffalo, they surely are in other places.

Gerry says, "My mother-in-law lives in Alabama, where she has fire ant problems. She doesn't like to use harsh chemicals or gasoline on her lawn to rid herself of these terrible stingers, but she does want to get rid of them or at least partially control them. She boils a gallon of water and pours it down the center of the nest."

Birdcage Stand *Makes* a Great Garden Perch

You may find a discarded birdcage stand in the attic or at a yard sale. If it's not a valuable antique or suitable for an indoor cage, put it in the garden. (You may have to stake or tie it if it's in a windy location.) The stand can hold a hanging plant, and it will attract birds, who will perch on top of it. If you provide the home, the birds will patrol your garden for insects. Some birds will even make their nests in the plant. Perhaps the birds know the stand was designed to give them a place to hang out.

Invite birds to your garden to help in reducing the bug population. Birds need places to perch, and a hanging basket on an old birdcage stand will be irresistable to your feathered friends.

Post *a* Perch *for the* Birds

If you don't have the space for living perches, and your garden lacks bean poles or teepees, welcome insect-eating birds with a tall (8- to 10-foot) perch made from a pole topped by a wooden crosspiece of any length. You can use a ½-inch wooden strip, a piece of molding, or any small scrap of lumber for the cross-piece. However, a bird's little feet may feel best perching on a smooth piece of dowel.

Neighborhood birds will help to rid your garden of insect pests, as long as you give them a place to perch while they watch for bugs.

Tomato Cages **Help Birds** Hunt Insects

Birds eat insects—an impor-tant source of protein for them and their young—in summer, just when you and your garden need the help. Make their hunting easier by pro-viding perches at high points around your garden. Tall tomato cages provide perches, but the birds will find your garden more attractive if there is at least one stake that is 1 to 2 feet higher than the tops of the cages. Put a short cross-piece atop each tall "perching" stake where birds can rest while they scan for insects.

"Plant" **Toads** *in the* **Peas**

Few things are as good for your garden as a resident toad—or two. You can't ex-actly *plant* a toad, but you can try to attract them to the pea patch. Toads love pea aphids and a lot of other pest insects; they even eat slugs. So offer toads shelter, such as an in-verted clay pot with a "door" chipped out of the lip, and some water. A small sunken pool or even a shallow dish will do fine. Put these near the pea patch and the toads will come. And, when you find a toad around your yard, move him into your garden.

homegrown HINTS

SUPPORT BIRDS WITH SUNFLOWERS

A planting of sunflowers or any other tall annuals or perennials can help bring the birds to the garden, but the plants must be strong enough to offer a place to perch that doesn't collapse when the birds land there. If you have tall plants that are too wobbly to support even a bird's weight, try putting up a fence on the less visible side, or put up a wire cage around them. The flowers will add beauty to your garden while they attract birds and beneficial insects. And the birds and beneficial insects will help manage any pests that dare to venture into your garden. If you hope to save any sunflower seeds for yourself, cover one or two flowerheads with a piece of plastic mesh just as the seeds start to ripen.

Be Patient with Aphids

You can beat aphid attacks just by using a little patience. Aphids have so many predators that they rarely become a problem if you encourage predation and have a little patience. Something will come along to eat them—but only if you wait a little while and don't spray them!

If you *do* spray—organic, botanical, or otherwise— you'll probably kill off or discourage beneficial insects as they arrive. Or, you'll at least cut down the population of the attractive aphids just long enough so that the predators won't discover your garden. As a result, the aphids that survive the spraying (the strongest ones) will suddenly multiply, and there will be no army of predators ready to handle them. So you'll have to spray and spray again, and the problem continues.

If a particular crop or specific plants are seriously threatened by aphids while you're waiting for the beneficials to arrive, just spray them hard with a hose once a day until you see your insect allies arrive. You'll be glad you waited for reinforcements.

problem SOLVER

APHIDS ARRIVE AFTER YOU PRUNE!

You can avoid a lot of aphids by pruning most of your trees and shrubs when they are dormant. The reason you find aphids on the tips of plants or on new leaves is that they are seeking nitrogen, which is concentrated in areas of new growth. Pruning your trees and shrubs, including roses, gives the plants a signal to produce nitrogen-rich new growth. So by trimming your plants while they're dormant, you'll make sure there is no nitrogen signal to attract aphids, and few, if any, aphids to attract anyway.

Note that some shrubs, such as lilacs, should be pruned during the growing season, after they finish flowering. But these shrubs seem to be less prone to aphid problems and have already produced their new leaves and flowers.

To keep aphid problems in check in your perennial beds, go light on nitrogen when you fertilize. It triggers the nitrogen-rich, aphid-attracting growth that follows summer pruning.

Trench Warfare *Topples* Armyworms

Armyworms sometimes march into the garden from neighboring fields and can do an impressive job of destroying beets, corn, and other vegetable crops. (This is especially true of the fall armyworm, which likes almost everything edible in its path.)

Armyworm problems are most severe in the southern and central United States, but these voracious pests sometimes work their way quite far north. Here's the trick to stopping these determined soldiers in their tracks.

If you have a big crop, dig a narrow (2-inch) trench along the sides of the garden, 6 to 8 inches deep. If you have a "ditch witch" or other trenching equipment—the equipment used when laying pipe or cable—available, the job is easy. Even if you have to dig the trenches manually, it's worth it. The worms will fall into the trenches before they can destroy your crops.

Keep a heavy pipe the width of the trench nearby. From time to time, drag it along the tunnel to squish the worms.

Garlic Is a Gardener's Friend

Planting garlic near cabbage or lettuce can help prevent pest problems, but it may be hard to grow enough garlic to do the job right.

Dave Swaciak, horticulture educator for Cornell Cooperative Extension of Cattaraugus County in New York, recommends, "If you grow hardneck garlic and use every clove for cooking or for planting next year's crop, then you can let one or two of the scapes mature." (Scapes are the flower stems that produce a bulblike part on top. The usual advice is to cut them off so they don't steal nutrients from the developing bulb.) Each scape holds a flower, which produces about a dozen tiny bulbs called bulbils. You can plant these bulbils throughout the garden and they will sprout the same year. Leave the bulbils in the ground over winter, remove them when you prepare your garden in the spring, and re-plant them after you have mixed in your soil amendments. Or leave them in the garden while you prepare your bed, and they will usually still find their way up! After a few years, they will even produce cloves that you can divide for further planting or cooking.

Don't let any of your garlic go to waste. Dave recommends that you chop any scapes that you do cut off for use in cooking—or use them as the basis of an insect-repelling spray.

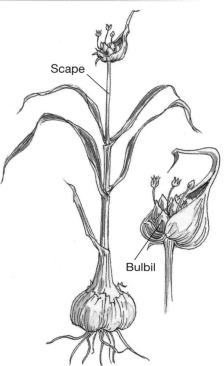

To get enough garlic to eat and to use for pest control, let a couple of scapes mature, and plant the resulting bulbils.

homegrown HINTS

CATCH CUCUMBER BEETLES WITH OLD SQUASH

Spotted cucumber beetles chew holes in all sorts of vine crops as well as in corn, potatoes, and some fruit crops. Even worse, they can spread serious diseases to your garden. But smart gardeners can put a stop to these troublesome pests early in the season.

If you have winter squash in storage, keep some until spring—even if they are getting soft. Scoop out a hole in each squash, and place it by the vulnerable crops soon after planting. Once these traps hold lots of cucumber beetles, toss squash and pests in the trash.

Battle **Birds** with *Fantastic Plastic* Bottle Baffle

If the birds are tasting your grapes before you are, try bottling them on the vine! "Bottling is easier than bagging," says Pennsylvania gardener Bill Dailey.

To guard your grapes from marauding birds, try Bill's simple technique. He cuts the neck off of a 1-liter plastic seltzer bottle, then makes a slit down the length of the bottle. To prevent condensation inside the bottle, Bill pokes a few holes in its bottom. Then he simply snaps the bottle over a developing fruit cluster. Bill adds that he always tries to slip the top of the slit bottle over a neighboring vine to help support the weight of the growing grape cluster.

"I put the bottles on when the grapes are about half-size, and I usually just do a few a night over a couple of weeks," he reports. Bill's reward is perfect, unpecked grapes at harvest time, with no disease or rotting.

Apple **Maggots** *in the* Bag

For years, organic gardeners have used red sticky balls, coated with Tanglefoot or another sticky substance, to simulate ripe apples so that they can catch the flies that lay apple maggot eggs. The problem is the sticky balls can be quite messy, and they need to be changed frequently. You have to hang two to eight traps per tree in the middle of June and leave them all summer. When the sticky traps become coated with flies or other debris, they are useless, and you have all the trouble and expense of changing them.

To avoid this end-of-summer mess, slip your new, clean balls into plastic sandwich bags, using twist ties to close the bags. (The twist ties can double as hangers, or you can use inexpensive red Christmas ornaments, complete with wire hangers.) Coat the bags with your sticky substance, and then hang them in the apple tree. When the sticky bags become too bug-encrusted to be effective, simply slip off the old bags and tie on new ones.

Lots of apple growers lure apple maggots to red sticky balls and away from ripening red apples. You can make the whole process less messy, however, by putting the balls in plastic sandwich bags first, and then coating the bags instead of the balls. Simply toss out used bags, and reuse the red balls.

homegrown HINTS

CABBAGEWORMS DON'T LIKE RED

Are cabbageworms ruthlessly butchering your cabbage? To save some for yourself, try planting red-leaved cabbage. Studies indicate that cabbageworms don't like them as well as they like green-leaved varieties. (And maybe the gardener can see the pest better and will hand-pick it more often!) It is also true that cabbages that have smoother leaves are attacked less frequently than crinkly leaved varieties.

To protect green cabbage varieties, try turning the leaves of broccoli, cauliflower, cabbage, and brussels sprouts white by dusting them with white flour. (It sticks best after a rain or on the morning dew.) Caterpillars eat the flour, get bloated, and die.

Sheer Protection from Cabbageworms

Row covers are a great way to protect members of the cabbage family, including broccoli and cauliflower, from imported cabbageworms and cabbage loopers. But row covers aren't practical if your garden is interplanted with flowers you would like to enjoy or if you don't plant in rows.

You can still protect your cabbage and broccoli, though, with their own personal covers made from your used nylon stockings or the legs of panty hose. Put the stockings right over each individual vegetable, and they will stretch as the cabbages or heads of broccoli

The sheer, stretchy fabric of nylon stockings offers perfect protection for growing vegetables. Air and light get through the fabric, but the snug fit keeps insects from eating your crops.

grow. However, if you threw the stockings out because of holes, the cabbage butterflies will find those same holes and lay eggs there! Avoid using the parts that are torn.

Spread the Sheets under the Pines

Conifer sawflies are a serious problem for pine and spruce trees in many parts of the country. To catch a lot of them in late spring, spread old bedsheets around the base of your evergreen trees. The conifer sawfly larvae will drop to the ground to pupate. You can gather them up and carry them to the trash or the bonfire before they have a chance to develop.

Timely tip

A brisk whack or shaking the tree a few times will encourage some of the conifer sawfly larvae to drop sooner than they expected!

Plant a *Winning Combination*

"This is not a new idea, but it's definitely underused," says Sally Cunningham, author of *Great Garden Companions*. "Everybody should plant rows of potatoes alternating with wide rows of bush beans."

Sally says this really works. Mexican bean beetles and Colorado potato beetles are both repelled by the mixed planting. "The pests just don't find their targets!"

Outsmart Mexican Bean Beetles

Master Gardener Fran Evans of Hamburg, New York, uses this timing trick to beat Mexican bean beetles.

The timing may differ in your zone, but the principle is the same. Plant snap beans as early as possible. Then pick the beans until the crop begins to dwindle. Pull up all the bean plants or mow them down and till them into the soil by the third or fourth week in July. "About 90 to 95 percent of the time, weather cooperating, you will be finished with the beans before the Mexican bean beetles can lay eggs and establish themselves," says Fran.

homegrown HINTS

SCOUT FOR CUTWORMS AFTER DARK

One old-timer who gardens in New York State suggests that after your first big planting day, when your body aches all over, sit for a while with a cool drink. But before you lie down, take one more walk out to the garden in the dark. Bend down and pick off those cutworms before they get going. Those last few bends and stretches won't kill you—but losing the crop by morning just might!

Nail Those Cutworms!

Stick a nail in the soil next to each seedling. Any size nail will do. Simply place it about ¼ inch away from the stem. The nail keeps cutworms from wrapping around a plant's stem, which is how they feed on—and sever—young plants.

Lure **Cutworms** with Clover

Cutworms like fresh-cut grass or clover, so make a few piles of it right in the garden near new seedlings. Look under it in a while for cutworms. If you find them, either discard the worms or pour boiling water over the whole pile, taking care not to get boiling water on your seedlings.

Old Forks Keep Cutworms at Bay

Keep some old forks stuck among your young plantings. Garden tools are too coarse and many are not handy to use around little seedlings. Instead, gently scrape and poke with a salad or dinner fork around the base of seedlings to dislodge the cutworms as they approach the tender stems of your transplants.

It's especially important to keep a careful eye on your transplants during the first few days after planting to keep cutworms away from your young plants. Keep old forks and other anticutworm equipment close at hand. Once the plants grow a bit older and tougher, cutworms will look elsewhere for tasty treats.

The **Bottle** Tree

One apple grower, Bill McKentley, stopped a lot of traffic with his "bottle trees." Before his apple trees were in bloom, he hung clear empty soda bottles from the branches, suspending them horizontally with ribbons tied at the neck and bottom. Why? He was catching codling moths in a mixture of vinegar and molasses, which he placed in every bottle. There are several methods for using vinegar and molasses combinations, but here's one easy method. Mix about 1 cup of molasses in ½ gallon of vinegar in the blender. Put just enough of the mixture into each bottle so you can lay the bottle sideways and the liquid won't spill out. (Bottles vary, but you'll need from 1 to 2 cups per bottle.)

Be sure to replace the bottle caps while you are hanging the bottles. Use twine or ribbon to attach the bottles to the tree. Tie one piece tight around the neck of each bottle with enough length to tie it to a branch. Use a second piece of twine in the form of a sling to suspend the lower half of the bottle so that it hangs parallel to the ground. If your area is windy, it helps to wind the twine once rather tightly around the bottle. Take the caps off, and you're ready to catch some moths.

Prevent codling moths from damaging your apple crop by capturing the moths—before your trees blossom—in homemade soda bottle traps.

Vinegar and molasses mixture

Three Cheers for No More **Caterpillars**

Eastern tent caterpillars and fall webworms are destructive caterpillars that make white or gray webs or "tents" in trees.

While you can cut out the affected branches, here's a less invasive way to deal with the problem. A former cheer-leader attached her old pom-poms to a pole and poked them into the nests to pull out the offenders.

Dust Mop to *the Rescue*

Here's another clever way to rid your trees of tent caterpillars. One gardener recommends drenching a dust mop in *Bacillus thuringiensis* (BT) and shaking it over the nest to try to saturate the nest with the caterpillar poison. (BT is a biological stomach poison for leaf-eating caterpillars, but it does not harm birds or other creatures. It can kill the larvae of butterflies, however.) The long-handled dust mop makes it easier to get the BT through the webbing and onto the pest caterpillars inside.

Screwdriver Can *Prevent* Tents

Karen Soltys, garden book editor at Rodale Press, reports that she, too, had an annual problem with eastern tent caterpillars on her trees.

"Every year I'd have to cut out a branch or two from my weeping cherry tree when the tents appeared. Then I got smart and started looking for the caterpillars in my tree before they crafted their tents."

Karen now uses a screwdriver to lightly scrape the caterpillars out of the trees. She lets them fall onto paper on the ground below, then wraps up the paper and tosses the caterpillars out with the trash. There's nothing magical about the screwdriver. You can use any tool narrow enough to fit in branch crotches.

Flea Beetles Get Mixed Up

"My eggplants were the first plants to be riddled with flea beetle holes," reports Sally Cunningham, the author of *Great Garden Companions*. But Sally proposes a solution that relies on using the mixed plantings that are typical of her companion-style approach to gardening.

Japanese Beetles Drop & Disappear

Every Japanese beetle you catch early is one that can't lay eggs to make more. So early in the season set your alarm clock early—before 7 A.M.—to get out there and get the beetles.

Spread a sheet under the

Sally says, "One year I planted eggplants all alone in one area, and in another place, I interspersed eggplants with marigolds and basil. Guess what? The 'solo' eggplants were full of holes, but the other ones were camouflaged enough that they squeaked through the season undiscovered! Flea beetles are easily confused."

plants the beetles prefer. Some say roses suffer the most, but there are hundreds of target plants—everything from grapevines to fruit trees. Then shake the plant or whack it with a broom and watch the beetles fall down and "play dead." Toss them into soapy water or put them in the trash.

problem SOLver   CATCH FLEA BEETLES AS THEY JUMP

A Buffalo gardener had trouble with flea beetles in a community garden and risked some odd stares from fellow gardeners when she performed her clever jumping flea beetle ritual.

She coated a wide board with a homemade sticky substance (Tanglefoot would do) and brushed it along the top of the row,

just touching the plants. She enlisted the help of a friend, who used a ruler to jiggle the plants just enough so that the flea beetles all started jumping. They stuck to the board and were never heard from again!

Repeat this trick for three or four days in a row, and you'll have fewer flea beetles jumping about and feeding on your garden.

homegrown HINTS

THE FOUR-O'CLOCK CONNECTION

Companion gardener and author Sally Cunningham reports this tip, first offered by Clarence Mahan, an expert in Japanese iris with experience in Japan as well as America. Clarence has many gardeners planting drifts of four-o'-clocks (*Mirabilis jalapa*), a wonderful, fragrant, old-fashioned annual, slightly away from the garden. They are a favorite of Japanese beetles, and they work as a trap.

When you notice beetles attacking the four-o'clocks, hand-pick and squish them all in one place, or knock them off the flowers into a can of soapy water. In theory, you can even scoop up and discard your entire planting of four-o'-clocks, Japanese beetles and all—but upon seeing and smelling the flowers, who could?

Less Turf *Equals* Fewer Beetles!

According to nurseryman Skip Murray of Murray Brothers' Nursery in Orchard Park, New York, "Beetles like turf to lay their eggs." Skip explains, "In our nursery we have very few Japanese beetle problems—and it's not because we spray a lot of pesticides, because we don't.

"We're surrounded by fields, trees, and some groundcover. It's those massive suburban lawns—one after the other—that are perfect for breeding beetles!"

So, if you replace some of your lawn with more groundcover or garden areas, and keep the birds around with food, shelter, and water sources, Japanese beetles and other lawn grubs won't be as much of a problem.

Japanese Beetles *Like It Wet*

Female Japanese beetles only feed for about two days before laying their eggs. And many of the eggs that are laid in dry soil dry out and cannot mature. So, let your lawns and gardens dry out well between waterings. The adult females may seek other, damper, places to lay their eggs, which means they may even be drawn away to feed elsewhere while getting ready to start the new generation.

Spider Mites and the *Wet Blanket*

If spider mites are a problem on some of your landscape plantings (they especially like junipers), use the wet blanket trick. Spider mites dislike cold, wet conditions, so when you have a cold rain, make the most of the situation. Put a blanket over the shrub, and keep the blanket wet for a few days. (Don't deny your plant light for too long, of course.)

Or, if the blankets are too much trouble with a larger planting, just keep hosing the shrubs every day to simulate a cold, wet spring. Besides discouraging the problem mites, you will be helping beneficial predatory mites, which eat the "bad ones." Unlike problem mites, the beneficial mites happen to thrive in moisture, so you'll be skewing the odds in favor of the good guys!

Vaccinate the Vines

Gardener Craig Vogel of Eden, New York, takes care of squash borers with a hypodermic needle. He uses it to inject liquid *Bacillus thuringiensis* (BT), a stomach poison that only affects caterpillars, right into the stems of squash and pumpkin vines, wherever he suspects a squash borer may be lurking.

After the first discovery of a squash borer, Craig reports that he had no further problems with this pest. "An extra benefit," said Craig, "is that butterflies aren't affected. We have a butterfly garden, and I couldn't use BT where other caterpillars could get sick from it. But when the BT is right in the plant stems, only the vine borers get it."

Once you're sure you've eliminated borers from your squash vines, mound moistened soil over any damaged stems. Keep them well watered and they'll root and keep right on growing.

Instead of sprinkling BT crystals on squash plants, where any caterpillar can ingest them, try injecting the liquid variety directly into the squash vines, where it will affect only the squash vine borers.

High-Pressure Hosing for Squash Vine Borers

This tip is best performed in a bathing suit. Where you see yellow frass (insect excrement), which indicates a squash vine borer, make a small hole and a slit in the vine. Take your garden hose, and pump the water full force into the hole.

According to Craig Vogel of Eden, New York, the pressure knocks the "worm" right out or drowns it. Plus, your garden gets watered and you get quite a cooling shower in the process.

Squash Vine Borers *Skewered* Again

There are many ways to impale this pest, which can decimate a whole squash plant from the point where the stem meets the soil. Pennsylvania gardener Karen Soltys uses the jumbo-size paper clips to go after both squash vine borers and peach borers. "Paper clips are cheap, readily available, and easy to unbend and poke into the squash stem or tree bark to kill and remove damaging caterpillars," says Karen.

Skewer Your **Wireworm** Woes

A time-honored trick to trap wireworms is to bury pieces of potato where you plan to plant. Then dig up and discard the infested potatoes. However, sometimes people lose the potato pieces, resulting in even more well-fed wireworms!

To solve the missing potato pieces problem, some gardeners put the pieces on a stick. But that can lead to another problem—the sticks sometimes soften or rot in the spring rains.

Instead, use metal shish kebab skewers or fondue forks. (You can sometimes find these at bargain prices at yard sales.) Skewer the potatoes and bury them with half the handle showing above ground. Pull up the potato and the culprits to discard them, and bury another piece until the wireworms are gone. A few other equally good "skewers" include chopsticks, cocktail stirrers, plastic forks, and row-cover staples (U-shaped pins) that won't be in use until after planting, when the wireworm hunt is over.

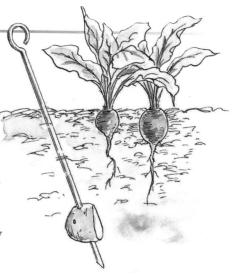

Raw potato wedges will attract wireworms away from your plants. Spear the potatoes on metal shish kebab skewers or fondue forks so that you can easily remove the bait once it has done the job.

Baking Soda *Is Still News*

Not only is baking soda the key ingredient in a well-respected home recipe for fungicide, but now it's legal! Many people have used the baking soda formula to control black spot on roses, rust on hollyhocks, and powdery mildew on many plants with considerable success.

But extension offices and those in the horticulture industry were careful about passing on the information to gardeners and farmers, because baking soda had not been listed by the United States Department of Agriculture (USDA) for fungicide use.

Well, now it's official— baking soda has been approved by the USDA as a fungicide. If you have plants that are suceptible to rust or mildew, here's the formula:

Baking Soda Formula

1 teaspoon baking soda

1 tablespoon horticultural oil or light summer oil (acts as a sticking agent)

1 quart water

Mix together baking soda, horticultural oil, and water, and use it in any clean spray bottle. Spray on the vulnerable plants every seven to ten days. You'll need to reapply the spray after a heavy rain.

Timely tip

Although there are no reports of plant injuries caused by the baking soda treatment, it's always wise to test any treatment on a small portion of a plant and watch for a day to be sure that the cure is not worse than the problem.

Hosiery *to the* Rescue

If your row covers rip, you can patch them with pieces of discarded stockings or panty hose. The stretchy fabric is perfect for the job and the earth-tone colors are nearly invisible (unless you wear hot pink!). Simply cut the hosiery into patch-size pieces and whipstitch them in place with a few hand stitches.

Row Covers Stop *Diseases* and **Pests**

Row covers can prevent the spread of diseases by stopping insects that spread diseases. For example, "mosaic virus" is a name given to many strains of viruses that affect beans, tomatoes, and other crops. Leafhoppers and aphids spread mosaic virus. The damage these pests do is small compared to the damage caused by the diseases they spread. Use row covers to keep insects out and you'll block disease, too.

Timely tip

Buy extra-wide row cover fabric to make it extra easy to cover your crops. A 6- or 8-foot-wide cover can protect an entire raised bed or a couple of wide rows.

problem SOLVer   BURY YOUR BROCCOLI FOR SAFER SOIL

To banish the deadly verticillium wilt from your soil, make sure it eats its broccoli. It doesn't matter which part of the vegetable you use, so go ahead and eat your favorite parts, and save stems, leaves, or whatever parts don't suit your fancy for the garden.

"It's true—decomposing a dose of broccoli or other cruciferous (cabbage-family) vegetables in soil creates a toxic gas that can reduce, if not completely rout, verticillium wilt and other soil-based fungi that afflict tomatoes, eggplant, and other garden yummies," says plant pathologist Themis Michailides of the University of California at Davis. One caution: Strawberries won't do very well in the treated soil, so try another solution for that crop.

For scientific measuring purposes, Dr. Michailides uses vegetation dry enough to be ground into a powder, but fresh works too, he says. Just keep in mind that much of the bulk of fresh vegetables is water, so use lots of veggies, chopped as finely as possible. Or, if you prefer, dehydrate the vegetables by cooking them in your oven, microwave, or dehydrator (time will vary according to the amount). Then, push the dried stuff through a fine-meshed sieve. Mix the vegetables thoroughly into the top 6 inches of soil. Dr. Michailides uses a 1 percent mixture, or 1 part cruciferous vegetables to 99 parts soil.

After mixing the vegetation into the soil, wet the soil completely for proper decomposition. Then cover the soil with a sheet of plastic to prevent the crucial gases from escaping. "How long it takes depends on the temperature. Warmer is better," Dr. Michailides says. Keep the soil covered for about a month, then wait a few more days after that before planting anything in the treated soil.

out in the Garden

EVEN AFTER YOUR GARDEN is up and growing, you can improve it and keep it at its very best by following some expert advice and homegrown good sense. From helpful hints for more vigorous vegetables to a wealth of ways to fine-tune your flower gardens, these chapters are packed with great ideas for the many different kinds of gardens you grow. Learn new ways to bring colorful butterflies and cheery songbirds to your yard. Produce a bumper crop of fresh fruit that's both delicious and care-free. You'll get more from every part of your garden with these smart ideas and clever techniques.

great

Vegetable Gardens

Of all the things we do in the garden, growing vegetables delivers the most tangible rewards: luscious ripe tomatoes, bumper crops of beans, delicate asparagus spears, and so much more. And getting your vegetable garden to deliver bigger, earlier, better yields is what ingenious gardening is all about. Dig into this chapter and discover a treasure trove of unbeatable tips and techniques for clever crop combinations, super ways to solve everyday problems, and helpful how-to hints for humongous harvests.

From *Packaging* to **Pathways**

Clever gardeners across the country have discovered the many advantages of using layers of newspaper and mulch materials to turn sod or weedy areas into new garden beds. To create paths in and around new gardens, Master Gardener Margaret Ferry of Timonium, Maryland, recommends raiding your recycling for something a bit sturdier—cardboard boxes.

"Instead of newspaper, use cardboard cut to the size of the pathway you desire. Wet it down and cover it with 3 to 4 inches of wood chips," advises Margaret.

To make a pathway that's both free and built entirely from recycled materials, Margaret notes that it pays to be on the lookout for tree trimmers in your neighborhood. "They're usually glad to leave their wood chips at a nearby site, rather than haul them longer distances for disposal," she explains. "Just be sure you know the type of tree they're removing, and try to avoid getting a delivery of chips that include poison ivy or oak, sumac, black walnut, or thorny vines."

Garden Thrives *within* Bale Borders

There are a lot of advantages to having a few bales of straw around the vegetable garden, reports Master Gardener Teena Bailey of Germansville, Pennsylvania. Teena really means *around* the garden—she actually surrounds her entire garden with a border of straw bales each spring and finds that her garden really reaps multiple benefits.

"We place intact bales of clean straw around the edges of our garden to accomplish several things," Teena says.

"When my husband cuts the lawn around the garden, seed-heads from grass or weeds—yes, our lawn has weeds!—aren't blown into the garden, and the bales act as a bit of a barrier against the strong winds in our area."

The bales also reduce the amount of grass that creeps into the garden from the lawn, Teena adds. "When the bales begin to break down, we use them for mulch and replace them with fresh bales—any weed seeds or leftover grain they contain has probably sprouted by then and doesn't contaminate the garden."

Summer Plastic **Beats** Fall Weeds

The weed control you get from black plastic mulch lasts even after you remove the plastic, says farmer Jim Crawford of Hustontown, Pennsylvania. For example, when you're ready to replace a summer crop such as broccoli that's planted in black plastic with a winter crop like fall snap peas, Jim says it's time to take the plastic off. Removing the plastic reveals a completely weed-free planting bed for your fall vegetables because the heat beneath the black plastic has killed the weed seeds.

"Or you can put down black plastic with the idea that you'll leave it on for three to four weeks, then pull off the plastic and save it to reuse elsewhere in the garden," Jim says. "When you remove the plastic, it has the same effect—the weed seeds are dead. You can even shallowly till the top 2 inches of the bed, and there is no viable weed seed," he adds.

Till **Soil** for Crops, *Not* for **Weeds**

Save time and effort this spring by tilling only where you plan to plant, says Sharon Thompson of Boone, Iowa. There's no need to till the paths between rows and beds in your garden, she explains. And by tilling only where you intend to plant, you avoid walking on and compacting tilled soil. Your feet stay on whatever weeds have dared to poke through the untilled parts of your garden, Sharon adds.

As a result, your boots stay cleaner, and your plants enjoy tilled soil while weeds languish in the uncultivated paths. Weeds grow more slowly in untilled soil, Sharon points out. "Hold off on any pathway tilling until it's needed—when the weeds grow enough for you to notice them or when they're large enough to compete with your vegetables."

Timely tip

Untilled paths also make a fine place to toss any weeds that you pull from your garden beds. There's little chance they'll root in the inhospitable pathway, and you can stay out of the mud as you tread on your fallen foes.

Wipe Out Weeds with Fall *Freezer Wrap*

To get a jump on spring planting and weed control, Dan Tawczynski, a farmer from Great Barrington, Massachusetts, prepares some of his planting beds in fall. Dan tills, adds organic fertilizer, and covers the beds with clear plastic. "We lay the clear plastic in October, then the weeds sprout and get frozen over winter. Come spring, we have no weeds under cover," he explains. Dan says this method works great for early spring transplants such as lettuce and broccoli.

Choose Chips for **Cheap**, *Natural* Weed-and-Feed

For good, cheap weed control and fertilizer, use wood chips, says gardener Eber Wright of Pierpont, Ohio. "It's better than sawdust, because it doesn't restrict water and oxygen like sawdust," he explains. Eber mixes wood chips and composted manure to make a combination mulch and fertilizer. "It gets the plants off to a good start, and it provides good weed control."

Tough on Weeds, **Easy on You**

For smart and simple cultivating, organic farmer Scott Case of Aaronsburg, Pennsylvania, says the best thing you can do is put aside that heavy, worn-out garden hoe and get one that's user-friendly.

Many older hoes are unnecessarily heavy and clunky and simply aren't productive tools for efficiently cutting out the weeds. Scott suggests novice gardeners check out the hoe descriptions in garden catalogs to see which features are most suited to their needs. He says he prefers a collinear hoe, like the one designed by Eliot Coleman and sold by Johnny's Selected Seeds of Albion, Maine. The 70-degree blade/handle angle lets you stand straight and use a comfortable thumbs-up grip while you easily remove the small, seedling-size weeds that can all too quickly overtake your vegetable seedlings.

Scott says he also appreciates the advantages of stirrup hoes, which come in various widths. These hoes feature an oscillating steel stirrup that cuts through weeds just below the soil surface.

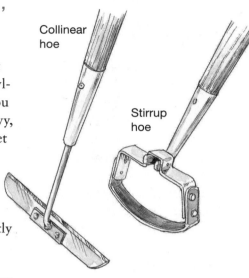

A top-quality tool takes a lot of the hard work out of hoeing weeds. Choose a lightweight hoe that has a sharp blade to easily skim weeds off the surface of your garden.

Timely tip

Give weeds an early shot at your garden, then wipe them out before they know what happened, suggests Bruce Butterfield, research director at the National Gardening Association in Burlington, Vermont. Before you sow seeds, prepare the soil—work it up, rake, and tamp, then wait, Bruce says.

"As the weed seeds emerge, cultivate again, so you get rid of practically all the weeds," he says. Then you're ready to sow the crop that you want to grow there.

Flame Away
Weeds Around
Slow-Rising Crops

Flame weeding is perfect for slow-emerging crops such as carrots, parsnips, dill, cilantro, and parsley, says Jim Crawford, a farmer in Hustontown, Pennsylvania. He explains that flaming lets you wipe out weeds at exactly the right time to give slow-to-germinate vegetables and herbs the advantage they need.

And flame weeders have become very affordable, Jim adds. The basic equipment, which is available from many mail-order garden suppliers, is a propane torch with a long wand and a portable propane tank.

Jim recommends these steps for flaming away weeds before your slow-emerging crops appear:

1. Prepare the soil, moisten it, and let it sit for two days.

2. Sow your crop seed.

3. Wait until the fifth or sixth day, then check the row for weed seedlings. When weeds start to appear, go over the rows with the flame weeder. "This kills the weeds and gets the crop off to a great start," Jim says.

Use a flame weeder to turn up the heat on weeds and give slow-starting crops like carrots and parsnips a fighting chance against their quicker competition.

Every Space
Has a Use

Even the most efficiently planned garden will have the occasional unused or awkward spaces in it. And if you don't fill the empty spots in your garden, Mother Nature will quickly fill them for you—especially if the soil is completely bare. Instead of letting problems arise, with a little thought and advance planning, you can find clever, garden-enhancing uses for those empty or underused spots, says Darrell Frey of Sandy Lake, Pennsylvania.

At Three Sisters Farm, Darrell makes curved raised beds that follow the contour of the rolling land. But gardening on the contour means that some places are too wide and there is excess space where the vegetable beds don't fit.

"We make those places useful," Darrell says. "That's where we put our compost piles or manure tea buckets, or where we plant something like raspberries. Or, we let the area go naturally wild to attract beneficial insects. There's no reason to waste space, even if it's unused space."

homegrown HINTS

TIME PAPER PLACEMENT TO WIN OVER WEEDS

Newspaper mulch makes a great weed blocker around crops such as potatoes, says gardener Sharon Thompson of Boone, Iowa. But it's important to mulch at the right time to stop the weeds without slowing down your vegetables, she explains.

As potato plants grow, Sharon notes, their size makes it hard for the gardener to weed between the rows. Yet the weeds can still sneak in there with no trouble. To stop weed problems before they start, Sharon waits until her potatoes are growing and well established but not yet filling in the rows completely. Then she hoes between the plants one last time and lays down a two-sheet-thick layer of newspaper. "Toss a little soil on the edges to hold the paper down, or cover it with grass clippings or straw for cosmetic appeal," she says. The timing of this mulch gives the potatoes a boost and will save your back in weeks to come. Sharon's system works well for beans and other crops too, but she cautions against laying down a newspaper mulch too early in the season, noting that it's important to let the soil warm up first.

Use **Vine Crops** as Mulch

Many small seeds, including weed seeds, need light to germinate, and shade is your best weapon for preemergent weed control, says Mac Cheever, a market gardener from Milton, Wisconsin. "So use your vine crops as a mulch," he advises.

"Interplanting your taller plants with smaller vine crops won't affect either crop's yield much, but it will significantly reduce the need to cultivate," Mac says. "Flowers and vegetables mix nicely, too. Small-leaved cukes will do well under peppers or eggplants, for example, as well as around tall flowers like cleome and sunflowers."

Plant low-growing vines like cucumbers under taller crops like peppers to shade the soil and stop weed seeds from germinating.

Timely tip

Mac gets another season's use out of tall crops such as sunflowers—he turns them into next year's stakes! "Tough, old sunflower stalks may very well be next year's tomato stakes, or supports for the snap peas," he says.

Paper Your Way to *Problem-Free* Fencerows

Good fences make good neighbors, but they also make a refuge for weeds and other pests that can plague your garden. Diane Matthews-Gehringer of Kutztown, Pennsylvania, puts newspaper under the fence around her garden and puts a stop to its weed-harboring ways.

Diane's method is simple: She centers an open section of newspaper under the fence, then tops it with a little straw, and covers it with a layer of black plastic mulch, secured at the ends. "Make sure there's no gap where the fence meets the plastic," Diane warns, adding that her technique doesn't work with electric fencing. But around her garden, it keeps weeds at bay in this hard-to-maintain area, and it removes a favorite hiding place of garden-eaters like rabbits and voles.

Double-Cropping *Delivers* **Multiple** Benefits

Intelligent double-cropping can lead to higher yields, greater diversity, and more enjoyment of your garden. It can also help prevent pest problems and even give you mud-free paths, says Mac Cheever.

In his Milton, Wisconsin, market garden, Mac replaces early radishes with beans or peppers—which he starts in gallon containers to help them develop big root systems. He puts late broccoli where the peas were or plants late cabbage after the early lettuce.

"By double-cropping, you get two crops in the same space, and you have the opportunity to clear-cultivate once again (annual grasses are a plague in Wisconsin). You

Well-chosen crop combinations can cut down on weeds in the garden. Young tomatoes enjoy the company of maturing cabbages—the cabbages' large leaves make the shady soil beneath them an inhospitable place for weeds to grow.

also provide some simple rotation, which can alleviate pest buildup," he explains.

Mac plants cabbages between his rows of tomatoes. The broad leaves of the cabbage inhibit weeds. Sometimes he doesn't remove the large basal leaves after cutting the cabbage heads so that he can use the leaves as a natural, mud-free path to pick tomatoes. Otherwise, he removes the plants and lets the mature tomatoes fill the space after one more pass with the tiller.

Laugh at **Weeds** and **Mud** with *Living Mulch*

Chillicothe, Illinois, gardener Keith Crotz doesn't like walking in the mud. And he doesn't care much for weeds, either. "So we intercrop hairy vetch with our sweet corn," he says. The hairy vetch smothers the weeds, keeps the soil moist, and makes a living mulch that climbs up the corn stalks.

But that's not the limit of the benefits this mulch delivers: "If you inoculate it, the hairy vetch will pump about 50 pounds of nitrogen into the soil," says Keith, who also teaches college biology. Inoculation is a seed treatment that coats the vetch seed with beneficial bacteria that helps it "fix" or convert to a form plants can use—atmospheric nitrogen. You can order inoculants from most seed catalogs; applying an inoculant is usually a matter of moistening seeds slightly and then shaking the inoculant over them before you plant.

Keith says he plants his sweet corn on 36-inch centers to accommodate the width of his mower. "When the corn is about 1 foot tall, we broadcast the vetch seed. After a rain, the vetch comes up and within two weeks it's 8 to 10 inches tall." He warns against confusing benevolent hairy vetch (*Vicia villosa*) with its much more aggressive legume cousin crown vetch (*Coronilla varia*), which can easily take over your garden and everything around it.

When it's time to harvest the sweet corn, Keith uses a 26-inch mower to mow the hairy vetch between the rows. "We never have to worry about walking in mud because of the thick carpet of vetch," he adds.

Hairy vetch is a soil-building cover crop that makes an attractive, weed-smothering, moisture-conserving, plant-feeding, so-you-don't-have-to-walk-in-the-mud living mulch for a stand of sweet corn.

Weeds for Dinner Equals Sweet Revenge

Not only are many of the weeds that plague your garden edible, but they're also some of the best-tasting natural foods around, says Darrell Frey of Three Sisters Farm in Sandy Lake, Pennsylvania. That's why Darrell adds tender baby wild edibles to his gourmet salad mix, which is one of the most popular mixes he sells.

The wild edibles Darrell gathers for salad include chickweed, dandelion, lamb's-quarters (you can also cook the young shoots as you'd cook spinach), pigweed, purslane, and more. "Chickweed is a favorite of our customers," he adds.

"With the baby wild edibles, you get two crops in one space," he explains. "The wild edibles grow with the head lettuce, which takes four to five weeks to mature." Darrell harvests baby wild edibles both before and after the main crop of lettuce or other vegetables, then he tills the remaining "weeds" into the soil as a green manure.

If you gather wild salad greens from anyplace other than your own organic garden or lawn, make sure they haven't been sprayed. Better to have a boring salad than one dressed with herbicides or fertilizers!

Get even with weeds and stop them before they take over your garden: Call them "baby wild edibles" and eat them in a delicious dinner salad!

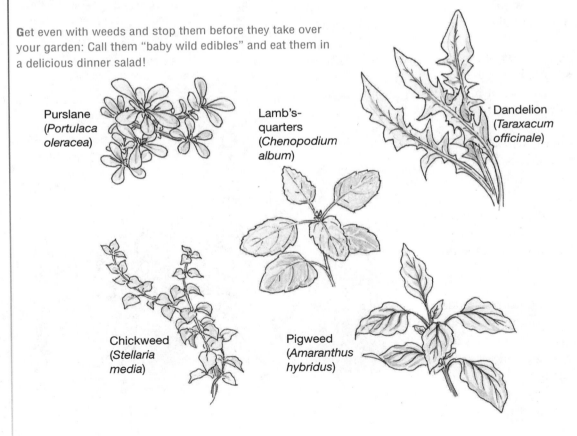

Purslane
(*Portulaca oleracea*)

Lamb's-quarters
(*Chenopodium album*)

Dandelion
(*Taraxacum officinale*)

Chickweed
(*Stellaria media*)

Pigweed
(*Amaranthus hybridus*)

Add *Cover Crop* at Last Cultivation

"On the last cultivation of my fall crops, especially broccoli and cabbage, I usually plant a cover crop like rye between the rows," says organic farmer Don Kretschmann of Rochester, Pennsylvania. "It takes a little while for the rye to get going, and this is a great time for it." The rye provides soil protection over the winter and helps keep any weeds from taking hold.

Here's how to use rye as a soil-building fall cover crop:

1. Cultivate around fall crops, sow the rye around them, then rake or hoe lightly to mix the seed into the soil.

2. The rye will sprout and grow to provide winter cover and prevent weed growth.

3. The following spring, at least two to three weeks before planting, mow the rye and till it into the soil.

Rye is a great soil builder, but it can suppress germination of other seeds when it's tilled in. Allow a couple of weeks between turning under the rye and planting spring crops.

Build Your Soil with a *Birdseed* Cover Crop

There are a lot of fancy plants that you can use for garden cover crops, says gardener Craig Cramer of Cortland, New York. Planting cover crops in the time between harvesting an early crop and planting a fall crop will help prevent erosion and keep weeds from invading, Craig points out. "But they're pretty pricey in small amounts, and you never seem to have them around when you need them," he says.

"So if it's hot, and you have an empty space in the garden, throw in some cheap birdseed mix. It's mostly millet and sorghum that will come up fast and give a quick summer cover you can dig into the soil before planting fall crops."

Timely tip

For an end-of-summer cover crop, Craig recommends cheap, cool-season covers such as annual ryegrass, rye, and wheat. Craig says annual ryegrass usually makes up the bulk of the "quick lawn" grass mixes, while rye is becoming more widely available in garden centers. You can also find cover crop seed in your grocery store's bulk food section—look for "wheat berries" if you want to sow a winter cover crop of wheat that you'd till under in the spring.

Leftover birdseed mix can be a handy source of seed for a summer cover crop.

A *New* Role for Rocks

If you have land that seems to grow rocks, turn them into a garden asset, says Master Gardener Teena Bailey of Germansville, Pennsylvania. After cold weather killed some of her grapevines during their first winter in the garden, Teena used rocks to give the replacement vines a fighting chance against the cold.

She filled clear plastic bags—the heavy-duty kind that sand is sold in—with rocks that "grew" in her garden. "We set partially filled bags on the windward side of the young vines," Teena explains. "The bags helped protect the grapevines from the strong wind, and the stones held enough solar heat to give the grapes the extra margin they needed until they got established."

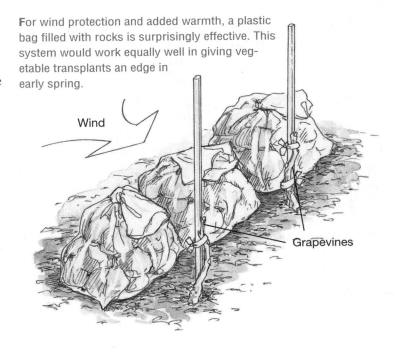

For wind protection and added warmth, a plastic bag filled with rocks is surprisingly effective. This system would work equally well in giving vegetable transplants an edge in early spring.

Wind

Grapevines

problem SOLVer   SHADE CLOTH HELPS BLOCK THE BREEZE

Woven polyester—that stuff sold as shade cloth to help protect greenhouse crops from overexposure to the sun—is also a great garden protector, says Bruce Butterfield, research director at the National Gardening Association in Burlington, Vermont. When it's attached securely to fencing around your garden, shade cloth makes a terrific windscreen for your plants, Bruce explains.

He compares the way the screen works to a person seeking shelter outdoors from chilling winds, noting, "Plants like a little protection, too." The semipermeable fabric cuts the worst of the wind but still allows some air movement in the garden.

If you have wooden fence posts, Bruce recommends attaching the shade cloth with 1 × 2-inch strips of wood nailed to the post. If your fence posts are metal, you can fasten the cloth to them by sticking pieces of wire through the cloth and twisting the ends around the post.

In addition to shielding your plants from damaging winds, the shade cloth also warms things up a bit, Bruce adds, noting that a warm plant is a happy one.

Trellis Away Vine Troubles

If humidity hampers your vine crops in the summer, try this creative way to keep your plants happy and healthy, says Maryland Master Gardener Margaret Ferry. Margaret uses trendy—and unusual—trellises to keep the air moving around vining plants like cucumbers and melons as well as pole beans and morning glories.

Good air flow is important, she explains, because it helps keep diseases at bay when the humidity climbs in the summer months. But it's important to have some fun while you're fighting fungal problems, she

adds. "When it comes to trellises, you can use yard sale and flea market finds like ladders, old broom handles, bamboo fishing rods, and refrigerator shelves, especially from commercial units that are long and narrow."

Other innovative trellises might include the skeleton of a beach umbrella, with strings attached for a cascade of cucumbers and morning glories; an old hat rack transformed with scarlet runner beans (*Phaseolus coccineus*); or a vine scarecrow dressed in hyacinth beans (*Dolichos lablab*) and gourds.

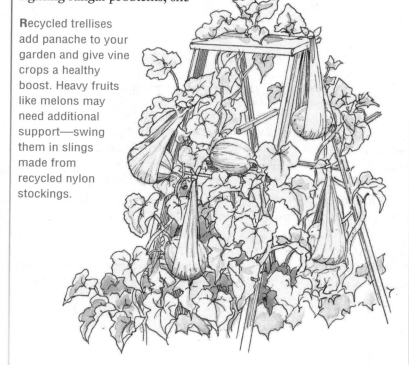

Recycled trellises add panache to your garden and give vine crops a healthy boost. Heavy fruits like melons may need additional support—swing them in slings made from recycled nylon stockings.

Pipe Up Your Climbing Crops

Turn plumbing supplies into low-cost, custom-built supports for your garden's climbers, says Pennsylvania gardener Nancy Ondra. To make lightweight trellising for climbing vegetables, shape supports from long-lasting PVC pipes and connections. Or, do as Nancy does and use copper water piping and copper fittings to create attractive, durable supports for flowering vines. Nancy says she uses a tubing cutter to cut the pipes to the desired lengths and secures the joints with plumber's adhesive.

Crops **Cooperate** on Teeming Trellis

Combining climbing crops on one trellis makes smart use of space for gardener Sharon Carson of Delmar, Delaware, and the plants work to support one another. Sharon plants a trio of twining cucumbers, tomatoes, and beans together and enjoys good results. "The twining beans hold up the tomatoes, especially cherry types, quite well," she says. She grows small, pickling-type cucumbers, like lemon cucumbers.

Sharon uses sturdy wire mesh with 4-inch-square holes, fastened to rebar posts, to support her climbing crops. She says a strong trellis is important when you're counting on it to hold up three climbing crops. "But we get lots more food and save space with vertical planting."

New Life for Leftover **Drip Tape**

"We use leftover drip irrigation tape to secure the plastic on our hoop houses, instead of buying the usual stapling or greenhouse tape," says Martha Daughdrill of Newburg Vegetable Farm in Newburg, Maryland. The used drip tape holds the plastic well, Martha explains. "And it seems we have plenty of it left over each year, with no other use after its time in the field," she says.

To find a steady supply of used irrigation tape, check with an area nursery or market gardener. Or substitute a worn-out soaker hose. The tape is useful for attaching plastic to any wooden frame to keep the plastic from ripping.

problem **solver**   BE FIRM WITH SEEDS SOWN IN DRY SOIL

In 1874, Peter Henderson, known as "the great-grandfather of truck farming in America," did experiments showing that "trodding on" rows when the soil was dry increased germination and maturity of corn, beet, spinach, and turnip crops. More than 100 years later, Emmaus, Pennsylvania market gardener Melanie DeVault read of Peter Henderson's results and tried his method in her own garden.

In a year when Melanie's garden was in constant need of watering, she walked on rows of newly sown late turnips and spinach, and left other rows less firmed. "It really made a difference," she says. "Germination was consistent in the firmed rows, and the others were really spotty. I can still picture the difference.

"Peter Henderson found big differences in corn germination under dry conditions—4 days in firmed rows compared to 12 days in unfirmed ground. And in late spinach and turnips, firmed rows germinated well, while unfirmed rows germinated poorly." She adds that this method doesn't work in really wet weather.

"Firming the rows makes sense," Melanie says. "It's something so simple, and it has such a big payback. I've been walking on rows—and reading old gardening books—ever since trying Henderson's method."

Hide Your Heap with *Hungry Tomatoes*

If you circle your tomato plants around your compost pile, you'll enjoy several benefits, says California gardener Paul Barina. You'll have well-nourished tomatoes and a compost pile that's conveniently close for tossing garden waste into. And you'll save precious gardening and composting space while building your garden soil for future crops.

Here's Paul's method for creating a space-saving, soil-building, tomato-boosting compost garden:

1. Start by making a combination compost bin and tomato cage. Use a cylindrical cage about 6 feet in diameter, made of 48-inch-tall galvanized wire fencing with 2 × 4-inch mesh. Be sure it's galvanized, or it will rust badly.

2. Space six 6-foot metal fence posts evenly (about every 2 feet) around the cage, about 10 inches outside the fence.

3. Plant tomatoes halfway between each post.

4. Tie sisal twine from post to post, about 6 inches above the ground.

5. As the tomato plants grow, keep adding lines of twine about 6 inches above the previous one.

"As you accumulate compostable material—young weeds, grass clippings, leaves, spent annuals, kitchen waste—throw it into the compost and keep it moist," Paul says. "Don't worry about anything that falls through the mesh of the cage—it will serve as mulch." Watering the compost also helps keep the tomatoes watered, and nutrients wash into the soil to nourish the tomatoes. As the tomatoes grow, they shade the compost pile, helping to keep it more evenly moist.

Warm Those Transplants

Garden transplants really take kindly to soil that's been warmed up well before transplanting time, says farmer Dan Tawczynski of Great Barrington, Massachusetts. Dan says he has found that you can successfully transplant just about anything. He likes to get started earlier in the season to improve his odds of success by warming the soil with a layer of plastic mulch before he starts to plant.

But if you want to get your transplants in early, Dan says, you have to get your plastic down earlier. "The most common mistake people make is putting the plastic on too late," he says. So often, gardeners lay the poly mulch right before setting in their transplants. "To really benefit, the plastic has to be on a few days ahead of time to warm up the ground," he advises.

Timely tip

Putting down plastic mulch in early spring can be a bit tricky, Dan notes. He suggests waiting for a calm day to do this job, to avoid wrestling with sheets of plastic flapping in the breeze. To lay your mulch, use a hoe to make a trench down one side of the bed. Lay the plastic so that its edge is in the trench, then hoe along the edge of the trench to push the soil onto the plastic. Do the same along the other side of the bed, stretching the plastic across to make it taut, and bury the ends in the same way.

Good Use for Old Gallon Pots

Get that stack of gallon-size nursery pots out of your garage and into the garden, advises Jo Meller of Five Springs Farm in Bear Lake, Michigan. Jo turns empty plastic pots into useful watering tools for her vegetable garden.

"Bury a pot in the middle of a hill of summer squash or between four Swiss chard plants or two tomato plants," she says. "The pot should be most of the way in the ground—with 2 to 3 inches sticking out so that the holes of the pot are down by the roots. Then just fill the container two or three times when you water.

"It all goes to the roots, and the plants are so happy," Jo adds. "We even filled the pots half full of composted manure, so we made manure tea as we watered." It worked great, Jo says, "and it saved me a lot of anguish with our sandy soil."

Empty Pots Hold Rocks and *Don't Roll*

Don't toss out large, leftover nursery containers—use them in your garden, says Darrell Frey, owner of Three Sisters Farm in Sandy Lake, Pennsylvania. Darrell puts large plastic pots at the corners of his gardens, along the pathways—where the hose tends to whip over newly planted seedlings. Then, as rocks appear—as they always seem to—he pitches the rocks into the pots.

"The pots guide the hose through the garden, keeping the plants safe," Darrell says. But that's not the only benefit he gets from his pots full of rocks: "When you need rocks to hold row covers down, they're right there," he adds.

When It Rains, Don't Lose a Drop

Gardener Tom Gettings of Center Valley, Pennsylvania, captures treasure—liquid treasure—in a trash can. Tom has rigged up a simple water-collection system, using a plastic trash can, to create a convenient water source that's close to his garden.

He started by redirecting a downspout from his roof into a 30-gallon plastic trash can. "I put a spigot on the side near the bottom so that the height is just right for the watering can," Tom says. He cut a hole in the plastic trash can using a linoleum knife, and he made the hole just big enough to insert the spigot (available at any hardware store). He used plumber's glue around the faucet to prevent leaks, then set

his new rain barrel under the downspout, right next to his garden. "Anytime I need water, I just turn on the spigot and fill the watering can," Tom says.

Meant for trash—but filled with treasure. The addition of a spigot turns a plastic trash can into a convenient water supply for your garden.

homegrown HINTS

STAKES YOU CAN HANDLE

Stakes aren't a high-cost item in Eber Wright's garden budget. The Pierpont, Ohio, gardener says you can get inexpensive wooden stakes for your garden from woodworking shops. And sawmills often have hardwood drying sticks that make fine stakes, he adds.

Emmaus, Pennsylvania market gardener George De-Vault has a similar stake success story: He buys "reject" hoe handles from handle mills. "I was visiting my parents in Delaware, Ohio. Driving by the Union Fork and Hoe Co., I saw a sign out front: 'Tomato stakes 25¢.' I pulled right in and piled 100 of them into the back of my pickup.

"They were 5 feet long or longer. Some were a little thicker at one end than the other. Others had some minor cracks or extra grooves. That's why they ended up in the reject bin. The company had thousands of them!"

The handles George bought were white ash. "Despite the minor defects, they're nice and sturdy and will last years and years," he says. "One end is rounded, which makes them very easy to drive into the ground with a sledgehammer. The handles are also big enough to take staples for pea trellis or even light fencing." George adds that since they're unfinished, many of the handles are a bit rough. He recommends wearing gloves when carrying or handling them to avoid ending up with a handful of splinters from your discount stakes.

Still *Generous,* but *Thrifty*

"I'm always giving away plants," says Pennsylvania gardener Nancy Bubel. Her favorite low-cost container is a half-gallon milk carton. Nancy cuts the carton lengthwise down the center on one side, then across the ends. She folds the resulting flaps inside the carton and staples them to the sides, then pokes drainage holes in the bottom. "I don't have to worry about people returning pots," she says.

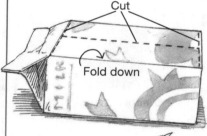

Modified milk cartons make it easy to share plants with friends without the expense of containers or the clutter of returned empty pots.

Holey Hose Does the **Drip Trick**

To provide efficient and inexpensive "drip irrigation" for his intensive plantings of peppers and tomatoes, Illinois gardener Michael Contratto simply took a nail and poked a bunch of small holes in an old length of regular garden hose. He capped one end of the hose and hooked the other end up to a faucet. "The water seeps out just as if you're using a soaker hose. Just don't turn the pressure up all the way or it comes out too fast," Michael cautions.

Buckwheat Keeps Gardens *Buzzing*

Planting buckwheat is a sure-fire way to bring bees into your garden, advises Bud Glendening of McGrann, Pennsylvania. And bees in the garden are a surefire way to improve pollination and yields, Bud explains.

"Buckwheat definitely works," he says, noting that its attractiveness to bees makes it a perfect addition to small gardens or orchards that bees otherwise might not find on their own.

Bud plants buckwheat wherever he has an extra square foot of space. As the owner of Fox Hollow Seed Co., his goal is to lure the bees *away* from his crops so he can gather uncrossed seeds.

If you plant buckwheat, bees will come. And while they're in your garden, they'll pollinate your vegetables and fruits, and you'll have a bigger harvest.

Flower Power— Nature's Pest Control

Permaculture advocates say you should provide plenty of habitat for beneficial insects around the edges of your garden. If that's good, reasons organic market gardener Steve Gilman, why not go one step further and put the habitat right in the middle of the garden? On his Ruckytucks Farm in upstate New York, Steve experimented by leaving 28-inch-wide grassy strips between his permanent raised beds.

"By allowing seasonal wildflowers to self-sow in the sod strips, we provide a pollen and nectar source that attracts honeybees, little wasps, and many other beneficials." Steve says the wildflowers range from dandelions and Queen-Anne's-lace to asters.

"After they produce pollen and nectar, but before the seed stage, we mow and blow them into the rows as a mulch because we don't want to create more problems," he says. Steve also sows Dutch white clover in the strips to ensure a steady supply of flowers for beneficials. "The grassy pathways also keep harvesters dry during the wet, muddy season," he adds.

Steve's system really works. "For the last four years," he says, "we have used no pest controls at all. We haven't noticed any ill effects, and we've seen a lot of good effects."

Battle *Slugs* with **Big** Leaves

Here's a simple way to get slugs out of your garden without hand-picking. All you need are some big-leaved veggies, such as cabbage, kale, or rhubarb, growing in your beds. Trim off a few leaves and lay them on top of the soil. The slugs will visit the leaves—and not your vegetables—for a meal, and they'll hide beneath the leaves when the sun comes up. Gather the leaves and dunk them in soapy water to get rid of the slugs. Or, lay the leaves—slug side up—where hungry birds can snatch up the slugs.

Toothpicks *Ward Off* Cutworm Troubles

To prevent cutworm damage, Wanda Boop of Briar Patch Organic Farms in Mifflinburg, Pennsylvania, places a toothpick next to each transplant's stem, with 1 inch stuck into the soil and 1 inch above the ground. Because of the toothpick, "the cutworm cannot completely circle the plant stem and cut it off at soil level," Wanda explains. "It works."

homegrown HINTS

STOP SLUGS WITH NIGHTTIME SNIPFEST

Don't get mad when slugs come after your young plants, and don't worry about having to touch the slimy pests to get rid of them. Gardener Nancy Bubel of Wellsville, Pennsylvania, doesn't do either of those things. She gets even with the voracious nighttime marauders—and she does it without hand-picking.

Nancy waits until well after dark when her unwelcome visitors are once again gorging themselves on tender young lettuce and other seedlings in the greenhouse. Then, with a pair of sharp scissors, "I go out there at night and snip the slugs in half." Don't worry, the half-slugs can't regenerate themselves the way earthworms can.

Comfrey Wrap Keeps **Cutworms** Away

Comfrey was the answer to the cutworm problem at Five Springs Farm in northwestern Michigan. Jo Meller and Jim Sluyter found relief from this persistent pest by wrapping their seedlings in comfrey leaves. The leaves seemed to protect young plants from cutworms, and "they also increased our production—we think from the calcium boost," say Jo and Jim.

If you grow your own comfrey, be careful: This plant can grow out of control and become a weed that spreads more quickly than mint.

Flea Beetles Can't Escape Simple Trap

There's nothing elaborate about the simple but effective trap recommended by Pennsylvania market gardener Cass Peterson to help reduce flea beetle populations in the garden. Cass suggests making a trap from a 6 × 6-inch piece of Styrofoam packing or a small Styrofoam plate.

"Attach it to a bamboo stick with some duct tape, coat it with Tangle-Trap, then put it out there in the garden like a little lollipop," she says.

Painting the trap yellow will attract the most beetles, but unpainted traps work, too.

Deer Detest Strongly *Scented* Soap

If deer are devastating your garden, give them a whiff of something that will send them hoofing, says Emmaus, Pennsylvania, market gardener George DeVault. "In our case, it's Irish Spring soap. But any really fragrant brand of soap will do," he says.

"Just cut a bar into several chunks and tie each piece in a recycled net bag or an old nylon stocking leg," George advises. "Tie the bags to fencing, fence posts, or stakes at intervals around your garden. And remember to replace the soap with the fresh, whiffy stuff every few weeks or so, when you notice the scent fading."

Repel Deer with Runaway Mint

At last there's a use for the excess of mint that almost inevitably follows the planting of this fragrant herb. Maryland Master Gardener Margaret Ferry contains mint's runaway nature by planting it in recycled plastic pots that she sinks at intervals throughout her flowerbeds. She recommends planting containerized mints in areas of the garden where deer tend to browse, especially along the semishady edges of flowerbeds. "The potted mints planted in these beds will not invade the rest of the planting, and they will deter nibbling deer," she says.

Deer Netting Deters Birds, Too

Distressed by birds feeding on his strawberries, organic gardener Tom Gettings of Center Valley, Pennsylvania, set out to foil the robbers. He bought some inexpensive plastic mesh—the really wide kind that's sold for use as tall fencing to keep out deer. Then he cut some tomato stakes into 18-inch lengths.

Tom drove the stakes into the ground at 4-foot intervals around the outer edge of the bed and stapled the netting to the tops of the tomato stakes. He stuck taller green bamboo stakes in the middle of the bed to hold up the netting so that the patch was nicely tented.

"The sides flip up so you can pick easily, and you can take the netting apart at the end of the season and reuse it year after year," Tom explains. "Don't worry about pollination—the bees can get through the netting just fine."

Plastic mesh deer fencing is great when you need to protect a block of sweet corn seedlings from hungry birds. Use stakes to support the mesh.

Avoid Fungal Disease Woes

Whether you're watering in a greenhouse or in the garden with a watering wand or sprayer nozzle, don't drop it on the ground, says Cass Peterson, of Flickerville Mountain Farm and Groundhog Ranch in Warfordsburg, Pennsylvania. "Put the wand on a bench or table, up off the floor. It'll pick up fungal spores from the ground," she warns. In the garden, hook your hose nozzle over the fence or on the handles of your cart.

homegrown HINTS

CALL HIM "CAPTAIN HOOK"

Keeping the watering wand or nozzle off the ground helps keep you from spreading soilborne disease organisms when you water. To help fight the spread of fungus, Emmaus, Pennsylvania, market gardener George DeVault put a few handy hooks around Pheasant Hill Farm. George put two plastic-coated screw-in hooks about a foot apart on the greenhouse potting bench to hold the watering wand. He added more hooks to a bench in the center of the greenhouse.

In the garden, single hooks placed here and there on wooden stakes make convenient hose nozzle holders. Not only do they help reduce the spread of disease spores, but they also save you from bending over so often to pick up the nozzle!

Pick Wisely to Avoid Spreading Disease

At Food Bank Farm, a community-supported agriculture operation in Hadley, Massachusetts, farmers Linda Hildebrand and Michael Docter make many successive plantings to ensure both consistent quantity and quality of produce. You can do the same thing, by starting more than one planting of your favorite crops, including lettuce, cucumbers, beans, tomatoes, and more. Just plant each crop at two- to three-week intervals to keep a steady harvest coming.

Linda and Michael explain that careful harvesting is the key to keeping all these slightly different stages of crops healthy and productive. When that second or third planting comes into production, they say, begin your harvesting in the newest section first and move from there into the older sections. That way you avoid spreading diseases such as anthracnose and powdery mildew that commonly appear on plants as they start to near maturity.

"On crops such as tomatoes, summer squash, peppers, and eggplant, which have a longer growing season, we always wait until the foliage has dried before we enter the field," Linda adds, explaining that this also helps prevent the spread of diseases like blight. Linda and Michael also remove diseased crops promptly. As soon as yields and quality start to decline, "we disk it in and plant a cover crop," Linda says. "Since we do not use sprays of any kind, this cultural practice is critical for disease management."

Early Fencing *Outfoxes* Groundhogs

You can create an inexpensive little fence in a short amount of time to outfox the nosiest—and hungriest—groundhogs and rabbits. The key is to start early enough, says organic farmer Don Kretschmann of Rochester, Pennsylvania.

"The important thing is to get the fence up *before* the groundhogs get used to feeding on anything in the garden," Don says. "They won't know what's on the other side."

Don pounds 2- to 3-foot-tall stakes—whatever you have on hand is fine—every 15 feet or so, then runs twine between the tops of the stakes. Then he takes pieces of used greenhouse plastic cut in strips about 3 feet wide and hangs the plastic from the twine with clothespins. He buries the bottom of the plastic in the soil. Don says his simple fence is a success at keeping the critters out of his garden, and it has the added benefit of preventing wind damage.

If you don't have used greenhouse plastic on hand, ask a local nursery owner or greenhouse grower. Most likely they'll have leftover plastic that they don't have a use for. Or you can purchase sheets of plastic at a hardware store or garden center.

Combine stakes, twine, clothespins, and used plastic greenhouse covering to make a simple, critter-stopping, wind-blocking fence for your garden.

Wood Ash *Works* on "Wascally *Wabbits*"

Melinda Ingalls of Copper Rose Farm in Howard, Ohio, had trouble with rabbits wreaking havoc on her tomato plants. Then she heard that wood ash would help keep the critters away.

"It really works!" she enthuses. Melinda has no trouble collecting enough wood ash—she heats her home with wood. "I just keep a big tub near the stove, and we save most of the ash. I sprinkle a little in a circle around the base of the plant as we put them out, and replenish it when I see that it's disappearing," she explains. She sprinkles the ashes 1 to 2 inches away from the base of each plant.

Melinda says she and her husband, Jim, also sprinkle wood ash on the leaves of bean plants when they're still damp with dew, replacing as necessary. The ash keeps the rabbits from eating the tender young plants.

"I don't know if it has anything to do with the wood ash, but I've even seen a decrease in tomato worms since I started sprinkling it," Melinda adds.

Proper Harvesting **Keeps** Produce *Pleasing*

Nothing keeps the zing in vegetables like proper harvesting, say Linda Hildebrand and Michael Docter. The farmers of Food Bank Farm in Hadley, Massachusetts, advise picking ripe tomatoes—for best flavor—into plastic buckets. Remove the stem from each fruit so that it doesn't pierce the other tomatoes. Fill your buckets only half to three-quarters full to avoid squashing the tomatoes on the bottom. Some heirloom varieties, such as 'Brandywine', need more careful handling: Fill your bucket only one-third full. Once out of the garden, sort the tomatoes onto single-layer trays to reduce further bruising of thin-skinned varieties.

Save the rough stuff for overgrown zucchini, and harvest tomatoes gently. Remove their stems and use a smooth plastic bucket.

To Increase Vegetable Yields, **Pick Early!**

The best way to increase your garden's vegetable yield, says Bruce Butterfield, research director at the National Gardening Association in Burlington, Vermont, is to pick early. "A plant's purpose is to reproduce seed. Be diligent in picking, and the plant will always try to play catch-up," he explains.

The best example is broccoli, Bruce says. "Don't wait until a huge head has formed. I'll cut it at 3 to 4 inches across, and I get a lot more broccoli in the long run through sideshoots."

Beans and zucchini are other good examples. Keep picking them young, and they'll keep right on producing.

Keep tabs on plants so you know when to start picking. When flowers appear on your beans, you can plan to start picking within seven to ten days, Bruce says. For zucchini, the flower watch is particularly important. Once they start blooming, zucchini will appear—seemingly overnight—and grow to the size of baseball bats if you don't check daily from that point on.

Let's Hear It for Volunteers

"When I go out to till in spring, I always find interesting volunteers there," says Nancy Bubel, author of *The New Seed-Starter's Handbook*. Nancy says she saves these unexpected—but not unwelcome—volunteer seedlings. "I just pot them up and set them aside for another day. It helps me save a lot of perfectly good volunteers," she says, noting that her "free" seedlings have included spinach, two peach tree seedlings, and lots and lots of lettuce.

Interplant Asparagus *and* Cherry Tomatoes

New York State gardener Lois Morton interplants cherry tomatoes in her asparagus bed and enjoys two wonderful benefits: excellent weed control and reduced asparagus beetle infestations.

The weed control is most helpful around the beginning of July when the asparagus goes to seed, Lois says. The cherry tomatoes are leafy, vigorous growers that shade out weed seedlings, she explains. Lois adds that because cherry tomatoes self-sow readily, she only had to plant them once to have a steady supply of tomato seedlings amid the asparagus every year.

Let frost kill the tomato plants in the fall, Lois says. In early spring, lightly till the bed, and mulch as usual—Lois likes to use straw manure around her asparagus.

Tomatoes didn't eliminate her asparagus beetle problems, Lois says, "but when I compared rows where I interplanted tomato plants to a row in another portion of the garden, I didn't have as much defoliation of the asparagus."

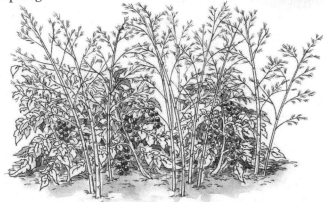

Weeds can't compete with vigorous cherry tomatoes growing in your asparagus bed. The tomatoes seem to deter asparagus beetles, too.

Help Crops Keep Their Cool

"Pick lettuce and other fragile greens before the sun comes up—before they've accumulated any field heat," say Linda Hildebrand and Michael Docter of Food Bank Farm in Hadley, Massachusetts. Then immerse the greens in cold water as soon as possible. A plastic tub filled with cold well water works beautifully; you could also cool lettuce in a sinkful of cold water. Lettuce can soak for a half hour or so, but even a short dunk helps keep it crisp. After the cold bath, store your greens in a covered plastic container lined with dry paper towels, Linda adds.

"We wash most of our produce, with the exception of summer squash, spinach, basil, cilantro, and tomatoes," she says. For short-term storage, Linda and Michael cover the greens with wet burlap so that they will stay cool and crisp.

Timely tip

When it comes to crops in the cabbage family—kale, collards, broccoli, and others—Linda cites another benefit of a half-hour soak in cold water: "Not only does this reduce field heat to prolong life, but it also gets the cabbage loopers to the bottom of the barrel," she says.

ingenious RECIPES

Too Many Beans?

"Never!" says Beth Seagraves of Westlake, Ohio. At least not since she started making good old-fashioned pickled beans. "I ask my husband to plant more," she laughs. Beth says she stumbled across a pickled bean recipe, tried different versions of it, and came up with her personal favorite. She started giving her preserved treats as gifts, and people started asking for more.

Just about every canning book has some basic recipes for pickled or "dilly" beans. Beth says the trick is to use a long, straight variety of bean, and to pick the beans on the same day that you preserve them. "You can adjust the flavor by adding different types of hot peppers," she says.

Beth's recipe is a secret, but she says the following instructions will get you started. To give the flavors enough time to blend, let the beans age for 12 weeks after canning before you eat them.

BASIC PICKLED BEANS

7½ cups water
5 cups vinegar
½ cup pickling salt
About 4 pounds green beans
8 heads of dill
8 slices onion *or* 8 cloves garlic
4 teaspoons mustard seed
8 hot peppers

Combine water, vinegar, and pickling salt, and bring to a boil. Wash beans and trim to fit pint jars. Use eight sterilized jars, and work while they're hot. Put a head of dill, a slice of onion or a clove of garlic, the mustard seed, and a hot pepper in the bottom of each jar, pack tightly with beans, and pour the boiling brine over them to fill jars, leaving ¼ inch of headspace. Wipe jar rims to ensure a good seal, then top with hot lids. Process 10 minutes in a boiling water bath or 5 minutes in a steam canner— Beth's favorite method. Yield: 8 pints

Beans and Peas Share Space, Save Time

To get double duty out of a single trellis, let your beans sort of run over your peas, says Steve Moore, of Wilson College's Center for Sustainable Living in Chambersburg, Pennsylvania. Plant your peas in early spring—when conditions are right in your area— Steve instructs. When the peas are producing well and around the time of your last frost date, plant pole beans 6 to 8 inches away from the peas so that the peas are between the beans and the trellis. Steve recommends scarlet runner beans or 'Fortex', an extra-long variety of pole bean, for this trellis-sharing technique, explaining that these climbers grow tall enough to bridge the distance over the peas to get to the trellis.

"When the beans are 1 to 2 feet tall and wanting to run, the peas are usually done and can be pulled out," Steve explains. Then, he says, apply a layer of mulch between the trellis and the beans to prevent weed problems. Put more mulch on the other side of the row of beans to push them gently toward the trellis.

Borage *Brings* in the *Bees*

To boost bean yields, plant borage, say Steve and Carol Moore, of the Center for Sustainable Living at Wilson College in Chambersburg, Pennsylvania. The borage attracts bees to your garden, and more bees means more beans, Steve explains.

You only need one borage plant for every 100-foot row of green beans in order to enjoy a bigger bean harvest, Steve says, adding that having borage nearby benefits smaller bean plantings as well. You can order borage seed through many catalogs, and it's easy to grow from seed, says Steve. "We let it self-seed, putting a little stake in to remind ourselves where the plants are."

Carol and Steve also enjoy the borage itself. "We pick the blossoms and toss them in salads. Carol absolutely loves them," Steve says.

Dainty borage flowers are just the thing to bring bees to your beans. The starry, edible blue blossoms make an attractive addition to salads, too.

Flea Beetles *Flee* Broccoli for Chinese Cabbage

If flea beetles are about to make you give up on late-summer broccoli, get some relief by interplanting with Chinese cabbage, recommends Pennsylvania market gardener Cass Peterson. "I plant Chinese cabbage among the broccoli and the cabbage to attract flea beetles," Cass says. And the flea beetles—which are a real problem for fall broccoli—like the Chinese cabbage better. "But Chinese cabbage is a rugged plant.

Enjoy pest-free broccoli in late summer, while the flea beetles dine on nearby Chinese cabbage. When cooler weather ends the flea beetles' feasting, you'll also get a nice crop of Chinese cabbage.

When autumn brings cooler temperatures, and the flea beetle population drops, the Chinese cabbage will bounce back and produce a crop," Cass explains.

Radishes *Help* Mark Carrot Rows

Hoeing to keep weeds away from a young carrot crop is risky because you can't always tell where your carrots are, explains organic farmer Scott Case of Aaronsburg, Pennsylvania. And crusty soil can make the growing tough for slender carrot seedlings.

To solve these carrot woes, the Patchwork Farm grower recommends radishes—not *instead* of carrots but *with* them. "I sow radish seeds right in with the carrot seed," Scott says. "The radishes are up in a couple of days, so they mark the rows, and they also help break the soil. And radish seed is cheap."

Save Your Old *Net Bags*

Beth Seagraves of Westlake, Ohio, says save those old potato, onion, or fruit bags—the ones made of netting with good air circulation. She uses them to store bulbs, hanging them from the ceiling in her basement. They're also good for keeping harvests of onions, shallots, or garlic from your garden well into winter.

Celeriac Offers Celery Flavor *All Winter*

Coaxing tall, leafy stalks of celery from the garden is more work than most gardeners want to invest in the quirky crop. But you can enjoy the flavor of celery without all the work by planting its relative, celeriac, also called celery root. Jim and Moie Crawford plant celeriac from transplants in April on their Hustontown, Pennsylvania, farm. "It's easier to grow than traditional celery," Jim says.

A type of celery grown for its big, white round root, celeriac has nearly fiberless flesh and pure celery flavor. On their New Morning Farm, the Crawfords harvest celeriac in November— "and it keeps until April," Jim says. "Just refrigerate it, keep it moist with some dirt on it, and you can use it all winter. It's good as a side dish with dinner, raw, or in hearty soups and stews," he says.

Most seed catalogs offer celeriac. Sow seeds 10 to 12 weeks before you want to transplant seedlings outdoors. Seedlings emerge in 2 to 3 weeks. When the seedlings have two true leaves, transplant them to cell packs, then transplant them outdoors when the weather is settled. You can harvest celeriac from late summer through fall when the roots reach 3 to 5 inches in diameter. To enhance celeriac's keeping qualities in storage, dunk the plants in cold water after harvesting to remove field heat before storing.

There's no need to struggle to get celery flavor from your garden when you plant easy-growing, long-keeping celeriac instead of the more tempermental celery.

Keep the **Oomph** in Cukes

Few things are more disappointing than cucumbers that vine everywhere but go nowhere. *Organic Gardening* contributing editor Jeff Cox of Kenwood, California, uses a two-pronged approach to ensure cucumber success: hand pollination and an anti-mildew spray.

"A lot of times the female cucumber blossom doesn't get pollinated," Jeff explains. "If you hand-pollinate, your cucumbers will set more fruit." Insects usually do the job of transferring pollen from the cucumber's male blossoms to its female flowers. You can do the same thing, using a small paintbrush, a cotton swab, or your fingertip.

To figure out who's who among the cucumber flowers, check the base of the blossom. If there's a small cucumber-shaped swelling at its base, the flower is female. Pick a male flower (one with no swelling) and rub the male flower's anthers (the yellow-tipped stems that protrude from the center of the blossom) on the central stigma of the female flower. Or brush pollen from the an-thers with a small paint brush, then "paint" the pollen onto the female flower's stigma.

To prevent powdery mildew, Jeff mixes 1 table-spoon of baking soda in 1 gallon of water. He sprays this solution on his young vines every week and continues as they start to produce cucumbers.

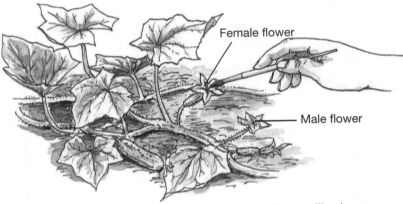

Hand-pollinating cucumbers helps to guarantee that you'll enjoy a healthy harvest of cukes. To make the most of your efforts, take a moment to be sure of the difference between female and male flowers before you begin.

problem SOLVer   PLEASE DON'T SMOOSH THE FLOWERS

There's more to salad than grocery store croutons, bottled dressing, and hard-boiled eggs. Harborside, Maine, organic gardener Barbara Damrosch recommends edible flowers to give salads a boost in both flavor and color. Barbara, the author of *The Garden Primer,* says, "Sometimes I'll add a few Johnny-jump-ups or calendula. Sometimes nasturtiums—both flowers and leaves—and daylilies. They taste sweet."

But Barbara only adds flowers to a salad *after* it is fully dressed. "If you put the flowers in before you mix it all up, they all get smooshed."

Keep Crops
Coming with
Careful Cutting

When you harvest leafy crops like spinach, cut the leaves high enough to preserve the plant's growing tip, recommends Linda Hildebrand of Food Bank Farm in Hadley, Massachusetts. The plant will produce more leaves and you'll get more food from the plants.

This means leaving 1 to 2 inches at the base of the leaves for the plant to regrow from when clipping mature crops. Be sure to keep the base plants watered after harvesting. "We recut spinach, kale, broccoli rabe, mustards, and Swiss chard," says Linda.

Eggplant *Thrives*
with **Mulch**
and **Cover**

To achieve true success with your next crop of eggplant, try a special system that protects the young plants from flea beetle damage and gives them the warm soil they prefer. While working at the Rodale Institute Experimental Farm near Kutztown, Pennsylvania, Diane Matthews-Gehringer compared the effects of poly mulch (black plastic) and insect barrier (floating row cover) on eggplant production. She found that eggplant grown in poly mulch and covered with a floating row cover did much better than eggplant grown without either, and it also surpassed eggplant grown with just the poly mulch.

Today, Diane uses the winning system in her own garden at Gehringer Farm. She plants the eggplant in soil warmed by the poly mulch and covers the entire planting with a double width of floating row cover stapled together. She buries one side along the length of the 4-foot bed and rolls the other side, anchoring it with bricks, stones, or 2 × 4s to allow room for the plants. As the eggplant grows, she unrolls the fabric a bit to give the plants more room.

"It's very important to watch for blossoms," Diane says. Once the plants begin to flower, she recommends opening the cover for a couple of hours in the morning if you're not getting fruit set, or if fungus mold develops on the blossoms. Eggplant flowers don't need insects for pollination, but air movement helps them, she explains. Or remove the cover when the plants start to bloom, since then they're big enough to withstand attacks from eggplant's number one enemy: flea beetles.

Fend off destructive flea beetles with a protective row cover over your eggplant. Black plastic mulch gives eggplants the warm soil they need for phenomenal growth and productivity.

Clip Kale for **Super** Crop

For a bumper crop of
kale that is easier to
harvest and is not
riddled with flea
beetle damage,
Bud Glendening
of McGrann,
Pennsylvania, says
the secret is all in the
clipping. Bud, who plants
1,500 to 2,000 kale plants
annually on his farm, says he
harvests every leaf that's
more than 8 inches long.

As the plants develop, he
goes through the field and
removes every leaf that has
grown to more than 8 inches

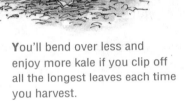

You'll bend over less and
enjoy more kale if you clip off
all the longest leaves each time
you harvest.

Trimming kale makes the plants
grow taller, and it reduces flea
beetle troubles, too.

in total length—and gets
them out of the field. This
has a shocking effect on the
kale, encouraging the plants
to grow really fast. He leaves
the plants alone for two
weeks, then returns to his
kale planting for another harvest of all the leaves that are
more than 7 to 8 inches long.

Bud says this method pro-
motes rapid growth that
seems to diminish the effects
of any flea beetle feeding. As
a result, the kale he harvests
is nicer, with few holes in the
leaves. At the same time, his
method encourages the plants
to grow tall and upright,
making them easy to harvest
with less bending.

Harvest Lettuce *All Summer*

Forget about lettuce that
turns bitter and bolts in
summer's heat. By planting
heat-tolerant lettuce varieties
and using a midday misting to
help the crop keep its cool,
you can grow lettuce all
summer, says Jim Sluyter, of
Five Springs Farm in Bear
Lake, Michigan.

Jim says at Five Springs
Farm they select "slow-to-
bolt" or "heat-tolerant" varieties such as romaines, 'New
Red Fire', and Batavian types
(sometimes called summer
crisp). All of these lettuces are
unsurpassed in their tolerance
for warm weather. "We grow
them quickly in fertile soil with
adequate moisture," Jim says.

"On hot days, we cool off
the lettuce with a spray of
water. We use misters from a
drip irrigation supplier.
Punched into a special hose at
about 5-foot intervals, we run
the misters for an hour or two
each day when it's hot. This
changes the microclimate
around the lettuce plants
without overwatering them,"
Jim says. Misters and other
irrigation tools are available
from local or mail-order
irrigation equipment suppliers.

homegrown HINTS

SUMMER COOLING SOWS LETTUCE SUCCESS

To keep leftover lettuce seed in peak condition for late-season planting (or even for next year's garden), store it in your refrigerator for the summer. Steve and Carol Moore, of the Center for Sustainable Living at Wilson College in Chambersburg, Pennsylvania, say that lettuce seed stored in the refrigerator during the summer germinates better than lettuce seed that's not kept cool in warm weather.

Carol says they keep their lettuce seed in the refrigerator during June, July, and August, because they notice improved germination rates in seed that's kept cool. They simply put the extra seed back in the packet, put the packet in a plastic bag, then close the bag with a twist tie. The bag can go anywhere in the fridge, says Carol. During the rest of the year, they store their lettuce seed on a shelf. Many market gardeners routinely store their seeds in a cooler or refrigerator year-round, since cool temperatures do tend to prolong seed life.

Baby Your Lettuce

Cass Peterson of Flickerville Mountain Farm and Groundhog Ranch in Warfordsburg, Pennsylvania, says one of the best ways to use garden space wisely is to grow baby lettuce. It matures more quickly than standard-size lettuce so that you can harvest more greens from the same space. You can plant baby lettuce as close as 6 inches apart, and it only takes five to six weeks to mature from transplants. Cass says her favorite is 'Diamond Gem' baby romaine; 'Red Lollo' is another popular baby lettuce.

Or if you grow some French crisphead and Batavian varieties that form a rosette of small leaves at the "baby" stage, you can plant them closer than normal and harvest every other plant as baby lettuce, leaving the remaining plants to grow to standard size. Good varieties for this treatment are 'Sierra' and 'Nevada'.

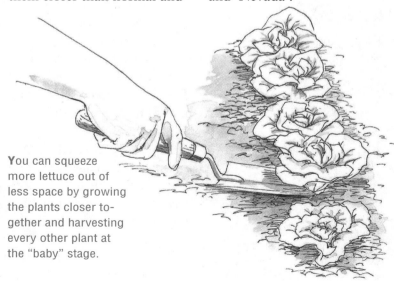

You can squeeze more lettuce out of less space by growing the plants closer together and harvesting every other plant at the "baby" stage.

Lettuce and Glads Go *Great Together*

At her Common Ground Farm in Spring Mills, Pennsylvania, Leslie Zuck mixes up an unlikely planting combination that's both eye-catching and smart: head lettuce and gladiolus. Using staggered rows of head lettuce with glads planted in between, Leslie gets two crops from the same space while enjoying a pretty-as-a-picture planting.

"We'll plant a row of lettuce, two trowel-blade-lengths apart in each direction," Leslie says, explaining, "when you're in the field, that's an easy way to measure." Leslie grows her lettuce-and-glad combo in raised beds that hold three rows of lettuce.

The second row of lettuce is staggered from the first, then the third row is planted so it's even with the first row. "The glad bulbs go in between the lettuce. They come up at the same time, and you waste no space!" she enthuses.

An application of compost gives the plants what they need to get a good start, and a thick hay mulch keeps the weeds down before the lettuce takes off. The lettuce eventually fills in the space between the glads to provide further weed control. Once the flowers bloom—they're used for cut flowers—"it looks so pretty," says Leslie, "especially with green and red lettuce." She adds that this "glad" combination works well with leaf lettuce, too.

Kohlrabi Is a **Keeper!**

It may look like an alien vegetable, but kohlrabi will be very much at home in your garden. And the best thing about kohlrabi, say Jim and Moie Crawford, farmers in Hustontown, Pennsylvania, is its staying power. "We direct-seed in early August, harvest in November, and can keep it until March in plastic bags in the fridge," says Jim.

Kohlrabi is great sliced raw in salads or for dips, or cooked like potatoes and turnips and used in casseroles, stews, soups, or omelets. Peel the globes before cooking. The leaves are edible too, and can be cooked like cabbage.

Tell the kids that aliens have taken over the garden, but don't be turned off by kohlrabi's appearance—its crunchy texture and mild flavor make it a super low-cal snack.

problem **solver**   ROW COVERS GIVE GREENS THE GO-AHEAD

At Food Bank Farm in Hadley, Massachusetts, all greens are covered with row covers to keep flea beetles off and improve the texture, says Linda Hildebrand. If you've ever tried to start kale in mid- to late summer for a fall crop, you know what flea beetles can do—enough damage to give you nothing more than unappealing leaves filled with holes, Linda explains. The row covers keep the flea beetles away from the young plants and create conditions for healthy growth that give the greens a wonderful texture.

homegrown HINTS

LIMAS GIVE BRUSSELS SPROUTS A BOOST

Eber Wright of Pierpont, Ohio, interplants lima beans and brussels sprouts and gets a generous crop from both. How does he do it? His system uses a four-pole teepee to support pole-type lima beans, and he plants four brussels sprout plants under the teepee. The lima beans shade the brussels sprouts—giving the sprouts the cool conditions they prefer, keeping weeds to a minimum, and ensuring that Eber enjoys an ample harvest of limas and brussels sprouts.

Plastic *Keeps* Wandering Melons **Weed-Free**

Melons grow great in soil covered by plastic mulch. But limiting the mulch to just a 3- to 4-foot-wide strip—and limiting your melons to that same space—may be reducing the benefits you get from this method. Bonnie Wilson of Doylesburg, Pennsylvania, traded row-size strips of plastic for larger block-shaped sheets and says she and her melon crop will never go back to the narrower stuff.

"We planted watermelon and cantaloupe on row plastic for years," Bonnie says. "And it just did not work." The melons would wander off the plastic into the weeds, and the sun could not reach them.

Now Bonnie uses a system her father tried. "He took a 40 × 100-foot sheet of plastic from an old greenhouse, laid it on a patch, and planted into that." The plastic suppressed weeds around the melons and kept the soil warm and moist for the melons.

Bonnie explains that the larger mulched area has another benefit for her and for the melons—there's no "rearranging" the melon vines to put them back onto a narrow strip of plastic. That makes less work for her, and it's less disturbance for the plants. The planting holes in the plastic allow enough water to reach the melon roots, and they do fine with overhead watering. Bonnie adds that you can eliminate puddles of water on top of the plastic by puncturing low spots with the tines of a pitchfork.

To get a low-cost sheet of plastic for your melon block, ask local farmers or greenhouse growers for old plastic they'd like to get rid of. Or you can create bigger blocks of plastic mulch by overlapping the edges of row-size plastic sheets, making sure there are no gaps where weeds can pop up.

Timely tip

Plastic isn't the only thing that will keep your melon patch weed-free; cardboard works well, too. Cut up large cardboard boxes—like those appliances come in—and overlap the pieces on top of your patch. Then cut small holes out of the cardboard and plant your seeds through the holes.

Grafting Melons

Grafting melons is a practical technique that Chinese gardeners use to overcome serious problems with nematodes and soilborne diseases. "In southern China and Taiwan, virtually all melons are grafted onto a hardy gourd rootstock," says Missouri market gardener Steve Salt.

"It is extremely easy to graft," adds Steve. "It's cleft grafting, which is ridiculously easy at the two-leaf stage."

To try your hand at melon grafting, follow the steps described below. To make the cuts, you'll need a sharp razor blade. It's easier to graft in a greenhouse or on a potting bench than in your garden.

Grafting a melon onto a hardy gourd rootstock involves cutting a cleft into the rootstock and shaping a point on the melon seedling. Cover the grafted plant and keep it out of direct sunlight while the graft heals.

1. Make sure that the rootstock (the plant that will be used for its roots) and the scion (the plant you want to produce fruits) are well watered.

2. Start with young rootstock that has two true leaves. The true leaves look like the actual leaves of the plant; they are not the seed leaves, or cotyledons, that first appear when the seed sprouts. The stem diameter of the rootstock and the scion should be about the same.

3. "You essentially decapitate the rootstock. Take off the leaves down to the cotyledon," Steve explains. Cut a V-shaped cleft into the top of the rootstock stem.

4. Cut the root end off the seedling that you want to graft onto the rootstock: Just above the cotyledon, cut a pointed end on that scion piece, and fit it into the V on the rootstock.

5. Wrap the completed graft with paraffin sheets or tape to keep the graft moist. Cover the plant with a plastic bag or plastic sheeting for two to three days to hold in moisture until the tissue knits itself together. Keep the plant out of

direct sunlight. For larger plants, Steve recommends staking the graft with a popsicle stick and a twist tie.

You may lose some plants in the beginning, Steve says, but with practice, "nine times out of ten, the graft will take." He adds that this technique is very similar to one used for fruit trees, but the success rate is generally higher. Grafting vegetables is easier than grafting fruitwood, Steve says, but "it's just not what most people do." But he stresses the disease-preventing advantages of grafting melons and cucumbers onto hardy gourd and watermelon rootstocks over the technique's novelty.

Try Luffas Two Ways

Don't limit your thoughts of luffa gourds (*Luffa aegyptiaca*, also called sponge gourds) to the scrubby sponges you can make from their insides, says gardener Steve Salt of Kirksville, Missouri. "They're great in a stir-fry!" Steve exclaims. "I really like luffas!

"They're also called Chinese okra in some seed catalogs," Steve adds, noting that the gourds are not related to okra. "Just pick them when they're young. They're very crisp and tasty."

Steve says he usually harvests luffas for eating when they're only 5 to 6 inches long. When in doubt, he says, scrape the skin with your thumbnail. If the skin tears easily, the luffas are just fine for fresh eating. And if they're too mature, let them keep growing and harvest them for sponges later in the season.

Unlike zucchini, when luffa gourds outgrow their young, edible stage, they're still useful for the natural sponges you can harvest from their insides.

problem SOLVer

MULCH-BED GARDENING PLEASES PEAS

Gene Logsdon, author of *The Contrary Farmer's Invitation to Gardening* and a farmer in Upper Sandusky, Ohio, is a big fan of mulch-bed gardening, and he says the technique works especially well for peas.

Mulch-bed gardening, he explains in his book, is mimicking nature in the forest or on the prairie. You cover the soil surface with more organic matter each year. Leaves work beautifully, but anything that will rot into humus can be used. The plants or seeds go directly into these beds of rotting organic matter, and you keep right on mulching, Gene says.

"We plant peas into a mulch bed in spring," Gene says. He sets up two lengths of rabbit fence about a foot apart, and sprinkles pea seed into the mulch bed between the fencing. Rabbit fence is welded wire fence, available at garden centers, with narrower holes at the bottom and gradually larger openings near the top. He uses his foot to press the seed down into the mulch. "As the peas come up, I dribble compost on; I use finely chopped leaves with the compost," Gene explains. "The peas come up without the worry of weeds and cultivation. They grow up on the trellises, and best of all—for this part of Ohio, anyway—the trellis keeps the rabbits out!"

Gene says the mulch-bed system works well for various vegetables and lasts from year to year. He recommends giving your mulch beds a break every five to ten years and cultivating them for a year to put a stop to any weed problems that might be cropping up.

Peas and Gourds Make a Perfect Match

When you're planting a tall variety of pea, whether it's a sugar snap, a snow pea, or a shelling variety, Leslie Zuck of Common Ground Farm in Spring Mills, Pennsylvania, says it's just as easy to plan ahead for another crop at the same time. She plants a few gourd seeds right along with the pea seed. The gourd seeds can be planted early but require a long growing season—125 days for birdhouse or bottle gourds—so the double-teaming works well.

Here's how she does it: Leslie plants the peas in double rows—two rows parallel to one another, about 4 to 6 inches apart. She pounds in 4-foot high posts or stakes, spaced about 6 feet apart, and plants two gourd seeds at each of these posts. When the peas are about 6 inches high, she cultivates around them and puts up pea trellis between the posts. (Trellis is available at most garden centers).

Leslie uses a mulch of straw or grass clippings to keep the weeds down between the double rows of peas and in the 4- to 6-foot pathways between trellised plantings. The Executive Director of Pennsylvania Certified Organic, Leslie says she likes planting birdhouse gourds with her peas because the gourds have beautiful flowers, few insect problems, and are really prolific. But just about any vining gourd or melon crop will do. "The peas fix nitrogen, so they don't take away from the gourds," Leslie adds. "When the pea vine dies, the longer-season gourds continue to grow."

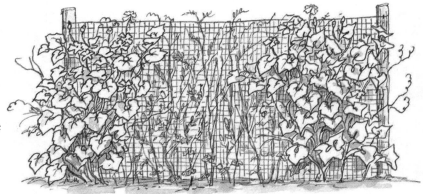

Sow long-season gourds with quick-growing peas to get two crops on one trellis. Birdhouse gourds look especially pretty as peas start to fade.

Transplanting Gives Peas a Snappy Start

Transplant sugar snap peas for a fast, dependable, earlier start, says Steve Moore of Wilson College's Center for Sustainable Living in Chambersburg, Pennsylvania. Plant peas (presoaked for 24 hours) into 3-inch-deep flats, using mature, sifted compost or a 1:1 mixture of compost and your best garden soil. Steve grows the pea seedlings in the flats for 10 to 15 days. "You shouldn't let them get above 6 to 8 inches," he says. "Plant the transplants on 1½- to 2-inch centers in offset row spacings." In just a few weeks you'll enjoy the pleasures of a successful and early harvest of sugar snap peas.

Check Out Fresh Peanut Flavor

Did you ever eat what Alan LaPage of Barre, Vermont, calls a *real* peanut? That is, a peanut picked fresh from the garden?

"They're called *pea*nuts for a reason," Alan says. "They're as sweet as a pea. The flavor is just phenomenal. It is a delight in cooking."

Garden-fresh peanuts are the magic ingredient in curries, peanut sauces, and other Indian dishes. Peanuts from the grocery store don't taste as sweet because their sugars long ago turned to starch. "But as a fresh vegetable, it is quite unique and really worth the effort," says Alan. He grows peanuts in central Vermont under floating row covers that stay on the whole season.

Many seed and garden supply catalogs, including Park Seed and Shumway, offer peanuts. Alan says he favors 'Virginia Jumbos'. "The smaller Spanish peanuts are much earlier, but they really suffer in a poor year," he adds.

Peanuts can be planted, either hulled or in their shells, as early as mid-April in Massachusetts. They grow best in humus-rich soil. For quick germination, plant the seeds 1½ inches deep in the North. In the South, plant peanuts at least 4 inches deep. In cool, cloudy weather, germination may take several weeks. Cultivate when the plants are 6 inches tall. Hill the rows as you would potatoes when they are a foot high, then mulch heavily between the rows. Peanuts are ready for harvest when the leaves yellow and the veins in the pods turn dark, often around the time of the first frost in your area.

But don't eat every peanut you harvest, Alan cautions. Save the very best ones for seed. "Gradually, you will end up with a peanut that is well-suited to your local conditions," he explains.

You don't have to live in the South to enjoy fresh peanut flavor. This intriguing crop is fascinating to watch as its flowers "peg" into the soil and form the peanuts below ground.

Spice Up Your Cooking

Enjoy a winter's worth of fresh-from-the-garden flavor with this simple mixture from gardener Beth Seagraves of Westlake, Ohio. All it takes are some hot-to-your-taste peppers, garlic, and butter.

"Bring a stick of butter to room temperature, mince one or two peppers, and crush garlic, to taste. Add a little lime juice, and mix it all up," Beth explains. She freezes the mix in "stick-size" quantities and keeps them in small plastic bags in the freezer.

Then when she's cooking, Beth slices off a bit of seasoned butter, and fresh garden flavor is at hand. It's great for sauteeing chicken, stir-frys, and vegetables, she says.

ingenious
RECIPES

Salsa Kit Delivers Garden Fun and Flavor

Brighten a friend's day with this new twist on gifts from the garden: Give him a make-your-own-salsa kit, complete with home-grown ingredients and your favorite recipe. Emmaus, Pennsylvania, market gardener Melanie DeVault says she had a great response from recipients of the salsa kits she created for subscribers to Pheasant Hill Farm's produce delivery program. Melanie packed fresh-picked tomatoes, onion, garlic, hot and sweet peppers, and cilantro in a 2-quart box topped with a piece of mesh to hold everything in. Then she attached her recipe for Salsa Cruda to each kit with a raffia bow.

"Our customers really liked it," she says. "They were so happy to have everything they needed to make their own fresh salsa. And the kit was a fun, easy thing for us to assemble—we grew everything that was in it." Here's Melanie's salsa recipe:

SALSA CRUDA

1 cup seeded, diced tomatoes
2 tablespoons diced onion
1 or 2 garlic cloves, minced
½ teaspoon sugar
Salt, to taste
1 seeded, minced jalapeno or serrano pepper
1 seeded, minced sweet yellow pepper
Chopped cilantro, to taste

Combine tomatoes, onion, garlic, sugar, salt, jalapeno and yellow peppers, and cilantro, and mix well. Let salsa stand for 30 minutes before serving.

Staggered Picking Spurs Pepper Success

Get the most out of your bell pepper plants by picking some fruit in the green, immature stage, then leaving the rest of it on the plant to color up and mature. Here are three good reasons to stagger your picking, according to market gardener Cass Peterson of Flickerville Mountain Farm and Groundhog Ranch in Warfordsburg, Pennsylvania.

➤ Peppers commonly form their first fruits in a center cluster. If you leave all of these fruits to ripen, they may rot from moisture trapped between them.

➤ Leaving the first flush of fruit untouched will discourage the plant from setting a second flush of fruit.

➤ Picking the first fruits is a bonus for green pepper lovers, since they're larger than later ones.

Timely tip

Pick peppers when they're slightly underripe, says Cass. This reduces the likelihood of rot and saves your colorful crop from being eaten by pests, she explains. "When we let peppers color up completely on the plant, we lose up to 75 percent of them to rot or to insect, bird, or rodent damage. If we pick when they're 50 to 75 percent colored, we lose almost none."

Store the peppers in a cool, dark area of your house, and they'll finish ripening naturally in a couple of days.

homegrown HINTS

PATIENCE PAYS IN POTATO PLANTING

Bonnie Wilson admits to having been skeptical when she first heard about planting potatoes at the end of June in central Pennsylvania. "But it worked for us," she says. Now, the motto at Highland Acres in Doylesburg, Pennsylvania, is "just be patient."

Bonnie says that by being patient and waiting to plant potatoes, "you miss the insect cycle. Those potatoes planted earlier come up just as the insects come out." Bonnie adds that potatoes planted earlier don't emerge until the soil is warm enough anyway.

"My dad put his in early in a cold, wet year, and they rotted," she says. But when she planted fingerlings and other potatoes at the end of June, there was no problem with rotting; the potatoes took off and grew well in the warm soil. Bonnie notes that the only concern with the delayed planting schedule is that the potatoes will need irrigation to grow during the summer in a really dry year.

Trick Those *Spuds!*

If you want more spuds per square foot, Steve and Carol Moore, of the Center for Sustainable Living, Wilson College, Chambersburg, Pennsylvania, say to plant potatoes in a 4- to 5-foot-wide raised bed. "Then put stakes and string around to keep the plants up, tricking them to continue to grow and make more spuds per square foot," Steve says.

He explains that the staked potato plants tend to grow for a longer period of time than unstaked potatoes. It's a hormonal phenomenon—normally, when the plants' tops fall over, the plants begin to wind down. Staking the potatoes so that they can't flop over as they normally would tricks them into continuing to grow, and they keep getting larger.

Staking also makes weeding easier, Steve adds. Having the potato tops growing up instead of sprawling all over the ground will leave weeds uncovered—and vulnerable to your waiting hands.

Jungle Warfare Dooms Potato Beetles

With clean cultivation between rows and crops planted in solid blocks, serious garden pests such as the dreaded Colorado potato beetle can ravage an entire vegetable planting like wind-whipped wildfire. But put a few roadblocks in their way, then fortify those defenses with legions of soldier bugs and other beneficial insects, and the beetles are "nowhere, man," says Steve Gilman of Stillwater, New York.

Steve plants all of his crops in 52-inch-wide permanent raised beds. Only occasionally does he mow the sod strips between beds. "Leaving the strips unmowed keeps pests isolated and turns the grass into a jungle, creating an ideal habitat for the predators that live there full-time," he says.

As if that's not enough, Steve plants potatoes four or five beds apart. When those nasty potato beetles go in search of food, they run into a fatal ambush of hungry soldier bugs in his homegrown jungle between the beds.

A *No-Dig* Potato Patch

Want to grow plenty of pest- and disease-free potatoes without digging a trench or making hills? All you need is some leaf mulch, wood chips, and wheat straw, says Minneapolis organic gardener Shar Feldheim.

Shar layers 6 inches of leaf mulch over 4 inches of wood chips on his 8 × 10-foot plot. He tops the leaf mulch with a sprinkling of dry, composted cow manure and a handful of bonemeal, then nestles his seed potatoes in the leaves. The leaf mulch helps to create the acidic growing conditions potatoes prefer. Shar covers the potatoes with wheat straw and lets them grow. Without any additional work over the course of the growing season, Shar says he harvests a satisfying amount— more than 20 pounds—of clean, scab-free potatoes from his potato patch. And he never has to lift a shovel to do it.

Free Fall **Radishes**!

By giving up a few of the radishes from her spring harvest, Sharon Thompson of Boone, Iowa, reaps a free fall crop of the crunchy roots. Sharon recommends letting one radish plant go to seed every 5 to 6 inches. "When the seed pods dry, till through the row of plants you left, and hope for fall rains," she says. Or you can water to help ensure that the seeds will sprout. "Later, you'll have a carpet of fall radishes—mild and crisp and free."

Don't despair if your radishes have bloomed and set seed pods. Although the roots are no longer worth bothering with, the young seed pods are crunchy and mildly spicy while they're still tender. Once they dry, you can till the pods into the soil and water them to get a free crop of fall radishes.

Santa Spuds?

While many gardeners strive mightily to get their early potatoes planted by April Fool's Day, Steve and Carol Moore, of the Center for Sustainable Living, Wilson College, Chambersburg, Pennsylvania, are already eating freshly dug new potatoes by then. One year, on the day after Christmas, Steve and Carol planted 'Red Gold' potatoes 8 to 9 inches deep in the double-dug beds inside their greenhouse.

The greenhouse is unheated, so it's like a big cold frame, Steve explains. For extra protection, they covered the potato beds with a layer of heavy plastic stretched over plastic bows.

Through winter, the growth was phenomenal. "We had to tie the plants back a bit so they wouldn't flop out into the walkway," Steve says. Then on March 20, they dug the first of their extra-early potatoes.

"We've grown bigger potatoes, but this was some of the best eating ever," Steve says. If you don't have a greenhouse for a winter potato crop, cover a raised bed with a sheet of plastic under a second plastic layer supported by hoops.

Grow Your Own "Great Pumpkin"

Ever wonder how those growers of large pumpkins at the fair manage to get them so big? Wanda Boop of Briar Patch Organic Farms in Mifflinburg, Pennsylvania, knows the secret. Here are her instructions for growing a megapumpkin of your own: "Sow 'Atlantic Giant' pumpkins indoors in pots approximately three weeks before your last frost," says Wanda.

"Meanwhile, incorporate lots of compost into your garden soil and put down black plastic to warm the soil for two weeks."

When the pumpkin seedling is approximately two weeks old and properly hardened off, transplant it into the warmed ground in the plastic, she explains. "Place a toothpick in the soil right next to the stem to deter cutworms, and spray the transplant with fish emulsion to help relieve transplant shock. Water the plant with fish emulsion every week. As fruit forms, choose the sturdiest-looking pumpkins and cut off the weaker fruits. Make sure the plants are always well watered."

As the plant gets larger, hill up the soil at the base of the plant to deter vine borers. "Then find a forklift," Wanda jokes. "You'll need one to get your pumpkin out of the garden!"

homegrown HINTS

EARLY SPRING SPINACH TAKES A 'BOUGH'

Jo Meller, of Five Springs Farm in northern Michigan, plants spinach seeds in late August for an extra-early spring harvest. "Cover the seedlings loosely with evergreen boughs to prevent compaction of snow; we use hemlock or juniper boughs," Jo says. You can protect the young plants before the first hard frost arrives in your area, she explains. "Uncover the plants in the spring, and let them continue to grow."

Use evergreen branches to keep snow from pressing down on a fall-sown crop of spinach. Insulated through the winter by their covering of snow and branches, the plants will really take off when spring arrives.

Bye-Bye Beer Nuts, Hello *Soybeans!*

Looking for a tasty and different snack food? Take a tip from the Japanese, who enjoy the buttery, crunchy flavor of *edamame*—fresh, green soybeans. "In Japan, they are certainly standard summer fare," explains Rick Davis, a long-time organic gardener who lives in rural Ashigawa, Japan. "They are eaten everywhere—in homes, restaurants, bars, and beer gardens."

But you don't have to go all the way to Japan to enjoy *edamame.* You can grow green soybeans in your garden. "They're easy to grow, have no pest problems, and are much faster than ordinary soybeans," says Rick. These beans grow anywhere that farmers grow regular soybeans. In fact, they are better adapted to northern growing conditions than lima beans, which they resemble somewhat in taste.

"We grow them here!" declares Robert L. Johnston Jr., president of Johnny's Selected Seeds in Albion, Maine. The two varieties in his catalog are 'Envy', a 75-day bean, and the 90-day 'Butterbean'.

"Most of the pods ripen at the same time," Rob explains. To harvest your green soybeans, clip the plants near the base when the soybeans are plump in their pods and just as the pods begin to lose their bright green color.

Strip the pods from the plants, rinse, and boil in salted water for ten minutes. Flush with cold water to cool the pods and enjoy by popping beans out of the pod. (You can also package the shelled soybeans for freezing at this point.)

"They go great with a cold

Fresh green soybeans look a lot like their field-grown relatives, but their flavor earns them the nickname "butterbeans."

beer at the end of the day!" exclaims Rick, who grows as many green soybeans as he can. "I can get only one crop of ordinary soybeans in a year, but can harvest *edamame* very often by staggering the plantings," adds Rick. He typically gathers his final harvest around the beginning of September.

problem solver

TRAP SQUASH TROUBLES BEFORE THEY START

To keep that age-old pest—the squash vine borer—under control, Sharon Carson of Delmar, Delaware, recommends setting out a little preventive medicine. "Take a gallon plastic milk jug and cut a big hole in the top of the side. Then put about a quart of water, 3 to 4 tablespoons of molasses, and a little vinegar in the bottom. Set your jugs out here and there when the squash are in bloom. It traps the moths that lay the eggs that grow into squash borers," she says.

homegrown HINTS

GIVE SQUASH AND MELONS A SUPER START

Start seeds of winter squash and melons inside in mid-May, recommends Jim Sluyter, of Five Springs Farm in Bear Lake, Michigan. Jim uses the molded brown cardboard containers sold in garden centers and garden supply catalogs. This lets him tear away the containers at transplanting time to avoid disturbing the young plants' roots.

When you start the seeds, also begin preparing the ground for your crops. "Make your hills by digging down 1 foot and filling the hill with composted manure. Then cover the hill with garden soil," he says. This warms the soil nicely and gets the melons and winter squash off to a good start, Jim explains, noting that it also makes the use of black plastic unnecessary.

Jim gives his squash and melon crops one last advantage to ensure success: "We also surround melons and winter and summer squash with hairy vetch," he says. "Any low-growing cover crop works well." He sows the hairy vetch when he transplants squash and melons, or shortly afterward. The vetch controls weeds throughout the growing season, and Jim tills it under in the fall to enrich the soil for future crops.

Choose *Wisely* for *Surefire* Sweet Potatoes

Although traditionally considered a southern crop, sweet potatoes can be grown just about all over the United States—if you pick the right variety. "A short-season variety such as 'Georgia Jet' works just fine in northern gardens," says Dr. Booker T. Whatley, a retired sweet potato breeder from Tuskegee University in Alabama.

"When I was an adjunct professor at Cornell University in Ithaca, New York, there was a professor there who was successfully raising sweet potatoes all the way up north in Ithaca! He was using 'Georgia Jet', a 90-day variety, and getting good yields.

"Besides the proper variety, you need well-drained soil, and a soil test to make sure your potassium level is relatively high. Other than that," Dr. Whatley says, "there is just not much to it."

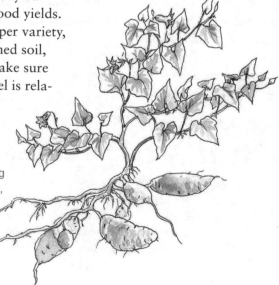

Don't rule out sweet potatoes if you live in the North. By choosing short-season varieties, you can enjoy these nutritious orange vegetables no matter where you garden.

To Enjoy **Sweet Potatoes**, Store Them Right

Few things are more frustrating than harvesting a bumper crop from your garden only to have it quickly deteriorate in storage. Unfortunately, that happens all too often with sweet potatoes. That's because there is no place in the average American home that has the proper conditions for storing sweet potatoes, says Dr. Booker T. Whatley, who developed the popular 'Carver' variety of sweet potato at Tuskegee University in Alabama.

"The only safe place to store sweet potatoes for any length of time is in your freezer. Coat each root with vegetable oil and bake in a conventional oven—not a microwave—at 375°F for 90 minutes. Once the roots have cooled, wrap each one in aluminum foil and put them in your freezer," advises Dr. Whatley.

"Any sweet potato recipe should be started with baked sweet potatoes," Dr. Whatley declares. "Dr. George Washington Carver recommended baking sweet potatoes over all other methods of preparing them almost 100 years ago. The only time you should use your microwave oven for sweet potatoes is to warm them up after they come out of your freezer."

Young Tomatoes Like It *Cool*

A big mistake gardeners tend to make with tomatoes is keeping them too warm at the seedling stage. Young tomatoes need to keep their cool during the day if they're in a hoop house, greenhouse, or even a bright window situation. They also like cool nights—50°F is perfect, says Michael Brownback, a certified organic commercial grower in Loysville, Pennsylvania. "Cool conditions keep seedlings fairly short. If they get too warm, they get leggy, and you want stocky, sturdy plants so they can withstand wind," explains Michael.

Tomatoes— A Month Early

If you're after those early tomatoes, try this method from Wanda Boop of Briar Patch Organic Farms in Mifflinburg, Pennsylvania. Wanda recommends starting a few short-season tomatoes in the greenhouse or under growing lights at the end of January. "Around March 20, set Wall O' Water plant protectors in the garden, fill them with water, and let them warm up the soil for approximately two weeks.

"Meanwhile, on really sunny days, start to harden off your seedlings a bit outdoors— only a couple of hours at a time," she says. Then, around April 1st, transplant the tomatoes with plenty of compost into your Wall O' Waters, making sure they close completely at the top.

As the weather warms and all danger of frost has passed, pull open the Wall O' Waters. Allowing more air and sun in begins preparing the plants for the outside temperature. After a few days, it's safe to remove the Wall O' Waters entirely. "The plants look a bit straggly but will perk up in a week or so," Wanda notes. "Stake the plants well. And enjoy those early tomatoes!"

Tomato Cages That Last *"Forever"*

He's tried all types of systems for staking tomatoes, but organic grower Scott Case of Aaronsburg, Pennsylvania, says he is sold on wire cages made of the heavy-duty mesh used for reinforcing concrete. "They're cheap to make, and they last forever," he says.

Scott buys 5-foot-tall wire mesh in a 150-foot roll. Then he just cuts off 6-foot sections with wire cutters and fastens them together into a circular cage. "We plant the tomatoes, and about a week later go through and cage them," he explains. "These cages hold up great and don't rust."

To make fewer cages, have your building supply center cut off only as much wire as you

The heavy wire mesh used to reinforce concrete also makes strong, long-lasting tomato cages.

need, or split a whole roll with a gardening friend. You can also use the sturdy mesh to protect young fruit trees or as a trellis for peas, pole beans, or other climbing crops.

Pamper Tomatoes with *Pruning*

James Weaver of Kutztown, Pennsylvania, started pampering heirloom tomatoes well before heirlooms became the rage they are today. And he found that one of the best ways to pamper the tasty gems—to pamper all of his field-grown tomatoes, in fact—is to prune them.

James and his son prune the suckers—sprouts that form in the angles where a branch emerges from a main stem—off the plants up to the first flower cluster. The pruning improves air flow and keeps the fruit up off the ground. "You get less fruit this way, but what you get is earlier, by a week or so, and it's much nicer and bigger," Jim explains.

Tomatoes *Need* Calcium

"Calcium is very important to tomatoes," says organic grower Michael Brownback of Loysville, Pennsylvania. In fact, he says ensuring that the plant has enough calcium and watering evenly are two critical factors if you want incredible tomatoes.

"Blossom-end rot can be aggravated if there is too little water and if there isn't enough calcium in the plant," he says.

The best way to know if your garden soil has enough calcium is to do a soil test. Specific recommendations are included in the test results. (Check with your local exten-

sion office for information on soil testing, or look in the "Resources" section, starting on page 317.) Too busy to test the soil for your tomato plants? Stir a handful of gypsum (available in small bags at most garden centers) into the soil at the beginning of the planting season to give your tomatoes a little boost.

Boost Tomato *Yields* in a Short Season

It may take a little more care, but Jo Meller, of Five Springs Farm in Bear Lake, Michigan, says it's possible to get big yields of great tomatoes even in short-summer areas. Jo recommends the following method: "Pick off blossoms, if any, before you plant each tomato plant in the garden, and bury the plant up to the top leaves," she says. Snip off the remaining leaves. "All of the stem that is under ground turns into roots."

Trellis the plants, keep them thinned to one or two stems, and trim off all suckers, she adds. "In late July, when there are five fruit/blossom clusters per plant, cut the top off and re-move any additional flowers as they form. This speeds the ripening time of the fruit, al-lowing much higher yields in a short growing season," Jo explains. At Five Springs Farm, the last frost is around the end of May and their first frost arrives in mid-October, so they've gotten used to hur-rying the tomatoes in order to produce a timely crop.

problem solver

DON'T SQUEEZE YOUNG TOMATOES

"The number one tip I can offer for growing tomatoes," says Michael Brownback of Loysville, Pennsylvania, is give them plenty of room at the seedling stage. Michael should know. He specializes in tomatoes at his 200-acre Spiral Path Farm.

Michael says his staff starts tomatoes by scattering seed in an open flat and covering lightly. When the seedlings develop their first true leaves—those that look like the leaves of a mature tomato plant—they transplant the seedlings into 4-inch or larger pots. Transplanting at this point gives the roots room to grow, and it also allows the tops of the plants to spread out. That way you get good buds and good tomatoes, without stress. "You have a balanced plant from the beginning," he says.

The system they use at Spiral Path Farm works equally well on a smaller scale. Simply sow tomato seeds indoors five to six weeks before your last frost date. If you sow more than one variety of tomato in a seed flat, sprinkle the seeds in rows and label them to avoid confusion later on. At the true-leaf stage, transplant the healthiest plants to 4-inch or larger pots. You'll be surprised at how much difference a little growing room makes.

Snatch Tomatoes from the **Jaws of Death**

Have you ever picked a gorgeous, perfectly ripe 'Brandywine' tomato only to find that one of your four-footed adversaries has already gnawed a big hole in it? Fight back by picking early, says Michael Brownback, a Loysville, Pennsylvania, or-ganic farmer. "Once a tomato has started to ripen, it doesn't need light. Pick it, and take it inside to finish," he says. "You'll have a perfect, firmer tomato." Once you have them indoors and out of harm's way, put your tomatoes in a cool spot to finish ripening. A base-ment shelf is great for this, but they'll ripen on the kitchen counter, too. Just keep toma-toes out of the refrigerator where too-cold temperatures will retard ripening and ruin their home-grown flavor.

Delay Effects of Late Blight

It's a little bit of extra work, but Bud Glendening of Fox Hollow Seed Co. in McGrann, Pennsylvania, says he finds the preventive work well worth the effort in delaying late blight on his tomatoes. "It'll get you eventually," he says, "but I find spraying with hydrogen peroxide really delays the effects of the disease."

Bud says you can use pharmacy-strength, 3 percent hydrogen peroxide solution, straight, to fend off late blight, which causes irregular, black, water-soaked patches on tomato leaves along with dark-colored spots on the fruits. Bud sprays the mild preventive on his tomato plants each evening starting in late August or early September. "It tends to perk up pepper plants, too," he says.

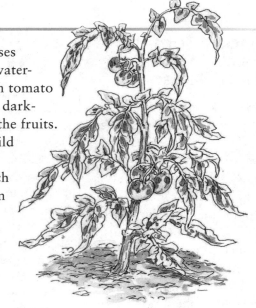

Fend off late blight with a simple hydrogen peroxide spray. Late blight usually appears during humid weather with cool nights (below 60°F) and warm days (70 to 85°F).

Hoops *Are a Must* for Undercover Tomatoes

"When we put our tomatoes out, we like to put row covers over them—with wire hoop support," says Michael Brownback. The Pennsylvania commercial grower explains that it's important to use hoops because plants like tomatoes can't take fabric row covers without support. Their stems aren't strong enough to hold up a "blanket" and be whipped around by wind. (In addition to the supported row covers, plastic mulch underneath gives the quickest heating of the soil, he adds.)

Michael uses 60-inch hoops, which leave about 18 inches of head room for the tomato plants underneath the cover. That gives his young plants plenty of unrestricted growing room, unlike the tight confines found beneath milk-jug covers and similar makeshift protectors. The ends of the rows are covered also, and the edges of the cover are firmly tucked in the soil to prevent the wind from getting under it and carrying it to Oz. Leave the row cover on until it begins to push against the tomatoes' tops or until their blossoms start to open.

Timely tip

Be careful with row covers on tomatoes, Michael cautions. "When the temperature is over 90 degrees, the pollen is affected. It can hurt a bud, and the bud won't be able to set fruit," he explains. So keep an eye on the weather, and be ready to ventilate or remove covers from tomatoes when temperatures start to climb.

A **New Twist** on Tomato Stakes

If you've yet to discover your "perfect tomato stake," take a look at the curvy creation called Spira-stake. Designed by gardener and artist Jim Jeansonne, Spira-stake provides both aesthetically pleasing support and a way to supply fertilizer directly to the roots. As the tomato plant grows, you simply guide it up the curves of the spiral-shaped support, eliminating the need for all those ties.

Made of UV-stabilized recycled plastic, Spira-stake is hollow, and the part that goes into the ground is perforated. This lets

you pour water and liquid fertilizers down through the hollow plant holder to emerge at the root zone. Late in the season, when the tomato plants in Jim's Louisiana garden are heavily laden with fruit, he uses horizontal connector rods between the stakes to provide additional support. The result is an uncluttered garden look, a productive root system, and unique, durable stakes that last for many years. (See "Resources," on page 317, for information on where to find this product.)

The twists in Spira-stakes offer no-tie support for your tomatoes. The hollow stakes also make it easy to put water and fertilizer right where they're needed.

Give Zucchini Some **Manure**

Coaxing earlier, more prolific production out of zucchini and other squash family members is as easy as starting with a shovelful of manure, says Wade Bitner, Utah State University extension horticulturist for Salt Lake County in Salt Lake City, Utah. When growing zucchini and other squash crops, Wade recommends this system: Dig a hole in your garden a shovel's depth and a shovel's width in diameter, and replace the soil with horse manure. Then cover it with the soil you removed from the hole. This makes a 4- to 6-inch mound of soil.

Make a 2-inch-deep trench around the mound to hold water, then plant the zucchini seed (one is usually enough unless you are willing to thin) on the top of the mound. When it gets moist, the decomposing manure warms up the soil to create the conditions squash thrive in. "And when the roots hit the manure, the plants practically shoot out of the ground!"

helpful
Herb Gardening Hints

Herbs are some of the most versatile plants you can add to the garden or landscape. Whether you want to harvest herbs for their medicinal value and culinary benefits or simply use them to enhance the beauty of your ornamental beds, herbs are the hottest thing going. Herbs have other uses, too—aromatherapy, craft projects, beauty aids, and more. In this chapter, you'll find tips and ideas to make your herb growing—and using—successful, from seed germination to the final harvest and beyond.

190

Save *Lavender* from **Winterkill**

In areas without reliable snow cover, lavender commonly suffers from winterkill. Typically, you can prevent winterkill with a thick layer of mulch, which acts as an insulating blanket over tender plants.

However, heavy mulches can inflict lavender with fatal "wet feet." What's a lavender-lover to do?

"Here's my solution," advises Barbara Steele, co-owner of Alloway Gardens and Herb Farm, located in Littlestown, Pennsylvania. "After Christmas, I cut the boughs off the holiday tree and stuff small branches around the base of the lavender plants. This loose mulch insulates against winter winds that can dry out the roots of the plants, without creating a wet spot."

Barbara doesn't worry about the acidic effect that the evergreen needles can have on the soil. To neutralize the extra acidity, Barbara says, "I remove the branches once the weather settles out and then sprinkle wood ashes around the plants."

Grow *Gorgeous* Lavender in **Mounds**

Lavender plants need full sun and good drainage to grow their best. Dr. Arthur O. Tucker, a renowned herb researcher and cocurator of the Claude E. Phillips Herbarium in the Department of Agriculture and Natural Resources at Delaware State University, recommends planting lavender in mounds in areas with less-than-perfect drainage.

"Preparing a mound for lavender plantings is well worth the extra effort," claims Dr. Tucker. "The plants look spectacular and have a much longer life span."

Dr. Tucker says it's ideal to prepare mounds in the fall before spring planting to allow time to solve any settling problems. However, unless you live in a bog, success is all but guaranteed, even without this advance planning. Here is Dr. Tucker's technique.

Mark the edges of the bed. Work in an area about 1½ to 2 feet wide and allow about 2 feet between plants. Loosen the existing soil with a spading fork.

Create a well-drained site for lavender by forming mounds of soil, sand, compost, and gravel.

Make a soil mix consisting of 1 part native soil, 1 part sand, and 1 part compost in a wheelbarrow. Mix in a third as much pea gravel, or mixed rock of about ½ inch in diam-eter, and about 1 cup of lime. You may use more or less, depending upon how big your mounds will be and whether your soil is acidic or alkaline.

Pour this mix onto the site and shape it into a mound from 8 to 18 inches high, using higher mounds in wetter areas. Taper the edges of the mound to meet the soil level. (Within a year, the mound will settle to about half its original height.)

To plant the lavender in the prepared mounds, make a cone of the soil mix (try to use mostly soil around the roots, brushing any gravel away), and spread the roots of the plant over the cone. Cover the roots with mix, and water thoroughly.

Place a bareroot lavender plant on each mound. Then cover with the soil, sand, compost, and gravel mixture.

Topdressing
for Lavender

"Top-dress lavender plants with 1 inch of white sand," suggests herb researcher Dr. Arthur O. Tucker. "The reflectivity increases the light available to the inner leaves of the plants. In my research, plants mulched with sand grew more quickly and also achieved better form."

Dr. Tucker adds that sand isn't the only mulch you can use. Light-colored mulches such as gravel, marble chips, or oyster shells would also work, but he warns against wood chips and peat moss.

Surefire
Lavender Cuttings

Timid about taking lavender cuttings? There's no need to fuss with bottom heat, perlite, and rooting hormone powder. When new growth starts in the spring, trim and shape plants, removing up to a third of each plant. Look through the trimmings for sturdy stalks with vigorous sideshoots. Rip sideshoots off the stem, leaving a piece of the stem, or heel, attached to each "cutting." Shove cuttings into soil under the existing lavender plant, and water well. Cuttings will be rooted in three to four weeks.

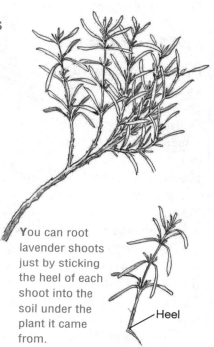

You can root lavender shoots just by sticking the heel of each shoot into the soil under the plant it came from.

Heel

problem solver

FRAGRANT HERBAL PATHWAYS

Drooling over photographs of garden pathways festooned with thyme and chamomile, but worried that they're too much work to achieve? "It's not that difficult," claims Nancy McDonald, cofounder and managing editor of the quarterly *The American Cottage Gardener,* and whose own garden in Grand Marais, Michigan, houses the northern test garden of the American Dianthus Society.

Nancy laid cement pavers for a pathway, spread fine sand in between them, and then sowed seed of English thyme between the pavers Nancy kept the area well watered, and by summer's end, she had a well-established herbal carpet. Talk about low maintenance—an annual mowing keeps it trimmed!

Nancy also recommends putting a weed barrier down before laying the pavers. She used cardboard; other potential weedproofing materials include thick layers of newspaper, old carpets, and commercial weed barrier fabric. She cautions, "Don't put a weed barrier where you plant the thyme. Too much mulch will make it difficult for the thyme roots to reach the soil below." Instead, Nancy used a layer of straw to block weeds until the thyme grew in and covered the area.

homegrown HINTS

FRENCH LAVENDER GROWS LARGER AND LIVES LONGER

Most herb gardeners love growing lavender, but *Lavandula angustifolia* and its cultivars, also known as true lavender, don't grow nearly as tall or live as long as French lavender, or lavandin. To boost lavender production in your garden, plant lavandin cultivars, instead of true lavender.

"Most of the lavender grown in France for the perfume industry is derived from lavandin (*Lavandula × intermedia*), hybrids that can only be grown from cuttings," explains Dr. Arthur O. Tucker, cocurator of the Claude E. Phillips Herbarium in the Department of Agriculture and Natural Resources at Delaware State University.

According to Dr. Tucker, lavandin will eventually usurp lavender's popularity in the home garden. In his research done in Delaware (Zone 7), lavandin is hardier than lavender and rarely succumbs to root rot, a fungus disease that plagues lavenders in humid climates. This disease resistance contributes to lavandin's longer life span of up to ten years, whereas a well-tended lavender plant rarely survives for longer than five years.

Lavandins are gradually making their way into garden centers but the term lavandin is rarely used. Look for such cultivar names as 'Dutch', 'Grosso', and 'Seal'.

Presto—You Have an Herb Garden!

If you want to plant herbs but you're deterred by the labor of preparing a garden site, take heart. There is an easier way. "Here's the easiest way to get growing," suggests Tina James, an herbalist and teacher in Reisterstown, Maryland.

Determine the dimensions of the garden. Mow the turf as low as possible. Cover it with newspaper—at least six pages thick—and drench the newspaper with water. Cover the wet paper with at least 2 inches of mulch. (Tina likes to use a mixture of green grass clippings and shredded leaves.) Wait at least three weeks for the sod underneath to begin decomposing—then dig holes right through the mulch and newspaper to set the transplants into the soil. Adjust the newspaper to make sure it's covering the sod. Add more mulch if needed around planted herbs. And you're done!

Tina says you can plant immediately where there is no sod or where the soil is loose. "My sister has a virtual sandlot for a backyard, so we were able to put the plants in the same day we made the garden. If you have sod or very hard soil, it will be a lot harder to plant, but herbs are tough!"

Timely tip

Tina adds that this bed preparation method is ideal to try in the fall, because there will be more time for the sod to break down. "To make things really mellow for spring planting, strip the sod and lay it back down with the roots face up before spreading the newspaper."

Bag-Dry Herbs in the **Fridge**

Some leafy green herbs, such as parsley, dill, and basil, are slow to air-dry and generally lose their bright color during the process. Here's a better way to dry them. Stuff herb stalks loosely in paper lunch bags, then label the bags and close them with clothespins. Place the herb bags in a frostless refrigerator. In a few days, the herbs will be perfectly dried, thanks to the refrigerator's dehumidifying action. You can leave the dried herbs in the fridge indefinitely. Tape the bags to the side of the refrigerator with masking tape to save space—or transfer the herbs to airtight containers and store them in a cool, dark place.

You can dry herbs and keep them green when you put them in a paper bag in a frost-free refrigerator.

Fall Sowing Saves Time in *Spring*

"Some herbs naturally lend themselves to fall planting," suggests Janika Eckert, manager of the herb seed program at Johnny's Selected Seeds in Albion, Maine. "I plant perennials like anise hyssop, angelica (a biennial), catnip, dandelion, horehound, Joe-Pye weed, lemon balm, lovage, ginseng, goldenseal, mullein, St.-John's-wort, marsh mallow, motherwort, mugwort, and valerian in late summer to early fall. Many of these herbs germinate better after a cold period. Annual weeds, often a problem in direct seedings, will winter-kill with this fall method of planting. Plus, this method saves time in the spring." Janika recommends sowing seeds in a protected area and then transplanting them after they germinate the following spring and have grown big enough to handle.

Janika has also found that many herbs self-sow, including catnip, calendula, yarrow, anise hyssop, holy basil (*Ocimum sanctum*)—the only basil that reliably self-sows—angelica, caraway, chamomile, chives, fennel, evening primrose, vervain, motherwort, mugwort, valerian, and echinacea (purple coneflower). Self-sowing is only a problem if you don't want the particular herb in your garden next year, but the "volunteer" seedlings can be weeded out easily.

Timely tip

If you're particular about where you want volunteer herb plants to pop up, harvest seeds from self-sowing herbs when they start to shatter, and plant them right away. After all, Mother Nature knows the best time for them to germinate!

homegrown HINTS

MAKE LEMON VERBENA LAST

Hate to lose your lemon verbena (*Aloysia triphylla*) over the winter? You don't have to, with this tip from Jim Long, author of *Herbs, Just for Fun—A Beginner's Guide to Growing and Using Herbs* and owner of Long Creek Herbs in Oak Creek, Arkansas. "Lemon verbena is actually a tropical shrub and will produce leaves almost year-round if well cared for," claims Jim.

Jim grows his lemon verbena in the herb garden throughout the summer. In the fall, he cuts the plant back to about 15 inches, digs it up, and trims back some of the roots before placing it in a clay pot. "Once you bring the plant indoors, it will drop all its leaves, but don't give up on it," insists Jim. "Keep the soil moist and place the pot near a sunny window or under a grow light where temperatures remain above 60°F. Within about ten days, the plant will sprout new leaves. In just a few weeks, you'll be able to harvest the tasty leaves again."

Jim replants his lemon verbena in the ground once the weather warms up the following spring and all danger of frost has passed. "Don't plant lemon verbena in the ground in a pot," he cautions. "This constrains the roots too much. Lemon verbena really likes to grow. Mine reaches 3 to 4 feet in one season."

Rejuvenate Muddled Mints

Here's a tip for keeping a bed of mint looking good and producing well. "Unless it is divided occasionally, a stand of mint becomes a dense mat, which literally chokes itself out after a few years," acknowledges Jim Long, the owner of Long Creek Herb Farm and author of *Herbs, Just for Fun—A Beginner's Guide to Growing and Using Herbs*.

Jim's solution is to rototill the mint bed every two years. He covers the bed with a bit of compost and then tills the area well.

The last step is to pull out and dispose of two-thirds of the roots. "Don't worry," Jim assures. "Within several weeks, the chopped-up roots will sprout and produce plenty of robust and flavorful mint all over again."

Timely tip

Here's another mint tip. Don't plant more than one variety of mint in the same area. Crossbreeding will blur distinctive flavors and aromas.

Divide All Your Potted Mints, Too

If you grow your mint in sunken pots rather than directly in the garden soil to prevent unwanted spreading, you can still spruce up your mint bed.

Every few years, you may need to unearth the pots, divide off several portions of the plant, and repot one section per pot back in the garden.

Use the leftover portions to give to friends, donate to a local plant sale, or make into refreshing mint tea.

homegrown HINTS

HERB WINDOW BOXES
FOR ANY EXPOSURE

Different herbs thrive under different light conditions. When you plan a window-box herb garden, be sure to consider the sun exposure it will receive.

Jane Kuitems, owner of Jane's Herb Farm in Webster, New York, plants stunning containers for her demonstration gardens. "Over the years, I've found several combinations that are absolutely ideal," says Jane.

For a spectacular pot for a sunny southern spot, Jane uses bronze fennel in the center flanked with a mixture of yellow miniroses, golden feverfew, golden lemon thyme, and 'Woodcote' sage. "I use a shallow container that is 24 inches wide and 8 inches deep for this planting," says Jane. "The bronze, yellow, and chartreuse color combination is really breathtaking."

For a western exposure, Jane plants an oblong wooden cradle with purple sage, common thyme, chives, 'Kent Beauty' oregano, prostrate rosemary, violas, and sweet marjoram. Jane says, "This spring-planted container thrives throughout the summer in a wave of mauve and green. The perennials in this planter have lasted for three years now, so I don't have to replace the whole container every season."

For a shadier eastern or northern exposure, Jane uses perilla (a purple-leafed herb known as shisho in Japan), curly parsley, and trailing helichrysum (a downy, gray-leafed beauty sometimes called licorice plant, although it's actually a type of strawflower), and then adds a few flowers likes pansies, impatiens, and torenia. "For northern exposures, this planting works best if placed up against the wall of a building," says Jane. "The reflected light is enough to keep these plants thriving even though sunlight is limited."

To give your window-box herbs something to sink their roots into, fill your containers with a quick-draining planting mix. Stir in a couple of trowelfuls of compost for light nourishment and so they don't dry out too quickly.

Lovely Lovage Subs for *Celery*

Lovage (*Levisticum officinale*) is a beautiful perennial herb with a distinct celery flavor, but it's much easier to grow than celery. You can either start from seed or buy transplants. Plant lovage in sun or partial shade in moist soil.

One or two plants will yield a continuous supply of leaves and stalks to mince in salads or stews. A little lovage goes a long way—use it in the same proportion as most other culinary herbs for seasoning.

And here's another bonus—the hollow stalks make tasty straws for Bloody Marys!

Lovage (*Levisticum officinale*) is an easy-to-grow herb that substitutes for celery in your recipes.

problem SOLVer

LOTS OF LEMON BASIL

Lemon basil is ideal for fish and chicken dishes, and it makes a delectable pesto, as well. The trouble is, the common variety generally bolts as soon as transplants take hold. For better results, sow lemon basil seeds directly in the garden once the soil has completely warmed rather than setting in transplants.

"For even more productive plants, try growing the heirloom 'Mrs. Burns' Famous Lemon Basil'," advises Maryland herbalist Tina James. "This unique variety is much taller—up to 3 feet—and very slow to flower, so yields are much greater. The flavor is distinctly lemon with an undertone of spice—it's great for seasoning seafood as well as for making tea and potpourri."

Great **Herb** Gardens-*to*-Go

Most culinary herbs make great container plants. Basil, savory, calendula, chives, tarragon, marjoram, thyme, rosemary, and oregano meet two important criteria for container growing: compact growth and drought resistance. The bigger challenge is finding enough large, inexpensive containers in which to plant.

"Bushel baskets are my solution," says garden writer Tina James. "They don't overheat the soil like plastic containers do, and they're large enough to save me from constant watering." Tina says she lines each basket with a trash bag, punches a few holes in the bag to ensure good drainage, and then fills the basket with her regular soil mix, consisting of 1 part sand, 1 part compost, and 1 part potting soil. To extend the life span of the basket, Tina places it on a slate or on a couple of bricks so that it's not sitting directly on the ground or on the deck.

"Bushel basket containers cost next to nothing and last for at least two seasons," claims Tina. "And here's another bonus. Bushel baskets have handles, so it's easy to take one as a gift—even up in the elevator to the 40th floor, as I did!"

Herbs Solve **Wet Landscape** Challenges, Too

While many herbs flourish in dry conditions, you can also turn to herbs when you have a wet site to landscape. Sweet woodruff, a May-flowering herb used in Germany to flavor May wine, will spread easily to form a low-maintenance carpet in a shaded spot.

Other choices for a low groundcover are pennyroyal and corsican mint. Both are noninvasive members of the mint family. Chervil, an annual with a delicate part-parsley, part-anise flavor, will form an attractive patch if sown from seed in the fall. It bolts quickly in the heat but will readily self-sow in a moist, partly shaded location.

Taller plants that thrive in moist locations include the perennials valerian, meadowsweet, bee balm, and lemon balm. Keep in mind, however, that these are not refined garden plants, and they will reseed and spread happily if you give them the right conditions. If you have a damp area to fill and an informal garden fits in your plans, these attractive plants will be good choices for you.

Herbs Suited to Shade

While lots of herbs prefer full sun and well-drained soil, you can grow herbs in the shade—especially medicinal herbs. "It's true—most culinary herbs perform best in full sun," says Maryland herbalist Tina James. "But I live in the woods, so I've chosen a different tack. Many native medicinal plants need shade, so I decided to give them a try."

Tina says that many woodland plants are difficult to start from seed. To find transplants, check local nurseries that specialize in growing herbs and wildflowers, or order plants from a reputable mail-order source (see "Resources" on page 317). To learn how to use woodland medicinals, consult one of the references listed in "Recommended Reading" on page 327, or take a course with a knowledgeable herbalist.

Although Tina grows many different medicinal herbs, here are the six that she likes the best—and that she says are easiest to grow:

➤ Black cohosh (*Cimicifuga racemosa*)

➤ Bloodroot (*Sanguinaria canadensis*)

➤ Bowman's root or Indian physic (*Gillenia trifoliata*)

➤ Wintergreen (*Gaultheria procumbens*)

➤ Solomon's seal (*Polygonatum biflorum*)

➤ Twin leaf (*Jeffersonia diphylla*)

Herb Forecast: Hot, *Dry*, and *Sunny*

If you have an extremely hot, dry, sunny site that seems just impossible to landscape, think herbs! Many herbs are as tough as weeds and can tolerate even the worst conditions. Not only that, you can harvest herbs for use in cooking, crafting, or healing.

Try planting some of the many varieties of thyme or oregano along walkways. Both are very useful groundcovers with attractive flowers. An added benefit is the scent that is released as you brush or step on the foliage.

Another useful, scented plant to use on a larger scale is sweet fern (*Comptonia peregrina*), which is not a fern at all but a deciduous member of the bayberry family that tolerates hot, dry sandy soils. Even in exposed, infertile sites, sweet fern will spread slowly to make a 4-foot-high, flat-topped colony with a fernlike appearance and a spicy fragrance.

Also, consider silver- or gray-leafed plants, such as lavender, santolina, lamb's-ears, and wormwood, which thrive in sunny, dry locations.

homegrown HINTS

HERBAL GROUNDCOVERS FOR SLOPES

Some groundcovers such as oregano, sweet fern, lamb's-ears, and wormwood can tolerate sloped terrain, while providing you with aromatic herbs for cuisine or crafts. In addition, you might consider planting mints, comfrey, or tansy along your slopes. But don't make your decision quickly. Because all three of these herbs spread by rhizomes, they are tough plants to get rid of once established, so choose their locations carefully.

Almost Instant Knot Garden

A knot garden, with its formal, mazelike design, can create a stunning focal point for the herb garden.

The trouble is, herbs such as germander, box, myrtle, and lavender—the traditional knot garden choices—grow very slowly and are often difficult to establish in some regions.

"Why not knot with lettuce?" suggests Tina James, an herbalist and teacher who gardens in central Maryland. "Select five to seven different colors and shapes of leaf lettuce. Start the seeds in a seedbed or buy transplants. Then lay out the knot design with lettuce plants!"

Tina adds that using lettuce gives you a chance to see the shape in three dimen-

This typical sixteenth-century knot garden design is very formal.

A contemporary knot garden design can be a bit more whimsical.

sions and make sure you like it before you invest in costlier herb plants. As an added bonus, you can eat the results in a salad!

"This year," says Tina, "I think I'll replant my knot garden, using different types of basil when the lettuce goes to seed."

problem SOLVer   QUICK-DRY HERBS

Want to dry herbs without the bother of hanging them up and waiting for them to dry? Here's a quick tip. On a warm sunny day, spread newspaper on the seats and floors of your car. Spread the herbs on the newspaper and then cover with another layer of newspaper. Leave the car windows just slightly cracked.

By the end of the day, most herbs will be crackly dry and ready to store in airtight containers. (Some herbs with thicker leaves, like sage, may take a few more sunny days to dry.) Handle the dried herb leaves with as little crumbling as possible to preserve their essential oils. The time to crumble the leaves is when you use them in cooking.

Stay Healthy with Juicy Herbs

Fruit and vegetable juices are refreshing on their own, but when you add herbs, they provide even more pleasure and health benefits. Maggie Oster, author of *The Herbal Palate Cookbook*, recommends adding 1 teaspoon of fresh herbs for every 1 cup of juice. If you're using an electric juice extractor, add fresh herbs as the juice is being made. For store-bought juices, allow minced herbs to stand in juice at least 30 minutes, then strain before serving. There's no need to strain juice made using a juice extractor.

FRUIT/VEGETABLE/HERB	HEALTH BENEFITS
Apple with sage or thyme	good for sore throats
Berry juice with mint	stimulates digestion
Carrot juice with marjoram or burnet	soothing
Celery juice with lovage, parsley or chives	mineral-rich
Cherry juice with lavender	eases headache
Cranberry juice with gingerroot or rosemary	relieves nausea
Grape juice with thyme	good for sore throats
Grapefruit juice with angelica or sweet cicely	calming
Papaya juice with marjoram	soothing
Peach or nectarine juice with coriander seeds	good digestive
Raspberry juice with rose geranium	soothing
Tomato juice with basil	eases headache

Spicy Nigella Seeds

Here's a spicy alternative to plain old black pepper. The seeds of *Nigella sativa*, sometimes called black cumin or black caraway, have a slightly peppery, nutty taste and have been used since biblical times to flavor breads, stews, salads, and condiments. In fact, nigella seeds dotted the first New York bagels.

You can easily grow this annual, which produces decorative parchment-colored seed pods that dry naturally on the plant and self-sow readily once established. The only hard part may be finding a seed source. Seeds of *Nigella damascena*, also known as love-in-a-mist, are readily available but have little flavor.

To use nigella seeds, leave them whole to season breads or flavor chutneys. Grind nigella seeds in a peppermill or crush them with a rolling pin to use them as a substitute for pepper on vegetables or mixed into soft cheese.

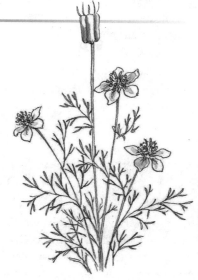

Black cumin (*Nigella sativa*) seeds are a flavorful substitute for black pepper.

Summer Cilantro for *Sizzling* Salsas

Cilantro (*Coriandrum sativum*) is a necessity for summer salsas, but it bolts readily in hot summers. Shade cloth prolongs the season for a week or two, but sooner or later, the plants poop out.

For hard-core salsa addicts, who want their summer and cilantro, too, Maryland herbalist Tina James suggests trying some of the cilantro "mimics," herbs that are reputed to have cilantro-like flavor but can take the heat.

"I've tried Vietnamese coriander (*Polygonum odoratum*), but to my taste,
you might as well use the common smartweed," says Tina. "So I switched to papalo (*Porophyllum ruderale* subsp. *macrocephalum*), a Mexican herb that grows to 8 feet, and quillquina (*Porophyllum ruderale*), a shorter plant (4 to 5 feet) from Bolivia. I wouldn't say that either plant tastes exactly like cilantro, but they're spicy-sweet and good in salsa."

Tina says these plants don't taste alike, but are similar. Her husband, who doesn't care for cilantro, is fond of these substitutes. Tina says, "I've used both these herbs to garnish all kinds of salsas—
tomato or fruit, sweet or spicy—they're all good!"

While Tina has enjoyed both of these plants, she cautions that planting one of each is more than plenty. Quillquina is tall and bushy with thinner leaves, while papalo has larger, more rounded leaves and is bushier than quillquina, according to Tina's results. Tina recommends growing either of these plants by planting seeds in a seedbed after danger of frost, then transplanting them to the garden. Since both of these cilantro stand-ins grow quickly, there's no need to start them indoors.

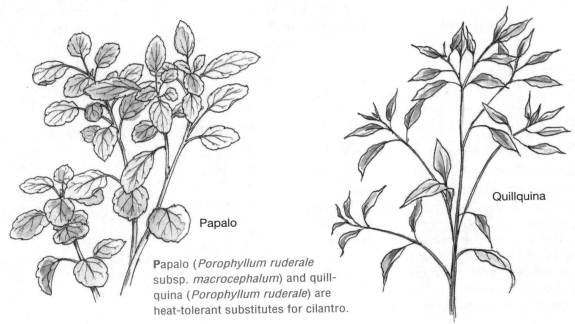

Papalo

Quillquina

Papalo (*Porophyllum ruderale* subsp. *macrocephalum*) and quill-quina (*Porophyllum ruderale*) are heat-tolerant substitutes for cilantro.

Sweet Success with *Lemongrass*

Lemongrass (*Cymbopogon citratus*) is a tender perennial native to southern India and Sri Lanka that gives an indispensable, unique flavor to teas, syrups, fish stews, poached or steamed seafood, and other delights associated with Asian cuisine. Given rich soil and full sun, a purchased plant or root cutting will form a billowy clump of lime-green blades by midsummer. So, asks the bewildered gourmet, how do you cook with this stuff?

To harvest lemongrass for cooking, choose outside stems that are about ½ inch thick. (Proceed carefully—those grassy blades are

Discard tips

Slice ends of stalk

sharp!) Use scissors to cut each stem at the base. Cut off and discard the leafy upper section. You can cut the stems into 2- to 3-inch lengths, or chop them. Unless very finely minced, the stems are removed from a cooked dish before serving because they're quite tough.

Lemongrass (*Cymbopogon citratus*) adds a wonderful flavor to Asian dishes.

Lemongrass is usually treated as an annual. The stalks lose most of their flavor if dried, but they freeze well. Wrap single stems in aluminum foil, label, date, and freeze.

ingenious RECIPES

Lemonade with a Rosemary Twist

Here's a refreshing twist on a summer standby from herb lover Sandra Seymour from Solihull, England. To extract the greatest amount of juice, Sandra uses lemons at room temperature and rolls them on a hard surface for a minute or two before cutting and squeezing. Sandra also freezes her lemon verbena leaves in ice cubes for added flavor and fun.

ROSEMARY LEMONADE

1 heaping tablespoon fresh rosemary leaves

1 cup sugar

4 cups water

4 lemons

In a covered saucepan, simmer the rosemary leaves and sugar in 1 cup of the water for 5 minutes. Add the remaining 3 cups water and the juice from the lemons. Serve ice-cold.

Yield: about 4 servings

ingenious RECIPES

Tender Tricks with Lemon Verbena

Lemon verbena has lovely fragrance and flavor, but the leaves remain tough even after cooking. Carol Costenbader, author of the *Well-Stocked Pantry* series as well as *The Big Book of Preserving the Harvest,* has a solution. "If you grind the dried leaves, the pieces will be small enough to use as seasoning even without cooking," Carol suggests. "The blender or a small food processor works great. But since ground herbs lose their punch quickly, make small batches."

Here's one of Carol's favorite spice mixes. "This blend has a complex Thai flavor that's great on rice as well as stir-fried vegetables."

ASIAN SEASONING MIX

4 tablespoons dried mint leaves

2 tablespoons dried lemon zest

3 teaspoons ground white pepper

2 teaspoons dried lemon verbena leaves

½ teaspoon ground cayenne powder

¼ teaspoon cumin

Combine all ingredients and mix well. In a blender or a clean coffee grinder, grind to a fine consistency only the amount you will use right away (to prevent flavor loss). Sprinkle over cooked rice or add to a stir-fry. Store the remaining mix in an airtight container in a cool, dark place until needed.

Yield: about ½ cup

Nasturtium Capers

Pickled nasturtium flower buds and unripened seedpods make great stand-ins for capers. Harvest the buds while they're still tight, and harvest seedpods before they harden.

Place buds and seedpods in a clean glass bottle, and cover with vinegar. They'll be ready to eat in three days, and they'll keep well for at least a year. And, there's no need to refrigerate.

Bud   Seedpod

Flower

Make your own capers from the seedpods and buds of nasturtium (*Tropaeolum majus*).

Use **Wood Sorrel** for **Lemon Juice**

Out of lemons? Pluck a few sprigs of wood sorrel (*Oxalis acetosella*), a common weed also called shamrock or sourgrass, which appears in late spring. Minced fine, the sour leaves give tuna, pasta, and chicken salads a lemony twist.

Wood sorrel (*Oxalis acetosella*) can give your recipes a lemony tang.

ingenious
RECIPES

5-Minute Kitchen Wreath

Here's a "recipe" for a completely edible herb wreath that you can twist together in five minutes from Jim Long, author of *Classic Herb Blends*. Jim has created many unique herbal crafts during his years at Long Creek Farm in Oak Grove, Arkansas.

EDIBLE WREATH

Gather the following fresh herbs:

Several leaves or flower stems of garlic or onion chives

2 or 3 sprigs of rosemary, 8 to 12 inches long

2 or 3 sprigs marjoram, 5 to 6 inches long

2 or 3 parsley leaves with long stems

1. To make the wreath, lay the chives together unevenly so that the ends do not meet.

Chive stems

2. Twist the chives together like a rope, then make a circle about 5 inches in diameter, pinch ends together, and hold with one hand to keep from unraveling.

3. Twist the first sprig of rosemary into the chives, then keep twisting as you add the remaining sprigs. Keep twisting to incorporate the remaining herbs, tucking the end of each herb under part of the previous herb.

Twist herbs together

4. Continue around the circle until you have a small wreath.

5. With a little practice, you can twist the wreath together and tuck the ends in and under so it will hold together by itself, but feel free to bind it together with string if it seems too loose. When finished, add a decorative ribbon.

6. Hang the cooking wreath in the kitchen, or use it to decorate a bottle of herbal vinegar. To use, remove the ribbon (as well as any string) and toss the wreath into soup or stew during the last half hour of cooking.

Finished wreath

ingenious
RECIPES

Gourmet Preserves with Herbs

Fresh herbs add a gourmet touch to home-made jams, jellies, conserves, chutneys, and other pantry treats. Simply place one or two fresh herb sprigs in sterilized jars before pouring in the hot preserves. The flavor and fragrance are subtle, providing an intriguing memory of summer flavors and fragrances.

Another idea is to place a pretty leaf like a rose-scented geranium on top of the fruit before sealing, using a sterilized spoon to submerge the leaf. It's more for looks than flavor, but it will make a sweet reminder of summer when you open the jar in January!

DELECTABLE PRESERVE-HERB COMBINATIONS:

Apple jelly with rose-scented geranium, cinnamon basil, or sage

Peach preserves with bronze fennel or holy basil

Grape jelly with thyme

Tomato jam with rosemary

Plum jam with anise hyssop or lemongrass

Pear butter with nutmeg-scented geranium or bronze fennel

Strawberry jam with lemon verbena, lemon basil, or lemon balm

ingenious
RECIPES

Pesto— Not Just for Basil!

Traditionally, pesto is made from fresh basil—lots of it—ground with fruity olive oil, garlic, Parmesan cheese, and pine nuts and is served hot or cold over linguine. But you don't have to wait for summer and a stand of fresh basil to make pesto. Try making pesto with watercress, spinach, parsley, mint, dill, cilantro, or chives—you can even try a combination of these herbs.

BASIC PESTO SAUCE

2 cups fresh greens or herbs (tough stems removed), coarsely chopped

2 cloves garlic, minced or chopped (more to taste)

¼ cup Parmesan cheese

2 tablespoons toasted nuts or seeds, such as pine nuts, walnuts, pistachios, sunflower seeds, or pumpkin seeds

½ cup extra-virgin olive oil

1 pound linguine, cooked

Salt and pepper (to taste)

Place fresh herbs or greens, garlic, cheese, and nuts or seeds in a blender or food processor. Add olive oil in a steady stream until you have a smooth puree. Toss pesto with linguini. Add salt and pepper, then garnish with more cheese and nuts, if desired.

Yield: about 1 cup of pesto sauce

ingenious RECIPES

Skinny Veggie-Herb Sauces

Looking for skinny sauces to dress up your favorite dishes? Vegetable juice sauces seasoned with fresh herbs are the perfect solution, and the technique is simple. Juice a few vegetables, simmer, add a little thickener such as arrowroot powder, then remove from the heat and whisk in some herbs.

Root vegetables like carrots and beets are good candidates for sauces and produce brightly colored, clear sauces that keep for up to two weeks in the refrigerator. Use these sauces with fish or meats—they also make good dips for raw or roasted vegetables.

Vegetable herb sauces are fat-free unless you add a small amount of browned butter to give the sauce a silkier texture. To brown butter, sauté unsalted butter in a small saucepan until it turns golden.

Here's one versatile gourmet herb-veggie sauce to add to your low-fat repertoire.

CARROT DILL SAUCE

2 large carrots, juiced in a juice extractor

1 teaspoon arrowroot powder dissolved in 2 tablespoons water

1 teaspoon rice vinegar or lemon juice

1 teaspoon fresh dill, finely chopped

1 teaspoon fresh chives, finely chopped

½ teaspoon browned butter (optional)

Whisk carrot juice in a small pan over medium heat until it begins to bubble. Add arrowroot mixture and simmer until sauce thickens. Whisk in vinegar or lemon juice. Remove from heat. Add dill and chives, and blend gently. Stir in browned butter. Serve sauce warm or cold. Try with grilled chicken, poached salmon, or baked potatoes.

ingenious RECIPES

Low-Fat Herb Mayonnaise

Here's an herbal spread that stands up to mayonnaise, without the fat or cholesterol. Use it on sandwiches as well as to dress leftover meats or poached fish. It doesn't keep long, so make small batches as needed.

HERB MAYONNAISE

2 tablespoons rice vinegar (or herbal vinegar such as tarragon)

2 tablespoons Dijon mustard

2 tablespoons minced capers or pickled nasturtiums

½ cup mixed fresh herbs and greens, such as sorrel, parsley, arugula, watercress, chervil, mint, and tarragon, stems removed, coarsely chopped

6 tablespoons extra-virgin olive oil

Salt to taste

Place vinegar, mustard, capers, herbs and greens, olive oil, and salt in a food processor or blender. Process until well blended. Serve immediately. Store any remaining sauce in the refrigerator, where it will keep for two to three days.

Yield: about ½ cup

Prevent the Itch of *Poison Ivy*

Instead of rubbing jewelweed plants on your skin to ease the itch of poison ivy, try drinking jewelweed tea to *prevent* the rash.

Mary Ann Burke, of Smallwood, New York, says, "In summer, I make jewelweed tea and freeze it. I drink the tea before poison ivy season starts—one cup in March, and another cup in April. That's all it takes." Mary Ann is highly allergic to poison ivy, but she hasn't had more than a few spots since using this tea.

To make jewelweed tea, Mary Ann simmers "a good handful" of the leaves in 2 cups of water for five minutes. Cool, strain, and freeze the liquid until spring.

Use jewelweed (*Impatiens capensis*) to make a tea that prevents poison ivy.

Help from **Honey-Herb** Mixtures

Preserving herbs in honey captures all of the plant's goodness—and the results are easy to swallow. "Honey has been used as a preservative since ancient times," explains herbalist Chanchal Cabrera, owner of Gaia Garden Herbal Dispensary in Vancouver, British Columbia. "In fact, honey is both sterile and an excellent solvent."

To make herb honeys, it's important to use only dried herbs because the moisture in fresh herbs may dilute the honey, enabling bacteria such as botulism to grow. Sterilize a glass jar: wash it, dry it, then fill it with boiling water and let it stand for five minutes. Let it air-dry completely. Fill the jar with the dried herb—chop or grind tough root parts or hard ingredients like rose hips first. Then cover the herbs with unpasteurized honey.

You should note that honey sold in grocery stores is usually pasteurized. Unless the label says otherwise, assume the honey is pasteurized. Gourmet shops and health food stores usually carry unpasteurized honey, or for a real adventure, search out a local beekeeper and buy your honey direct from the source.

Chanchal says she typically uses dried marsh mallow root, slippery elm bark, thyme, sage, or hyssop, all of which are used to soothe coughs and sore throats.

After preparing them, let your honey-herb mixtures steep in a cool, dark place for two weeks, then strain and rebottle them. To use herb honeys, take by the teaspoonful or dissolve a teaspoonful into a soothing cup of herbal tea.

Timely tip

Chanchal adds that local honey is beneficial even without herbs, so buy it whenever possible. "Exposure to the pollen gathered in the honey-making process helps build up natural immunity to potential allergens. One of the best remedies for hay fever is to take 1 to 2 teaspoons of local, raw, unpasteurized honey every day." (The heat of pasteurization can denature some active compounds.)

"For this method to work, it's important to get a head start. Begin taking local honey in the fall to prevent or alleviate spring allergy attacks," Chanchal recommends.

Grow Your Own **Echinacea**

Echinacea, widely known for its immune-stimulant properties, is now the top-selling herbal product in the United States. But at $13 an ounce, it makes sense to grow your own supply of echinacea by planting easy-to-grow purple coneflowers (*Echinacea purpurea*). And contrary to what you might have read or heard, you don't need to destroy the beautiful plants by harvesting the roots.

"Every part of *Echinacea purpurea* has active healing properties," claims Rosemary Gladstar, a well-known herbalist and author of *Herbal Healing for Women*, who makes her home in East Barre, Vermont. "You don't need to use any roots to make an effective echinacea tincture that helps ward off a cold or boosts your immunity after an illness. I harvest the flowering tops—the stalk, leaves, and unopened flower buds from new growth—throughout the season. The plant will keep growing and you can harvest again in a few weeks."

Purple coneflower roots were used in traditional Native American remedies when the plants were very abundant. "That doesn't mean that the other parts of the plant are useless— they just weren't studied," Rosemary says. "And because echinacea is now so popular, it's been overharvested from the wild by poachers eager to make a quick buck."

To help preserve the remaining stands of native coneflowers, which were once widespread in America's heartland, Rosemary urges everyone to grow their own echinacea for tincture or buy products that clearly state that they've been made from organic cultivated plantings of purple coneflower.

"*Echinacea purpurea* is the easiest variety to grow and makes an excellent tincture," Rosemary says. "It will grow almost anywhere in full sun to part shade. Two or three plants will spread into a generous clump in several years. You can begin making your own tincture from the flowering tops during the first year of growth," she says.

Homemade Tinctures

To make your own tincture from fresh herbs (which will be a lot less expensive than the store-bought variety), loosely fill a clean glass jar with the plant material. Cover with vodka, minimum 60 proof. (The ratio should be about 2:1, alcohol to plant.) Cap the jar tightly, label, and date it. Let the tincture steep for two to three weeks at room temperature, then strain it. Pour some tincture into an eye-drop bottle for daily use (again label and date it), and store the remainder in a glass jar in a cool, dark place. The tincture will keep for up to five years. Refill the eye-drop bottle as needed.

You can use the stalks, leaves, and buds of purple coneflowers—not just the roots—to make medicinal tinctures.

homegrown HINTS

HERBS FOR MEDICINE MAKERS

Pay attention to what you plant if you're interested in growing medicinal herbs to make homemade remedies such as teas, tinctures, and herb-infused oils (use only dried herbs for these). Look for strains of herbs developed for higher concentrations of essential oils and other chemicals responsible for the healing action of the plant when you're planning your herb garden.

Janika Eckert, manager of the herb seed program at Johnny's Selected Seeds in Albion, Maine, says they now offer strains of many medicinal herbs, including St.-John's-wort, calendula, valerian, marsh mallow, lemon balm, chamomile, marjoram, agrimony, caraway, dill, sage, summer savory, and yarrow, that contain significantly more essential oil in their leaves.

"Many of these cultivars have been developed in Germany, where extensive research has been done on the effectiveness of medicinal herbs," advises Janika. Some of the powerhouse herbs that you may want to try include 'Erfurter Orangefarbige' calendula, 'Bona' and 'Bodegold' chamomile (two varieties of German chamomile), 'Topas' St.-John's-wort, 'Aromata' summer savory, and 'Proa' yarrow.

Southern Exposure Seeds in Earlysville, Virginia, and Richter's in Canada also offer a selection of herb varieties specifically developed for medicinal uses.

Sage Cools "Power Surges"

"Sage (*Salvia officinalis*) is a great help for women in their menopausal years," says herbalist Susun Weed, author of *Menopausal Years—The Wise Woman Way*. Susun reports that there is no other herb as effective as sage for drying up sweats that accompany some women's hot flashes. "One dose can provide relief within two hours, and the effects can last for up to two days."

Susun finds that with regular use, the nutrients in sage (notably calcium, potassium, zinc, and thiamine) can ease nerves, headaches, dizziness, trembling, and emotional swings. Sage also has antiseptic and antioxidant qualities. As if that's not enough, using the tea as a hair rinse darkens graying hair!

If you use sage as a remedy, Susun cautions to not go overboard, as it will cause dry mouth. She recommends 1 to 2 tablespoons of very strong tea one to eight times daily (that's one cup of tea sipped throughout the day) or 15 to 40 drops of the tincture one to three times a week. Also, do not use sagebrush (*Seriphidium tridentatum*), which is also known as *Artemisia tridentata,* internally—that's a completely different plant.

To make the sage tea, use 1 ounce of dried sage or 2 ounces of fresh sage to 4 cups of boiling water; brew for at least one hour.

Herbal Calcium **Boosters**

Looking for an ingenious way to boost your daily dose of calcium? Try herbs!

Sage, nettles, yellow dock, chickweed, red clover flowers, oat straw (the stems of oats that are harvested when the oats are green rather than dried), parsley, raspberry leaves, plantain leaves and seeds, borage, and dandelion leaves are all excellent sources of dietary calcium and are easily absorbed by the body. Make some tea with these leaves, singly or mixed, and drink 2 cups daily. This tea will provide approximately 250 to 300 milligrams of calcium.

In addition, if you use a juice extractor, chickweed, dandelion, and parsley are excellent when juiced along with vegetables and fruits. Try them with a blend of carrot, apple, and celery.

Timely tip

As you're working to build your calcium intake, remember that certain foods, most notably soft drinks, coffee, sugar, salt, and alcohol, deplete calcium from the body.

Garden **Soother** for *Bee Stings*

For quick relief, look for plantains (*Plantago* spp.), a common weed that grows just about everywhere. Rub the leaf vigorously between your thumbs (or chew the leaf) to extract some juice, and press the juice on the sting. Whew! Repeat as needed until the pain is gone. Both the broad-leaved and the narrow-leaved plantain work, although the broad-leaved form is juicier.

Another way to take advantage of the healing power of plantain is to grow ornamental cultivars. Here are two varieties recommended by freelance garden writer and nursery owner Nancy Ondra, of Emmaus, Pennsylvania: purple-leaved plantain (*Plantago major* 'Rubrifolia'), which has purple foliage, and rose plantain (*Plantago major* 'Rosularis'), which has the well-known green leaves, but in place of the common flower spike, grows green bracts that look like tiny green roses.

Nancy says that both of these plants are fun to grow in the garden as ornamentals. But they will self-sow. To prevent that, simply pinch off the flower heads before they set seed. "Actually, there's no need to let the purple-leaved plantain flower spikes even bloom. The beauty of the plant is the foliage. For the rose plantain, simply pinch off the green roses as they start to fade."

Timely tip

If you happen to be in your garden when a bee stings, there are two garden flowers you can turn to for relief. Bee balm leaves (*Monarda didyma*) and calendula flowers (*Calendala officinalis*) also take away the sting. Use them just as you would a plantain leaf.

Broad-leaved plantain (*Plantago major*), *left,* and Narrow-leaved plantain (*Plantago lanceolata*), *right,* can be used to soothe bee stings and insect bites.

Magic Mint Mask

"Summer heat and sweat can cause even the nicest skin to get a little ragged," admits Stephanie Tourles, licensed aesthetician and author of *The Herbal Body Book* and *Natural Foot Care*. "For just pennies, this refreshing mask sloughs off dead skin cells, absorbs excess oil, and refines your pores."

To make the mask, you'll need ten large peppermint leaves, ⅓ cup water, and 1 tablespoon white clay (available at health food stores or through mail order sources). Put the peppermint and water in the blender, and puree until green and frothy. Strain out the solids.

Place the clay in a small bowl. Add enough mint liquid to make a spreadable paste. Spread paste onto your clean face, keeping it away from your eyes. Lie down and relax until the paste is dry. ("If the doorbell rings, don't answer it!" says Stephanie.)

Rinse your face with tepid water, then blot gently to dry. Look in the mirror and admire the beautiful results.

Homemade Herbal *Aftershave* Splash

Most cosmetic recipes are formulated for women, but here's an easy recipe for men from Rita C. Karydas, owner of Lunar Farms, who makes and sells her own line of herbal body care products in Gilmer, Texas.

This recipe focuses on homegrown herbs and pantry staples, with the exception of the optional addition of benzoin, a resin extracted from a tropical tree. "Benzoin is super for aftershave as it soothes dry cracked skin and helps retain skin elasticity," says Rita. "It also has fixative qualities, which enhance the fragrance of other ingredi-

ents." (To purchase benzoin, check your local health food store or order from an herbal supplier. For this recipe, look for liquid resin benzoin, rather than solid benzoin, because it will mix easily.)

"This recipe is just to get you started," adds Rita. "Experiment with herbs and spices that appeal to you. Vanilla beans are one of my favorites."

Herbal Aftershave

2 cups witch hazel

Handful of fresh rosemary and mint leaves, bruised

2 medium-sized fresh comfrey leaves, chopped

2 cinnamon sticks

10 whole cloves

2 to 4 strips each, orange and lemon peel

10 drops benzoin resin (optional)

1 sprig rosemary or mint

Place witch hazel, rosemary, mint, and comfrey in a large jar. Steep in a cool dark place for four to six weeks, or longer if you want a stronger fragrance. Strain liquid into a measuring cup to make it easy to pour into another clean bottle. Add cinnamon sticks, cloves, orange and lemon peels, and benzoin, as well as a decorative sprig of rosemary or mint. Label and date. Aftershave will keep for up to a year, or longer if stored in a cool place.

Yield: about 2 cups of aftershave

Easy-to-Make Herb Stamps

Have a favorite herb you'd like to use as a personal logo? There's no need to buy a rubber stamp when you have the real thing growing right there in your garden.

New Jersey artist Laura Donnelly Bethmann, author of *Nature Printing with Herbs, Fruits and Flowers,* offers an easy technique for leaf stamping. "The only materials required are a stamp pad and a leaf," says Laura, "but it's good to have waxed paper and tweezers on hand, too."

You can use Laura's technique to personalize recipe cards, labels for homemade goodies, stationery and gift wrap, or even an herb diary. "Stamp-pad ink adheres especially well with herbs that have downy, textured, or curiously shaped leaves, like lamb's ears, sage, wormwood, geranium, lady's mantle, or sprigs of oregano and rue," Laura suggests. "I've also had good results with feathery leaves like yarrow and chamomile. You may want to practice on bond or newsprint paper a few times until you get a feel for how much ink is needed and how much pressure to apply."

1. Lay the leaf underside down onto the stamp pad. (The leaf veins are usually more pronounced on the underside.) Sponge-type stamp pads sold for stamping projects work best.

2. Cover the leaf with a small piece of wax paper. Press all around, feeling through the paper. Make sure the ink adheres to the leaf, but don't ink it completely, or the texture will be lost.

3. Remove the leaf from the stamp pad with tweezers.

4. Lay the leaf on the project paper. Cover it with a small piece of newsprint paper, and press with the heel of your hand. If the leaf is large, hold it in place with the thumb of one hand, and press all around with the other hand. Remove the newsprint, and lift the leaf with the tweezers. If the print lacks detail, there's too much or too little ink. To remove excess ink, press the leaf onto the practice paper a few times. If the image doesn't improve, try a fresh leaf. The ink should dry within 15 minutes; then your project is ready to use.

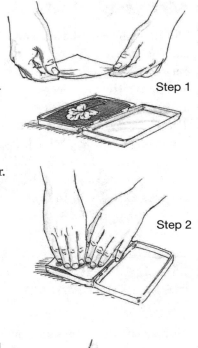

Step 1

Step 2

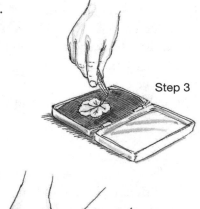

Step 3

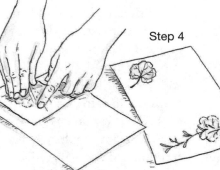

Step 4

Use leaves from your garden and a stamp pad to create beautiful customized stationery.

Herb-Dyed
Easter Eggs

"Coloring Easter eggs with natural plant dyes is an organic and wonderful way to introduce children to herbs," says Rhonda Hart, author of *Easter Eggs by the Dozen,* who has created and tested dozens of egg-decorating projects with her family in Chattaroy, Washington. "Eggs symbolize new life, hope, and joy. What better way to celebrate spring?"

Rhonda says the process couldn't be easier. Gather the plant materials, simmer them for an hour, and then add the eggs. "The mistake most people make is that they don't use enough plant material. It takes a whole pot of herbs to create good color. And don't expect the neon colors that artificial dyes render. Natural dyes reflect their source— beautiful earthy tones."

Use hard-boiled or raw eggs for this project. Raw eggs may be blown out after dyeing. Since a small amount of dye leaches into the egg through the porous shell, be aware that not all herb-based dyes are safe to eat. Also, never eat eggs that are unrefrigerated for more than two hours.

Loosely fill a 2-quart stainless steel or enamel stockpot with the chosen herb, and cover with water. Bring the water to a boil. Cover the pot and simmer for one hour. Let water cool to room temperature. Add hard-boiled or raw eggs to the pot of herbs, making sure to cover with water. Leave eggs in dye bath until they reach the desired shade—which may mean overnight. Remove eggs from dye bath, and blot dry.

Herb Dyes

Stinging nettle greens *(Urtica dioica)* yield khaki green

Sage leaves yield a soft greenish gray

Fresh dandelion flower heads yield bright yellow

Marigolds yield a deeper yellow or orange

Larkspur blossoms yield blue

Red onion peels yield red

Hops yield brown

Note: Here's an extra tip for harvesting stinging nettle. Wear heavy gloves, long sleeves, and let only your scissors touch the plant. Use tongs to handle the stalks once indoors.

Fresh Face
Herb Toner

"My recipe for an inexpensive facial toner is gentle enough to use on a baby's skin," says Katherine Glynn, owner of The Fragrant Garden in Port Perry, Ontario. "The lactose in the milk provides cleansing action while the butterfat softens the skin."

Note: Use fresh herbs, not dried.

Herbal Face Toner

1 cup buttermilk

2 tablespoons peppermint leaves, finely chopped

1 tablespoon rosemary leaves, finely chopped

1 tablespoon lavender flowers

Place buttermilk in a small glass or ceramic bowl. Stir in the peppermint, rosemary, and lavender. Cover the mixture with plastic wrap and let steep overnight in the refrigerator. Strain.

To use, dip a cotton ball in the infusion and gently wipe your face and throat. Rinse your face with tepid water and blot dry. Store any remaining toner in the refrigerator. Use leftovers within 3 days or freeze into ice cubes; thaw as needed.

Sweet Dreams with Herb-Stuffed Pillows

"Selecting herbs for dreams is a form of aromatherapy," explains Jim Long, owner of Long Creek Herbs in Oak Grove, Arkansas, and author of *Profits with Dream Pillows*. "Certain flowers and herbs have been found to evoke various kinds of dreams. In fact, 'comfort pillows,' as they were once called, were used in hospitals and sickrooms to ease the nightmares that the odors in those places can trigger."

Jim points out that dream blends are different from potpourri. "The fragrance is subtle and should only be slightly noticeable. During sleep, your head rolls around on the pillow, which lightly crushes the herbs to release their aromas."

He adds that you should begin to notice a change in the kind of dreams you have within a night or two. "For best results, use the dream pillow for seven to ten days, then remove it and sleep without it for that same length of time."

Jim also cautions against using any kind of essential oil in dream blends. Essential oils are so potent that the effects can be overwhelming after many hours of exposure.

Most people respond very well to dream pillows, but you may have allergies. The cure is simple—if you start sneezing, stop using your pillow.

Here's Jim Long's herbal blend recipe, formulated to stimulate quiet, peaceful dreams:

Peaceful Dreams Herb Blend

½ cup dried rose petals

½ cup dried mugwort

⅛ cup dried rosemary

¼ cup dried lavender flowers

1 tablespoon dried sweet marjoram

Combine rose petals, mugwort, rosemary, lavender, and marjoram. Seal them in a plastic bag to allow fragrances to blend for about 2 days.

To use, remove ¼ cup of the dream blend and place it in a little cloth bag, such as a 3 × 5-inch cotton drawstring bag—it's easy to make one yourself. Tie the bag closed and place it in your pillowcase. You'll have enough mix to make a pillow for a friend.

Make a Versatile Herbal Body Rinse

"Herbal body rinses are a snap to make and have multitudes of cosmetic uses," claims Stephanie Tourles, owner of September's Sun Herbal Soap Company in West Hyannisport, Massachusetts, and author of *The Herbal Body Book*. "I use this recipe as a body and hair rinse after showering to soften and restore the natural pH. It also makes a soothing and deodorizing soak for smelly feet."

Stephanie recommends fresh sage leaves for brunettes and chamomile flowers for blondes and redheads.

Multipurpose Herbal Rinse

½ cup chopped sage leaves or whole chamomile flowers, tightly packed

1 teaspoon borax (check the laundry aisle in the grocery store)

6 cups boiling water

½ cup apple cider vinegar

Place borax and sage or chamomile in a large saucepan or bowl. Pour in boiling water. Steep for 15 minutes. Stir in vinegar. Strain. Use liberally as a rinse for hair and body, or pour into a pan and soak feet. Refrigerate any leftovers for up to 10 days.

Fragrant Potpourri *Bookmarks*

Crafting an herbal bookmark like the one shown below is a fun way to use your home-made potpourri, and it makes a thoughtful gift—but be sure to make an extra one for yourself. You'll need to buy ½ yard of 2-inch-wide decorative ribbon. Stamped lace ribbon looks especially pretty.

Cut a length of ribbon into two equal-length pieces. Lay the pieces on top of each other with wrong sides together. Whipstitch the edges together, leaving an opening at one end to insert the potpourri.

Stuff the potpourri between the two layers of ribbon so that it's no more than ¼ inch thick, using a chopstick to push in the dried herbs.

Stitch the opening closed to complete the bookmark.

Quick and *Easy* Herb Soap for **Gardeners**

What gardener doesn't suffer from grubby hands and fingernails?

"Here's a fragrant way to scrub your skin clean without resorting to harsh soaps," says Katherine Glynn, owner of The Fragrant Garden, a Canadian mail-order company featuring imported potpourri, essential oils, and other scented delights. "The little bits of rosemary in my herb soap lift off dirt without scraping your skin."

Here's Katherine's method: Chop 1 tablespoon dried rosemary leaves. Place the leaves in a small saucepan. Pour ¼ cup boiling water over herbs and steep 15 minutes.

Meanwhile, grate 2 cups castille or glycerin soap. Place in mixing bowl. Reheat the herbs and water to boiling. Pour the mixture over the shredded soap and let it stand 15 minutes. Add five or six drops of rosemary essential oil, if desired, to increase the fragrance. Mold soap into balls or bars, and allow them to harden, which takes up to three or four days.

fun

with Fruits & Berries

From jugs of doom to blankets of straw, garden experts from around the country offer the benefits of their years of experience for making fruit growing fun and flavorful. With these ingenious tips, you'll discover how to keep your fruit and berry crops pest-free, and how to make tree and plant maintenance a snap. Planting the right variety or cultivar can also make a difference at harvesttime, so read on for advice on choosing the most scrumptious fruits and berries for your garden.

Early Ripening Means *Fewer* Bugs

"Organic growers have it tough when it comes to apples," asserts Michael McConkey, owner of Edible Landscaping in Afton, Virginia. The fruit takes so long to ripen that it's an inviting banquet for all kinds of insect pests throughout the growing season. But Michael has a simple yet ingenious solution. "If you plant a crop of early ripening apples, you can reduce that dangerous time and create a small window in which you have a great chance of getting good fruit."

"While I was growing up, the only really early apple was 'Lodi', which made good sauce but wasn't a dessert apple," says Michael. Now there are 'Williams Pride' and 'Pristine', which ripen near the end of June, the same time as 'Lodi', but which offer big, red, tasty eating apples. They're disease-resistant, too, notes Michael. Because 'Williams Pride' and 'Pristine' ripen much faster than other apple cultivars, your chances of getting bugged by bugs are minimized.

A **Snip** in **Time**

"Thinning my apples used to make my fingers sore," says Marie Bedics, a home gardener from Whitehall, Pennsylvania. "I can't believe it took me so long to wise up and switch to scissors!" Marie uses a pair of regular all-purpose scissors to snip off the extra apples from her trees so that she'll get bigger fruit from those apples remaining on the tree.

After the natural fruit drop (when the tree sheds lots of extras on its own), Marie steps in to thin the rest so that there's just one or two of the best remaining in each cluster. She says she used to pinch the fruit off, followed by an attempt at using pruners, but all that squeezing made her wrists sore. "Scissors are much faster and easier," she says. "They slice right through the stems."

Marie has another tip for new snippers—use orange-handled scissors. There's so much going on outside, she says, that she gets distracted and lays the scissors down to watch a bird or look at the flowers. Orange handles are easy to find, laughs Marie.

problem SOLVer

HENS: SUPER ORCHARD HELPERS

Squawk! Awk! Put a landscape crew to work in your orchard from dawn to dusk every day—for pennies! Even a small orchard will support a few chickens, and you'll have plenty to show for it besides eggs. Hens will gobble up pests, weeds, weed seeds, and disease-harboring dropped fruit. They'll provide your trees with nitrogen-rich organic fertilizer for super crops. And their loony carryings-on will brighten each and every gardening day. Just make sure your orchard is predator-proofed with a good fence before sending your "crew" to the site.

Fruitful Vines Produce *Privacy* Fast

Privacy is a problem for many of us, as more and more houses are built on smaller and smaller lots in planned communities. All the fencing solutions seem to have drawbacks—a solid wood or masonry fence is expensive, wire fences are unsightly, and hedges take forever to grow. What can you do? Solve your privacy problems with prolific fruiting vines!

Hardy kiwi vines are legendary for fast, luxuriant growth, with glossy dark green leaves and fragrant white flowers. And recent research shows that gram for gram, kiwis are the most nutritious fruits of all. Hardy kiwis are smaller and smoother than their fuzzy cousins, but they'll take winter lows of -20 to -25°F, making them hardy from Zones 5 to 9. Plant them 8 feet apart on a sturdy wire fence or a wood-and-wire trellis for beauty and bounty. Plant a male kiwi vine for every two or three females for good pollination.

Grapevines, with their beautiful foliage and delicious fruit, are also great for privacy and productivity. Choose a variety that's trouble-free in your area—for example, 'Concord', 'Niagara', and 'Canadice' are three of the best for the northeastern United States. Or try maypop (*Passiflora incarnata*), a cold-hardy species of passionfruit. This perennial vine has roots that are hardy from Zones 5 to 10, and it climbs readily on a fence or trellis.

homegrown HINTS

A NEW ERA IN APPLES

The introduction of disease resistance is the most important advance in apples, says Jim Cummins, retired fruit breeder at Cornell University's Geneva research station. A consortium (known as P.R.I.) of scientists from Purdue University, Rutgers University, and the University of Illinois have introduced more than 50 scab-resistant varieties. These low-spray varieties are certain to find a place in the home garden and in the specialty farmstand.

The most successful introduction from Cornell's program so far is 'Liberty'. There are three new varieties from the P.R.I. cooperative (often identified by the letters "pri" somewhere in their names): 'Pristine,' Enterprise,' and 'GoldRush'. 'Pristine' is an early-maturing variety, while 'Enterprise' and 'GoldRush' mature late and are designed for long-term storage. Even fruit fanciers in the Deep South may soon be able to grow apples without fungicides because a Brazilian offshoot of the P.R.I. program has developed a scab-immune apple called 'Primicia' that requires little winter chilling, says Jim.

Orchard Bees for Fruitful Trees

Haven't seen too many honeybees buzzing around your fruit trees lately? The low numbers may be due to the mite epidemic that's wreaking havoc on our beloved honeybees. While scientists search for a safe, effective remedy, you can do something right now to ensure that your crops are pollinated: Order a box of orchard mason bees to hang in your trees. These peaceful native bees are great pollinators, visiting thousands of blossoms every day, and they're immune to the mites. Raintree Nursery, in Morton, Washington, sells a starter pack of orchard mason bees and a "bee condo" to house them, as well as a book on mason bees and a video, too. With these nonaggressive bees in your orchard, you won't get honey, but you *will* get heavy fruit crops.

Best of the New Breed

If you hunger for the crunch of a fresh apple in December, look for an apple variety that's a "long keeper." Long-keeping apples retain their texture and flavor for months after picking in your refrigerator crisper drawer.

'GoldRush', a disease-resistant cultivar that's perfect for the backyard fruit grower, gets Jill Vorbeck's vote as the best of the new bunch of trouble-free apples. Jill tastes all kinds of apples every year as owner of Applesource, a company that ships samplers of popular and unusual varieties for taste-testing. With built-in resistance to such apple plagues as scab, 'GoldRush' bears bountiful crops and boasts great flavor. "This is the first new long-keeper we think has top quality," she says. It's a green apple with an old-fashioned look because it lacks the polished skin of modern favorites. But it's definitely a *keeper*, in both the figurative and most literal senses of the word, says Jill: "It keeps for as long as nine months in the refrigerator," she marvels.

Add *Living* Art with **Espalier**

Espalier, the technique of training fruit trees along wires in ways nature never intended, is much easier than it looks and can be a great way to add a work of art to a strictly functional garden, says Mark Trela, manager of Fragrant Farms in New Harmony, Indiana.

"The hardest part is deciding what shape you want the tree to grow into. Once you have that decided and have the wires in place, it's easy," he says.

If the tree will be against a wall or fence, Mark trains it with a straight vertical trunk and straight horizontal branches, but if it will be a free-standing tree, he angles the trunk on a diagonal to make it more interesting to the eye. "The tree looks great any time of year," he says, "because you've created a living work of art in the garden. I don't know which season I like best: spring, when it blooms; summer, when the branches get softened by leaves; fall, when it's dotted with apples; or winter, when you can appreciate the abstract form."

Here's Mark's technique for espaliered fruit trees:

1. Set two 4 × 4 × 10 posts into the ground about 8 feet apart with the young, flexible-trunked tree (dwarf fruit trees are the best candidates) halfway between the posts.

2. Stretch four parallel rows of wires between the posts, placing a wire about every 12 inches up the height of the posts, starting about 12 inches above ground level.

3. Coax the lowest branches into position by loosely tying them with rag strips to the lowest wires. Work up to the top branches in the same manner. Generally, Mark aims for four branches extending out from each side of the trunk. "Think in 2-D instead of 3-D," says Mark. "The espalier will appear almost flat when you look at it from the side."

4. As the tree and branches grow, cut off any shoots or branches that don't fit your plan. Snip back any side branches that sprout from the main limbs, leaving only short fruiting spurs attached. The spring is the best time to do any major pruning, but since the tree is growing constantly, you may need to do minor pruning throughout the growing season.

5. Add more ties to each branch as it gets longer.

Use espalier techniques to train young, flexible trees to grow along wires. You benefit in two ways: First, you can fit an espalier tree into a small area, and second, you add a work of art to your garden.

homegrown HINTS

BATS BEAT BAD FRUIT BUGS

Codling moths and other night-flying pests can turn your dream fruit crop into a holey nightmare. But help is at hand. Bats can eat up to 600 pests an *hour*, and they will take up residence in a special bat house you can build or buy.

Hang the house in your trees, and soon little brown bats (or another helpful species) will be on pest patrol for you every night. You can buy bat houses and easy-to-assemble kits at wild-bird specialty stores and through many mail-order catalogs that offer gardening supplies. When you hang one up, bear in mind that the bats will be resting in it during the day, so site it where it's shaded by branches and far enough off the ground to avoid predators.

Taste Test
Before You Plant

Catalogs are full of mouth-watering descriptions of apple varieties, but how can you tell how sweet "sweet" is, or how tart "tart" is, let alone understand esoteric descriptions like "complex flavor?" The best way is to sample the real thing, and Applesource, owned by Tom and Jill Vorbeck of Chapin, Illinois, lets you do just that.

Applesource will send you a listing of about 100 varieties so you can custom-make your own mix, or they will send a selection of one each of 12 varieties of their choice. Recent samplers have included such delectable beauties as 'Melrose' and 'Mutsu', and antiques such as 'Ashmead's Kernel', a connoisseur variety, which Jill says belies its intense flavor with a russet skin that makes it look like an Idaho potato. 'Esopus Spitzenberg' is another outstanding apple that was supposedly Thomas Jefferson's personal favorite, according to Jill.

Applesource features a wide selection of antique varieties that they get from specialty growers. "Antiques tend to have intense flavor," notes Jill. They're wonderful for cooking too. Applesource will ship apples from late October through early January. Once you have found your favorite apple, you'll know which cultivar to ask for at your local nursery in the spring.

Fruiting for
Small Spaces

Don't let a lack of garden space keep you from growing your favorite fruit. Many fruit varieties are self-fertile, so you only need one plant to produce fruit. But if your favorite apple, pear, or you-name-it fruit needs another variety to act as pollinator and you only have room for one tree, don't give up in despair.

If you have fruit-growing friends or neighbors or there's an orchard near you, just ask them for a flowering branch of a compatible variety, and tie it among your tree's branches. The bees will do the rest! Remember: Both of the varieties must be in bloom at the same time for this solution to work.

Foil "Curcs" with *Plastic Bags*

The dastardly plum curculio, or "curc," is an insect pest that plagues apple growers. Its larvae tunnel through the fruit's flesh, causing many of the apples to fall from the tree. Organic remedies don't offer total protection, but Michael McConkey, owner of Edible Landscaping in Afton, Virginia, has found a fool-proof way to outwit the pest—he bags his young fruits to keep bugs out.

At thinning time, Michael removes all but the "prettiest" marble-sized apple in each cluster of fruits. Then he slips a plastic bag over the little apple and staples it in place, close to the stem on both sides. The bag is closed loosely enough to allow some air to enter the bag and prevent moisture buildup, but it will discourage pests by hiding the fruit. "You might think it's a chore," he says, "but it's more work to spray the tree three or four times." Bagging the apples on a dwarf tree takes about an hour and a half, he estimates. To be successful, Michael adds, choose only blemish-free fruits to bag. "There's no use bagging a fruit that's already been damaged.

"The Japanese have bagged fruits for thousands of years," Michael notes. "Today they use different-size bags for different fruits."

Staple small plastic bags over apples to protect them from dreaded pests like plum curculio.

problem SOLVer — CHANCE ENCOUNTERS OF THE BEST KIND

After a chance encounter with a 'Golden Delicious' apple tree, Debbe Burdick of Mt. Vernon, Indiana, says she learned you can reap rewards by starting with the right variety. Leaning over a fence in the neglected backyard of a derelict downtown house was a venerable 'Golden Delicious' apple tree, its branches bending under the load of fruit.

Debbe was inspired by that long-forgotten tree, so she bought a young one and planted it in her yard. Her tree is 15 years old now, and it has never felt the touch of pruners, let alone sprays or fertilizer. But she gets enough almost-perfect apples from it that she has to give some away—and she feels like a successful fruit grower. "I'm the ultimate lazy gardener," laughs Debbe. "Plant it, forget it, and pick it—that's my motto."

Debbe says that the stout-hearted 'Golden Delicious' tree shrugs off the pesky problems that can affect specimens of less stalwart constitutions. It's a great choice for gardeners who'd rather spend their time on something other than pruning and spraying fruit trees.

Neatness Counts with Netting

Cherries seem to have a built-in homing device for attracting birds, and tried-and-true mesh netting is still the best antibird bargain around, says Mark Trela, manager of the all-organic Fragrant Farms in New Harmony, Indiana. He stores his netting from season to season on large cardboard tubes—the kind you'd find at carpet stores. He cuts the long rugged tubes into easy-to-manage lengths, then rolls the flattened netting onto the tubes. To protect the netting during winter storage, just cover the tubes with plastic.

Getting the netting on the tree isn't always an easy job, but Mark says he just swoops it over the tree top, then uses sticks or brooms to maneuver it into place. The swooping technique takes a little practice and a little patience, so don't despair. If wind is a problem in your area, Mark suggests using 2-liter soda bottles partially filled with water or small weights tied to the netting to keep it from lifting up or blowing away.

homegrown HINTS

FRIGHT IN THE TREETOPS

"Scare-eyes balloons really work," asserts fruit grower Bill Hall, owner of Country Heritage Nurseries and Seed in Hartford, Michigan, who recommends the devices to protect fruit crops of any kind. He not only sells a lot of them, but also uses them himself. To get the very best results with the balloons, Bill recommends hanging them from a tall pole, about 12 feet high, that has some give—like a cane fishing pole. Then the balloons can wiggle around a lot and scare off flying fruit thieves.

The 18-inch balloons are made of tough plastic, with vivid scary eyes on four sides, so there's always a new frightful face coming into view. The devices aren't totally foolproof, admits Bill. They don't keep robins away, he says, but in most cases they do make a difference.

Time to *Avoid* Avian Temptation

Sweet and sour cherries and blueberries are so appealing to birds that many a gardener despairs of ever getting more than a taste of the crop. Netting or caging the plants with wire screening is one way to outwit the feathered fiends, but Michael McConkey, owner of Edible Landscaping in Afton, Virginia, has learned another trick. "An Amish friend from the Lancaster, Pennsylvania, area tells me that 'Ulster' cherry is one of the best cherries a backyard gardener can grow. It ripens late, so the birds eat local wild cherries first when they're hungriest, during nesting time, instead of bothering your cherries." By the time 'Ulster' ripens, says Michael, the birds have apparently lost interest and moved on to a new menu.

Michael's own trials with blueberries have illustrated the same principle. His rabbiteye and hybrid berries, including 'Tifblue', 'Misty Blue', 'Powder Blue', and 'Climax', ripen late in the season. By the time the crop is ready in August, says Michael, there's not a berry-eating wood thrush around!

Making *Pawpaws* Feel *at Home*

Large, lush leaves and rich, tropical-tasting fruit have made the native American pawpaw tree a *cause célèbre*, as pawpaw fans extol the plant to an ever-growing audience. But a gardener's burst of enthusiasm is often tempered by the cautions about pawpaws being difficult to transplant and slow to establish. Hector Black, founder of Hidden Springs Nursery, in Cookeville, Tennessee, has grown hundreds of pawpaws over the years and has found a simple way to establish the plants successfully. "If you have access to a pawpaw patch, take a handful of its soil and put it in the hole when you plant a pawpaw tree," he urges.

Hector surmises that soil from a pawpaw patch may contain beneficial mycorrhizal fungi that help generate better root growth (each type of plant responds best to particular fungi).

Hector says that bareroot trees establish themselves as well as container-grown specimens do. The trees grow slowly, so don't be discouraged, says Annie Black, Hector's daughter and co-owner of the nursery. During the first few years, most of a pawpaw's growth takes place underground because it's developing a long taproot, she says. Pawpaws require well-drained, fertile loam soil, but otherwise you'll need to do very little maintenance in the proper conditions.

Add a handful of soil from an existing pawpaw tree when you're digging a hole for a new pawpaw to generate better root growth.

Try **Pest-Free** Asian Pears

If you're looking for a fruit tree that produces sweet fruit and has virtually no pest woes, try an Asian pear tree. "It's not bothered by 90 percent of the pests that commonly bother other fruits," says Ed Fackler, president of North American Fruit Explorers and a commercial orchardist. And compared to other fruits, it's easy to grow.

Prune Asian pear trees as you would an apple to keep the tree's branches open and to keep the fruit in easy reach, Ed says. Asian pears are so productive that the fruits must be severely thinned to just one per cluster as soon as you see them developing. The heavy, yellow fruits are "crisp and sweet," he says, but flavor quality varies among the varieties. Ed grows some 70 varieties of Asian pears, but has two top favorites. "'Korean Giant' and 'Chojuro' have excellent flavor, almost a butterscotch nuance," he says. With a mouthwatering recommendation like that, who could resist adding an Asian flavor to the garden?

homegrown HINTS

MEET FELLOW FRUIT FANCIERS

In the good old days, folks could gather around the potbellied stove in the general store or chat at the post office about their gardens and crops. But unless you show up at the local diner to have breakfast with the farmers, you probably don't have much chance of swapping tales and learning lessons from others who share your gardening fancies. Enter the North American Fruit Explorers (NAFEX), a modern-day alternative to the cracker-barrel conversation. "It's the best $10 you can spend!" says president Ed Fackler, who doubles up his executive duties with ownership of Rocky Meadow Orchard and Nursery in New Salisbury, Indiana. "It's great for networking with people who share your interests."

Some of the 2,700-plus members dabble in exotic fruits like kiwis, persimmons, and pawpaws, while other members grow classic tree fruits, brambles, grapes, and other goodies. Most members are "backyard people," says Ed, although commercial growers also belong. Membership includes: a quarterly journal, with articles that members write about growing their fruits; a lending library that includes videos; and an annual meeting, often at a research university. And the group is as close as your computer. Many members are online, so advice is just keystrokes away. Visit NAFEX online at www.nafex.org, or obtain membership information from NAFEX at 1716 Apples Road, Chapin, IL 62628.

Painting Peaches

Wet or chilly spring weather can cause a dramatic decrease in your crop of peaches, because pollinating insects stay home instead of visiting the flowers. You can cross your fingers when weather like this persists while peaches are at peak bloom, or you can pull out a paintbrush and give the insects an assist, suggests home gardener Marie Bedics of Whitehall, Pennsylvania.

Using a soft watercolor paintbrush, swipe the brush against the anthers of a blossom to pick up pollen, then wipe the pollen against the stigma of a different flower. It goes a lot faster than you'd think, says Marie, who learned the trick from an elderly gardener from Europe. Marie's trees reach about 10 feet tall, so she can't reach all the blossoms. "You can tell the difference between the branches I 'painted' and ones I didn't get to," she says, "because that's where the peaches are!"

When pollinators are scarce, use a paintbrush to pollinate your peach tree. Swipe the anthers of a blossom to pick up pollen, then brush the pollen onto another flower.

Mulberries *without* the Mess

"Mulberries are just as good as blueberries in a muffin," declares Michael McConkey, owner of Edible Landscaping in Afton, Virginia. But the notorious purple stains from the fruit, spread far and wide by birds, are an unwelcome side effect of growing mulberries. So it's white mulberries to the rescue! As Michael says, the fruits are white (or pale lavender), and they lack the problematic purple juice.

His favorite is 'Beautiful Day', a cultivar that can reach 30 feet, but which grows slowly—it can be kept bushy by pruning during the summer months. The mulberries are 1 inch long and about ⅝ inch in diameter, the perfect size for popping in your mouth. Or cut them in half and drop them into muffin batter.

Weeping mulberries, dwarf or regular size, are another option, says Michael. The berries drop within the narrower branch line of the tree instead of all over the place, so you're less likely to track the staining fruit into the house. (But birds may still make unwanted "deposits" elsewhere.) And while you're waiting for berries, the privacy within the drooping branches of the tree "makes a great playhouse for kids," notes Michael.

Weeping mulberries produce delicious fruit in the late summer and create the coolest natural playhouse for kids.

Mulberries Lure Birds from *More Luscious* Fruits

Most of the year, gardeners love to have birds in our backyards. But when our homegrown fruits start ripening, our formerly welcome guests can become unwanted pests.

To keep birds from plundering your cherries and digging into your other tree fruits, plant a mulberry nearby. Birds prefer mulberries to all other fruits—they'll ignore *your* favorites while they feast on the mulberries. Gardener Pam Ruch of Macungie, Pennsylvania, even protects her blueberries by using a mulberry tree as a decoy.

There are several varieties of mulberry that have been bred specifically for flavorful berries, including 'Illinois Everbearing', 'Wellington', and 'Oscar', so you may find yourself munching on a handful as well—if the birds leave any.

But remember: Never plant a mulberry tree near a path, sidewalk, or parking space—mulberry-colored bird droppings will get all over everything.

Get Your Fill of Fresh Berries

If sun-warmed raspberries are ambrosia to your palate, make the berry-picking season last by planting cultivars that bear in succession. A couple of bushes of each variety will give you plenty of berries for your breakfast cereal and your after-dinner ice cream, so you can fit a season's worth of fruit into a single strip of berry plants.

Michael McConkey, a confirmed berry lover and owner of Edible Landscaping in Afton, Virginia, suggests starting with early summer bearers. "Blackcaps are the earliest ripeners," he says,

"followed by red raspberries like 'Latham' and 'Citadel'." Planting early, midseason, and late varieties of red raspberries will give you many weeks' worth of berries. In late summer, fall-bearing raspberries come into their own, with cultivars like 'Autumn Bliss', 'Heritage', and 'Golden

Harvest' extending the berry season until frost. Make your berry-picking easy by planting the bushes in the order they ripen, with early bearers at one end of the row, midseason in the middle, and latecomers at the far end.

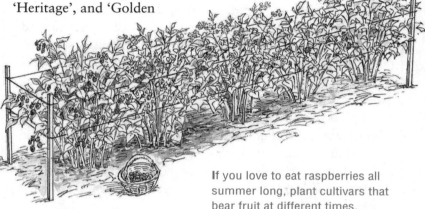

If you love to eat raspberries all summer long, plant cultivars that bear fruit at different times.

Make the Most of Strawberry Flavor

Many newer strawberry cultivars produce firm, long-lasting fruit that holds up better during shipping, but lacks flavor.

Strawberry lovers should steer away from the varieties grown for the supermarket, says Bill Hall, owner of Country Heritage Nurseries and Seed, Inc., in Hartford,

Michigan, and look for older varieties that have both flavor and some disease resistance.

> ➢ 'Sparkle'—ripens late; Zones 4 to 7.

> ➢ 'Honeoye'—ripens midseason; Zones 4 to 6.

> ➢ 'Jewel'—ripens midseason; Zones 4 to 6.

> ➢ 'Allstar'—ripens midseason; Zones 5 to 7.

To maximize the flavor potential of your berries, plant them in full sun, in a warm, protected site, says Bill. Loam and clay soils, which must be well drained, add to the taste, too. Sandy soils may make berries less flavorful. Avoid planting strawberries in an area that was used for peppers, tomatoes, melons, or raspberries. These crops may leave behind diseases that affect strawberries.

homegrown HINTS

STRAWBERRY FIELDS FOREVER

If you'd rather not replant your strawberry bed every year, try this: Treat your strawberries like perennials. Create a rich, well-drained bed for them; keep them mulched, watered, and fed during the growing season; and remove energy-draining runners. Your plants should get bigger and more productive every year. If the day dawns that the plants start losing steam and aren't producing a lot of fruit, just let them form runners that year, remove the mother plants, and start over.

Mix Up a Jug of Doom

Like many gardeners, Jeanette Manske, of Stoddard, Wisconsin, learned the basics at her mother's knee. One trick that Jeanette uses has cut down dramatically on the insect pests around her fruit and berry plants. To use her trick, you'll need a plastic milk jug or deep plastic container (like an ice-cream bucket) with a lid. The liquid in the container will tempt insects to enter the container, and they'll fall to their watery doom.

Just mix up the recipe and set the jugs or buckets among your raspberries, strawberries, apple trees, or other garden plants. One batch will usually last through the summer, but you may need to renew the recipe if the liquid in the container evaporates to less than 4 inches deep. You may also want to leave the jug in the garden until after cold weather comes so that it won't smell so bad when you discard it. The mixture has become a regional favorite, passed on from one gardening friend to another.

Liquid Doom

1 gallon-size plastic milk jug or similar-volume plastic container with lid

1 cup sugar

1 cup white vinegar

Water

2 banana peels

Pour sugar and vinegar into the container. Fill with water to a couple of inches from top. Fasten on lid. Shake well. Open lid and push in banana peels. If you're using a milk jug, keep the lid off and set the jug in the garden. If you're using a wide-mouth container, cut a few 1-inch triangular flaps in the lid and bend them back so bugs can get in.

Mix up a jug of doom to lure insects away from your fruit crop. The pests will head for the enticing liquid, then fall to their watery grave inside the container.

What to Do When the **Icemen** Cometh

Mulch and a garden hose are two weapons strawberry-loving gardener Jeanette Manske of Stoddard, Wisconsin, has learned to rely on to protect her early blooming berry plants from the tough Wisconsin weather.

"Sometimes in May, the 'Icemen' come," she cautions, explaining that this is her name for the unexpected and heavy late spring frosts that can nip the tender strawberry flowers or young fruit. To ward off the Icemen, Jeanette keeps her strawberries mulched with a generous scattering of straw from fall until after berry season. The soil doesn't soak up the early spring warmth and so stays cooler longer, slowing down bloom time. And if a nip of unusual cold does come along, she's ready with her garden hose, out before the sun to wash the frost from the plants before it can damage the buds or berries.

"I have way too much garden," laughs 74-year-old Jeanette, a lifelong gardener. Through the years, she's discovered ingenious ways to deal with garden problems.

A *Groundcover* Good Enough *to Eat*

Biodynamic gardener Mark Trela of New Harmony, Indiana, uses strawberries as a groundcover for a slightly sloping hillside on his property. "I used to spend a lot of time keeping my strawberries under control," says Mark. One summer, he tried a new approach and planted pinched-off runners on the slope where he planned to use a groundcover. The strawberries filled in quickly, sending runners to cover every bit of open space.

To plant runners, Mark merely pushes the crowns of the plantlets, many of which are already rooted, into the moist, loose soil with his thumb, making firm plant-to-soil contact but being careful not to cover the point where the leaves emerge. The berries are much smaller than those of the coddled plants in his garden, he says, "but they taste just as good." Mark also uses strawberries, and the hybrid pink-flowered 'Pink Panda' to edge sidewalks. He likes to plant them along curbs and walls, where they can sprawl over the edges, and he says, the leaves and white flowers are very pretty. Some of his gardens are along public sidewalks, and Mark says he especially enjoys seeing tourists who come to visit his historic hometown stop to snitch a berry.

Strawberries make great groundcovers! Just pinch off excess runners from your plants, then push the roots of the runners into the soil, tamping the soil with your hands.

Double Your Pleasure with *Edible Landscaping*

Why plant the usual boring shade trees and hedge plants that everyone else does when you can fill your yard with flavorful fruit *and* beauty at the same time? If your soil is acidic, plant a beautiful blueberry hedge, and enjoy its gorgeous red fall foliage as well as a bumper crop of luscious berries.

If your soil is neutral or more alkaline, rugosa roses with their purple, pink, or white blooms make a gorgeous hedge complete with deeply crinkled foliage and huge, vitamin C–rich hips. Or try cranberry bush, gooseberries, or currants. If you need a groundcover, strawberries are a delicious choice. Choose grapes or hardy kiwis rather than roses on trellises. And you'd be surprised at how many trees bear fruit or nuts while providing shade.

For nuts, think walnuts, pecans, butternuts, hickory nuts, and tree filberts. Fruits include apples and crabapples—'Centennial' is an apple-crabapple cross with bright red, sweet fruits for fresh eating—persimmons, pears, cherries, and Juneberries. For an exotic look, try pawpaws in the North and citrus in the Deep South and Southwest.

A Blanket of Insurance for Blackberries

Myron Nixon of Chesterfield, Illinois, a pioneer in selecting his own cultivars of thornless blackberries (though, as he says, other breeders' introductions "beat him to it"), is a big fan of the fruits. But he knows that some of the thornless commercial cultivars are less hardy than their prickly cousins. His Zone 5 winters can be rigorous, so he tucks in his bushes for the season by slipping straw bales under the arching canes for support and burying the branches in a layer of loose straw "until you can't see them."

If the canes freeze back, the new growth won't bear until the following year, causing you to lose out on a summer of delicious berries. To protect his berries, Myron covers his plants during the last week of

November and uncovers them the last week of March. You can use the method for any bramble fruits that are of questionable hardiness for your area. "Whether to bother with this kind of insurance," laughs Myron, "depends on whether you like berries or leaves."

A little blanket of straw goes a long way toward protecting brambles from cold weather. Slip bales of straw under the canes to support them, then bury the entire bush in loose straw.

Easy Access with Slip-Through Wires

Maintaining a row of trellised brambles means maneuvering over, under, and between the wires you use to hold up the canes. Myron Nixon, a blackberry grower from Chesterfield, Illinois, uses a system of slip-through wires to make maintenance a snap. He attaches the wires, one down each side of the row to turn-buckles on the supports he uses at either end of his row. The supports are hand-me-down telephone pole crossarms he re-ceived as castoffs when the local phone company switched to using underground cable.

His support wires are also freebies from the phone company—they're the wires that used run along the roadways. But whether your wire comes from Ma Bell or your local home supply store, you can adapt his method. At the end of the season, Myron unhooks the wire from the turnbuckle and pulls it right through the row, coiling it up. Then he performs any needed maintenance on the patch with

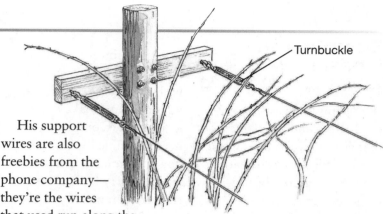

Turnbuckle

A wire trellis makes bramble maintenance a snap. Just unhook the wire from the turnbuckle, pull the wire through the row, and coil it up. Now you have access to the canes without reaching through the support wires.

free access. Replacing the wires is easy because you've pruned the long canes.

problem SOLVer

MAKE ROOM FOR WINEBERRIES

Raspberries and blackberries are well known, but one of their relatives has es-caped notice by most gardeners, even though it's a favorite among many berry connoisseurs. "Wineberries are wonderful!" exclaims Michael McConkey of Afton, Virginia, because of their complex mix of sweetness and tartness. As owner of Edible Landscaping, Michael grows a lot of different berries, but he ranks the flavorful, jewel-like wineberry number one.

For an unusual and ornamental planting with berries, try planting an arching bush of wineberries between stalwart, upright ornamental grasses, like pampas grass (*Cortaderia selloana*) or maiden grass (*Miscanthus sinensis*), says Michael. These grasses mellow to tan in winter, providing a beautiful backdrop to the fuzzy red canes of the wineberry. Wineberries naturalize like black raspberries—the canes will arch and root from their tips. The canes are hardier if they go through the winter with their tips in the ground; they produce berries on second-year wood. It may be necessary for you to prune the canes to control their steady spread, especially if they're planted between ornamental grasses.

ingenious RECIPES

Better Than Blueberries

"I like Juneberries best in a pie," says fruit fancier Hector Black of Cookeville, Tennessee. "They're better than blueberries. And if you know me, you know that's saying a lot!" Juneberries (also known as serviceberries) are delectable, and they're pretty plants too, with early blooming white flowers. Unlike most fruiting plants, Juneberries don't need pruning to bear a good crop. They aren't fussy about soil pH, and they have few pest problems.

Hector's favorite is 'Regent' Juneberry (*Amelanchier alnifolia* 'Regent')—only 3 to 4 feet tall and shrubby. It's not invasive and it's very productive. The flowers are ornamental, and the leaves turn red and yellow in fall. Hector likes everything about Juneberries, even the seeds, which are tiny, like those of blueberries. The seeds have a delicious almond flavor that comes out when you bake them, he says. And garden writer Sally Roth's recipe for Easy Juneberry Crisp will have your mouth watering in no time.

EASY JUNEBERRY CRISP

Topping
1 cup unsifted all-purpose flour
½ cup rolled oats
1 cup light brown sugar, packed
½ cup butter or margarine, melted

Filling
4 cups Juneberries, or 2 cups Juneberries and 2 cups sliced fresh peaches
½ cup sugar
¼ cup unsifted all-purpose flour
⅛ teaspoon ground nutmeg
½ cup water

Heat oven to 375°F. Combine flour, rolled oats, and brown sugar; stir in butter with a fork to make a crumbly mixture. Set aside. Grease an 8 × 8 × 2-inch baking dish. Combine Juneberries, sugar, flour, and nutmeg in a dish; stir in water. Sprinkle topping over filling. Bake about half an hour until the crumbs are golden. Let stand for 10 minutes while juice thickens. Serve warm with vanilla frozen yogurt.

Let the Sun Do It

Open your fruit trees to good health by letting the sun shine in. Longtime fruit grower Ed Fackler of New Salisbury, Indiana, says "early morning dryout is one basic thing that really helps." He prunes so that the sun can reach into the interior branches of the tree, encouraging flower bud development and successful fruit ripening. "You want to be able to see clear through the tree with no obstructions."

When branches are dense, the drying rays of the sun can't evaporate the moisture and remove the humidity that bring insect and disease problems. Dwarf trees are very easy to prune, notes Ed, and they're easy to fit into even the smallest yard. With fewer branches and less vigorous growth to contend with, you can hone your pruning techniques in a hurry, leading to bountiful crops of good fruit on a healthy, sunlit tree.

fabulous

Flower Gardens

Add a sense of adventure to your flower garden. Experiment with some wonderful new annuals and perennials or some unusual ways to use your tried-and-true favorites. Try some clever tricks to make maintenance easier and more fun. Learn about the latest plant introductions and creative combinations, then discover great ideas for soil preparation and propagation. These hands-on projects and ingenious tips will brighten your landscape and keep you in blooms all season long.

No-Fuss Zinnias

When the weather turns cool and humid, zinnia foliage often turns ugly with powdery mildew. To avoid the mildew mess, try hybrids like 'Profusion Cherry' and 'Profusion Orange'. These mildew-tolerant charmers grow about 1 foot tall and bear single 2-inch-wide flowers.

"They combine the good looks of garden zinnia (*Zinnia elegans*) with the durability of narrow-leaf zinnia (*Z. angustifolia*)," says Nona Wolfram-Koivula, executive director of All-America Selections and the National Garden Bureau.

After the Tourists Leave

When summer comes to Florida, impatiens and geraniums fizzle. But there are heat-loving annuals that provide much-needed color when the temperature turns torrid. "The best annual for heat and drought is the French marigold (*Tagetes patula*)," says Marina Blomberg, garden columnist for *The Gainesville Sun*. "Salvias, verbenas, and moss rose (*Portulaca* spp.) also do well during the summer here."

Scattering the Cosmos

There's no need to start annual flowers indoors, says Pam Ruch, a Pennsylvania garden designer. She has learned from experience that the most reliable way to establish reseeding annuals is to sow seeds directly into the garden and go easy on the mulch. "The time to sow is when the plants are dropping their seeds, anytime from midsummer on, depending on the flower," she says.

Pam carries a supply of envelopes to collect seeds when she visits gardening friends. When she gets home, she empties the seeds into her garden. By the following June, her seedlings are usually well established. Some annuals to start this way include:

➤ Rocket larkspur (*Consolida ambigua*). Upright spikes of blue, pink, or white flowers.

➤ Love-in-a-mist (*Nigella damascena*). Feathery foliage; low-growing blue or white flowers. Decorative seedpods follow the flowers.

➤ Jewels of Opar (*Talinum paniculatum*). Chartreuse green foliage; delicate sprays of tiny, red jewel-like flowers.

➤ Cleome (*Cleome hassleriana*). Showy, bushy, rosy pink to white flowers.

➤ Cosmos (*Cosmos bipinnatus, C. sulphureus*). Robust plants with abundant daisylike blossoms in a variety of colors.

Pinwheel Plant Labels

For colorful flower pinwheel labels, Tennessee gardener Dawn Flagg gets the neighborhood kids busy with crayons. Dawn asks them to draw pictures of the flowers she plans to plant. Then she traces the flower outlines on squares of medium-weight cardboard that are marked as shown in the illustration at right. She has the children color both sides of the cardboard with crayons, and then she cuts along the diagonal lines on the cardboard to separate the pinwheel "petals." She also pokes a hole at each corner of the cardboard square, and one in the middle.

To make a pinwheel, Dawn bends two opposite petals backward and the other two petals forward, so that all four corner holes align with the center hole, as shown below.

She pushes a straight pin through the aligned holes to hold the petals in place. Then she pokes the pin through a plastic straw, bends the sharp end of the pin down and tapes it against the straw.

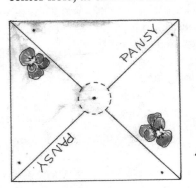

For fun flower labels that twirl in the breeze, decorate cardboard squares and shape them into pinwheels. Attach each pinwheel to a plastic straw "stem," and it's ready for the garden.

Great Blooming Groundcovers

Use annuals as bright groundcovers! It's easy to give your garden a whole new look from year to year just by changing the color scheme of the flowers you select. Try spreading colorful annuals around other flowers in a sunny border, using them to brighten the base of shrubs and trees, or cascading them out of containers. Any of these terrific annual groundcovers will fit the bill:

➤ 'Purple Wave' petunia is a favorite of garden writer Susan McClure. 'Purple Wave' will spread about 4 feet across on long-blooming stems. In addition to 'Purple Wave', you can find newer varieties such as 'Pink Wave', 'Rose Wave', and 'Misty Lilac Wave'.

➤ Tapien verbena hybrids include 'Blue-Violet', 'Lavender', 'Pink', 'Powder Blue', and 'Soft Pink'. They feature lacy foliage and long-blooming flower clusters on 3- to 4-foot-long creeping stems. These heat-loving, mildew-resistant plants are bred for use in hanging baskets or planters. They also grow well in rock gardens or along retaining walls. Ron Ferguson, horticulturist for Bear Creek Gardens in Oregon, likes to plant Tapien hybrids 18 to 20 inches apart to create a carpet of color.

➤ Temari verbena hybrids include 'Bright Pink', 'Bright Red', and 'Violet'. They have large leaves and dramatic baseball-size flower clusters on 3- to 4-foot-long stems.

homegrown HINTS

TROPICALS AS ANNUALS

If you're tired of the same old annuals, look into the increasing array of tropical flowers you can substitute for them. Debbie Lonnee, horticulturist for wholesalers Bailey Nursery in St. Paul, Minnesota, says, "There are many new plants that offer the same long-season interest as plain old geraniums, but these plants have a different look." Try one or all of the following tropicals during the frost-free growing season for a change of pace:

● Mandevilla (*Mandevilla* X *amabilis*): Pink, trumpet-shaped flowers with golden throats emerge all season on large-leaved, drought-tolerant vines. Debbie allows this vine to grow up the handrail at her back step. Plant in full sun.

● Egyptian star cluster (*Pentas lanceolata*): Large clusters of star-shaped pink, lavender, or red flowers on plants that can grow 10 inches high and wide, making an interesting geranium replacement in a container or patio garden. Plant in full sun.

● Candle plant (*Plectranthus forsteri* 'Marginatus'): This trailing plant with white-edged scalloped leaves makes an interesting alternative to periwinkles (*Vinca* spp.) as a groundcover or filler. Plant in sun or shade.

Coax Kids With a *Floral Clubhouse*

An age-old way of fostering a love of gardening in kids is to provide their own garden space. For an ingenious new twist, let them build an easy teepee frame and cover it with annual vines, suggests Dawn Flagg, the youth gardening chairman for the Tennessee Federation of Garden Clubs, Inc. "My kids love their teepee. They take books out there and read for hours," Dawn says.

Start with a dozen 7-foot-long bamboo poles. Space the poles evenly in a 3-foot-wide circle, then insert one end of each pole about 6 inches into the ground at an angle. Tie the tops together with wire or twine to pull the poles into a teepee shape.

Have the children plant some quick-growing vines, such as scarlet runner beans or morning glories (remember to soak the seeds overnight to crack their shells and ensure quick germination). Dawn says, "Annuals are better than perennials because annuals give kids a chance to replant every year."

Create a garden space for kids by building a teepee frame, then help them plant quick-growing annual vines around its base.

problem SOLVER

UPLIFT YOUR ANNUALS WITH BAMBOO

If your potted flowers droop, use bamboo loop supports to keep the stems up. Bamboo, a staple in Japanese gardens, is commonly used in its upright form for tomato staking. To support annual flowers, look for bamboo that has been molded into arches or more upright loops. The arches and loops are perfect for supporting floppy plants like cosmos, which have a tendency to lean.

They also make great supports for vines like periwinkles (*Vinca* spp.) and nasturtiums that like to grow up and over nearby plants. Bamboo is stronger, more flexible, and much more attractive than metal of the same thickness, plus it's lighter and less expensive, says Phil Hallam, bamboo apprentice with Eastern Star Trading Company in Libertyville, Illinois.

Mini-Petunia Equals *Maxi*-Bloom

For more flowers than you can imagine, plant Million Bells *Calibrachoa* hybrids. This hybridized wild Brazilian relative of the petunia has hundreds of tiny, bell-shaped flowers, each one no larger than a quarter, and it blooms for an exceptionally long time, says Jim Sims of Bear Creek Gardens in Oregon. It also tolerates drought more readily than many petunias.

problem solver

SURFINIA PETUNIAS LOVE SUMMER HEAT

For more color and lavish growth than you can imagine from a hanging basket, treat yourself to Surfinia petunias. These tender perennials grow and flower nonstop through the heat of summer, reaching 3 to 4 feet in length. Their extra-vigorous nature stems from their parentage—a large-flowering, creeping, tropical Brazilian petunia that relishes heat. "Fertilize Surfinias each time you water them. They need to be well fed to display their superior vigor," says Charlene Harwood of Bear Creek Gardens in Oregon. Use compost tea or liquid kelp for best results.

Victorian Annuals for Modern Gardens

Look to the past to fill your garden with fragrant flowers. During the opulent Victorian era, every annual garden wafted floral perfumes, reports garden historian Doris Bickford-Swarthout. Here are three easy-to-find annuals that were mainstays in many Victorian gardens:

> Sweet peas (*Lathyrus odoratus*): Sweet peas, fragrant-flower vines that thrive in spring, were a Victorian standard. Beloved favorites still available today are 'Blanche Ferry' (with crimson, pink, and white flowers), 'Butterfly' (with white and mauve flowers), and 'Painted Lady' (with white and rose-pink flowers that climb from 4 to 6 feet high).

> Flowering tobacco (*Nicotiana alata*): Another favorite was flowering tobacco, with long white, pink, or red floral trumpets and a height of 2 to 3 feet. White flowers were popular in Victorian white-night gardens.

> Common heliotrope (*Heliotropium arborescens*): Bearing blue flowers in tight slightly domed clusters, this 2-foot-high beauty was coveted. This annual was originally called by the name cherry pie, despite its vanilla scent.

Fuchsias That Scoff at Heat

If you have trouble with fuchsias that falter in the summer heat, try two new Angel Earrings fuchsia cultivars (*Fuchsia* Angel Earrings hybrids). They continue to thrive after most other fuchsias have given up the ghost.

Bred from wild fuchsias found in hot, tropical Brazil, these great garden annuals revel in heat as long as the soil is kept moist, but not wet. 'Dainty' is compact, growing 9 inches high and 24 inches across. It has small fuchsia-pink petals and purple bells, and its upright habit makes it an ideal bedding plant. 'Cascading' can grow to 4 feet wide and has pink petals and purple bells.

"These fuchsias are really revolutionary. While others collapse in heat, these stay nice and lush," says Ron Ferguson, horticulturist for Bear Creek Gardens in Oregon. He recommends fertilizing Angel Earrings fuchsias three times during the growing season with Epsom salts in addition to using a balanced organic fertilizer like compost tea regularly.

Cherry Tomato Basket **Protects** Bulbs

You can keep burrowing herbivores from chewing on a prized lily, amaryllis, or tulip bulb without paying a cent for protective gear. All you have to do is remember to save plastic mesh baskets from the grocery store, and to place one bulb in each basket when planting. The mesh forms a barrier on the bottom and sides and limits access for hungry critters.

Deep Planting Frustrates Voles

Plant tulip bulbs 10 to 12 inches deep in the soil instead of the usually recommended depth of 6 to 8 inches, and you might escape the destructive tunnels and voracious appetites of voles, says Master Gardener Jan Adams. Voles tend to dig shallow tunnels, so they won't find deep-planted bulbs. Planting extra-deep may also help tulips perform better for a longer time, since it discourages bulbs from multiplying.

Color Fun with **Tulips**

Add a touch of drama to an early spring garden by planting a tulip that changes color as the days go by. 'Georgette', a favorite of Master Gardener Jan Adams, produces a cluster of flowers on each flowering stalk and provides a color-filled show in the garden. "The flowers open a light cream color and then deepen to yellow with a red edge," Jan says. The color changes will provide daily interest.

Bold Foliage *with Bananas*

Bananas aren't just for slicing on cereal and yogurt anymore. Their huge, oblong leaves make them outstanding foliage plants. Dan Benarcik, a horticulturist for Chanticleer Foundation, a public garden in Wayne, Pennsylvania, often uses bananas as a garden high point, surrounding them with other annuals and perennials. Here's a sampling of his favorite plant combinations:

➤ Blood banana (*Musa zebrina*, also known as *M. sumatrana*) is a burgundy-leaved variety that looks wonderful with 'Inky Fingers' coleus or the red stems of vining Malabar spinach (*Basella alba*). It can grow to 6 feet tall.

➤ Pink banana (*Musa velutina*) has pale pink flowers that complement purple-leaved 'Chameleon' spurge (*Euphorbia dulcis* 'Chameleon'). The banana plant may grow to 5 feet.

The huge, burgundy leaves of the blood banana make an eye-catching combo with 'Inky Fingers' coleus.

Submerged Pots Stop Vole Damage

One of the main threats to spring-flowering bulbs are voles, which may burrow in tunnels 6 to 8 inches deep, feasting on crocus, hyacinth, and tulip bulbs. Voles may also travel through mole runs to reach your bulbs. One easy way to stop their predations, says Maryland Master Gardener Jan Adams, is to plant susceptible bulbs in plastic pots with drainage holes, setting the pot rim at the soil surface.

"Voles won't go through the plastic, nor will they come up to the surface to get to the bulbs through the top of the pot," Jan explains.

Protect your spring-flowering bulbs from hungry voles by planting the bulbs in plastic pots with drainage holes.

Circling the Wagons for Tulip Safety

Growing elegant, rainbow-colored tulips is a risky proposition if you have hungry, bulb-eating rodents around who sweep through a planting, eating every bulb. You can defend your tulips, however, by hiding a cluster of tulip bulbs within a circle of daffodils. The daffodils contain bad-tasting, poisonous alkaloids that these pesky herbivores detest.

As host of the Saturday morning radio talk show *Planting for Pleasure with Jan*, in Salisbury, Maryland, Master Gardener Jan Adams has offered this antirodent advice many times to her callers.

"I call this the covered wagon method, and in my experience, it seems to work," says Jan. She says to dig a large, flat-bottomed hole 6 to 8 inches deep. Set a cluster of 5, 7, or more tulips of a single cultivar in the center, spacing them 1 to 2 inches apart. Surround them with 11, 13, or more bulbs of a single cultivar of daffodils, also spaced 1 to 2 inches apart. Refill the hole with soil, and rest easy, says Jan.

Foil bulb-eating rodents by planting tulip bulbs within a cluster of daffodil bulbs. The bad-tasting daffodils help deter rodents before they reach your tasty tulips.

problem SOLVer

PLEASING TRANSITIONS

Interplant your beds with daffodils, verbena (*Verbena* spp.), and liriopes (*Liriope* spp.) so that you have flowers in bloom throughout the growing season and great foliage cover to boot, says Maryland Master Gardener Jan Adams.

Jan likes to set daffodils such as 'King Alfred', 'Mt. Hood', and 'Salome' behind 'Silvery Sunproof' liriope (*Liriope exiliflora* 'Silvery Sunproof') and 'Sissinghurst' verbena. The daffodil flowers shine as the cream and green liriope leaves emerge. When the daffodils are fading, the verbena fills in to hide their yellowing leaves. From July to September, liriope sends up dense spikes of purple flowers to finish out the season of color.

Interplanting
Bulbs for Dazzling Color Blends

Just as you might underplant a tree with ivy or a rose with violets, you can get double the flower power in your bulb bed by interplanting bulbs of varying heights that bloom at the same time. The resulting two-tiered flower display has more dramatic contrasts in color and texture than ordinary single-species clumps.

In autumn, plant large bulbs deeply, and put a more shallow layer of small bulbs above and around them. In spring, you'll find lower-growing bulbs carpeting the earth beneath taller bulbs. You can also mingle early tulips with later daffodils for a lighthearted blend of colors.

Combining flowers with different textures, colors, and heights creates unique multi-level displays, says Tim Schipper, a third-generation Dutch bulb merchant.

Here are three surefire pairings Tim suggests:

➤ 'Princeps' tulip and 'White Splendour' Grecian wind-flower (*Anemone blanda* 'White Splendour')

➤ 'Thalia' daffodil (Triandrus Division) with Armenian grape hyacinths (*Muscari armeniacum*)

➤ 'Red Emperor' tulip with 'Ice Follies' daffodil

Bulb Storage Success

Wilt-Pruf, an antitranspirant used on evergreens to reduce windburn in winter, also will help tender bulbs overwinter indoors without shriveling. Apply it in the fall, just after you dig up tender bulbs such as cannas, glads, and dahlias. Rinse or shake off any clinging soil and allow the bulbs to dry. Mix a solution of Wilt-Pruf (make a 1:10 dilution with water) and use it to coat the bulbs. Let them dry outdoors in the daylight. Wilt-Pruf will bond into a film that acts as a protective coating to hold in moisture. Store the treated bulbs in boxes of peat moss in a cool basement.

Wilt-Pruf was invented after World War II when people resumed landscaping in the middle of the summer. It was so hot that Dr. Luther Baumgartner came up with the idea of making an anti-transpirant that would reduce wilting problems in newly planted landscapes. Brad Nichols of Wilt-Pruf says that the product is derived from a pine oil resin and can be used to coat foliage, bulbs, or dormant plants.

homegrown HINTS

FUN WITH TULIP FOLIAGE

Instead of expecting the show to be over when tulip flowers fade, try planting a large mass—20, 40, or 60 bulbs of a tulip—with handsome mottled foliage. Tim Schipper, third-generation Dutch bulb merchant, recommends both 'Amazon' and 'Red Riding Hood' for their flowers and foliage. The planting will look great from the moment the leaves appear in spring until they begin to fade weeks later.

Sparkling Complementary Colors

While traditional gardens celebrate spring with massed plantings of identical bulbs, go a step farther by mingling equal parts of two compatibly colored, simultaneously blooming cultivars. "Integrate, don't segregate," says Tim Schipper, third-generation flower bulb merchant.

Start with two tulip cultivars that will flower at the same time in spring and that will look handsome together. Gently toss a large quantity of bulbs over a prepared planting bed, letting them mingle naturally. Plant them where they fall, and adjust the spacing of the bulbs if necessary so that they are no more than 4 inches apart.

"The mix of colors looks great together, even when a few bulbs of the same color end up in a bunch. Like fireworks or a snowflake, no two displays are alike," Tim says. Any of these tulip combinations will provide exciting color next spring:

- 'Orange Emperor' with a deep purple tulip from the Triumph Group

- Red 'Oxford' with white 'Purissima' (also known as 'White Emperor')

- Maroon 'Queen of Night' with yellow 'West Point'

- Pink and white 'Meissner Porzellan' with red 'Kingsblood'

- 'China Pink' and 'White Triumphator'

Forget Flowers, Focus on Foliage

Instead of growing a canna for its flowers, think of its tropical leaves as the star of the show. The brilliant 'Tropicanna' (also known as 'Phasion') has exceptionally vivid foliage and is striped with burgundy, red, pink, yellow, gold, or green.

Judy Glattstein, instructor for the New York Botanical Garden, says, "As foliage plants, cannas are really coming along and can produce the look of the tropics wherever they are planted. I much prefer the leaves to the flowers on modern hybrids and most usually just snip the flowers off."

Judy grows 'Tropicanna' in a large, 22-inch-wide pot beside a half whiskey barrel bearing an apricot-flower angel's trumpet (*Brugmansia* 'Charles Grimaldi') and a black-leaf sweet potato (*Ipomoea batatas* 'Blackie'). 'Tropicanna' is perennial in Zone 7 and south and can grow to 6 feet tall. Further north, dig the rhizome in the fall after the leaves die back, and store it in a cool, dry place until the danger of frost passes in spring.

How to Plant **100 Bulbs** in a Half Hour

Tim Schipper, third-generation bulb merchant, has been planting bulbs the fast-and-easy way for years. His method takes a little muscle, but is extremely efficient and successful.

1. Strip sod from a 5 × 5-foot area of your yard. Remove the soil to a depth of 7 inches, and place it on a large sheet of plywood or on a tarp.

2. Spread 100 tulip or daffodil bulbs across the bulb bed, setting them with their pointed ends up and root ends down. Don't worry if a few tip slightly to the side; they can naturally align themselves for proper growth. Try to avoid planting upside down because this may cause premature bulb failure.

3. Slide the soil off the plywood or tarp and over the bulbs, leveling it with a rake. Firm up the soil with the back of a shovel. When spring arrives, this planting will reward your efforts with a spectacular display of flowers that will outshine an equal number of individually planted bulbs.

To plant a lot of bulbs in a little time, start by digging the soil from the bulb bed and placing it on a sheet of plywood.

Next, spread the bulbs across the bed with their pointed ends up. Once the bulbs are in place, slide the soil from the plywood back over them.

The **Stars** Are Out in Summer

Make your summer extra-spectacular with big-blossomed summer bulbs and color-coordinated summer perennials. Try these combinations from Viki Ferreniea, horticulturist for Breck's:

➤ Leichtlin camass (*Camassia leichtlinii*), 'Wargrave Pink' Endress cranesbill (*Geranium endressii* 'Wargrave Pink'), and 'Mrs. Franklin D. Roosevelt' peony. If partial shade is available, add 'Peach Blossom' astilbe and common bleeding heart (*Dicentra spectabilis*)

➤ Ornamental onion (*Allium ostrowskianum*), 'Silver Brocade' beach wormwood (*Artemisia stelleriana* 'Silver Brocade'), and Chilean shamrock (*Oxalis adenophylla*)

➤ Star of Persia (*Allium christophii*), 'Royal Purple' purple smoke tree (*Cotinus coggygria* 'Royal Purple'), and white rose campion (*Lychnis coronaria* 'Alba'). Cut the smoke tree branches to the ground each fall to control its size.

A *New Direction* in Climbing Roses

Instead of training climbing roses upright, pin them to the ground, says Judith McKeon, chief horticulturist and rosarian for Morris Arboretum in Philadelphia. The horizontal habit can make roses produce more flowers than ever before. When you use wire "staples" to pin floppy-stemmed roses to the ground, they'll root along the stems and produce strong, upright shoots that bloom heavily—that's why they make great groundcovers. You can try this technique with many of the older roses that have floppy habits like Bourbon and damask, as well as cultivars like 'Louise Odier' and 'Reine des Violettes'.

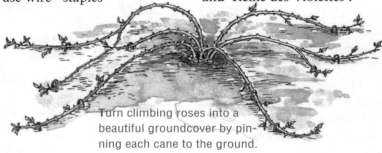

Turn climbing roses into a beautiful groundcover by pinning each cane to the ground.

Crabby Climbing Roses

Instead of building a trellis for a climbing or rambling rose, use a bare crabapple trunk to support its lovely, lanky stems. In northern climates, try this with super-hardy, disease-resistant Explorer roses, including the unbeatable 'William Baffin'.

Plant a young rose 3 feet from the tree, positioning the rose so that the stems lean toward the trunk. Build a framework of bamboo stakes to support and direct the rose stems up the bottom of the trunk. When the rose canes reach the first tree branch, they will be able to climb on their own.

"I've enjoyed this so much that I used up every crabapple I could find and now am on a quest to find other trees for rambling roses," says Judith McKeon, chief horticulturist and rosarian for Morris Arboretum in Philadephia.

homegrown HINTS

IMPROVING THE BOTTOM LINE OF SHRUB ROSES

Camouflage the barren and prickly bases of mature shrub roses with pretty perennials that offer a beautiful veil of foliage and flowers. Mixing old-fashioned and species roses with other garden plants maximizes their best assets—their height, their bright and fragrant flowers, and their colorful hips—and it minimizes their limitations, including a single season of bloom and occasional naked knees, says Judith McKeon, chief horticulturist and rosarian for Morris Arboretum in Philadelphia. Judith says there are a number of ingenious ideas for dressing up the area around shrub roses.

Remove lower limbs from large rose bushes. Prune just enough to let in sun, and leave space for the spontaneous growth of self-sowing foxgloves (*Digitalis* spp.), larkspurs (*Consolida* spp.), and annual poppies. The colorful annuals will arise around, under, and through the thorny stems.

Underplant with perennials that bloom at the same time. Judith suggests blending yellow-flowered golden rose of China (*Rosa xanthina f. hugonis*) with the petite blue blossoms of Siberian bugloss (*Brunnera macrophylla*). Since complementary, or opposite colors, are so pleasing, you may want to try 'Harison's Yellow' rose (*Rosa × harisonii* 'Harison's Yellow') with 'Purple Sensation' Persian onion (*Allium aflatunense* 'Purple Sensation') or 'Johnson's Blue' geranium (*Geranium* 'Johnson's Blue'). Another good combination is wine-colored French roses (*Rosa gallica* hybrids such as 'Tuscany') with orange-red campions (*Lychnis coronaria*) or yellow-flowered 'Happy Returns' daylily.

Feature a foliage plant at the knees. Underplant lower-growing roses with silver-leaf 'Powis Castle' artemisia. The base of the rosebush will be clothed in a veil of silver with just the bright flowers and hips of the rose emerging through. Silvery lamb's-ears (*Stachys byzantina*) also make handsome partners for low-growing roses. Choose a nonflowering cultivar such as 'Silver Carpet'.

Lobster Traps Lend **Roses** *Lasting* Support

Finding sturdy, weatherproof supports for climbing roses can be difficult, but The Roseraie at Bayfields has discovered that lobster trap metal can be molded into pillars and pyramids and is durable enough to last for years in outdoor conditions. The supports are made from vinyl-coated heavy-gauge wire—the same durable wire that has been used to make deep-sea lobster traps for years. "If it survives in the ocean, you can imagine how well it holds up in the garden," says Lloyd Brace, owner of the mail-order rose nursery.

Instead of being woven into lobster traps, however, the weather-friendly wire mesh has been formed into decoratively shaped supports to hold climbing roses. Lloyd says the support practically disappears from sight as the roses climb and fill out. The three-legged tripod design and four-legged pyramidal shapes should be planted with a rose beside each leg for best coverage. Or one or two legs of the shapes can be planted with clematis for foliage and texture variations.

Moving Made Easy

In an ideal world, you could plant a rose and let it live its entire life in that location—growing bigger and better with age. But in the real world, encroaching shade, a house sale, or a change in your plans for your yard may mean your roses need to move to a new spot. Lloyd Brace, owner of The Roseraie at Bayfields, has a no-fail method for moving roses. "Skeptics who have tried this have had fabulous results. For such a simple thing, it works so well," he says. Here are Lloyd's step-by-step directions for successfully transplanting rose bushes:

1. Scrape out a shallow basin of soil above the rose roots.

2. Attach a spray nozzle to your hose, set it for a hard stream, and turn the water on full blast. Push the nozzle into the soil all around the basin, transforming the entire area into a mud pie.

3. When the earth becomes liquid, you can tease the rose out without losing roots, especially the delicate feeder roots responsible for liquid intake.

4. Transplant the rose immediately, replanting at the same depth it grew at before and watering it well.

Making mud makes it easier to move a rose bush while keeping most of its roots intact.

A *Lover's* Salad

Toss a little love into your next salad with cabbage rose petals. The old-fashioned cabbage rose (*Rosa × centifolia*) is as edible as it is beautiful, says Barry Dimock, lecturer and writer. "Roses have been a symbol of love for centuries," he says. But he cautions that you should use only organically grown roses from your own garden—never those from a florist.

To use cabbage rose petals, snip off the bitter white base of the petals first, then toss the velvety petals with the rest of your salad ingredients.

For a very special picnic, try dainty rose petal sandwiches (made with homemade bread, butter or cream cheese, and lots of petals).

7-Up for Cut Flowers

Extend the vase life of edible flowers like tulips, roses, pansies, pot marigolds (*Calendula officinalis*), and chives—and keep them edible—by adding a little 7-Up to the water. Mix one part 7-Up with two parts water in a vase before adding the fresh-cut flowers. Don't use florist's preservatives on flowers you might eat.

Fabulous Foliage and Flowers, Too

Instead of growing a rose for flowers alone, try growing one with spectacular leaves. Red-leaf rose (*Rosa glauca*) has tall, arching red canes with eye-catching purple leaves. The single, petite pink flowers play second fiddle to the interesting foliage. "I love this rose for the foliage," says Susan Beard, garden designer and lecturer in Oakbrook, Illinois. Susan also says that wonderful rose hips follow the unassuming flowers. The hips turn orange first, then orange-pink, red-orange, and finally red, she says. And they brighten the garden all winter.

Susan's choices for perennials and shrubs that look stunning next to the beautiful purple foliage of the redleaf rose include:

➤ White and pink peonies.

➤ 'Louise Odier' rose, with gray-green leaves and pink flowers.

➤ 'Purpurea' ground clematis (*Clematis recta* 'Purpurea'), a bush clematis with purple leaves and white flowers.

➤ 'Roseum' European cranberrybush viburnum (*Viburnum opulus* 'Roseum'), with simultaneously blooming white flowers.

➤ 'Purple Sensation' Persian onion (*Allium aflatunense* 'Purple Sensation'), with deep purple flower globes.

➤ Pink Asiatic hybrid lilies and early-blooming lilies in many colors.

➤ Fall-blooming asters, with mounds of daisylike blooms in rich colors.

Two-for-One Trellises

Get double-duty from your trellises by having them bear an early-summer blooming climbing rose and a later-blooming clematis. Train an old-fashioned climbing rose such as 'Honorine de Brabany' on a trellis or pillar for flowers in early summer. Once the blooms are past, the rose provides quiet greenery through fall. To keep the color coming later in the season, plant a summer- or fall-blooming clematis on the same trellis, suggests Judith McKeon, chief horticulturist and rosarian for Morris Arboretum in Philadelphia. Judith says the clematis will twine up, over, and around the rose and provide a second floral show for late summer.

problem solver   FIBERGLASS PLANTERS IMPROVE WITH TIME

If you like the classic look of planting in big metal urns but can't bear to haul their heavy bulk around, consider using a lightweight fiberglass alternative. New fiberglass planters from Claycraft (available from Smith and Hawken, Gardener's Supply, and Plow and Hearth) have actual metallic finishes fused onto fiberglass resins, which gives the pot an authentic look. The bronze finish develops a verdigris patina as it ages, and the cast iron finish turns a rust color.

"These containers improve with age, like fine furniture does. When their newness wears off, they blend better than ever into the landscape," says Martin Gottlieb, horticulturist. A large pot usually sells for over $100.

homegrown HINTS

IRRIGATION-LESS CONTAINER GARDENS

If you're a city dweller and have a container garden on a rooftop, balcony, or windowsill, you have to make the most of intensely sunny and arid conditions. Instead of running unsightly hoses or irrigation tubing through these "every-inch-counts" gardens, consider the easiest solution: Plant drought-tolerant plants from the aster family (Asteraceae), which includes plants such as marigolds, zinnias, sunflowers, and black-eyed Susans.

Although they will still need water, even daily during hot dry weather, these plants are more likely to survive occasional shortages than impatiens, hostas, and other plants from moisture-loving plant families. Add extra compost to the planting mix, then mulch with cocoa or buckwheat hulls to help retain moisture and further reduce your container garden's water needs.

"These plants evolved in many of the world's hottest and driest geographic locations—Africa, Central and South America, and the Great Plains of North America, for example. They luxuriate in summer's heat and tolerate incredibly lean soils," says Scott D. Appell, urban garden designer, lecturer, and director of education for the Horticultural Society of New York in New York City. Here are Scott's top plant selections for sunny urban container gardens that don't have to be shackled to a tangle of irrigation tubing:

- Mexican sunflower (*Tithonia rotundifolia*), a Mexican annual growing to 7 feet tall and bearing bright orange-red flowers.

Attracts hummingbirds and butterflies even to urban rooftops.

- Common sunflower (*Helianthus annuus*), especially some of the newer, shorter, and less top-heavy cultivars such as 'Pastiche' (a yellow, red, and buff mixture) and 'Italian White' (crisp off-white flowers 4 inches across). Adds height to container plantings and provides a steady supply of cut flowers.

- Narrow-leaf zinnia (*Zinnia angustifolia*), a dainty little plant glowing with orange flowers.

- Signet marigold (*Tagetes tenuifolia*), a diminutive Central American species featuring cultivars such as 'Golden Gem' and 'Lemon Gem'. Has lacy foliage, small blossoms, and some have a citrus odor. A similar species, Irish lace marigold (*Tagetes filifolia*), has finely cut foliage and tiny yellow-green flowers.

- Black-foot daisy (*Melampodium paludosum*), a 12-inch-tall plant covered from early spring to frost with metallic yellow blossoms.

- 'Moonbeam' threadleaf coreopsis (*Coreopsis verticillata* 'Moonbeam'), a hardy and long-blooming perennial for summer and fall. Has creamy yellow flowers and fine feathery leaves.

- 'Magnus' purple coneflower (*Echinacea purpurea* 'Magnus'), produces crimson red coneflowers for about six weeks in summer. Leave the spiky central cones for winter interest and food for goldfinches.

Light Mulching Pleases *Peonies*

To be sure your peonies give you the best bloom, go easy on mulch. "Don't mulch peonies between their stems, and you may not want to mulch them at all," warns Shelia Brackley, perennial production and sales assistant at Bigelow Nurseries, Inc., in Northboro, Massachusetts. Too much mulch around peonies can have the same effect as planting too deeply: They won't bloom. So plant bareroot peonies in early fall, covering the buds, or "eyes," with about 2 inches of soil. Firm the soil from the sides, not the top, so you don't break off any buds.

Fill a Space with *Fragrance*

If you've removed a dying shrub and need to fill a 3-foot-square space, plant the perennial 'Blue Fortune' giant hyssop (*Agastache* 'Blue Fortune'). The leaves have a licorice scent while the steel blue flower spikes attract butterflies and bees, says Mary Ann McGourty, co-owner of Hillside Gardens, Norfolk, Connecticut.

Double-Decker *Decorating*

If you need to liven up a patio or yard for a special occasion, use two-tiered topiaries for quick, yet dramatic, floral displays. The two-tiered topiary system was patented by Mike Ruibal, a garden center owner in Texas, and features a moss- or coco-lined basket supported on a pole that rises from a clay pot bottom.

"I generally use this system when I decorate golf courses for professional tournaments," says Jim Kerwin of Terrona Farms in Peotone, Illinois. Jim plants a showy blend of flowers and interesting foliage to create the "really big show" that he needs for the event. The two-tiered system is also perfect for ivy and seasonal annuals.

The topiary system is available from Ruibal's Topiary Systems, The Horchow Collection, and Alsto's Handy Helpers catalogs; see "Resources" on page 317.

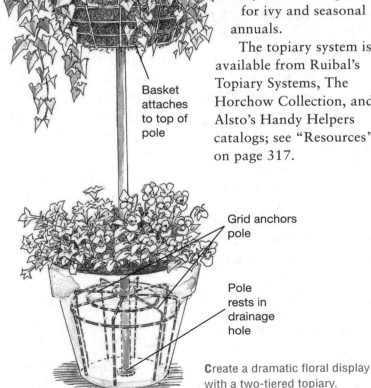

Basket attaches to top of pole

Grid anchors pole

Pole rests in drainage hole

Create a dramatic floral display with a two-tiered topiary.

problem SOLVer

NEW BEE BALM NEEDS NOTHING EXTRA

Bee balm, which has an enticing fragrance and attracts hummingbirds and butterflies, also can get leggy and have mildew problems. These disadvantages disappear with new 'Petite Delight' bee balm (*Monarda didyma* 'Petite Delight'). "It has tight internodes (the sections of stem between sets of leaves), making it half the size of other bee balm cultivars," says Debbie Lonnee, horticulturist for Bailey Nursery in Minnesota. "You can bring it to the front of the border and enjoy its nice foliage and pleasant clump shape." 'Petite Delight' bears clusters of rose-lavender flowers on 12- to 15-inch-high plants.

To care for 'Petite Delight', provide organic-rich, well-drained soil in full sun. Fertilize lightly in spring, remove faded flowers in summer, and cut back the old foliage in fall.

Topsy Turvy No More!

If you like to grow tall bananas, large upright flowers, and other plants that can catch the wind and cause a pot to tip over in a gust or storm, fill the bottom half of the pot with compost. Moist compost, which is heavier than peat-based mix, will help stabilize the pot, says Dan Benarcik, a horticulturist for the Chanticleer Foundation.

Plants for *Doting* Urban *Gardeners*

If you grow potted flowers on a shady balcony or courtyard in a city setting, and you like to water and pamper your plants, try growing calla lilies (*Zantedeschia* spp.) and Jack-in-the-pulpits (*Arisaema* spp.). Members of the arum family (Araceae), these plants love compost-laden, manure-rich, moisture-retentive soil, says Scott D. Appell, urban garden designer in New York City. They also thrive in deep shade.

If you're a hands-on, likes-to-fuss gardener, try these plants in the arum family for container gardens in moist, shady locations:

➢ Italian arum hybrids (*Arum italicum* hybrids), have striking winter foliage in silver, white, lemon-lime, and purple. Cream-color flowers arrive in spring and are followed by clusters of orange berries.

➢ Caladiums (*Caladium bicolor*, also known as *C. hortulanum*) have large, flamboyantly colored leaves. 'Miss Muffet' has creamy chartreuse foliage flecked with raspberry, and 'Pink Gem' has straplike leaves that range from apricot to raspberry to deep green.

➢ Mouse plant (*Arisarum proboscideum*) is a little charmer with flowers that resemble mice running with their tails up.

➢ 'Black Magic' taro (*Colocasia* 'Black Magic') has powdery purple-black leaves that grow to 3 feet long.

➢ Giant taro (*Alocasia macrorrhiza*) has enormous shield-shaped leaves. 'Hilo Beauty' has smaller, apple green leaves with cream and white variegation. Tolerates full sun if kept moist.

➢ Imperial taro (*Colocasia esculenta* 'Illustris') has broad, emerald green foliage with black markings. Tolerates full sun if soil is kept moist.

There's Nothing *Cooler* Than Cocobaskets

Make an easy-care flowering basket by using a woven, long coconut fiber (also know as coir) liner in a wire basket frame. Called cocobaskets, these containers have a pleasant earthy color and natural texture. "As growers, we like cocobaskets because they keep plant roots cool. White plastic pots heat up so severely in summer that they can cook the roots," says Fiona Brinks of Bordine Nursery in Detroit, Michigan.

You don't have to water cocobaskets quite as frequently, Fiona says, because the baskets are extra large and hold more soil. Plant roots can even grow into the coconut fiber. If emptied in fall and stored in a dry place during winter, some liners can be reused for three to five years, she adds.

Fiona likes to plant baskets with a combination of yellow, pink, red, and blue flowers and often includes geraniums, Swan River daisies (*Brachycome iberidifolia*), English ivy, marigolds, and impatiens for an interesting, colorful display.

Peat Takes a Back **Seat**

Replace ordinary potting soil and peat-based planting mixes with coir planting mixes for great performance from potted plants. Coir planting mixes, made of coconut husk fibers and available in some garden centers, hold both nutrients and moisture similarly to composted bark and aren't hard to rewet, like peat-based mixes. They're also naturally richer in phosphorus and potassium. "Although coconut fiber mix is more expensive than peat, plants seem to grow better in it," says Jim Kerwin of Terrona Farms in Peotone, Illinois.

homegrown HINTS

THRIFTY PLANTING MIX DOES SUMMER MAGIC

If you're spending more than you'd like on peat-based potting mix, you can cut your expenses in half and get great performance, to boot. Dan Benarcik, horticulturist for the Chanticleer Foundation in Wayne, Pennsylvania, says compost is the perfect substitute for potting mix.

Dan fills the bottom half of his pots with well-rotted compost—worms and all. Then he tops the pot with peat-based growing mix. "Young plants root fast in the peat mix. By the summer, they have tapped into the moist, rich, and cool compost, which helps them keep growing even when the weather is hot," Dan says.

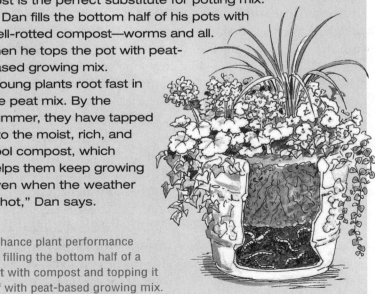

Enhance plant performance by filling the bottom half of a pot with compost and topping it off with peat-based growing mix.

Making Hosta **Bonsai**

Oriental bonsai, specially trained dwarfed trees or shrubs grown in small trays, is no longer limited to woody plants. Miniature herbaceous perennials and grasses are now accepted in bonsai with a style and grace all their own. Harry Abel Jr., a bonsai enthusiast who's been experimenting with hosta bonsai for 23 years, has an easy, step-by-step procedure for gardeners who want to try their hand at creating hosta bonsai.

1. Dig up a dormant hosta plant before the leaves emerge in spring. Wash the soil off the roots. (If the soil is dry enough, shake it off first, then wash the roots.) Cut off the thin, white roots 1 inch below the thick rhizome.

2. Cut the rhizome to any desired length, but be certain it has at least one growth bud—the tiny white bumps at the base of last year's growth.

3. Select a bonsai bowl that is 1½, 3, or 6 inches deep. Cover the drainage holes with a piece of mesh screen to keep the soil in place.

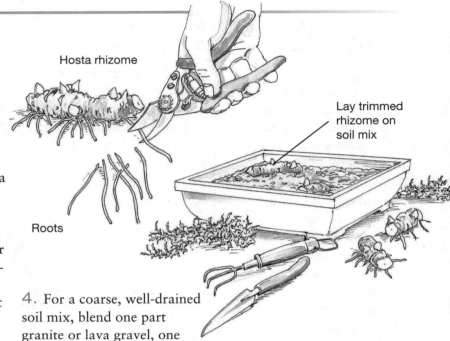

Hosta rhizome

Lay trimmed rhizome on soil mix

Roots

4. For a coarse, well-drained soil mix, blend one part granite or lava gravel, one part high-fired clay, one part ground pine or fir bark, and one part compost. Add 1 pound of organic fertilizer to each wheelbarrow load of planting mix. Harry doesn't recommend making substitutions because the soil mix's particle size is important to its success. This soil mix will need regular watering.

5. Set the rhizome pieces horizontally on or just beneath the soil surface. You can cover the soil surface with low-growing mosses or little club mosses (*Selaginella* spp.) to hold the soil in place and decorate the surface.

Make your own hosta bonsai by trimming off the thin, white roots of a dormant plant to one inch below the thicker rhizomes. Fill a bonsai bowl with a well-drained soil mix, and lay the rhizome on top of the mix.

6. Once the leaves emerge, place the pot in as much sun as possible without burning the leaves. The leaf size of the hostas will be reduced proportionately to the container size, but flowers will remain large. Remove any oversize leaves that look awkward. You may want to clip off flower and seed-bearing stems after they're done blooming.

Hosta Ideal for Bonsai

These are Harry Abel Jr.'s favorite hosta cultivars for bonsai.

Small Hosta
'Blue Cadet'
'Butter Rim'
'Chartreuse Wiggles'
'Ginko Craig'
'Ground Master'
'Kabitan'
'Vera Verde'

Large Hosta
'August Moon'
'Halcyon'
'Love Pat'
'Patriot'
'Sum and Substance'
'Wide Brim'

Banana Peels for Roses

Roses love potassium, so Lynne Kosobucki, a home gardener from Philadelphia, uses banana peels as a source of organic potassium. "I'm pretty low-tech with the peels. I just lay them on the ground at the base of the rosebush about 2 to 4 inches away from the stem. I've never had a problem with insects being attracted to the peels," she says.

Match Foliage to Flowers

Mix startling shades of foliage with vivid flowers to create a memorable hanging basket. Judy Glattstein, instructor at the New York Botanical Garden, recommends combining a yellow-and-purple coleus with orange-flowered lantana and purple-leaf 'Purpurea' spiderwort (*Tradescantia pallida* 'Purpurea', also known as *Setcreasea pallida* 'Purple Heart'). "I clearly like to mix it up," Judy says.

Self-Watering Pots for Busy Folks

Container gardening, although it can be easy, fast, and floriferous, requires regular attention to watering. An easy solution to this time-consuming task is a self-watering pot. "It's a relief to know if I go out of town for a weekend, my self-watering potted plants will still look good when I return," says Susan McClure, garden writer.

The Bemis pot, available at nationwide retailers Target and Home Base, uses a perforated platform to keep plant roots above a water reservoir. Feeder roots grow through slots in the bottom of the pot into the moisture below. An opening in the base of the pot lets you re-fill the reservoir and lets fresh air reach the roots.

problem solver

A TRUE ROCK GARDEN

Instead of growing flowers in plastic or terra-cotta pots, grow them in purchased pumice boulders. These lightweight gray volcanic rocks come drilled with 4- to 6-inch-wide openings—perfect for slipping a pot or plant inside. There's even a drainage hole in the bottom to prevent waterlogged soil. "I like to put bushy plants like mums and ferns in my rock planters on the patio," says Linda Gillespie of Far West Forest. "The natural color of the stone looks good with any kind of flower."

Garden-Lite rock planters, available from Frank's Nursery and Crafts, Gardener's Supply, and Whatever Works catalogs, come in 12- to 18-inch and 18- to 24-inch sizes.

Overwintering
Bananas Indoors

If you like big, languid banana leaves in your garden but tire of treating them like annuals and buying pricey new plants every year, try overwintering existing plants indoors. "You don't need a greenhouse—any basement will do," says Dan Benarcik, horticulturist for Chanticleer Foundation in Wayne, Pennsylvania. Leave the banana plant outdoors until just before the first fall frost. Cool weather will slow growth and prepare it for complete dormancy indoors.

Here is Dan's step-by-step process for overwintering bananas indoors.

1. Dig up the plant, leaving a 12-inch-wide rootball for a plant with a 6-inch-diameter trunk or an 18-inch-wide rootball for a multi-stemmed clump.

2. Tease most of the soil off the roots with a garden fork.

3. Wrap the base of the plant (up to about 3 feet high) in a heavy-duty, black plastic garbage bag. Tie the top snugly, but not tightly, around the trunk to hold in moisture.

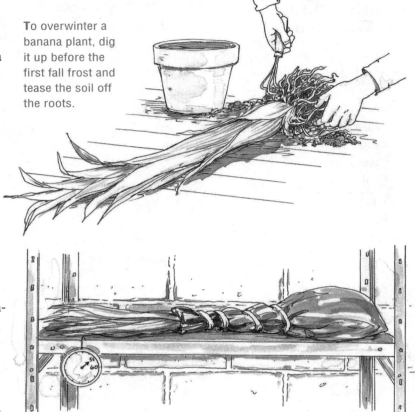

To overwinter a banana plant, dig it up before the first fall frost and tease the soil off the roots.

Wrap the base of the plant in a garbage bag before placing it in a cool, dark basement until spring.

4. Move the banana plant to a dark basement with a temperature of 50 to 70 degrees. It will go dormant and need no further attention until spring.

5. In mid-April, repot the banana plant and move it to a sunny location in the house. Resume watering and fertilizing the plant as you did during the growing season.

6. As the last spring frost date approaches, harden off the plant by moving it outdoors into increasing sunshine for gradually longer periods. Once it is acclimated and the weather is frost-free, the banana plant can stay outdoors in a pot or you can transplant it into a garden bed to grow in the ground until next fall.

problem SOLVer

PERENNIAL MEADOW FOR WHEELCHAIR USERS

Wheelchair users can also be gardeners with their own easily tended colorful pocket meadow. Even the smallest meadows, just a few square yards in size, can bring great joy, says Steven Davis, former executive director of the American Horticultural Therapy Association. Choose easy-care perennials that don't need lots of hugs and kisses from the gardener, such as spike gayfeather (*Liatris spicata*), Ozark sundrops (*Oenothera missouriensis*), black-eyed Susan (*Rudbeckia hirta*), and purple coneflower (*Echinacea purpurea*). These perennials need only simple care—deadheading, watering, weeding, and winter cleanup.

Start the meadow by broadcasting seed, a task that can be done from a wheelchair. You'll need to thin the seedlings to avoid overcrowding—this can be accomplished fairly easily if the gardener has a lightweight, long-handled hoe. Use the corner of the hoe to uproot individual or small clumps of unwanted seedlings when they are only several inches high. "The key is to involve gardeners with disabilities in the gardening tasks and have them benefit physically as well as mentally from working the garden," Steven says.

Sense-Stimulating **Perennials** for Seniors

"Flowers are a great way to reach out to older adults, especially those who once counted gardening as their favorite pastime," says Steven Davis, former executive director of the American Horticultural Therapy Association. If you plant flowers and grasses that stimulate the senses of smell, touch, sound, and sight, your garden will appeal even to older people who may have weakened senses.

Plant scented geraniums or heirloom roses (especially fragrant cultivated varieties more familiar to older adults) and furry lamb's-ears (*Stachys* spp.) that will provide tactile pleasures. Long-leaf ornamental grasses will add sound to the garden as their leaves rustle in the breeze, and butterfly-attracting plants like butterfly bushes (*Buddleia* spp.) will delight the eyes.

Pulmonarias for *Foliage* and *Flowers* in Shade

When planting a shade garden, look to the new pulmonarias for stunning silver leaves and attractive flowers. These silvery *Pulmonaria* hybrids make great groundcovers and look terrific with purple-leaf heucheras (*Heuchera* spp.) and silver-variegated Japanese painted fern (*Athyrium niponicum* 'Pictum'), says hybridizer Dan Heims of Terra Nova Nurseries in Oregon. He's also excited about the flowers on these cultivars. "The flowers are borne on compact stems instead of the old ungainly stalks that flop or break in the wind. They were selected for their rosette shape and shortened petioles, so they don't flop in the wind," Dan says.

Dan's pulmonaria hybrids have exciting features like ruffle-edged silver leaves, undulating silver foliage complemented by raspberry-pink flowers, and silver leaves edged in green. Ask your local garden center to order some of Dan's plants, or order them by writing to one of Terra Nova Nurseries' vendors (see "Resources" on page 317).

problem SOLVer

NEW KID ON THE BLOCK

Move over hostas, there's a new foliage plant for the shade garden, says Tony Avent, hybridizer at Plant Delights Nursery in Raleigh, North Carolina. It's the sacred lily of Japan (*Rohdea japonica*), a treasure seldom seen in America. Sacred lilies grow easily in dry, shady soil in Zones 6 through 10. In Zone 5, they die back during winter and take longer to reach full size.

The species has 1-foot-long and 2-inch-wide straplike leaves and grows into a vase-shaped clump about 2 feet wide. In the fall, the plants display clusters of red berries that harmonize with the surrounding autumn colors.

Fancy-leaf forms include 'Asian Valley', which has wavy green leaves bordered with a narrow edge of creamy white. 'Mure Suzume', a miniature, makes small rosettes of white-streaked leaves. 'Suncrest' has black-green leaves with a white dragon crest running down the center of each.

No-Spray Garden Phlox

While many forms of garden phlox (*Phlox paniculata*) suffer from powdery mildew unless sprayed regularly with fungicides, one cultivar stands alone for exceptional disease resistance. 'David', a beautiful white phlox, is not quite mildew-proof, but it does come close, says Mary Ann McGourty. 'David' is fragrant, grows to about 4 feet high, and bears large flower trusses from July to September.

A Collection for Small Spaces

If you like to experiment with a variety of new perennials, devote a special part of your yard to making a collector's garden. Ruth Rogers Clausen, perennial collector and horticulture editor for *Country Living Gardener* magazine, suggests starting in a small space and focusing on just a few plants. For example, put a few alpines in a stone trough, or devote an area to just one genus like *Dianthus* (pinks). "When you focus on specific plants, you'll have an opportunity to dig into their folklore, uses, and other interesting details that make the garden so much richer," Ruth says.

She also says to forget about elaborate garden designs and concentrate on giving your plants the best growing conditions you can. Ruth tries to duplicate the plants' original habitat, soil makeup, and moisture needs. She often grows the same plant in several different parts of the garden, then compares results before finding a permanent location for that special plant in her collection.

This Astilbe Will Be *Big*

A perfect perennial for milder areas, the monstrously large, purple-leaf giant astilbe (*Astilbe grandis*) has a 5-foot-wide basal rosette and a 5-foot-high flower spike. Growing from seed to flowering size in just 1½ years, this new discovery was found in Asia, where plant collector Tony Avent of Plant Delights Nursery travels in search of promising perennials. This astilbe will make an exciting conversation piece for your garden, says Tony.

Save Time with Hedge Shears

Use handheld hedge shears for fast and easy trims of bushy plants like asters, mums, and boltonias (*Boltonia* spp.), says Tracy DiSabato-Aust, author of *The Well-Tended Perennial Garden*. The long blades can do the job in 1 or 2 cuts instead of the 10 to 20 required by shorter pruning shears. Most perennials benefit from pinching, shearing, or cutting back to keep the rest of the plant looking nice during spring, summer, and fall, says Tracy. She uses hedge shears for the following jobs:

Shearing back the tips of mums, asters, and sedums in spring to encourage bushier, self-supporting plants.

Cutting off old flowers on

Make quick work of removing old foliage from ornamental grasses by simply trimming them with handheld hedge shears.

pinks (*Dianthus* spp.), thrifts (*Armeria* spp.), rock cresses (*Arabis* spp.), and others after they bloom.

Removing old foliage of ornamental grasses and cone-flowers (*Echinacea* spp,) in spring, or old leaves of peonies and other perennials in fall.

A Tidy Drink of Water

Allentown, Pennsylvania gardener Deb Martin has found an easy way to water the plants on her office windowsill without making a mess. She fills a sport-top water bottle with water, then directs the water stream at the plants' roots. The plants get the moisture they need, and Deb's windowsill stays moisture-free.

homegrown HINTS

BONSAI SCISSORS FOR TIGHT SPACES

Have you noticed that the new buds emerging on long-blooming perennials like bellflowers (*Campanula* spp.) and balloon flowers (*Platycodon* spp.) are commonly right next to the fading flowers you're trying to deadhead? If your handheld pruning shears tend to damage future flowers, use slim and sharp bonsai or never-dull scissors to slip into the smallest spaces and remove dead flowers.

"Bonsai scissors allow for careful deadheading and are the right size for small hands, too," says Tracy DiSabato-Aust, author of *The Well-Tended Perennial Garden*. Look for bonsai scissors at well-stocked garden centers, or order from mail-order garden and specialty suppliers.

homegrown HINTS

UMBRELLAS FOR VINES

When Richard Szalasny found a discarded table-size umbrella, he put it to good use in his garden: He removed the fabric cover and inserted the pole into a pipe that he'd driven into the ground. He planted morning glories and let them spill over the skeleton of the umbrella. "With the right vine, all the spokes can be covered," says Dick, a Master Gardener from Eden, New York. You could also create a smaller version by using a regular hand-held umbrella.

Wintering Mums under Plastic Pots

If your chrysanthemums seldom survive winter, they may be perishing due to intense cold or soggy soils. You can avoid both problems by wintering your chrysanthemums in a double-deck set of pots in your garage. "I saved

Holes for air circulation

six plants using this method last year. They came through like real troupers and awed me with flowers from late July through September," says David Glasier, Ohio experimental amateur gardener and television critic. Here is David's step-by-step method:

1. Cut down mum shoots to 1 inch as soon as the plant has finished blooming.

2. Dig up the rootball and gently knock away excess clods of soil. Put about 2 inches of fresh potting soil in the bottom of a pot. Place the rootball in the pot, then cover the rootball with potting soil.

Save your chrysanthemums from winter's elements by cutting them back, digging them up, and keeping them in a pair of pots in your garage.

3. Water the soil enough to make the roots moist. Let the pot sit outside for a day to drain well.

4. Cover the pot with a slightly larger, inverted plastic pot that fits snugly rim to rim. The top pot must have drainage holes for air circulation.

5. Store the double-deck pots in a protected but unheated place, like a garage or shed.

6. Several weeks before the last frost date, remove the top pot. The plants will have sent up yellow-green sprouts. Water and lightly fertilize. Gradually move the mums into brighter light until the leaves green up.

7. Plant the mums out in the garden after the danger of spring frost passes.

Reliable, **Easy**, and a **New** Look to Boot

Even though some gardeners consider the bell-shaped flowers of Jacob's ladder (*Polemonium caeruleum*) the stars of the show, the foliage on a new variety, 'Brise d'Anjou', will give the pretty flowers a run for their money. 'Brise d'Anjou' flaunts creamy-edged, fernlike foliage that looks like the rungs of a ladder.

Gary Doerr, owner of wholesale Peppergrove Nursery in Lapeer, Michigan, says 'Brise d'Anjou' grows in Zones 4 to 8 and should be planted in light to full shade and moist, rich, well-drained soil. It combines nicely with goat's beards (*Aruncus* spp.) and can be massed with astilbes, bergenias (*Bergenia* spp.), hostas, Lenten rose (*Helleborus orientalis*), and sweet woodruff (*Galium odoratum*).

problem solver

INSECT-EATING PERENNIALS IN A POT

Put perennials to work eating unwanted flies, mosquitoes, and other pests by planting insectivorous pitcher plants in a containerized bog garden. Karen Colini, landscape horticulturist with Sweet Bay Gardens in Ohio, says the bog garden is beautiful, easy to maintain, and fascinating to watch in action.

Pitcher plants, which naturally grow in sterile, acidic bogs, use insects as fertilizer. Their tube-shaped leaves contain insect-attracting nectar. Flies and other creatures slip down into the tube and are held there by a barrier of downward-pointing hairs. The insects break down into nitrogen and other necessary elements for pitcher plant growth.

Karen grows pitcher plants with sphagnum moss, bog cranberry (*Vaccinium macrocarpon*), and bog rosemary (*Andromeda polifolia*) in a black plastic cement mixing tub filled with water. She uses hardy species of pitcher plants that can stay outside during winter without any problem. "All I do to take care of them is fill the tub with water when it begins to get dry," says Karen.

For pitcher plant sources, see "Resources" on page 317.

The *Glories* of the *Gazing Ball*

Don't be an outsider in your own garden! "Gazing balls allow you to see yourself in the garden, rather than just being a passive admirer," says C. Colston Burrell, garden writer and lecturer. Bask in the glory of all that growing by adding a gazing ball—a mirrored globe of blue, purple, gold, green, or another color—to your flowerbeds.

Cole has five gazing balls in his garden. He says that gazing balls are an important color element, and he coordinates them with the colors of nearby flowers. He uses bright yellow and blue gazing balls in his shady garden, and purple gazing balls beside yellow and purple perennials in his sunny garden.

Timely tip

Instead of placing gazing balls on the ground where they might be hidden by surrounding foliage, make them seem even more magical by raising them up on nearly invisible supports. Cole suggests elevating a gazing ball on the bottom of a metal tomato cage or tall votive candle holder, which can raise a gazing ball 1 to 3 feet high.

The More, the Merrier

Double your perennial garden pleasure by planting two perennials in a single space, says Illinois garden designer Harriet Kelly. Dual plantings provide the extra color and support that make a perennial garden beautiful, right from the start.

"If you only put a single plant in each space, perennials like 'Johnson's Blue' geranium (*Geranium* 'Johnson's Blue') will flop until a couple years down the road when the garden gets crowded enough to hold the plants together," Kelly says. Plant 'Johnson's Blue' close beside purple coneflowers (*Echinacea* spp.) or 'Zagreb' threadleaf coreopsis (*Coreopsis verticillata* 'Zagreb') because they provide support and a summer season of bloom, she says. Here are other effective interplanting ideas:

➤ 'Mrs. Kendall Clark' meadow cranesbill (*Geranium pratense* 'Mrs. Kendall Clark') with cardinal flower (*Lobelia cardinalis*).

➤ Bigroot cranesbill (*Geranium macrorrhizum*) with daylilies.

➤ Armenian cranesbill (*Geranium psilostemon*) with betony (*Stachys macrantha*).

➤ Drumstick chives (*Allium sphaerocephalum*) with bluebeard (*Caryopteris* × *clandonensis*).

Peonies That Won't Flop

Peonies, which have one short, glorious bout of bloom in spring, can be knocked flat by a drenching downpour. You can eliminate that problem by selecting plants carefully, says Harriet Kelly, landscape designer for Kelly Gardens. "People in the Chicago area complain a lot about flopping peonies," Harriet says. "That's why I try not to plant big, full-headed peonies, and I stick with smaller-flower Japanese singles, instead. The singles don't get heavy and water-logged, nor do they fade and look like old tissues."

Selecting peonies based on flower type alone is not enough, though. Harriet inspects the bottom of the stem of a nursery plant, checking the distance between the leaf nodes. A shorter internode, the space between leaves, means a stockier stem and a self-supporting plant. 'Dawn Pink', a single pink-flower peony, 'Heritage', a semi-double red-flower peony, and 'Doreen' garden peony, a single pink, have passed Harriet's internode test for self-supporting peonies.

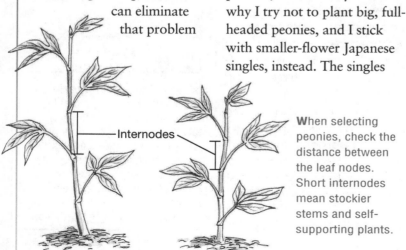

Internodes

When selecting peonies, check the distance between the leaf nodes. Short internodes mean stockier stems and self-supporting plants.

Dry Summer? Try a Durable Daisy Tree

Most gardeners recognize a daisy flower, but there aren't many people who have seen a daisy tree. This drought-tolerant plant comes from South Africa and is perfect for a large pot on your patio. "The daisy tree (*Euryops pectinatus* 'Viridis') blooms all summer, even when I forget to water it," says Julie Andracki, an Indianapolis-based member of the staff of Monrovia Nurseries. "It doesn't mind drying out be-cause it's a desert plant. If it wilts, it pops back up as soon as it gets water."

The so-called daisy tree, which is actually a shrub known as the golden shrub daisy, features finely cut, bright green leaves and 2-inch-wide golden daisylike flowers. Provide full sun with a little afternoon shade in the heat of the day for best re-sults. Because the golden shrub daisy is hardy only to Zone 8, Julie discards it in fall. In warm climates, she says, you can enjoy its flowers for years.

homegrown HINTS

THIS FALSE SUNFLOWER IS TRULY UNIQUE

Consider planting a mass of brilliant new 'Loraine Sun-shine' sunflower heliopsis (*Heliopsis helianthoides* 'Loraine Sunshine') for the unusual variegated foliage as well as its golden flowers, says Brent Hanson, plant introducer from Rhinelander Floral Company in Wisconsin. The remarkable foliage is white with green veins and is the only variegated false sunflower known in the world, says Brent. The plant was named in memory of Rhinelander employee Loraine Mark, who discovered it growing in her garden.

The sunflower heliopsis will grow in a wide range of conditions, but it does best in full sun and average soil that doesn't dry out. The plant will reach 30 inches tall, grows in Zones 3 to 9, and blooms from July until frost.

Pretty as a Picture

Make your perennial garden look beautiful the first year by adding unusual annuals and tender perennials to fill out the spaces between the young perennials, says C. Colston Burrell, garden writer and lec-turer. He likes to use fast-growing flowers that have a natural look. Cole says moss verbena (*Verbena tenuisecta*) is a good choice because it weaves nicely between the smaller perennial plants.

Cole also recommends Texas sage hybrids (*Salvia coccinea* hybrids), nicotianas (*Nicotiana langsdorffii, N. sylvestris*), tall hybrids of flowering tobacco (*Nicotiana alata*), and Brazilian vervain (*Verbena bonariensis*).

Timely tip

For a quick-maturing perennial garden that's full of just peren-nials, plant cranesbills (*Geranium* spp.), coreopsis (*Coreopsis* spp.), bee balms (*Monarda* spp.), ajuga (*Ajuga* spp.), creeping phlox (*Phlox stolonifera*), gold-and-silver chrysanthemum (*Chrysanthemum pacificum*), and Japanese anemone (*Anemone tomentosa* 'Robustissima'), suggests Cole.

Getting **into** *the Swim* with Cannas

Instead of growing cannas in soil, slip a few into a bog, water garden, or pond for a colorful garden scene that won't need weeding or watering. Cannas love a lot of water and are swamp plants in the wild, says Judy Glattstein, instructor for the New York Botanical Garden. She says to pot the rhizomes and set the pot in a shallow pan of water. After several days, increase the depth of the water. Keep increasing the depth of the water every few days until water covers the top of the roots—this will gradually acclimate the root system. Try this with 'Tropicanna', 'Taney', and 'Erebus' cannas.

Purple-Leaf Cannas Shine in Good Company

For a spectacular display of color in a garden of green foliage, combine purple-leaf cannas with blossoms of clear red, green, or purple, says Judy Glattstein, instructor at the New York Botanical Garden. Or use maroon-highlighted flowers for a more subtle color mix.

Start by planting 'Black Knight', 'Red King Humbert', or 'TyTy Red' cannas, then add any of the following: gladiolus (*Gladiolus callianthus*), clear red zinnias, green-flower 'Envy' zinnia, nicotiana (*Nicotiana langsdorffii*), or purple-flower Brazilian verbena (*Verbena bonariensis*).

Hot Daylilies for Warm Climates

If you want to grow daylilies in hot climates, says Florida garden writer Marina Blomberg, choose heat-tolerant evergreen cultivars with light-colored flowers, such as the following (most are available through mail order from Daylily Discounters; see "Resources" on page 317):

➤ 'Apple Tart', red with a green throat.

➤ 'Becky Lynn', rose with a white midrib.

➤ 'Cosmic Hummingbird', pink-peach with honey yellow.

➤ 'Green Glitter', yellow with a green throat.

➤ 'Irish Elf', lemon-chartreuse.

More Daylilies for Your Money

While conscientious deadheading keeps daylilies looking neat, it eliminates a propagation possibility. On some daylily cultivars, the old flower stems produce proliferations (minature plants that emerge on the stem below a faded flower). Dr. Winston Dunwell, associate professor of horticulture at the University of Kentucky, says, "If you can use the profilerations to multiply a $100 plant into two plants, you will come out ahead."

Watch for proliferations in late summer. They arise from a bud that grows into a little cluster of leaves and, by August and September, also sprouts tiny roots. Cut them free, roots and all, and move them to a separate pot. Or plant them beside the mother plant for easy identification, suggests Dr. Dunwell.

Some of the daylily cultivars that may sprout proliferations include: 'Coral Crab', 'Fairy Tale Pink', 'Lullaby Baby', 'Prairie Blue Eyes', and 'Siloam Red Toy'.

Have Your *Daylily* and *Eat It Too*

Don't limit yourself to a visual feast when your daylilies are in bloom. Use their flowers and buds as unique vegetables. Barry Dimock, plant consultant, lecturer, and writer, says fresh daylily flowers, minus their pistils and stamens, are a great addition to a salad. You can use the chopped petals, whole flowers, or about-to-open buds. "Lightly sauteed buds (in unsalted butter, of course) make a delightful vegetable offering to many dishes," says Barry. "And people who have a good collection of these enduring perennials in their garden can enjoy dining on the varieties as they bloom in sequence."

Even **Watering** Top to Bottom

If the water runs out of the holes in your strawberry pot when you try to water your

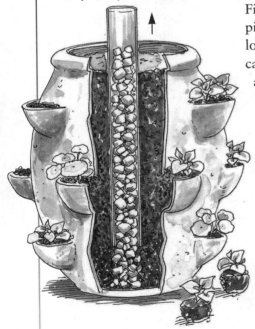

To create a watering channel in a strawberry pot, add planting mix around a cardboard tube filled with pebbles. After planting, slide the tube out.

plants, Pennsylvania landscape architect Joan Meschter has a solution that helps the bottommost plants in the jar get the crucial water they need. First, hold a cardboard wrapping paper tube (at least as long as the pot is tall) vertically in the center of the pot and fill it with pebbles, perlite, or sand. Then add soil mix and plants around it, working up from the bottom holes. Wrap each seedling in sheet sphagnum moss to protect the roots from drying out.

When the pot is fully planted and is filled with planting mix, gently slide the tube out, allowing the draining medium to settle into place. Plant the top, leaving the center open for watering. Now when you water, even the bottom plants will get their share.

Prevent Winterkill with *Summer Water*

To prevent winter losses among your roses, be more conscientious about summer watering, says Lloyd Brace, owner of The Roseraie at Bayfields. In August, roses produce fewer flowers and begin to store energy for the spring in their roots. Even though it doesn't look like the roses are growing, it's vital that they have enough water during this time in order for the roots to support new spring growth. A typical rose plant needs 2 to 3 gallons of water every five to seven days.

Plan to water your roses during the whole growing season, right up until the ground freezes, says Lloyd. If you can't be home, he recommends hiring a neighborhood kid or installing an automatic watering system.

Put a **Pomegranate** on *Your* Patio

The pomegranate (*Punica granatum*), a tropical shrub hardy in Zones 8 to 10, is well known for its juicy red fruit. But you don't have to live in warm southern climates to enjoy the pomegranate's delightful foliage and flowers. "I leave my tree out through a light frost or two until it drops its leaves and goes dormant. Then I slide it over to my attached, unheated garage and leave it there until spring," says Julie Andracki, an Indianapolis gardener and staff member of Monrovia Nursery.

Pomegranate stems arch like a fountain, reaching about 4 feet high when grown in a 12- to 18-inch patio pot. The glossy foliage is blushed with red when it emerges and matures into handsome dark green. The tree should be watered generously until it's growing strong, then it can tolerate some drought.

Try fancy-flower pomegranate cultivars like 'California Sunset' (coral red flowers with light stripes on the petals), 'Nochi Shibari' (double-flower and dark red), 'Toyosho' (double-flower, pale apricot, and shaped like a tree peony flower). Annuals that make bright combinations with pomegranates include red-leaved amaranth, 'Strawberry Fields' globe amaranth, and red- or orange-flowered New Guinea impatiens.

homegrown HINTS

BANANAS BEYOND THE TROPICS

Even if you live in a cool climate, you can enjoy the tropical lushness of growing banana plants without hauling tender plants in for the winter. Try Japanese banana (*Musa basjoo*), which is hardy to Zone 7 and even persists in protected areas in Zone 6. "It can be a real pleasure to grow a banana that provides repeat performances in moderately cold climates," says Dan Benarcik, a horticulturist for Chanticleer Foundation, Wayne, Pennsylvania.

Peanuts for Cannas

If peanuts used for packing drive you nuts, use them to help canna roots overwinter, says Erie County, New York, Master Gardener Tom Smith. Pack your canna roots in recycled packing peanuts and sprinkle lightly with water for winter storage. "The past two years I've placed canna roots in the peanuts inside both cardboard boxes and empty dog food bags and stored them in a cool corner of my basement. They've weathered the winter quite well," says Tom.

Squat Pots *Minimize* Watering

If you'd like to water your potted plants less often, plant your container garden in squat pots. Squat pots are large-diameter pots, about half the height of standard upright pots but twice as wide. Because of the squat pot's shape, less water drains out of it, giving you double the moisture reserves of standard pots. And the more moisture that stays in the soil, the less you have to water.

problem solver

CAPTURE 'NEARLY WILD' ROSES

For untamed color with minimal effort, plant large clusters of 'Nearly Wild' rose (*Rosa* 'Nearly Wild') in your sunny flower and shrub gardens. 'Nearly Wild' has five-petaled pink flowers and blooms vigorously from late spring through the middle of fall. It grows into handsome rounded bushes 3 to 4 feet high and is one of the most durable roses, resisting most diseases.

'Nearly Wild' looks particularly good when mass-planted and paired with anything containing blue or gray, like Russian sage (*Perovskia atriplicifolia*) or 'Longwood Blue' bluebeard (*Caryopteris* × *clandonensis* 'Longwood Blue'), says Tim Wood, horticulturist for wholesale Spring Meadow Nursery in Grand Haven, Michigan.

Mycorrhizae Give Roses a **Healthy Start**

Help your newly planted bareroot roses regain the beneficial mycorrhizal fungi that were lost when the plant was prepped for selling and shipping. Use mycorrhizal mycelium, a vegetative fungal growth that has been dried and chopped until it looks like cornmeal, as a soil amendment or fertilizer supplement. Mycorrhizal fungi are important because they help roses, flowers, trees, and other plants gather phosphorus when the soil is lacking in nutrients. The mycelium is available from The Roseraie at Bayfields; see "Resources" on page 317.

Roses that are sold bare-root are subject to all kinds of fungal invasions when they're stored and shipped, says Lloyd Brace, owner of The Roseraie. "We do all we can to keep the roots clean, including sterilizing them with a diluted bleach solution. This, unfortunately, kills any natural mycorrhizal fungi as well as disease organisms." Lloyd believes it's important to return rose roots to their natural balance, putting back the mycorrhizal fungi that were washed off. He says it's particularly helpful in new or nutrient-poor gardens where the mycorrhizae make conditions better for rose growth.

Quick Color from Coleus Cuttings

When a pot of annuals faded into obscurity at midsummer, Deb Martin, an Allentown, Pennsylvania, organic gardener, wanted something to fill the gap in her container garden. Spotting some coleus that needed to be pinched back, she nipped off the tops from a few of her favorites and stuck them into the moist potting soil of the empty pot.

"I was really pleased when they rooted and started growing," Deb says. "All it took was careful attention to keeping the cuttings well-watered for a couple of weeks, and I ended up with a free pot of coleus."

Timely tip

Location is everything when it comes to container plant survival, Deb says. "I've killed many potted plants over the years by putting them in spots where I didn't see them very often." This year, Deb created a large container garden along the sidewalk leading to her front door. "I walk past those plants at least twice a day—so they always get water when they need it."

lively
Landscaping Techniques

When you look around your yard, the view

should make you sigh with contentment.

After all, your landscape is a reflection of

your own style and taste. In this chapter,

we'll help start you down the path to a

landscape you'll love—or help you make

a good one even better—by offering tips

on plant selection, problem solving,

maintenance, design, and more. We've

chosen ideas that are ingenious, yet rel-

atively simple to execute. That way, you'll

still have time to sit back and enjoy the

fruits of your labor at the end of the day.

Uniting Soil and Water

When designing a water garden, you might want to forgo rocks piled around the edges. They can be over-bearing and unnatural-looking, especially in small settings, says Edd Harris, who has been a pond gar-dener in Pueblo, Colorado, for 16 years. Instead, con-sider preserving the lawn as close to the edge of the water as possible and using a con-crete and gravel slope or edge as a buffer between the water and the soil.

A concrete and gravel edge that extends about 6 inches into the lawn and about 2 feet into the pond water has a much more natural look, Edd says. Plus, this type of edge works well for hiding the pond liner. It's also stur-dier than a rock edge, which may cave in if you step on it.

This type of edge allows for easy mowing around the pond, too. Remember to run the mower so that the grass clippings are blown into the yard instead of into the pond. You may want to catch the clippings in your mower bag or rake them up afterward to keep them out of the water.

Stone Substitution

If you use heavy stones to hold down a water garden liner, they may cause the sides of the pool to collapse, especially if the water overflows during a heavy rain, warns Doug Akers, Purdue Cooperative Extension Educator for Boone County, Indiana. To avoid a collapse, edge your water garden with thin stone, such as Pennsylvania flagstone. Thin stone has another advantage, Doug points out. It's lighter, so it's easier to handle.

Wise Ways with *Wheelbarrows*

A wheelbarrow is essential for many landscaping projects, but simply lifting and pushing a wheelbarrow can be enough to land you in the examining room. To avoid injuring your back, the secret is to balance your load properly. Always put the load or the heaviest part of the load to the *front* of the wheelbarrow, advises Andrea Morgante, co-owner of Siteworks in Hinesburg, Vermont. "Keep your knees and elbows bent as you lift the load, then straighten them out when you're on your way."

problem SOLVer   WATER GARDEN HARDWARE

Looking for inexpensive water garden containers? Take a walk around your local hardware store, suggests Brian Greary, owner of Northern Lights Landscape in Williamsville, New York. Barrel inserts are readily available and work well for 2½- to 3-foot-deep water plantings. For plants that prefer shallow water, such as cardinal flower (*Lobelia cardinalis*) and chameleon plant (*Houttuynia cordata*), 8-inch deep plastic cement mixer trays are ideal.

Keeping Corners Square

Here's how to maintain a square corner when installing a fence manufactured in 4-foot sections. Tie a string to the post at the corner and measure out 3 feet toward where you want the next post to turn the corner. Temporarily mark your place by tying the string around a stake. Measure with the other end of the string 5 feet back to the next-to-last post from the end, and tie the string to the post. Adjust the stake until the string is taut. You can use multiples of these ratios, such as 6, 8, and 10 feet, if your fence sections come in 8-foot lengths.

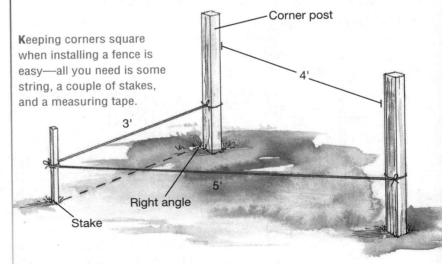

Keeping corners square when installing a fence is easy—all you need is some string, a couple of stakes, and a measuring tape.

Corner post

4'

3'

5'

Right angle

Stake

No More
Chain Links

If you need a fence to keep crit-ters out and pets in, but you don't care for the look of chain links, try this setup. Install cedar post-and-rail fencing, and staple green vinyl-coated wire mesh to the posts and rails. Plant your favorite vine next to the fence, and soon you'll hardly see the mesh. Plus, the cedar posts will resist rotting and will weather natu-rally without requiring paint.

Fence
Face-Lift

You can dress up an ugly stockade fence with lattice. Simply buy ready-made lat-tice at a home improvement store or construct your own. Once attached, the lattice becomes a support for climbing vines such as clematis, honeysuckle, or trumpet vine. Or be more creative and use it to support specially pruned trees and shrubs, such as espalier.

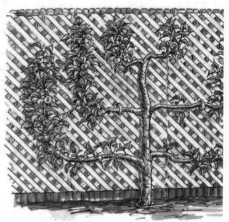

Prefabricated lattice turns an unsightly stockade fence into a trellis for vines or espalier.

Keeping
Posts Plumb

Installing fencing can be tricky, especially on a slope. The key is to keep the posts plumb. Here's how: As you set each pole in place, hold a carpenter's level against the side of the post, and adjust the post until the level is plumb. Then carefully backfill the hole, making sure you don't push the post out of position as you work. When you install the fencing, follow the slope, twisting the sections a little to climb the slope as you go (there's always some give in the framework). Or, step the sections up the slope as shown in the illus-tration below.

When installing fencing on a slope, put the posts in first and use a construction level (right) to make sure they're truly upright. Then attach the fencing to the posts, stepping the sections up the slope as you go.

problem SOLVer

THYME-LY ADVICE

A bit of borax can help keep a thyme groundcover growing strong when the heat is on. Low-growing thyme is one of the best groundcovers to plant between stepping stones, because it can withstand being stepped on—it even gives off a pleasant herbal scent when crushed underfoot. But in the middle of summer, when rainfall is scarce and the hot summer sun beats relentlessly down on surrounding paving stones, the heat can burn thyme foliage. So before your thyme dries out in hot weather, water it with a mixture of 1 tablespoon borax to 1 gallon water. "Water with this mixture only once a year, and it will prevent the burning," says Shelia Brackley, perennial production and sales assistant at Bigelow Nurseries, Inc., in Northboro, Massachusetts.

Three Cheers for **Perennials**

To get three extra benefits from your perennials, wait until early spring to cut them back, recommends Connie Gardner, assistant manager at Horsford's Nursery in Charlotte, Vermont. First, the yellowed, dried foliage and stems will add color and interest to your garden during the winter. Second, birds and wildlife will visit to eat seeds from dried seedheads and probe the stems for overwintering insects. And third, the stems will trap snow, which insulates roots and bulbs from severe cold.

Wisteria **Boost**

Even though you've pruned, watered, and coddled your wisteria, it still isn't blooming with the bravado you expect. "What it's missing," says Shelia Brackley, perennial production and sales assistant at Bigelow Nurseries, Inc., in Northboro, Massachusetts, "is Epsom salts!" To encourage wisteria to bloom, Shelia suggests watering once in the fall with a solution of 1 tablespoon Epsom salts to 1 gallon of water. Dose the plants with the Epsom salts solution again in April, and in late spring, you should see a wealth of wisteria flowers.

Paint-Free Fencing

You won't have to spend valuable gardening time painting fence posts if you install PVC post-and-rail fencing—it never needs painting! The fencing is available from Saratoga Rail Fence and Supply, Inc., in two- or three-rail sections as well as in ornamental pickets. For more information see "Resources" on page 317.

Fencing **Sense**

When installing yards of fencing, save yourself time and aggravation by digging the holes for one section and then installing the posts and rails *before* moving on to the next section. Digging all of the holes first leaves room for error—if one hole is off by a few inches, it quickly becomes a 6-inch problem. And who wants to redig all those holes?

Timely tip

If you install fencing, be sure the posts are set securely in the ground. A good rule of thumb is to bury them 6 inches deep for every 12 inches of post exposed above the ground.

Dogwood Signals Drought

How do you know when your plants are getting drought stressed—*before* it's too late? Keep your eye on your flowering dogwood, one of the first landscape plants to show symptoms of drought. "The first sign that your dogwood is suffering is wilting leaves in the heat of day," says University of Georgia Extension Service horticulturist Jim Midcap. "That's your signal to set out a soaker hose early the next morning." (Early morning is the best time to water because the water soaks into the ground before the day's heat can evaporate it—and because any water on plant leaves dries before evening, reducing the spread of disease.) And what happens if you don't quench your dogwood's thirst?

"The cells on the outside of the leaves begin to die, subsequently turning the leaf edges brown," Jim explains. Other plants may not be so obvious about their stress level, however, so watch your dogwood carefully for the signal to water your other trees and shrubs, too.

problem SOLVer

PLANTS LIKE GRAY WATER

When summers are dry, do you worry about restrictions on garden watering? End your worries by tapping some of the waste water from your everyday household activity. "You can use alternative watering sources, such as the gray water from your washing machine and showers, provided you use biodegradable soap," says Charlie Plonski, garden center manager of Horsford's Nursery in Charlotte, Vermont. Check local ordinances to be sure your community allows a separate gray water pipe. You may need the services of a plumber to set up a system to divert and store gray water for your garden.

Be Safe, Not Sorry

Working smart when you're cutting down a tree can be a life-or-death matter. If you need to cut down a small or midsize tree in your yard, whizzing through the trunk with a chain saw may seem like a fast and easy approach. But for safety's sake, don't cut to the point of letting the tree fall. Instead, stop your cut short and use wedges to force the tree over. "This affords much more control and eliminates having to worry about a running chain saw in the event of an emergency," says Steve Tworig, president of North Branch Landscape Co., Inc., in Stamford, Vermont. When the tree is notched and ready for the last cut, shut off the saw and insert one or more plastic wedges into the notch. Use a maul to hammer the wedge in, and watch out for the falling timber.

A smart way to cut down a tree is to stop your cut short, insert plastic wedges into the notch, and use the wedges to force the tree over.

homegrown HINTS

TARPS SAVE CLEANUP TIME

Take a small tarp along when you prune or plant for quick and easy cleanup. Peter Baecher of Davis Landscape Company in Lisbon, Maine, suggests spreading a tarp where it will catch most of the trimmings when you prune a shrub or tree. Then it's a quick and easy job to haul the trimmings to a brush pile or load them into a vehicle to take to your neighborhood composting site.

Landscape designer and author Jane von Trapp finds her tarp handy at planting time. She recommends spreading the tarp beside the planting site and piling the soil on the tarp. Once the plant is positioned in the hole, spread a few shovelfuls of soil around the roots, and then simply pour the rest of the soil off the tarp and into the hole. Planting goes quickly, and there's no soil to rake off the lawn when you're finished with the job.

Rope Up a Brush Pile

Here's a trick of the trade that landscapers use when they have a lot of brush to haul across a yard or in a pickup truck. Lay a thick rope in a straight line on the ground in the area where you'll be piling the brush. Stack the brush on top of the rope, laying it perpendicular to the rope, with all cut ends facing the same direction. Then wrap the rope around the pile and tie it securely on top. When you pull on the rope, the whole load will come with you, making the hauling seem like a piece of cake.

Andrea Morgante, co-owner of Siteworks in Hinesburg, Vermont, advises pulling the load with the cut ends of the brush facing toward you. "This method works great in the back of a pickup truck, too," Andrea says. "Lay the rope across the back end of the bed of the truck, pile the brush on top, and tie. When you want to dump the load, just pull on the rope, and it all comes out at once!"

Soil Sample for *Measuring* Moisture

Deep watering encourages your lawn to send roots farther into the soil, so your lawn can last longer between rains or watering without becoming stressed. But how can you tell whether you're watering deeply enough? The answer is underground. Start by giving your lawn at least 1 inch of water. After the water soaks in, use a spade to cut 3 to 5 inches into the soil. Then make a second cut about 1 inch away, and lift the sample of soil out of the ground. You should be able to feel the point where water penetration stopped. If it's less than 3 inches below the soil surface, you didn't water long enough.

Timely tip

You can also help your lawn survive with less watering by mowing high. "In hot summer months," says Clayton Johnson of New England Turf, Inc., in West Kingston, Rhode Island, and president of the New England Nursery and Landscape Association, "raise your mowing height from 1½ to 2½ inches, which will help conserve the moisture in the ground."

problem SOLVer

A CYCLONE SPREADER SAVES TIME

Make the most of your time when spreading grass seed or organic fertilizer on your lawn by using the right tool for the job. In this case, that means a broadcast spreader. A broadcast spreader works better than a drop spreader because it sprays, rather than drops, the material from the canister, allowing you to cover a larger area of lawn in less time. It also ensures that you'll get a pretty even distribution of seed or fertilizer over your lawn. (Adjust the baffle inside the spreader to avoid spraying seed on walkways, in swimming pools, and so on.) Cover your lawn in straight rows going one direction, then walk with the spreader perpendicular to those rows to ensure that you don't miss any spots.

Control Cattails with a Snip

Here's an easy way to control cattails that have gotten out of control in your water garden, says Fiona Wood of Baltimore, Ontario. In late fall, cut all the leaves off the plant to below the water level. Once the pond freezes, the cattails will drown because they can't breathe. Although this method isn't foolproof, it will prevent cattails from taking over the pond.

Smart Dos are Don'ts

Sometimes the smartest things you do in your landscape are the things you *don't* do. Here are some landscaping tasks that are better left alone:

➤ Don't waste water by spraying it high into the air with a hose or sprinkler. Instead, use a soaker hose or drip irrigation to put water right where it's needed.

➤ Don't fertilize landscape plants after midsummer. The resulting late-season growth is tender and easily injured by fall frosts.

➤ Don't prune heavily after midsummer—unless you

want to promote growth. Pruning during the second half of summer stimulates new growth that doesn't have time to harden before cold weather arrives.

➤ Don't pile mulch directly around the trunks of trees and shrubs. While mulching conserves moisture, it also provides ideal conditions for fungal diseases if the mulch is piled directly against woody plants.

➤ Don't plant a tree without doing a little research. The tree will probably outlive you. Take the time to check its mature size and habit, ideal growing conditions, and potential disease and

insect problems. You can find this information at your university cooperative extension office.

➤ Don't top-prune your trees. And if your tree service suggests topping your trees, get a second opinion. Topping trees makes them more prone to disease and encourages a flush of unsightly, witches'-broom regrowth.

➤ Don't forget that your landscape is for your pleasure more than for that of passersby. Check out the views from your windows; sit on your back porch; walk your pathways—and only then decide where and what to plant.

No More *Scarred* Trunks

Prevent scarring on trunks by annually pruning one lower branch off each of your young shade trees, says Charlie Proutt, landscape architect and owner of Horsford's Nursery in Charlotte, Vermont. Pruning shade trees while they're young instead of waiting until they're mature helps them heal quickly and completely. And removing only one branch per year also helps the tree keep its natural look. Allow about 7 feet between the lowest limb on the tree and the ground if the tree is next to a walkway or patio.

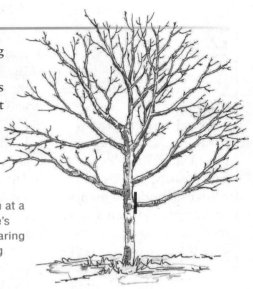

Remove only one low branch at a time to maintain a shade tree's natural appearance while clearing a path for walking or mowing under it.

Removable Latticework

You can grow vines on a fence or on the side of your house and still easily maintain and paint the fence or siding behind them. The trick is to attach a lattice to the house or fence with hinges at the bottom and hooks and eyes at the top. Make sure you fasten spacers (1-inch-thick blocks of wood or porcelain electric fence insulators) at various intervals between the lattice and the other surface. (All fastening hardware should be galvanized to prevent rust stains.) Grow the vines on the lattice. When painting time comes, simply unhook the hooks and carefully lay the lattice down on the ground with the vines still attached. Be gentle as you bend the lattice and vine outward. If the vine is woody, rest the lattice against the top of a stepladder instead of folding it clear to the ground. Not only are you able to paint behind the plants, but you've created an air space that minimizes the risks of rot and mildew on house and fence surfaces.

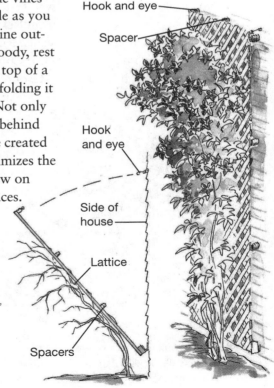

Create a removable lattice by attaching the lattice to the side of your house using hinges, hooks and eyes, and spacers. When it's time to paint your house, simply unhook the lattice and lay it down on the ground.

Dressing Up Concrete

Concrete wall systems are reasonably priced and weekend-warrior friendly when it comes to construction. The wall blocks fit together easily, and it's only a matter of putting a good base of gravel (from 6 to 12 inches, depending on how deep the ground freezes in your region) under the wall and leveling the first set of blocks. But concrete is concrete, and if you don't like the man-made look, you're stuck. Or are you?

For a little more money, you can cap (add a finishing layer) the wall and steps with a nat-ural material like bluestone. Use 1½-inch-thick pieces cut at the quarry to the desired width and length. Bond the bluestone or slate to the last layer of blocks with a wet concrete slurry so that it doesn't move. The gray-blue color of bluestone blends well with the color of the concrete. If you use stone that is slightly wider than the concrete blocks and project it over the edge of the blocks, you'll have your guests thinking the concrete is as natural as the bluestone! Concrete wall systems are available from Keystone Retaining Walls, Risi Stone Systems, and Ideal Concrete Block Co. (See "Resources" on page 317.)

Give a natural look to a concrete wall system by using bluestone to finish off the wall. Or, you can use stone that's slightly wider than the concrete and project it over the blocks to achieve the same effect.

Frozen Drinks for *Thirsty* Plants

A midwinter thaw can mean death to your plants. That's because a thaw triggers plants to grow, and if the roots can't find water, the plants will dry out and die. To keep your plants alive, water them until the ground freezes. Then when a thaw strikes, the water frozen in the ground will be readily available for those thirsty plants.

Although all plants, even established ones, will benefit from such watering, newly planted evergreens really reap the rewards. Pam Tworig, treasurer of North Branch Landscape Co., Inc., in Stamford, Vermont, recommends *heavily* watering newly planted evergreens right before a freeze. She says it doesn't matter what time of day you water; just make sure to concentrate your efforts on the base of the tree—watering the foliage won't do the tree any good. Pam also notes that you can give newly planted evergreens supplemental watering during any deep thaws that occur throughout winter.

Slow Drip *Saves* Time

Drip irrigation can save you lots of time and effort on watering plants in containers, and with a homemade system, you can have the convenience of drip irrigation with little cost. Your container plants dry out fast in hot weather, and they may need watering once—or more—every day.

To provide your plants with the water they need, simply attach a timer and an old garden hose to an outdoor faucet near your containers. Punch holes in the hose, string it through the containers, and plug the end. Test the pressure to make sure the water will drip out slowly, then set the timer to turn on the water several times a day. Your plants will never be thirsty again.

To make your own drip irrigation system for container gardens, punch some holes in an old garden hose. Plug one end of the hose, attach a timer to the other end, and hook it up to an outdoor faucet.

Simple *Silt* Barrier

A layer of fabric is the secret to keeping silt from seeping through a retaining wall. Simply place a layer of woven landscape fabric up against the back of the newly built wall before you add backfill material behind the wall. Leave a flap of the fabric exposed at the top of the wall. Once you've put the backfill stone in place, spread the flap over the stone. Then spread soil on top of the fabric. This prevents the soil from being washed down into the backfill stone, so you can plant right up to the edge of your wall.

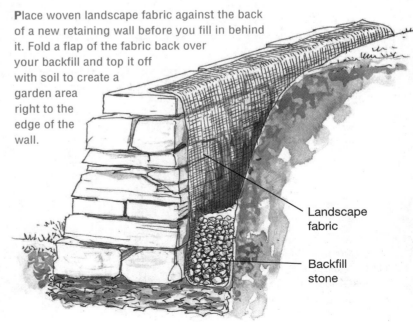

Place woven landscape fabric against the back of a new retaining wall before you fill in behind it. Fold a flap of the fabric back over your backfill and top it off with soil to create a garden area right to the edge of the wall.

Landscape fabric

Backfill stone

Checking
the Pitch

With a few simple props you can check whether the soil around your foundation is graded to allow water to flow away from it. (Water that flows toward your foundation can run underneath it, eventually cracking it.)

Cut two wooden stakes, each about 4 feet long, and drive one of them about a foot into the ground right next to the foundation. Walk at least 8 feet away (more is better) perpendicular to the house and drive the other stake into the ground. Tie a string between them and attach a line level to make sure the string is level from stake to stake. Use a measuring tape to measure the distance from the ground to the string at various intervals, beginning at the house and moving out to the other stake. If your measurement increases as you move to the outer stake, you have positive grade and the water will flow correctly. You need only 1 inch of pitch (slope) in 8 feet of length. If you don't have enough pitch, you can easily shave off the top inch or so of soil at the problem area so that the water flows in the right direction.

Check whether the soil around your foundation is graded properly. All you need are two 4-foot-long wooden stakes, string, a line level, and a measuring tape.

Wooden stake

Tape measure

String

Line level

Wooden stake

Share and **Save**

"It's much cheaper to rent a tool for a day or two than to own it for a lifetime," says Roger Cook, landscape contractor on television's *This Old House* and *The Victory Garden*. So if you need a large, elaborate tool for a landscape project, check the cost of renting it. The price may be more affordable than you think, especially if you share the rental with a neighbor who has a similar project going in his yard.

A sod stripper is a good candidate for a rental share. Or, if you're doing grading work, rent a skid-steer loader for excavation and moving boulders and soil. It's fairly easy to run and speeds up those tedious, backbreaking jobs. If you want to create a big bed on soil that's never been turned before, a large-size, rear-tine tiller (8 horsepower or more) is another good piece of equipment to rent. You take the machine for the morning; your neighbor has it for the afternoon, and the day's rental is minimal for both of you. Sure beats a wheelbarrow!

homegrown HINTS

SPRUCE UP THAT STOOP

You can dress up an old concrete stoop and steps as long as they don't have large cracks in them or pieces of concrete missing. Here's how you do it. First, thoroughly clean the concrete with muriatic acid to remove any old oil or grime that have built up over time. Repair small cracks with mortar. Then coat half-brick pavers or bluestone with a slurry of powdered cement and water. Brush the mixture onto the stoop too, then cover the stoop with the pavers or stones, keeping the joints as tight as possible. (If you cover the vertical portions of the stoop as well as the horizontal ones, you'll need to prop up the pavers with shims until the slurry has dried.) Let the stone dry for a day, then mix up a batch of grouting material in a wheelbarrow. Use about ten shovelfuls of sand, one-half bag of powdered cement, and a little water to make a mixture the consistency of thick, dry peanut butter. With a jointer, fill in all of the joints with this grouting mixture. Let the grout dry for a day before using the stoop. Now your stoop wears a coat of a different color—and for just a little bit of work!

Give an old concrete stoop a face-lift by attaching half-brick pavers with a slurry of powdered cement and water.

Screened Coverage for Potted Plants

Use a piece of window screening instead of pebbles to cover the drainage hole in the bottom of a clay pot. Screening "keeps stuff like roots and soil in, while keeping out slugs, which you wouldn't want to bring into the house when you over-winter your plants," explains Ray Rogers, award-winning flower show entrant and senior garden editor at DK Publishing, Inc., in New York City.

Wrought-Iron Alternative

Like the look of wrought-iron fencing but not the expense or maintenance? Aluminum is a great alternative. It doesn't cost as much, and you don't have to scrape and paint it regularly. Sections come in 4-foot lengths. With a post-hole digger and concrete, you can give your landscape a Victorian look. Aluminum picket-style fencing is available from Delgard Aluminum Ornamental Fencing and Jerith Manufacturing Co. (See "Resources" on page 317 for details.)

Containers *on the* Cheap

Container gardening is the hottest craze, but you needn't spend hundreds on pots for the garden and patio. Instead, use your imagination and you'll keep those dollars in your wallet. Punch a few holes in the bottom of an old plastic kiddie pool and fill it with a few tomato plants bordered by pest-repelling marigolds. An old watering can or a galvanized trash barrel can add a dash of creativity to an otherwise boring deck. A salvaged animal trough can take on new life when planted with annuals such as impatiens. And terra-cotta flue tiles have a pleasing rectangular shape and raise an arrangement of succulents such as hens and chicks to new heights.

Turn terra-cotta flue tiles into creative containers for plants, including succulents like hens and chicks.

Natural **Trellises**

Instead of buying a trellis, why not make your own with supplies from your backyard? The supple wood from willows, apple trees, and grapevines makes natural, attractive trellises. It's best to make your trellises in spring, when the new growth is green and flexible. Figure out how high you want your trellis to be, double that number, then allow for the width of the arch. (For example, for a 4-foot trellis, cut 10-foot sections of branch.) Bend some of the branches into an arch. Twist other branches around the arch and weave or twist the branches to form a structure. When the branches dry, they'll hold their shape. You can insert small trellises in containers to support climbing ivy and other vines, and use larger trellises right in the garden as props for drooping delphinium, peonies, and other lazy perennials.

Timely tip

Cut torn panty hose into pieces and use the pieces to tie plants to a trellis, says Charlie Plonski, garden center manager at Horsford's Nursery in Charlotte, Vermont.

Turn supple wood from your own backyard into a beautiful, natural trellis.

Flood Relief
for Your *Lawn*

Heavy rains can lead to temporary flooding around your yard from surface runoff. When the water subsides, don't be too concerned if there's a layer of flood-deposited soil on the grass: It may actually do your lawn some good if you know what to do with it. And that might be nothing, says extension educator Sally Cunningham of Erie County, New York.

"If your lawn has an inch or so of soil over it, don't walk on it or do anything at all until the soil dries," suggests Sally. Walking on the wet lawn and compacting the soil even more is the worst thing you can do to the already-stressed turf.

"In most cases," Sally says, "the silt and muck will gradually filter down through the grass and disappear, and can actually improve your lawn by acting as a mild fertilizer." After the muck settles, Sally recommends testing your soil's pH, just in case the runoff included some highly alkaline or acidic substance. Give your lawn plenty of time to recover, and don't let it suffer from drought later in the growing season, she says.

Sally adds that trying to wash excess soil off your lawn with a power hose only makes things worse: "It compacts the soil and adds even more water—the last thing the drowning roots need. You'll be surprised at how many lawns will grow right past this problem, and will do better if you do less!"

Timely tip

When flooding deposits a thick layer—2 inches or more—of soil on your lawn, you may want to lift or slice off some of the excess, says Sally. She suggests you try using a broad, flat snow shovel to scoop off the soil, and standing on boards to distribute your weight more evenly and to keep from sinking into the mire. "The goal is to avoid further damage to the lawn from compaction," Sally notes.

problem SOLVer   A SECOND LIFE FOR SOD

Construction in your yard means a muddy mess, but if you're working in a small area, there's an easy way to solve the mud situation: Reuse the grass. If you remove the grass carefully and store it properly, it will take hold again (this technique works best when the construction project will take only a couple of days). Using a spade, cut through the grass in straight strips about 4 feet long, 18 inches wide, and 2 inches deep. Roll the sod up and store it in the shade until it's needed. Then regrade and rake the soil in the construction area, unroll the sod on top, tamp it down firmly, and water well until the grass reroots (you'll know the grass has rerooted once you see topgrowth).

If the construction is long-term, lay the strips grass-side-up on an empty bed. Keep them watered, and they'll root in. When it's time to replace the sod, dig under it in the same way that you did originally, leaving at least 2 inches of roots. Immediately re-lay it on the raked and graded area, tamp it down, and water well.

homegrown HINTS

TAMING YOUR WILD MEADOW

Creating a natural area in your yard is great for wildlife—and it can cut your maintenance work in a big way, too. But if you just stop mowing a part of your yard, the transition from lawn to wild meadow may look awkward. To set off the wild area nicely, try defining the boundary with a fence. Decide how much of your yard you want to keep under control, and install a fence around that part. Even a see-through post-and-rail fence is often enough to set off the wild areas.

Give *Your* Garden the **Hose Test**

A garden hose is a great prop to use when laying out garden beds, and you can also use it to test whether your bed layout will work with the way you use your yard. "The flexibility of a hose lends itself to smooth curves," says Peter Baecher of Davis Landscape Company in Lisbon, Maine. "Leave the hose in place for 48 hours and live with the shapes you've chosen before you cut out the beds," adds Roger Cook, owner of K&R Tree and Landscape Co. in Burlington, Massachusetts, and landscaper-in-residence on television's *The Victory Garden* and *This Old House*. You may discover that your bed layout is awkward to walk around or that it intrudes into a play area. If so, you can adjust the hose until you have exactly the right shape for your bed. Then just cut the sod right along the line of the hose, says Peter.

To test a proposed site for a garden bed, use a garden hose to outline the bed, and leave it in place for a few days. A stake or shovel stuck in your chosen spot can help you decide whether planting a tree there is a good idea.

Timely tip

Roger also has a clever method for testing whether he's chosen the best site for planting a tree. He "plants" stakes or a shovel in the ground at the proposed spot and lives with the surrogate "tree" for a few days before digging the planting hole.

Screen with a Natural *Scene*

To give your yard privacy and the feeling of a natural forest at the same time, don't just plant a wall of trees. "If you want to create a natural screen between you and your neighbors, mix up the sizes and varieties of the plants you use," says Andrew Brodtman, landscape designer at Twombly Nursery in Monroe, Connecticut. "How often do you see all the same size trees in a pine forest?"

To create a beautiful, forest-like screen, start at the edge of your property. Plant a back-drop of some stiff-needle trees like spruce with soft-needle trees, using a mix of 8- to 14-foot trees at staggered intervals. Add a few small, flow-ering trees, such as crabapples and dogwoods, in front of them. As a final touch, plant small flowering shrubs and perennials in the foreground.

To get the most from a planting to add privacy, use a mix of trees, shrubs, and perennials of different heights.

Spilled Milk Garden Design

When dreaming up the shape for an island bed, "picture a glass of spilled milk," suggests Holly Weir, co-owner of Rocky Dale Gardens in Bristol, Vermont. Then mow around the shape and let the grass grow within it, suggests Bill Pollard, Holly's husband and co-owner of Rocky Dale Gardens. Seeing the relief will help you decide if you like the shape. Then you can cut and remove the sod and build your dream bed.

problem SOLVer   THE RULE OF FOUR

When you plan a new garden bed, you need to make sure you have plenty of space for everything you want to put in it. A good rule of thumb is to allow 4 square feet per plant, says Holly Weir, co-owner of Rocky Dale Gardens in Bristol, Vermont. Divide your total square footage by four, and you'll know how many plants will fit in the bed. "An empty bed looks huge, and most people don't make their planting beds large enough," Holly remarks. "They cram too many plants into the space, and it quickly becomes overgrown and un-sightly." Of course, when you actually plant, you'll space some plants closer and others farther apart. Small mounding perennials like columbines may need only 1 square foot. Peonies and strong spreaders like yarrow require more than 4 square feet of growing room, and so do clethra, hy-drangeas, boxwood, and other shrubs.

Work Some Winter Wonder

Berries, branches, and bark can change a garden from dull to dramatic in the winter. "Winter can be an exciting time in the garden," says Andrew Brodtman, landscape designer at Twombly Nursery in Monroe, Connecticut. To create winter interest in the garden, think beyond flowers, he suggests. Plant some trees and shrubs such as crabapples, viburnums, and winterberry (*Ilex verticillata*), which hang onto their berries into winter and will add color to a stark land-scape. Try Harry Lauder's walking stick (*Corylus avellana* 'Contorta') and other shrubs with twisting branches—they become garden sculptures once their leaves drop. The peeling bark of birches and cherries, the red and yellow barks of certain dogwoods, and the green-and-white striped branches of striped maple (*Acer pensylvanicum*) add appeal to a humdrum land-scape, too. And winter flowers aren't out of the question, Andrew notes. Just plant Chinese witch hazel (*Hamamelis mollis*) for flowers in February.

Evergreen shrubs are the mainstay of winter landscapes, but to really make your yard something special in winter, add shrubs with beautiful bark or unusual branches to the scene.

Pathway to *Paradise*

To add a sense of romance and interest to a flat site, make a sunken garden like the one created by Bill Pollard, co-owner of Rocky Dale Gardens in Bristol, Vermont.

"I had a wooded plot to make into a new garden," Bill says. "My lot was flat and I felt it needed some topography, so I dug the pathways to about 18 inches deep and threw the soil to each side into the garden to build the garden up as I went. Since the plot was a woodland, I planted it with groundcovers, ferns, fast-spreading campanulas, and lots of other woodland wildflowers. The result is a sort of tunnel-like pathway system through a woodland garden. The feeling is cool and magical."

Pathways need not be reserved just for flat sites, however. Bill notes that he always likes to start with the pathways when he develops a new area of his landscape. That way the garden areas are completely accessible both for maintenance and for enjoyment.

It's Just a Landscape Phase

Creating a master plan for your yard is a smart idea. Planting it in phases is even smarter. Of course, planting in phases is easier on the budget than undertaking a whole-yard makeover at one time, but there are other solid reasons to implement your changes in phases, as well. When you work in phases, "there's more chance of having many small successes instead of one big failure," says Dale Pierson, owner of Pierson Nurseries, Inc., in Biddeford, Maine.

Here's the best order in which to tackle a master landscape plan:

1. Plant trees and other large plants that are sited relatively far from your house. These are the biggest chore to plant, so it's best to tackle them right away, when you're the most enthusiastic. Large trees and shrubs also take the longest time to grow, so get them started right away.

2. Plant foundation shrubs and large plants near the house. As you do this, "make a large project into a series of smaller ones," suggests Roger Cook, landscape contractor on television's *This Old House*. "It's very easy to lose interest after spending several weekends trying to complete a large project."

3. Plant small border plants like groundcovers and perennials last. These ornamentals are the icing on the cake, and they are also the easiest to plant when you are running out of steam.

Timely tip

When you create a master plan for your yard, leave the door open for future changes. For example, you may decide to put in a swing set next year, or even to put an addition on your house. "Don't place barriers to change that are costly to overcome," warns Dale. So try to dream ahead, and don't plant a beautiful shade tree on the site where you may eventually want to build a sunroom or install a swimming pool.

problem solver   FILL YOUR FOUNDATION WITH COLOR

If you want a foundation bed that's colorful from spring through fall, break the annuals habit and choose a mix of bulbs and perennials instead, recommends Andrew Brodtman, landscape designer at Twombly Nursery in Monroe, Connecticut. A mix of spring-, summer-, and fall-blooming perennials will provide season-long color. Plant a layer of tulips, daffodils, and alliums at the front of the bed, and overplant them with perennials. That way you'll have early spring color, but the perennials will bloom in time to hide the bulb foliage as it dies back. Creeping phlox (*Phlox stolonifera*), irises, and hardy cranesbills (*Geranium* spp.) are all reliable early bloomers that you can plant and then forget about until they fill the spring garden with vibrant color next year.

"People will drive past your place and wonder why their house doesn't look as good as yours!" Andrew says.

Helpful *Hint* for **Picking** Plants

Visit a botanical garden or a yard with mature plantings to help you decide what will look good in *your* yard. By seeing the plants in the landscape—rather than in pots at a garden center—you'll gain clues about how they'll behave in your garden. For example, you may decide you want a narrower-growing plant, or one that's wider at the base. Plus, you'll be able to see the plants at their mature size. Stick to the garden center for checking flower color or leaf texture.

Take the **Long View** on Landscapers

Landscape designers like to advertise their work by putting signs on their newly installed landscapes. You've probably seen some in your neighborhood, and the yard looked fresh and fancy. But don't be fooled by initial appearances. The smart way to judge landscape designers is by visiting their mature designs—those installed five years ago or more. That way, you'll be able to see if the design still looks good and if the plants are holding up well. Ask friends or staff at your local garden center for names of landscapers they'd recommend. Then make your final decision by looking at time-tested results.

Timely tip

Having a landscape installed professionally can be a hefty expense, but you can keep costs in line by hiring a firm that both designs and builds the landscape. Such firms usually have a higher profit margin built into the construction phase of the project, so the design plan is greatly discounted or even free.

A **Rock-Solid** Idea

It's fun to include large boulders in your landscape, but to make them look like they really belong there, "plant" them the way Mother Nature might have, recommends Roger Cook, chief landscaper on television's *This Old House* and *The Victory Garden*. Big rocks work well as backdrops for tall and short perennials and shrubs, but not if they're just plopped down on the soil. For the most natural effect, decide which part of the rock looks best, and be sure that side will face forward. Then dig a hole large enough so that one-third to one-half of the rock will be below ground level. Use a crowbar to move and turn the rock until you manipulate it into the hole. Slide the end of the crowbar under the large boulder, and then place a small rock up against the crowbar. The small rock will give you extra leverage when you push on the bar.

A sturdy crowbar and a smaller rock for leverage will give you the necessary oomph to "plant" large boulders in your landscape.

Brighten Up Bracing

Gazebos, arbors, and trellises can add interest to any landscape, but the extra bracing these structures need to keep them sturdy may be less than appealing. One clever way to hide shear braces is by hanging plants on brackets attached to the braces. Good choices for hanging plants include geraniums, petunias, and tuberous begonias. If hiding the braces isn't an option, you can purchase old ornamental braces from an architectural salvage shop.

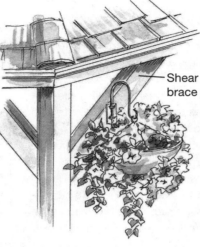

Shear brace

Hide less-than-attractive shear braces on gazebos, arbors, and trellises with hanging plants. Simply attach brackets to the braces to hold the plants.

Fence Defense

No one wants to argue with the neighbor over painting fences or pruning hedges that run along the property line. To maintain harmony with the folks next door, position all property dividers, live or otherwise, a few feet in from your property line. You'll lose a little bit of your yard, but you'll avoid potential hassles. Plus, you'll have a buffer zone that's legally yours to work in when you need to paint or prune.

Shady Way to a Prettier Deck

Pep up a wooden deck roof with open slats and add shade at the same time by planting fast-growing vines like morning glories or scarlet runner beans at the base of the deck posts. You can also plant vines in large pots next to the posts. (You may need to help the vines start climbing by gently tying them to the posts with twine or old panty hose.) The plants will climb and cover the posts and roof, adding visual interest while protecting you from the summer sun's rays.

homegrown HINTS

WHITE HOT IN THE SHADE

Want dazzle in your shady nook? White flowers can be just as hot in the shade as any pink flower is in sunlight. Lots of white-flowering, shade-loving plants are available to electrify the darker areas of your yard. Try shrubs like clethra (*Clethra alnifolia*) and viburnums, perennials like striped violet (*Viola striata*) and double-flowered dropwort (*Filipendula vulgaris* 'Flore Pleno'), and annuals like impatiens. And don't forget about plants with variegated and silvery leaves. Hosta, pulmonarias, and 'White Nancy' spotted lamium, which shines like tinfoil, are just a few of the possibilities. Make sure you mix up your plantings so you have lots of different sizes, shapes, and textures to add interest.

Landscaping 101

Ever wonder how to get that professional look for your landscape without calling in the professionals? The key is to establish one theme and stick to it throughout the design. In other words, if the planting beds are curved, use the same curved lines in the walkway or patio. If you use brick for the walkway, use similar material throughout the landscape. Try to build with stone that's found naturally in your area or with materials that complement the architecture and materials used in your house. The best designs are simple and subtle—not like a Hollywood movie set!

Cool Colors for Depth

Create the illusion of depth in a narrow flowerbed by using two tricks that professional garden designers use. First, simply plant layers of cool-colored flowers amid bright, hot colors. Cool colors, such as blues, whites, and greens, recede from your eye. Second, vary plant height. For example, plant tall, spikey delphiniums behind clumps of midsize flat flowers like scabiosa. By combining these two techniques, you'll make your garden appear bigger without having to put in the work required to increase its actual size.

Mixing It Up with Annuals

Have some vegetable beds that need a little oomph—especially as the veggies wax and wane? You can easily brighten things up by adding annuals to the mix. "Try tucking marigolds, petunias, or other annuals in at the ends of rows, at the corners of raised beds, or along edges of pathways," says James Lawrence, publisher at Microcosm, Ltd., a company that produces books on ponds and water gardens, in Shelburne, Vermont. You'll find that your garden will be more colorful and interesting with little extra work on your part. Cosmos, zinnias, or other tall annuals that grow quickly and flower to frost can also effectively frame an otherwise ordinary vegetable garden, James notes.

Timely tip

When brightening up vegetable beds with annuals, you can gain an added benefit by planting annuals that attract beneficial insects to your vegetable garden. Some good choices include calendulas, cosmos, sunflowers, sweet alyssum, zinnias, and marigolds.

Tie It Up with Ribbon Grass

Don't let your water garden stick out like a sore thumb from the rest of your landscape. Instead, use ribbon grass (*Phalaris arundicancea* var. *picta*) as an accent plant to tie your water feature to its surroundings. Ribbon grass, with its green-and-white striped foliage, adds a nice contrast to the dark greens of aquatic plants, says Janice LaCorte of Stone Ridge, New York. Plant the grass in a bare spot of soil next to your water garden, and watch as its green-and-white spikes and tall seedheads blend the land and water garden together. Be aware, however, that ribbon grass can spread rapidly. If you'd like to plant something that's not as invasive, try Japanese sedge (*Carex hachioensis*) instead.

Japanese sedge

Use a moisture-loving grass like Japanese sedge to tie your water garden to the rest of your landscape.

problem solver   QUICK COLOR FILLER

Do you have a little more empty space between the wall of your house and that line of trees or hedgerow than you'd like? A quick-and-easy solution is to install a prefabricated trellis between the trees and the house walls. Plant quick-growing annual vines like sweet peas and morning glories near the trellises each season, and they'll scramble up in no time, filling the void with color.

Swimming Pool Shade

You *can* have shade trees around your swimming pool—without the hassle of skimming leaves off the water. Just plant oak trees near the pool. The leaves on oaks hang on the branches well into winter, long after you cover the pool.

Make Way for Moss

Want the well-used, cool, and classic garden look of moss growing on your brick walkways and terra-cotta pots? Spray the area with sour milk and in a couple of weeks, your pot will be covered with moss, says Bill Stockman, owner of Spider Web Gardens in Center Tuftonboro, New Hampshire.

Clematis Cover

Clematis is not only a great climber, it's also a great spreader. Train it to grow horizontally, and you'll have a unusual flowering ground-cover. To make a truly special combination, train the clematis over an evergreen shrub.

homegrown HINTS

DIVERSITY FOR DURABILITY

Protect your landscape from pest and disease disasters by mixing up your plant selections. A large group of the same kind of plant, like hostas, is susceptible to the same disease and insect problems. So a serious infection or infestation can wipe out the entire planting. Choose several different kinds of trees, shrubs, and perennials instead of fixating on one or two favorite species of each. The result will be more interesting, more natural looking, and also more pest-resistant.

Shady Solution

Is there an area in your yard where the sun doesn't shine and the lawn doesn't grow? Plant shade-loving groundcovers in the space and watch those bare spots disappear. Groundcovers like pachysandra and periwinkle take a few years to fill in, but once established, they will continue to spread and will take quite a bit of abuse. Other shade-loving groundcovers to try include ajugas, lily-of-the-valley, hostas, and lamium.

Turn a Shrub into a Trellis

Plant a clematis vine near a small ornamental shrub like a viburnum or spirea, and you'll have an instant trellis for the vine—and waves of flowers, too. Just train the vine on a short stake at the base of the shrub, and the clematis will grow up into the shrub. This pairing works best with a hybrid clematis that won't get big and that you can cut back to a couple of bud sets each year in early spring before growth begins. A good choice is 'Comtesse de Bouchard'. Ray Rogers, garden editor at DK Publishing, Inc., in New York City, likes sweet autumn clematis (*Clematis paniculata*) planted with American holly (*Ilex opaca*). The white-flowered clematis complements the holly's green foliage.

Quick Fence Fix

A smart way to get a living fence going is to plant quick-growing trees and shrubs, such as Lombardy poplar (*Populus nigra* 'Italica') and Russian olive (*Eleagnus angustifolia*). But the quick growth of these plants means they're weak-wooded and short-lived—not the ideal for a living fence.

To plan for their eventual demise, plant long-lived, sturdy evergreens and shrubs, such as fir (*Abies* spp.) or hemlock (*Tsuga* spp.) in the same area as the quick-growers. Evergreens and shrubs grow more slowly but will be ready to take the place of the faster-growing plants when they're removed so that your living fence remains intact.

Timely tip

If you're using your living fence as a windbreak, make sure you plant trees that can take the breeze. 'Austriaca' Austrian pine (*Pinus nigra* 'Austriaca') and Scotch pine (*Pinus sylvestris*) are two types that grow well in windy spaces. Avoid trees like white pine and hemlock that burn easily in the wind.

Balanced Entryway

Mirror-image plantings of sculpted evergreens are a popular choice for foundation plantings, but for something more exciting, try a design that breaks the traditional mold. You don't need exact symmetry for a successful entrance planting—you just need a feeling of balance in your design. You can achieve balance by placing one large plant on one side of your entryway and three smaller plants on the other side. For example,

try a flowering shrub such as a lilac against barberry. Or balance one bed with two smaller beds. Without a mirror image, you'll create a more casual-looking design.

Forgo symmetry in your entryway planting and still achieve a balanced look by planting two smaller beds opposite a larger bed.

A Whole "**New**" Walkway

Dress up a boring walkway that's still in good shape (and that you don't want to remove) by installing precast concrete pavers on either side. It's eas-

iest to install a double row of brick-shaped pavers because you don't have to cut the pavers. On each side of the existing walkway, dig a trench about 8 inches wide and 6 to 12 inches deep. The depth depends on how deep the ground freezes in your region—the colder it

is, the deeper the trench should be. Fill the trench with ¾-inch plant mix (a gravel with mixed sizes ranging from stone dust to ¾-inch stone) to make a base for the pavers, leaving room for the thickness of the pavers and 1 inch of coarse bedding sand. Compact the gravel by tamping it down with your hand. Top the gravel with a 1-inch-deep layer of coarse sand. Bed the pavers in the sand and arrange them in a staggered running bond pattern, as shown at left, so that the joints don't overlap.

Pavers

You can give a boring walkway a face-lift by installing concrete pavers along the sides.

Gravel topped with coarse sand

problem SOLVer

GREEN DISGUISE FOR EYESORES

Hide ugly electric meters, junction boxes, wellheads, basement hatch doors, and propane tanks with flowers, shrubs, and trees. Plant in layers with large evergreen plants near the object and smaller shrubs and flowers in front of the evergreen backdrop. This layered approach looks less contrived than if you just plant a ring of shrubs around the object you want to hide. What you end up with is a bed or island forming an attractive focal point, disguising the eyesore behind it. Just remember to leave access for the person who services the monstrosity or he may drip oil on or trample your hard work. A few stepping stones will show him exactly where to step.

Emphasizing the Right Entrance

If you have two doors on one side of your house, do guests know which is the main entrance? You can minimize confusion by installing a low picket fence outside the door you don't want guests to use and planting an island bed filled with perennials next to the fence. Both the fence and the bed will separate the door from the main walkway and will help guide visitors to the preferred entrance.

Help emphasize the right entryway into your home by installing a low picket fence and an island bed to shield a secondary entrance.

Create an Edible Landscape

Gardener Angie Eckert of Belleville, Illinois, uses vegetables as ornamentals and gets double the benefit. "Some vegetables offer uniquely beautiful attributes," she says. "Celery, rhubarb, cabbage, and asparagus are excellent candidates for use in flowerbeds."

Asparagus, with its tall but soft lacy fronds, is perfect for anchoring the background of a perennial garden, yet it can be harvested early in the season for eating, says Angie.

"The large, coarse leaves and brilliant red stems of rhubarb add color and texture to the garden," she adds. "Deep purple leaves of red cabbage can be used to fill gaps in the perennial garden. Cabbage adds color interest to the garden in the early spring. It can be replaced with flowering annuals as the weather starts to warm."

So if a vegetable garden sounds like too much work for you, Angie says, "Simply tuck veggies into your ornamental beds for an attractive, edible landscape!"

homegrown HINTS

WET-SITE WONDERS

Do you have a wet area in the yard where grass won't grow? Make a planting bed and fill it with plants that love wet feet. Many shrubs and trees enjoy the moisture, and you can make a layered planting that includes moisture-loving perennials, too. Try corkscrew willow (*Salix matsudana* 'Tortuosa') with twisted twigs and branches, or dwarf purple osier (*S. purpurea* 'Nana') with blue-green foliage and purple branches. Red-osier dogwood (*Cornus stolonifera*) and yellow-twig dogwoods (*C. stolonifera* 'Flaviramea') love wet feet, as do swamp azalea (*Rhododendron viscosum*) and blueberries. For the foreground, many irises, marsh marigolds (*Caltha* spp.), and primroses are quite at home in a wet site.

Delight the Kids (*and Yourself!*)

Everyone likes surprises, so for a great treat, tuck everbearing strawberries everywhere: under the foundation plantings, in the flowerbeds, in a pot on the back porch, by the side yard walkway, and at the lawn's edge, suggests Jeff Cox, an *Organic Gardening* contributing editor. "Then enjoy sweet little morsels throughout summer everywhere you walk on your property!"

Garden Books Aren't the Gospel

"Don't always take what you read as gospel," warns Jeff O'Donal, president of O'Donal's Nursery, Inc., in Gorham, Maine. Many garden books and catalogs cite zones where a plant is hardy, but it's smart to double-check that information with local certified nursery and landscape experts at your garden center, extension service, or garden clubs.

"Many references, including major nursery suppliers, will cheat a zone, listing a plant as hardy in a zone where it's only marginally hardy. This results in more plants sold, but it sets people up to fail," cautions Jeff. Also, a book's advice that a plant will grow in a certain zone doesn't mean the plant will survive or thrive anywhere in your yard.

When you call an expert, be prepared to tell her about wind conditions, outbuildings, and exposure in your yard. "There are many places within a hardiness zone where plants will not survive because of frost pockets or exposure," Jeff says. For example, your property at the bottom of a slope may be more prone to frost than other nearby sites.

Small Plants Are a *Smart* Buy

"Bigger isn't always better," says Jeff O'Donal, president of O'Donal's Nursery, Inc., in Gorham, Maine. "Research has shown that younger plants recover faster than older plants after transplanting." So when you go to the garden center, choose small, vigorous plants over bigger, more mature ones. You can buy more plants for your money, you're less likely to have to replace them, and they'll catch up to older, larger plants in no time because of their youth and increased vigor.

Light Up the Night

Add a new twist to landscaping that's been in place for years by installing outdoor

Uplighting

lighting. Low-voltage lighting is a good choice because the fixtures are subtle, but the light can be powerful and plentiful, depending on bulb wattage. And you can achieve lots of interesting effects while still providing enough illumination to light your way. Use downlighting when you want light to spill down from a branch of a tree to the ground for interest and lighting tasks. Uplighting shows the nooks and crannies on the bark of trees and shrubs, and it shines like a beacon to guide you down a dark path. Place backlighting behind an object, like a trellis or plant, to project its shadow onto a wall.

Timely tip

Low-voltage lighting can be more effective at deterring burglars than traditional spotlights. When you hang low-voltage lights in trees or install them at ground level, the lighting directs light toward your house, which is best for discouraging would-be intruders. Spotlights attached to the upper corners of your house walls shine light out, leaving shadows and darkness near the windows and doors of your home, and inviting burglars in.

Downlighting

Backlighting

Uplighting works well for illuminating a dark path and for showcasing bark on trees; use downlighting when you want to light small trees or shrubs from above; generate interesting silhouettes with backlighting.

Buy in *Full Bloom*

"You get what you pay for," goes the old adage. Maybe so, warns Leonard Perry, extension ornamental horticulturist at the University of Vermont. "When buying plants, always try to buy flowering shrubs and perennials in full bloom, not because you need to know what the flowers look like, but because the plants may be mislabeled." This is especially important when buying for a certain color, such as a purple versus a white lilac. There is really no way to tell what color the flowers will be if the plants are the same species. Leonard has found mix-ups stemming from everything from handling problems at the grower's nursery to well-meaning customers who removed a tag to read it and then put it back on the wrong plant.

If you can't buy when the plants are in bloom and you end up with a mislabeled plant, take it back to the nursery where you bought it and ask them to replace it for you. Nurseries that grow their own plants have less potential for offering mislabeled plants.

Best Plants for **Living Fences**

If you're creating a living fence along the edge of your yard, you'll want as much privacy as you can get. The best plants to use are those that have branches down to the ground, such as firs (*Abies* spp.), red pine (*Pinus resinosa*), and Austrian pine (*P. nigra*). Beware that several types of evergreens lose their lower branches with age, which may defeat the purpose of the planting. In particular, avoid spruces (*Picea* spp.), because they defrock themselves over time. If you have a living fence that's lost its lower branches, try planting a layer of shrubs in front to screen the opening.

Dwarf Species for *Tight* Places

Don't miss out on wonderful plants such as spirea, lilacs, or crabapples simply because you think they'll get too big for your landscape. Plant dwarf species and cultivars, instead. 'Snowmound' Nippon spirea (*Spiraea nipponica* 'Snowmound') has the familiar white flowers in spring but only grows to 5 feet tall and wide. Dwarf Korean lilac (*Syringa meyeri* 'Palibin') has lavender flowers and grows only 6 feet tall. Sargent crabapple (*Malus sargentii*) is a slow-growing 8-footer with white flowers and excellent disease resistance. Check garden centers for small varieties of your favorites.

problem SOLVer   FAST-GROWING POND PLANT

Need some fast-growing plants for your water garden? Do as Judy Bechtel of Merced, California, does and hop over to your nearest grocery store to pick up a bunch of watercress. Place the watercress (still tied together) in your pond, close to moving water, such as a fountain or waterfall, if you have one. In a mere two days the watercress will start to root, and in another three it will start to spread, giving you a lush green plant—and sandwich filler, too. (Keep in mind that watercress will remain green year-round in tropical or moderate temperatures, but will die in cold weather.)

Under the *Walnut*

If you're having trouble keeping rhododendrons and birch trees alive near your majestic old black walnut trees (*Juglans nigra*), you're not alone. Those are just a few of the plants damaged by juglone, a chemical substance released into the soil by black walnut roots, buds, and nut hulls.

Juglone can be present even beyond the canopies of the walnut trees and can remain in the soil for years after trees are removed. But this doesn't mean that the ground under your walnut tree has to remain bare.

You can resolve the problem by building a raised bed. The walnut roots won't penetrate it, and you can toss a sheet of ½-inch black plastic mesh over the bed to keep it free from leaves and nut hulls. Be sure to empty the mesh (which is barely visible) often to keep it from being weighed down by nuts or wet leaves. (Don't compost the nuts or leaves.) In addition to making raised beds, you can also plant juglone-tolerant plants, listed at right, near walnut trees.

Good Neighbors *for* Problem *Walnuts*

Because walnut trees produce a substance called juglone that harms many types of plants, the easiest way to garden near walnut trees is to stick with plants that can tolerate exposure to the toxin. Below are some good juglone-tolerant flower, shrub, and tree choices:

Perennials
Ajuga (*Ajuga reptans*)
Astilbes (*Astilbe* spp.)
Chrysanthemums (*Dendranthema* spp., also called *Chrysanthemum* spp.)
Cinnamon fern (*Osmunda cinnamomea*)
Tawny daylily (*Hemerocallis fulva*)
Hostas (*Hosta* spp.)
Siberian iris (*Iris sibirica*)
Garden phlox (*Phlox paniculata*)
Pulmonarias (*Pulmonaria* spp.)
Showy stonecrop (*Sedum spectabile*)
Lamb's-ears (*Stachys byzantina*)

Annuals
Fibrous and 'Non Stop' tuberous begonias (*Begonia* spp.)
Morning glory (*Ipomoea tricolor*)
Pansy (*Viola* × *wittrockiana*)
Horned violet (*Viola cornuta*)

Bulbs
Crocuses (*Crocus* spp.)
Daffodils (*Narcissus* spp.)
Common grape hyacinth (*Muscari botryoides*)
Darwin Hybrid, Greigii, and Parrot Group tulips (*Tulipa* spp.)

Trees
Canada hemlock (*Tsuga canadensis*)
Japanese maple (*Acer palmatum*)

Vines and Shrubs
Knap Hill-Exbury hybrid azaleas (*Rhododendron* Knap Hill-Exbury hybrids)
Late, large-flowered clematis cultivars, such as 'Rouge Cardinal' clematis (*Clematis* spp.)
February daphne (*Daphne mezereum*)
Weeping forsythia (*Forsythia suspensa*)
Tatarian honeysuckle (*Lonicera tatarica*)
Rose-of-Sharon (*Hibiscus syriacus*)

problem SOLVer

PLANT HIGH IN HEAVY CLAY

Heavy clay soils drain slowly, which can restrict the root growth of newly planted trees and shrubs. But there's a way to help plants cope: "If the soil is heavy clay, plant trees nearly on top of the ground," suggests Connie Gardner, assistant manager at Horsford's Nursery in Charlotte, Vermont. Dig a shallow hole to accommodate just the base or lower half of the rootball. Make the hole twice as wide as the rootball. Amend the soil removed from the hole with equal parts of sand and peat moss to lighten it. Then set the plant in place, and mound the amended soil around the rootball. "The new roots will have the benefit of the lighter mix to get established, and they'll adapt much more easily than if they're smothered in thick, wet clay," Connie says.

Bag the Burlap Wrap

If you plant your broadleaf and needle evergreens wisely, you won't need to use ugly burlap to protect them from winter sun and wind— elements that can harm evergreens beyond repair. Simply give these plants a northern or eastern exposure near house or garage walls, which will give them some protection from sun or wind damage.

Treat *New Trees* to Drip

When watering newly transplanted trees, a little goes a long way, says Todd Kennedy, past president of the National Landscape Association. He advocates using a drip irrigation system rather than hand-watering with a hose.

According to Todd, "Three days of drip is better than three hours of standing with a hose." The result? Transplanted trees establish themselves more quickly, and you'll have fewer casualties.

If you don't have a drip irrigation system, you can improvise one by attaching a filter with a pressure regulator to the end of your garden hose and then attaching a small emitter hose to the pressure regulator (you can find these items at most garden centers). Position the emitter hose so the emitters will release water to the root zone of the new trees.

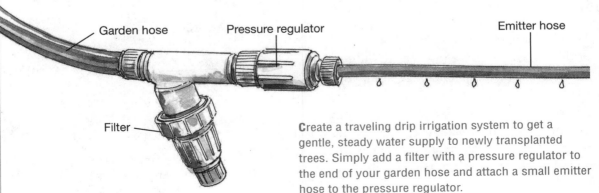

Garden hose   Pressure regulator   Emitter hose

Filter

Create a traveling drip irrigation system to get a gentle, steady water supply to newly transplanted trees. Simply add a filter with a pressure regulator to the end of your garden hose and attach a small emitter hose to the pressure regulator.

problem solver

TRY A PERENNIAL TRANSPLANTING TRICK

When you plant a perennial bed, it's best to leave plenty of space between plants so that they have room to grow to their mature height and spread. That means your bed will have lots of gaps for the first few years after you plant it. You can plant colorful annuals in the gaps, but you'll have to buy new plants each year. Instead, with a little extra planning, you can plant "filler" perennials that you'll eventually transplant elsewhere, explains Mike Guidosh of Klyn Nurseries in Perry, Ohio. "Careful planning is time well-spent on the front end of any planting project," Mike says. Just select some other spots in your yard where you'll eventually want perennials. Plant your new bed densely with perennials, and then transplant them as the bed becomes crowded. You'll save money and beautify other planting beds year after year!

Creating a Lush Lawn

To get the most out of seeding a new lawn, keep the top inch of soil moist after you sow. You can keep the soil moist by setting up an oscillating sprinkler on a timer early in the morning (about 5 A.M.) and letting it run for two hours. (Avoid watering at night because the cool, wet conditions can promote fungal disease.) Keep using the sprinkler system as needed until you've mowed your new lawn twice.

Speedy Bulb Planting

Here's how to plant lots of bulbs fast, while still getting that natural look, according to Charlie Proutt, a landscape architect and the owner of Horsford's Nursery in Charlotte, Vermont.

1. Dig a 24-inch round hole to the proper depth for the bulbs you're planting (cut right through the sod if you're planting in the lawn). Place the sod next to the hole, then put the dirt in a wheelbarrow and place the desired number of bulbs in the hole.

2. Take one giant step (about 2 to 3 feet) and dig another 24-inch hole, putting the sod aside. As you dig, throw the soil into the first hole to cover the bulbs. Then place more bulbs in the hole you just dug.

3. Repeat Step 2 until you have planted all of your bulbs. Use the soil that you put in the wheelbarrow to backfill the final hole. Then gently replace the sod on top of each hole.

2–3'

Take giant steps—between planting holes, that is—to quickly achieve a natural look with bulbs.

Success with *Sod*

If you spring for sod when you plant your lawn, you'll want to do everything possible to make sure it succeeds. Try these tips to give your new grass a chance to shine:

➤ Order only the amount of sod you can lay in one day (better to order less than more) because sod has no shelf life.

➤ When the sod arrives, store the pallets in dense shade or make a tent over the pallets to shade them. Don't lay plastic sheeting directly on the pallets of sod because they'll heat up and burn.

➤ Don't soak the sod as it lays in rolls because sodden sod is too muddy to handle. Instead, sprinkle lightly to keep the rolls from drying out.

➤ Stagger the joints when laying sod strips side by side. No two pieces should be lined up (staggering helps the joints knit together).

➤ Use a roller after the job is finished to ensure that the roots are in full contact with the soil. Any air pockets will result in dead sod.

➤ Protect any sod that adjoins a garden, walkway, or driveway from drying out on the edges by covering the sod with soil or mulch.

Once your sod is laid, make sure to water it well to help establish a healthy root system. And keep people (and pets) from walking on it until the roots have taken hold.

When laying sod, make sure to stagger the joints, instead of lining them up. And keep a hose nearby to lightly sprinkle the sod rolls so that they don't dry out.

Rock That Rootball

When you plant a tree, it's important that the top of the rootball be even with the soil surface. But what do you do if you dig the hole, slide the tree into place, and it's at the wrong height? Don't panic; you don't need to remove the tree to make adjustments. Just pull on the trunk a little to rock the still-intact rootball onto an angle. If the tree is set too low, add some soil under the rootball. If it's too high, remove some soil. Then rock the tree back in the other direction, and add or remove soil under the other side of the rootball.

Stomp Away *Air Pockets*

Boot out deadly pockets of air, which dry out the root systems of woody trees and shrubs. After digging the hole and placing the plant in, begin to backfill in layers. Shovel about one-third of the soil into the hole and then literally stomp the soil with the heel of your boot around the circumference of the rootball. Repeat twice more, and add extra soil if needed after the final stomping.

Rough Up the Roots

"Gardeners are too nice to their plants," says Amy Rose-White, perennial grower at Rocky Dale Gardens in Bristol, Vermont. Instead of handling container plants delicately, rough them up a little so that you don't end up with potbound plants whose roots continue to bind themselves after they're in the ground. Fred Dabney, owner of Quansett Nurseries in South Dartmouth, Massachusetts, suggests slicing the roots of a container plant vertically to

Give potbound plants some extra help in getting established by slicing the rootball before transplanting. Using a knife, make a slice 1 inch deep every 3 to 4 inches around the circumference of the rootball.

eliminate any possibility of girdling roots and to help stimulate new root growth. Turn the rootball in your hand and use a knife to carefully make a slice approximately 1 inch deep every 3 to 4 inches around its circumference.

Beware of the Flare

Confused about how deep to plant? "Proper planting depth is best determined by the location of the 'trunk flare,'" says Tom Vanicek, production manager at Quansett Nurseries in South Dartmouth, Massachusetts. Trunk flare is the area where the base of the trunk widens at ground level. Tom warns that after transporting and handling, the plant settles into the soil of the rootball and the flare is often covered up. So peel the burlap off of the rootball to properly locate the flare. Tom also recommends making sure the top of the ball sticks up 1 to 3 inches above what will be your finished grade around the plant. You'll know you have the trunk flare where it's supposed to be if you can see a slight arc from the rootball to ground level, says Tom.

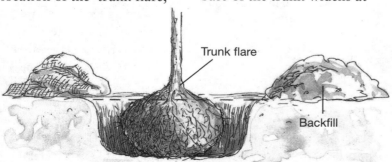

Locate the trunk flare—where the base of the trunk widens at ground level—and use that as a planting depth guide.

homegrown HINTS

RHODODENDRON SUCCESS SECRETS

You *can* have lush rhododenrons without having to tinker with soil pH—you just have to start afresh and plant them differently. Here are some secrets to getting rhododendrons to flourish from Pam Tworig, treasurer of North Branch Landscape Co., Inc., in Stamford, Vermont. Choose a shady site and amend the soil with rich, composted bark mulch (preferably softwood) and composted leaves. Rhododendrons don't like soggy feet, so raise them a little higher in the planting hole if you need to improve drainage. And never let the soil completely dry out.

Transplanting Trees in Full Leaf

Want to defy Mother Nature and transplant a young, established tree in full leaf in July? Here's a suggestion from Steve Tworig, president of North Branch Landscape Co., Inc., in Stamford, Vermont, and a director of the New England Nursery and Landscape Association. He has had excellent success with up to 1½-inch-thick sugar maples (*Acer saccharum*).

1. Thoroughly water the tree.

2. Strip off all leaves (you may want to remove the petioles, too, because they will look less than attractive if left on). Use a stepladder to reach the leaves near the top of the tree.

3. Wait a day or two, then dig up the tree and transplant it, making sure you water the tree thoroughly when it's settled in its new site.

4. Water the tree every other day during hot weather, and about three times a week throughout the fall.

By removing the leaves, you reduce moisture loss through them, which means there is more moisture available to help the tree establish itself in its new home. A second set of leaves will grow back before the end of the season.

New Use for Old News

Reuse your daily newspaper and help your plants in the process. Soak your paper in water, then line planting holes with pieces of the wet paper before you put in the plants. Tom Strangfeld, director of sales and marketing at Weston Nurseries, Inc., in Hopkinton, Massachusetts, says he and other gardeners did just that at the Public Gardens in Boston. They were following the advice of avid gardener Polly Wakefield, who says the papers slow the loss of moisture from the newly planted rootballs.

Easy Plant I.D.

Here are a couple of easy ways to remember what you planted, from Leonard Perry, extension ornamental horticulturist at the University of Vermont. To start, make permanent labels as soon as you get home from the nursery with new plants. Use plastic tabs (less expensive than metal labels) and write the name on the tab with a #2 pencil. Also, keep a log of the plant and its location in your landscape.

brilliant

Bird & Butterfly Gardens

Discover wonderful ways to bring more color and life into your gardens (and a little creature company, too!). From far-out feeders to flower favorites, find out how to entice your favorite birds to your backyard and provide food, water, and cover for your feathered friends. You'll discover that the right selection of plants is the easiest way to attract an interesting array of birds. To lure eye-catching butterflies to your flower garden, follow these gardener-tested tips and techniques that will bring flutters of brilliant color all season long.

Compass Plants Have Impact

"Birds love the seeds of the compass plant," says Jim Becker, who gardens with birds in Oregon. The compass plant looks something like a giant yellow hollyhock from a distance, with a spire of golden daisy flowers that can grow to reach 8 feet tall. An imposing clump makes a grand statement beside a garden gate—but make sure it's in easy view of an indoor window so that you can enjoy the parade of finches, juncos, sparrows, downy woodpeckers, and other seed-eaters who will be stopping by all fall and winter. Compass plant (*Silphium laciniatum*) grows best in moist, well-drained, humus-rich soil in full sun.

Christmas *Celebrations*

Winter birds love a Christmas feast even after the holiday. Set your Christmas tree outside where it's sheltered from the wind, then gather leftovers from holiday baking to make garlands of raisins, nuts, and dried fruit slices. Fill citrus rinds with peanut butter and fruit for ornaments.

Birds *Love* Love-Lies-Bleeding

Let things go to seed in your garden and you'll be surprised at the birds you attract, says Jim Becker, co-owner of Goodwin Creek Gardens in Williams, Oregon. "We grow amaranth and a decorative millet and sell the seeds, and we have to cover the plants when the seeds are ripe to fight off sparrows and juncos. But the birds love the seeds so much that we always leave some for them when we're done harvesting," says Jim.

Jim and his wife, Dottie, grow love-lies-bleeding (*Amaranthus caudatus*), an annual with long strands of deep pink flowers that look like thick, soft yarn, and 'Hopi Dye' amaranth, an upright, plumey type. "Both amaranths are great for dried flowers as well as for birdseed," Jim says.

Sow seeds outdoors after all danger of frost has passed and the soil is warm. Amaranth will ripen most of its grain 90 days after sowing.

Native sparrows, like this song sparrow, love the tasty, tiny seeds of love-lies-bleeding (*Amaranthus caudatus*), an old-fashioned garden annual.

problem SOLVer WITH BIRD FEEDERS, BIGGER IS BETTER

When you're hosting a lot of backyard birds, a feeder can empty quickly as hungry beaks snatch up sunflower seeds and other morsels. Save time refilling feeders by choosing large-capacity feeders that hold more seed. One ingenious option is hopper feeders that refill themselves as the seed level drops. Hopper feeders prevent waste, too, because windy, rainy weather doesn't soak the whole buffet, only the portion that's in the tray of the feeder.

Betsy Colwell, president of Droll Yankees, a company that's been making high-quality bird feeders for decades, says her favorite feeder is a large hopper model called the Jagunda. "I'm busy all week," she says, "so I can fill it up at the beginning of the week and not have to refill it until the weekend." When birds are depending on your banquet, a big feeder means they won't go away hungry when supplies run out and you're not home.

An A-**maize**-ing Hedge for Birds

Pauline Hoehn Gerard of Henderson, Kentucky, wanted to keep alive her memories of her childhood farm, so she planted a triple row of corn along her property line. "I planned to pick the ears for decorations, but the birds beat me to it. We had cardinals galore, blue jays, blackbirds, even woodpeckers feasting on our corn hedge," she says.

Pauline says she loves watching corn grow, and she needed a quick-growing hedge for privacy at her new home. Her corn grew quickly to towering heights, giving her home a farmlike feel, along with protection from prying eyes, and brought with it the added bonus of fun-to-watch birds at harvesttime.

Blue jay

Cardinal

Woodpecker

Plant a unique bird-attracting hedge by spacing sweet corn or field corn seeds 2 inches apart, in three staggered rows 6 inches apart, for maximum privacy.

Back-to-**Back** for Bluebirds

Bluebirds often face very stiff competition for birdhouses, especially from tree swallows. Since bluebirds aren't aggressive, the swallows usually end up with possession of the houses, but David H. Drake, president of Coveside Conservation Products, a birdhouse manufacturing company, says the solution is simple.

"Mount two bluebird houses back to back or very close together, and tree swallows and bluebirds will live happily as neighbors."

The key to this idea's success is knowing that birds of the same species, like two families of tree swallows, won't nest in adjoining apartments, even though they will nest as nearby neighbors. By putting the houses back to back, you play on the tree swallows' natural instinct not to share space. Birds of different species, however, will coexist contentedly even if their homes are very close together.

If tree swallows have been usurping your bluebird houses, mount a pair of nest boxes back to back. Swallows get one house, bluebirds get the other, and you get to enjoy two species of birds instead of just one.

problem SOLVer

FEATURE THE FOOD CHAIN

Prairie wildflowers, like coneflowers (*Echinacea* and *Ratibida* spp.), Joe-Pye weed (*Eupatorium* spp.), and many others, not only produce edible seeds for birds but are also unparalleled at attracting insects—the foundation of the food chain, notes Neil Diboll, chairman of Prairie Nursery, Inc., in Westfield, Wisconsin.

"Insects are the number one food for baby birds, so plant the prairie plants, attract the bugs, and feed the birds!" says Neil. When you plant perennial wildflowers that attract insects, you're bound to attract the birds that dine on them. If you buy large plants, you'll get flowers the first year you plant. After the flowers are finished, sparrows, finches, and other songbirds will enjoy the seeds from fall right through winter.

Slip-Sliding Away

"I love squirrels," says Heidi Doss, "but sometimes they get into my birdhouses and destroy the nests." So Heidi made simple baffles for her birdhouse posts out of 30-inch lengths of PVC pipe. She slips the pipe over the post and lets it slide to the ground, then she mounts the house on top of the pipe. The squirrels can't get a climbing grip on the slippery plastic barrier.

"My wrens are much more relaxed," says Heidi, a teaching naturalist at Wesselman Woods Nature Preserve. "It's as if they know the squirrels won't be able to reach their eggs or babies."

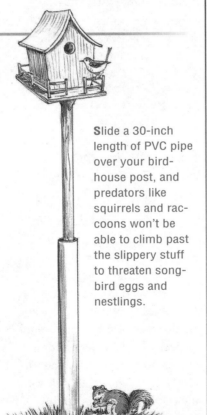

Slide a 30-inch length of PVC pipe over your birdhouse post, and predators like squirrels and raccoons won't be able to climb past the slippery stuff to threaten songbird eggs and nestlings.

Benefits of *Bayberries*

Bird lovers should try planting bayberry (*Myrica pensylvanica*), recommends Mike Hradel, owner of Coldstream Farm in Michigan. This easy-to-grow shrub not only offers evergreen shelter year-round, providing what Mike calls a "visual shield" to keep birds safe, but it also provides a winter banquet for birds. "It's unusual to find food and cover on the same bush in winter," he says.

Bayberry is tops with just about every bird that's around in winter. "More than 20 kinds of birds eat the berries," Mike notes, including pheasants, wild turkeys, flickers, downy woodpeckers, chickadees, Carolina wrens, and yellow-rumped warblers. "The one I could hardly believe is the tree swallow," he says. "I thought they ate only insects. But they love bayberries!"

The native shrub thrives in many soil conditions, including acid soils and poor, sterile, sandy soils, and is salt tolerant. Plant bayberry shrubs in full sun to partial shade in Zones 2 to 7.

The Cupboard *Gourmet*

Cleaning out the cupboards used to yield nothing more than a trash can full of stale food, so birdwatcher Deborah Burdick of Mount Vernon, Indiana, decided to make a special recipe for her backyard birds. "I emptied the last inch or two of all the cereal boxes, added some raisins that were hard as rocks, and mushed in the leftover oatmeal from breakfast," she relates. "Then I spooned out dabs of the stuff right onto the ground." Sparrows arrived before she even got back in the house, and they were soon joined by the local mockingbird and a bunch of noisy blue jays.

Now she crumbles stale crackers by hand so the pieces are smaller, and sometimes she treats her birds to a dollop of peanut butter for a tastier mix. Deborah says that natural cereals (without a lot of added sugar or preservatives) are best for the birds because they supply healthy calories that provide longer-lasting energy. Cereals with nuts or berries in the mix are always surefire favorites, too.

homegrown HINTS

A MIX OF MILLETS SUITS SPARROWS

Small seed-eaters like sparrows, juncos, buntings, and finches love the tiny, round seeds of millets, a group of annual grasses. Any type of millet is perfect for feeding birds from summer through winter because the birds pick every seed clean, says David A. Kester, owner of Kester's Wild Game Food Nurseries. Some millets shed their seeds and provide a banquet for sparrows and other ground-feeding birds. Other millets keep their seedheads intact on the plants, making sturdy landing pads for the finches who feed on the seeds.

David's company sells a millet mix that includes the familiar birdseed proso millet (*Panicum miliaceum*), which has an arching, branching seedhead that ripens in only 65 to 70 days. Siberian millet (*Setaria italica*), also called German millet, is another member of the mix. *S. berian* millet has interesting solid seedheads that "droop like a long finger," according to David. Seedheads like cattail pokers are the trademark of pearl millet (*Pennisetum glaucum*), another good bird plant. Japanese millet (*Echinochloa crusgalli*), with seedheads shaped like a turkey's foot, and several other types, round out the menu.

Plant *a Food Patch* for Birds

Tempt pheasants, quail, bob-whites, doves, and dozens of smaller birds with a patch of food plants just for them. David A. Kester, owner of Kester's Wild Game Food Nurseries in Omro, Wisconsin, encourages bird lovers to plant a special bird garden that includes both perennials and annuals. He recommends clovers, including bird's-foot trefoil (*Lotus corniculatus*), which sports clusters of sunny yellow blossoms, and bush clovers (*Lespedeza* spp.), which have small pink or purple pealike flowers. For fast payoff, include annuals like sorghum, buckwheat, and small-seeded soybeans and peas. Prepare a small planting bed, mix together a handful of seeds, and sow the seeds over the bed. Water generously until the seeds germinate, then take the low-maintenance approach—just wait for the bird visitors to arrive.

problem solver

SOME LIKE THEIR GARDENS WILD

Find a discreet part of your garden and let it go wild, and you'll get all kinds of pleasant bird surprises, says Jim Becker, co-owner of Goodwin Creek Gardens in Williams, Oregon. Birds love weed seeds even better than birdseed. "Let some weeds stand, and you'll have birds visiting until every seed is gone," he says, pointing to chicory and wild lettuce as two favorites of feathered friends. Goldfinches are particularly fond of both plants, he adds.

Lamb's-quarters, dock, and ragweed (if you don't have allergies) are top-notch, too. Jim says that even a small patch of weeds (about 3 × 3 feet), will provide plenty of great edibles for feathered friends. If you have room, let an even larger patch go wild, and you'll be on your way to creating a natural bird habitat. Be sure to keep your wild patch well away from your vegetable garden, though, so that stray seeds don't sow a crop of heavy labor for next season.

Warm Water in Winter

Second-story condo resident and bird lover Elizabeth Castaldi of Washington, D.C., says supplying fresh water in the winter to birds is a challenge. On cold days, she fills a clay saucer with warm water in early morning. "The birds have learned my schedule," she says. "They're already in line for baths when I bring the water outside." When she heads to work, she brings the saucer indoors until the next morning's birdie bath time.

Plant a Birdseed Garden

When bird-feeder traffic drops off in late spring, Heidi Doss of Evansville, Indiana, has an ingenious solution for getting rid of the last few inches of birdseed. "I know whatever's left won't last until fall, when feeding season picks up again, so I use it to plant a garden for my birds." Heidi prepares a bed just as she would for planting annuals, then she scatters the leftover seed and covers it lightly with soil.

Plant mixed seed so that you can learn what kind of plants grow from birdseed. "Buckwheat really surprised me—I had no idea it was so pretty," says Heidi. Let the

birdseed plants mature in place so that the birds can enjoy the seeds just as they grow. Birds will come and go in the patch all winter long, says Heidi.

Plant birdseed mix just as you would annual flowers for a true surprise garden. Many birdseed plants, like the buckwheat shown here, are as pretty as ornamentals.

Appreciating the Ordinary

Starlings, pigeons, and English sparrows were just "city birds" to Gretchen Harrison of Boston, but that changed when her two-year-old daughter, Erica, discovered the "birdies." Looking at the city bird life through fresh eyes, Gretchen found these birds as fascinating as any songbirds.

She and Erica feed their little troupe of feathered friends just what cosmopolitan birds like most—slices of sourdough bread, leftover French pastries, scraps of cream-cheese Danish, and the remnants of corned beef sandwiches. As the birds linger over the feast, Gretchen and her daughter learn their habits and personalities, and now they bird-watch daily on their sojourns through the city.

Once you change your outlook on city birds, you'll find they can be very interesting to watch. "Now I see how tender the pigeons are with their mates, and I love to watch the feathers on the starlings change colors in the sun, and listen to them sing," Gretchen says. "Even the English sparrows are pretty darn cute—especially if they're all you have!"

Wreath of Welcome

As soon as bird enthusiast Janice Ostock of Bethlehem, Pennsylvania, moved into her new home, she hung a grapevine wreath beside her front door. "I was still unpacking boxes when I noticed a house finch bringing sticks to the porch, and when I checked, I found a pair of them were making a nest in my wreath!" she exclaims.

Since finches, robins, and other songbirds often nest near human haunts, wreaths and hanging baskets located near the doorway all make great nest sites.

Janice's birds built their deep cup-shaped nest on the bottom of the wreath. "It looked just like the wreaths you see in the shops," she says, "except instead of an artificial nest, mine was real—and had birds in it."

Create an instant nest site for house finches or robins by hanging a decorative grapevine wreath near your front door. These friendly birds will let you enjoy a close-up look at how they raise a family.

problem solver   BIRDS AREN'T BREAD SNOBS

If you're baking and things don't turn out quite right, put the "failures" out for the birds. Like Janice Ostock of Bethlehem, Pennsylvania, you may find that you end up baking just for the birds. When Janice experimented with her new electric bread maker, the first loaves were rejects, so she tossed them outside for the birds. "When I finally gave up on baking, I saw the birds were still coming for the leftovers— except there weren't any. I couldn't let them down, so I still bake—just for them! They aren't fussy at all about how the bread turns out," she says.

A loaf of her dense, chewy bread, chock-full of nuts and raisins, probably costs more than the day-old bread she could buy at a bakery outlet, but Janice says she doesn't mind. She likes baking for an appreciative audience who relishes even the mistakes.

View Vines As Opportunity

With their tangle of stems and often luxuriant leaves, vines are favorite hiding places and homesites for many song-birds. Learn to look in vines and you'll discover lots of bird nests, says Marie Bedics, whose Pennsylvania farm-house has a wall covered with Boston ivy (*Parthenocissus tricuspidata*). The ivy shelters neighborhood wrens, spar-rows, and robins at night, and its thick growth also provides a home for a catbird that has lived in her yard for well over a decade.

Other vines favored by birds include: Virginia creeper (*Parthenocissus quinquefolia*), English ivy (*Hedera helix*), autumn clematis (*Clematis terniflora*), anemone clematis (*Clematis montana*), and grapevines. All are excellent bird homes and hideouts.

Marie says the best part of the ivy-covered nests is that you never know there are any birds there. "But at night, just before dark, I can hear them twittering as they settle down to sleep," she says. "And I watch the catbirds coming and going with food for their babies."

Keep the Neighbors Happy

Natural-looking gardens make birds and butterflies happy, but they may stir up trouble in a neighborhood of tradition-ally groomed lawns. Jean Hadley, whose natural land-scape covers acres in Solitude, Indiana, suggests a couple of simple tricks to keep neighbors content. "That feeling of the yard being out of control seems to be what bothers neighbors most," she says. "If you're making the transition from grass to plants in your yard, make sure you have nice, neat, wide paths going through it. That gives it a planned look that signals the plantings are intentional and not just noxious weeds left to roam."

Jean says that a fence helps, too—not to hide the gardens, but just to give them a civi-lized feel. A jumble of plants along a split-rail fence looks a lot better to most people than a so-called weed patch, she says. Even though you could have the same plants with either scenario, adding the fence can make a huge difference in how the garden is perceived.

WINTER FRUIT FOR WILD BIRDS

Most trees drop their fruit in fall, says Mike Hradel, owner of Coldstream Farm in Free Soil, Michigan, when there's more than the birds can eat. But in winter, when they really need it, there's little available. Good bird plants for wintertime, he suggests, are dogwoods and crabapples; he also recommends small-fruited crabapples like 'Sargent' and 'Zumi', which bear perfectly bite-size fruit for avian visitors.

Paint *Is for* People

"Birds would much rather be in a birdhouse that's made as inconspicuous as it could be," says David H. Drake, president of Coveside Conservation Products in Maine. "Otherwise it's easier for predators to find them." He recommends leaving nesting boxes *au naturel*, with no paint or decorations, so that they blend in with the landscape as easily as tree bark.

A coat of paint won't deter birds, but David adds, "Paint is for people—the birds don't care!" Sometimes paint can be a good thing, he says. If your spring weather swings from warm to cold, a dark-painted birdhouse will soak up heat and keep it cozy. If you put a birdhouse in full sun, a coat of white paint will keep it cooler inside by reflecting those warming rays.

Best Bets for Nest Building

Indian hemp (*Apocynum cannabinum*) and the very similar-looking dogbane (*A. androsaemifolium*) supply perfect nest-building materials for orioles and vireos, says Jean Hadley of Solitude, Indiana. Colonies of these plants grow at the wood's edge and in the meadow on Jean's property. All winter long, the stems of the plants weather in the rain and snow to become bird magnets by late spring. That's when Baltimore orioles, vireos, and the occasional yellow warbler descend to pull apart the old stems, stripping off thin, soft strings that are as tough as dental floss—just the thing for weaving nests. Plant dogbane and Indian hemp where the plants have room to spread naturally into a colony.

Get Wild with "Wild Ones"

If joining together with other nature lovers for seed exchanges, chats with kindred spirits, nature hikes, field trips, excursions, and tours of backyard wildlife gardens sounds like your cup of tea, get in touch with Wild Ones—Natural Landscapers, Ltd., a nonprofit group dedicated to educating and sharing information among "regular people" who love to learn about wildlife.

Members share information about gardening with native plants, attracting birds to their gardens and flowerbeds, and generally creating wildlife-friendly, ecologically sound backyards. For more information, write to Wild Ones—Natural Landscapers, Ltd., P.O. Box 23576, Milwaukee, WI 23576.

Keep the Peanut Eaters Happy

Peanuts are a big draw for woodpeckers, blue jays, chickadees, titmice, and nuthatches, but the nuts disappear fast when you offer them in an open feeder. The perfect solution is a tube feeder of stainless steel wire mesh with ¼-inch holes, says Betsy Colwell, president of Droll Yankees. The mesh holes are too small to let birds grab whole peanuts, but plenty big for woodpeckers and others to hammer through and get pieces.

The big draw for the peanut feeder is the woodpeckers, says Betsy. "They love peanuts! They'll bang away, just like they do on trees." Squirrels don't bother the feeder, she says, because they can't chew through the mesh.

If you're the handy type, you can make a homemade peanut feeder by replacing the plastic tube of an existing tube feeder. Here's how:

1. Measure the circumference and height of the tube of the existing feeder. (For example, some tubes measure 11 inches around and 12 inches high.) Buy a piece of stainless steel, ¼-inch wire mesh to correspond to the measurements you took. If you can't find stainless steel mesh, use hardware cloth.

2. Roll the wire mesh into a tube shape to fit the feeder's top and bottom, then bend the mesh over itself to anchor the edges together.

3. Fasten the feeder top and bottom to the mesh. Usually, the bottom of the feeder will hold tight when inserted into the mesh, and the top is held in place with the wire hooks at the ends of the handle.

Replace the plastic tube of a thistle feeder with ¼-inch wire mesh to make a whole-peanut feeder for woodpeckers, blue jays, and other nut lovers.

4. Insert the bottommost perch of the feeder.

5. Fill with shelled whole peanuts, and hang the feeder in a spot where you can watch the visiting birds.

Faking It

Many gardeners use red flowers to lure hummingbirds to their garden, where they'll stay to sample flowers of other colors, too, but natural-garden lover Jean Hadley of Solitude, Indiana, had trouble fitting fire-engine red into her romantic pastel color scheme. So she turned to subterfuge—a quick trip to the local discount store gave her an armload of red silk flowers that she wired to nearly everything in the garden. "It worked like a charm!" laughs Jean.

Now she has hummingbirds every summer, returnees who remember her garden of nectar-filled flowers, even though the red silk deception is long gone.

Shape **Is** What *Matters*

If you love hummingbirds, plant a garden specifically for them. Jim Becker, co-owner of Goodwin Creek Gardens, says flower shape, not color, is what matters most when planning a hummingbird garden. Tubular flowers, whether they're tiny mint flowers or 8-inch datura blossoms, are what hummingbirds seek. Their long, skinny beaks are exactly right for reaching the nectaries at the base of these flowers. "Red gets their attention, but they really like deep purples and blues, too," he notes.

Hummingbirds will go to just about any flower, Jim says. If it proves to be a good nectar source, they'll return to it over and over. One of Jim's favorite hummingbird flowers is a white-flowered selection of normally bright red cardinal flower (*Lobelia cardinalis*), which he selected from a batch of seed-grown plants.

Buying new annuals or perennials for your garden? Check the flower shape—if it's tubular, it will attract hummingbirds, no matter what size or color the flowers are. The penstemon, salvia, and bee balm shown here are three examples of the many tubular flowers you can use.

Natural Nectar

Hummingbirds are hungry after migratory flights, so treat them to nectar-rich early bloomers. Jim Becker, co-owner of Goodwin Creek Gardens in Oregon, suggests planting red flowering currant (*Ribes sanguineum*), a graceful shrub or small tree native to the Pacific Northwest that's also at home in Zones 6 through 8. A buffet table in a bush, dangling clusters of red-to-pink fragrant flowers decorate the branches very early in spring.

High-Rise Hummingbirds

Hummingbirds have such an eye for red that they'll go to great lengths—or heights—to investigate, says Elizabeth Castaldi of Washington, D.C. Trying to brighten her small second-story balcony, she added a pot of bright red zonal geraniums (*Pelargonium* spp.) that could take the all-day sun and heat. Within days, she noticed a male ruby-throated hummingbird at the flowers. When migration time came in early fall, she had a constant stream of tiny winged visitors humming with delight at her bright container garden.

problem SOLVer

BRING ON THE HUMMERS

"Hummingbirds return from migration in early spring, when there's not a lot blooming in the garden," says Jim Becker, who co-owns Goodwin Creek Gardens with his wife, Dottie. Luckily, the long-spurred, nectar-filled blooms of native American columbines are just hitting full stride when the zippy little birds return to the scene. Jim and Dottie grow both the eastern and western wild columbine (*Aquilegia canadensis, A. formosa*). Both are great garden plants as well as hummingbird plants. Columbines bloom for weeks, sustaining the birds until other plants come into flower.

Advantages of Agastaches

Their Latin name may be a mouthful, but perennials from the genus *Agastache* are sure-fire hummingbird attractors. Most plants have foliage with a delicious licorice scent, which has given more than one species the nickname licorice plant, or anise hyssop. But it's the whorled spikes of small tubular flowers that are the prime attraction for hummingbirds.

Many gardeners are familiar with anise hyssop (*Agastache foeniculum*), but there are many more to be discovered, says Jim Becker, co-owner of Goodwin Creek Gardens in Oregon. Native mostly to the American Southwest and Mexico, agas-

taches include many plants of surprising cold hardiness, usually to Zone 6.

Agastache species and hybrids offer a variety of flower color, including blue-purple, salmon, rosy orange, pink, and pale blue. Hummingbirds love all of them. Jim recommends 'Apricot Sunrise', whose beautiful orangey apricot flowers light up perennial gardens. 'Firebird' is a vivid orange-salmon flowered hybrid that creates a full, branching plant.

Richly fragrant rock anise hyssop (*Agastache rupestris*) has gray-green foliage and rich, rosy orange flowers; hardy to Zone 5, it blooms for almost two months straight. Plant in lean, well-drained soil in full sun.

Perch-Free Means *Predator*-Free

Perches on birdhouses are so common that it doesn't occur to most people that perches allow predators access to baby birds. If you're building new birdhouses, eliminate the predator threat by skipping the perches, or saw off the perches from an existing birdhouse, says David H. Drake, president of Coveside Conservation Products.

If you think about it, natural nesting cavities don't come with perches—nearby twigs and branches serve as landing platforms for arriving bird parents. Birdhouse perches offer raccoons or cats a balancing spot and allow them to reach an exploring paw inside the nest box, which often proves fatal to young nestlings.

Help **Birds** Get a Grip

Rough-sawed boards are cheaper than finished lumber and better for birdhouses, says David H. Drake, owner of Coveside Conservation Products. Rough-sawed boards make it easy for little bird feet to get a grip on the roof, sides, or front of the house.

Handy Hinges Make Cleaning *Easy*

Cleaning out a birdhouse is easy if the house has a hinged side or front, says David H. Drake, president of Coveside Conservation Products. On birdhouses with hinged openings, you'll need to undo the fastener, open the side, and make one swipe with your rubber-gloved hand to neaten things for the next resident. If you decide to clean out old nesting materials, it may be best to wait until the beginning of the breeding season to allow time for beneficial wasps to emerge from hibernation in the old nest. Wasps help control parasitic blowfly populations that can lower the survival rate of nestlings.

Hinged sides on a birdhouse make it easy to clean out old nesting materials.

Squirrel-Proofing Your Birdhouses

You may have visions of happy bird families when you mount that new birdhouse, but your neighborhood squirrels have other plans. Rambunctious squirrels often gnaw the entrance holes to enlarge them so the squirrels can move in instead of the birds. You can squirrel-proof nest boxes with a slate or metal barrier to keep out the varmints, says David H. Drake, president of Coveside Conservation Products, makers of high-quality wooden birdhouses fitted with antisquirrel devices. The guards are easy to cut and install, although you may find it easier to have a masonry or metal shop make them.

You will need a square of slate or sheet metal twice the size of the birdhouse's entrance hole. For example, if the entrance hole measures 2¼ inches in diameter, the slate or metal should be 4½ inches square. Drill a hole the same size as the entrance hole in the center of the slate or metal square, using a masonry drill bit if drilling through slate. Place the guard flush with the front of the birdhouse, aligning the holes. Drill into the wood along the outer edges of the guard, then attach it to the birdhouse, using the heads of the screws to anchor the guard in place.

A metal or slate squirrel guard will keep bushytails from using their teeth to enlarge the entrance hole to suit their own furry bodies.

Let the *Sun Shine* In

The latest bird-behavior research shows that house sparrows prefer a dark home to a light-filled one, so you can discourage them from monopolizing your birdhouses by retrofitting your existing houses to allow light in through the roof, says David H. Drake, president of Coveside Conservation Products.

You can test the theory in your own backyard by making a few quick changes to your existing bird boxes, but be sure to use this method only on boxes that are placed in shaded areas so that the interior temperatures of the boxes don't soar

when the sun pours in.

To discourage house sparrows, there are two methods that allow the sun to shine in, yet keep predators out. The first method (Steps 1–3) uses heavy-duty wire mesh and is the easiest to install, but it doesn't offer the birds any protection from the rain. The second method (the "Timely Tip" that follows) uses Plexiglas, requires a saw and an electric drill, and provides shelter from the rain if the birdhouse is in an open area.

You can easily discourage house sparrows from usurping your bluebird houses by retrofitting the houses with a Plexiglas or wire mesh roof. The added light will keep house sparrows away since they prefer to nest in darkness.

Both methods work for flat-roof and sloped-roof houses.

1. Remove the roof from the existing house.

2. Using wire cutters, cut a piece of ¼-inch or ½-inch wire mesh (as heavy-duty as possible) 1 inch wider than the inside diameter of the top of your birdhouse.

3. Bend the sides of the mesh up so that the mesh fits snugly within the width of the birdhouse. Using a staple gun and staples, staple the mesh securely to the inside of the house about 2 inches from the top edge. The mesh will let in sunlight but keep out predators.

Timely tip

To keep nesting birds protected from the rain *and* discourage house sparrows in the process, David says that you can also substitute a Plexiglas roof for the existing roof on your birdhouse. Using a coping saw or an electric saber saw and the existing birdhouse roof as a pattern, cut Plexiglas to fit the birdhouse. Using an electric drill, drill holes for screws to attach the Plexiglas roof to the birdhouse. Screw the new roof to the top of the birdhouse.

The **Magic** of Running Water

"I've read that birds are attracted to the sound of running water," says Heidi Doss of Evansville, Indiana, "but I'm a long way from the closest creek." So when Heidi found a small, battery-operated submersible pump for $20 at her local home-supply store, she set it right in her birdbath amongst the river stones. "I get to see all kinds of birds coming to drink—orioles, tanagers, warblers, vireos, plus the usual robins and catbirds—and I get to soak up that wonderful soothing sound," she says. She keeps her pump on the lowest setting so there's only a gentle gurgle through the outlet pipe, just enough to make the sound of water music.

Add a small submersible pump and stones to a pottery birdbath to create the sound of water music.

Poke Your Perspective

Pokeberries aren't people-friendly—they're poisonous—but birds devour them with great enjoyment. Mockingbirds, robins, thrashers, waxwings, thrushes, downy woodpeckers, flickers, and many others flock to pokeberries. "A lot of people think of poke as a weedy thing," says Jim Becker, co-owner of Goodwin Creek Gardens, but when a photograph of pokeweed (*Phytolacca americana*) and artemisias in a garden setting appeared in a national magazine, he noted that interest in the plant surged. "In the right setting it can be very pretty—those big, tall, arching, reddish purple stems and the purple fruits in fall."

Sometimes more unusual bird visitors show up. Jim notes he got a good look at a pileated woodpecker on his poke plant. The almost crow-size bird was hanging upside down to eat the fruit.

Don't pull every pokeweed seedling you see. Even though it's considered a common weed by some, bird watchers will be thrilled to see the visitors, like this mockingbird, that it attracts.

Pokeweed seedling

Mockingbird

Grasses for *Bird Safety*

Thick-growing prairie grasses or other ornamental grasses planted here and there in the landscape provide a safe haven for birds that need to make a quick dash to safety. They grow fast, too, making them useful from the first season they're in the soil. And most stay useful over winter, offering birds a tangle of sheltering stems, not to mention a bounty of nutritious seeds and nesting material in the spring. Neil Diboll, chairman of Prairie Nursery, Inc., in Westfield, Wisconsin, says that prairie grasses can play a starring role in a wildlife-friendly garden. "The plants of the prairie have the unique ability to combine both habitat and beauty," he says. Try these easy-to-grow prairie grasses: big bluestem (*Andropogon gerardii*), switchgrass (*Panicum virgatum*), and Indian grass (*Sorghastrum nutans*).

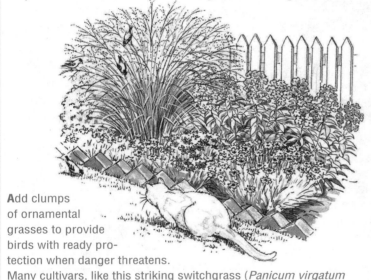

Add clumps of ornamental grasses to provide birds with ready protection when danger threatens. Many cultivars, like this striking switchgrass (*Panicum virgatum* 'Heavy Metal'), combine beautifully with pinks and garden phlox.

Timely tip

Because meadow flowers and field flowers are so good as nectar plants, people tend to forget the role that grasses play with butterflies, Neil says. "Many butterfly and moth caterpillars use grasses and sedges for food sources. Grasses also serve as resting areas for adult butterflies—when it's a really windy day, they go down into the grasses for protection," he adds.

Grasses serve as host plants for many species of skippers; sedges also attract skippers, in addition to satyrs. Native prairie grasses like little bluestem (*Schizachyrium scoparium*), switchgrass (*Panicum virgatum*), and others add beauty into a naturalistic or prairie garden.

Butterflies Zip for Zinnias

Marie Bedics of Whitehall, Pennsylvania, used to grow zinnias every year, but one spring she planted pricier perennials instead. "The difference was amazing," she says. "I was used to having lots of butterflies, and all of a sudden I had hardly any. They liked my cheap zinnias better than any of the five-dollar perennials I'd replaced them with!"

Now a patch of zinnias is always a standard part of her garden. "If you sit on my porch," says Marie, "you can watch the butterflies come across the field into my yard and head straight for the zinnias. Once they're here, they'll visit the other flowers, but they always hit the zinnias first."

Fruit Feeder Attracts *Butterflies*

Ripened fruit attracts many species of butterflies, says David Roth-Mark of New Harmony, Indiana. He offers butterflies all kinds of fruit buffets, and has discovered that they seem to like pears and bananas the best, "especially when the fruit is really soft and brown."

David surmises that the butterflies are more easily able to pierce the flesh of the fruit with their proboscis when it's overripe. He peels the bananas and slices the pears in half lengthwise before putting them on his feeder. "One pear can last for a week," he says, "so it doesn't cost much to keep them happy."

Instead of tossing overripe fruit into the compost pile, invite a few fluttery friends to dine on your past-prime leftovers.

Watermelon Magnet for Monarchs

Watermelon on the patio is a regular part of summer life—a slice of summer that butterflies, especially monarchs, enjoy, too, says nature lover Pauline Hoehn Gerard of Henderson, Kentucky. "I keep a chunk of watermelon on the deck rail just for butterflies," says Pauline. "In late summer, there might be a dozen butterflies eating at the same time." She adds that the butterflies seem to enjoy the watermelon most when it's overripe.

Swallowtails Think Purple

Many backyard butterfly enthusiasts have noticed that big swallowtails seem to prefer the color purple, and Jim Becker, co-owner of Goodwin Creek Gardens, agrees. "It seems that purple and swallowtails go together," he says. "Brazilian vervain (*Verbena bonariensis*) is absolutely excellent for attracting butterflies."

This tall, bare-stemmed perennial offers its clusters of tiny, soft purple flowers for months, until frosts stop it for

The Mutt and Jeff of the verbena clan—tall, skinny Brazilian vervain and low, sprawling 'Homestead Purple' vervain— are irresistible to swallowtail butterflies.

the season. It's easy to plant anywhere in the garden, but be sure to keep some near the front of the bed, where you can watch the butterflies that come to visit. Jim also recommends another verbena, a sprawling hybrid called 'Homestead Purple' that grows so fast you can use it as a groundcover.

Nature Versus **Nurture**

Sometimes Mother Nature's haphazard plantings teach the most useful lessons about gardening. "I planted all the flowers the books said in order to attract butterflies," says Pauline Hoehn Gerard of Henderson, Kentucky, "but I still didn't have many." Then she remembered how many butterflies she saw fluttering over the milkweed (*Asclepias* spp.), ironweed (*Vernonia noveboracensis*), and asters along the dirt lane to her house when she was a girl. She brought home some of these "weeds" from her mother's land, and she quickly found that butterfly visitations increased dramatically. It turns out that Pauline's old "weed" favorites are all-American natives that bloom from the middle of summer on, when butterfly populations are at their peak.

Barbara Trick, office manager for Aullwood Audubon Center and Farm, uses native trees to attract butterflies. Tulip trees, hackberries, maples, oaks, and white ash are nurseries for swallowtails, giant silk moths, and other winged beauties.

'Beefsteak' for Butterflies

When her 'Beefsteak' tomato crop swelled and cracked one year in the heat, Deborah Burdick of Mt. Vernon, Indiana, discovered that the cracked, leaking fruits turned out to be butterfly attractors. "I was walking out for my mail when I saw motion at the tomato plants. There were a bunch of butterflies—beautiful golden ones that I learned were hackberry butterflies, and some beautiful black and blue red-spotted purples! Now I leave some of my cracked tomatoes on the vine just for the butterflies."

All Around the Butterfly Bush

The single butterfly bush (*Buddleia davidii*) in the back of Janice Ostock's garden in Bethlehem, Pennsylvania, drew a steady stream of butterflies, but it was hard to get a glimpse of the butterfly visitors close up. So she created her own butterfly visitors' center by adding a path that circled the bush. The butterflies often retreat to the back of the bush when an observer comes near, says Janice, but the new walkway puts the nectar sippers in full view.

Give garden visitors a great view of visiting butterflies by making paths all the way around a butterfly bush.

Early Bloomers for *Early* Butterflies

When a few days of unseasonably warm weather late in winter coax early butterflies from their sheltered niches beneath bark, not many flowers are waiting to greet them. Nature lover Pauline Hoehn Gerard of Henderson, Kentucky, felt sorry for the early butterflies because there was no nectar to sip, so she planted early-blooming autumn-flowering cherry (*Prunus subhirtella* 'Autumnalis'), which she notes blooms not only in fall but also in late winter, whenever the weather turns mild for just two or three days.

Pauline also recommends winter-flowering witch hazel (*Hamamelis* × *intermedia* 'Arnold Promise'), whose ribbony-petaled flowers offer sustenance until real spring arrives. Pussy willow is another great food source for butterflies. When early butterflies such as the tiny blue spring azures and the elegant, understated mourning cloaks emerge from winter slumber, there's a banquet of rich nectar waiting for them.

Butterflies Think *Lavender Is Lovely*

Barbara Trick, office manager for Aullwood Audubon Center and Farm in Ohio, loves her patch of lavender. When the sweet blue-purple flowers bloom, "it's absolutely covered with butterflies and bumblebees," she says. "There are so many honeybees and bumblebees at it that the plants practically vibrate." Jim Becker, co-owner of Goodwin Creek Gardens in Oregon, concurs with Barbara about lavender. "Lavender has proven to be an excellent butterfly flower for us," he says, noting that his visitors include masses of skippers and western swallowtails.

Spritz the Bricks for *Butterflies*

As David Roth-Mark of New Harmony, Indiana, was watering the potted plants on the family deck one July, he noticed that butterflies were attracted to the wet spots on the bricks. So a couple of times a day, he wets down the bricks with the hose to give butterflies a drink. Many butterflies are puddle-sippers and seek out hospitable wet spots to congregate and drink. If you don't have bricks to wet with the hose, you can keep a spot of gravel wet or make a butterfly drinking station out of an old cookie sheet or big clay saucer lined with gravel or river stones.

Spray your brick walk or patio with the hose whenever you're out in the garden, and colorful, thirsty butterflies will soon become regulars.

Resources

To help you find great plants, garden supplies, and even more ingenious gardening ideas, we've compiled the following list of plant associations, gardening organizations, mail-order nurseries, garden suppliers, and product manufacturers. When you contact associations or specialty nurseries by mail, please enclose a self-addressed, stamped envelope with your inquiry. Notes in italics indicate particular products, plants, or services offered.

ASSOCIATIONS AND ORGANIZATIONS

American Dianthus Society
Rand B. Lee
P.O. Box 22232
Santa Fe, NM 87502-2232

American Horticultural
Therapy Assn.
909 York St.
Denver, CO 80206-3799
Phone: (301) 948-3010
E-mail: ahta@ahta.org
Web site: www.ahta.org

American Iris Society
Marilyn Harlow, Dept. E
P.O. Box 55
Freedom, CA 95019
Web site: www.iso
  media.com/home/AIS

American Rose Society
P.O. Box 30000
Shreveport, LA 71130-0030
Phone: (318) 938-5402
Fax: (318) 938-5405
E-mail: ars@ars-hq.org
Web site: www.ars.org

Backyard Wildlife
Habitat Program
National Wildlife Federation
8925 Leesburg Pike
Vienna, VA 22184-0001
Web site: http://nwf.org/nwf
  /habitats

Bio-Dynamic Farming
& Gardening Assn.
Bldg. 1002B
Thoreau Center
The Presidio
P.O. Box 29135
San Francisco, CA 94129-0135
Phone: (800) 516-7797
Fax: (415) 561-7796
Web site: www.bio
  dynamics.com

California Certified
Organic Farmers
1115 Mission St.
Santa Cruz, CA 95060
Phone: (831) 423-2263
Fax: (831) 423-4528

The Lady Bird Johnson
Wildflower Center
4801 La Crosse Ave.
Austin, TX 78739
Phone: (512) 292-4100
E-mail: nwrc@onr.com
Web site: www.wildflower.org

The Maine Organic Farmers
& Gardeners Assn.
P.O. Box 2176
Augusta, ME 04338
Phone: (207) 622-3118
Fax: (207) 622-3119
Web site: www.mofga.org

National Gardening Assn.
180 Flynn Ave.
Burlington, VT 05401
Phone: (802) 863-1308
Fax: (802) 863-5962
Web site: www2.garden.org
  /ngA

North American
Butterfly Assn. (NABA)
4 Delaware Rd.
Morristown, NJ 07960
Phone: (973) 285-0907
Fax: (973) 285-0936
E-mail: naba@naba.org
Web site: www.naba.org

North American Fruit
Explorers (NAFEX)
1716 Apples Rd.
Chapin, IL 62628
Web site: www.nafex.org

Northeast Organic
Farming Assn. (NOFA)
Web site: www.nofa.org
  /index.html
*An affiliation of seven state
chapters—CT, MA, NH, NJ,
RI, VT. Check Web site for
state contacts.*

Rodale Institute
Experimental Farm
611 Siegfriedale Rd.
Kutztown, PA 19530
Phone: (610) 683-1400
Fax: (610) 683-8548

Seed Savers Exchange
3076 N. Winn Rd.
Decorah, Iowa 52101
Phone: (319) 382-5990

Seeds of Diversity Canada
P.O. Box 36
Station Q
Toronto, Ontario
M4T 2L7 Canada
Phone: (905) 623-0353
E-mail: sodc@interlog.com
Web site: www.interlog.com
  /~sodc

Wild Ones–Natural
Landscapers, Ltd.
P.O. Box 23576
Milwaukee, WI 23576
*Nonprofit group dedicated to
educating and sharing infor-
mation among those who love
wildlife.*

BENEFICIAL INSECTS

Bountiful Gardens
18001 Shafer Ranch Rd.
Willits, CA 95490-9626
Phone/fax: (707) 459-6410

Gardens Alive!
5100 Schenley Pl.
Lawrenceburg, IN 47025
Phone: (812) 537-8650
Fax: (812) 537-5108

Gurney's Seed & Nursery Co.
110 Capital St.
Yankton, SD 57079
Phone: (605) 665-1930
Fax: (605) 665-9718

Harmony Farm
Supply & Nursery
P.O. Box 460
Graton, CA 95444
Phone: (707) 823-9125
Fax: (707) 823-1734
E-mail: info@harmony
farm.com
Web site: www.harmony
farm.com

The Natural Gardening Co.
217 San Anselmo Ave.
San Anselmo, CA 94960
Phone: (707) 766-9303
Fax: (707) 766-9747
E-mail: info@natural
gardening.com
Web site: www.natural
gardening.com

Peaceful Valley Farm Supply
P.O. Box 2209
Grass Valley, CA 95945
Phone: (530) 272-4769
Fax: (530) 272-4794
Web site: www.grow
organic.com

Territorial Seed Co.
P.O. Box 157
Cottage Grove, OR
97424-0061
Phone: (541) 942-9547
Fax: (888) 657-3131
E-mail: tertrl@srv1.vsite.com
Web site: www.territorial
seed.com

BIRD AND BUTTERFLY SUPPLIES

The Audubon Workshop
5200 Schenley Pl.
Lawrenceburg, IN 47025
Phone: (812) 537-3583

Coveside Conservation
Products
202 U.S. Route One
Box 374
Falmouth, ME 04105
Phone: (207) 774-7606
Fax: (207) 774-7613
E-mail: coveside@maine.com
Web site: www.maine.com
/coveside
Manufacturer of birdhouses

Down to Earth
4 Highland Circle
Lucas, TX 75002
Phone: (800) 865-1996
Fax: (972) 442-2816
E-mail: sales@downto
earth.com
Web site: www.downto
earth.com

Droll Yankees Inc.
27 Mill Rd.
Foster, RI 02825
Phone: (800) 352-9164
Fax: (401) 647-7620
E-mail: custserv@droll
yankees.com
Web site: http://droll
yankees.com
Manufacturer of bird feeders

Duncraft
102 Fisherville Rd.
Concord, NH 03303-9020
Phone: (800) 763-7878
Fax: (603) 226-3735
E-mail: info@duncraft.com
Web site: www.duncraft.com

Kester's Wild Game
Food Nurseries, Inc.
P.O. Box 516
Omro, WI 54963
Phone: (920) 685-2929
Fax: (920) 685-6727
E-mail: pkester@vbe.com
Web site: www.vbe.com
/~pkester

Wild Bird Centers
of America, Inc.
Phone: (800) 945-3247
Web site: www.wildbird
center.com

Wild Birds Unlimited
Phone: (800) 326-4928
Web site: www.wbu.com

Wildlife Nurseries, Inc.
P.O. Box 2724
Oshkosh, WI 54903-2724
Phone: (920) 231-3780
Fax: (920) 231-3554

BULBS

Breck's
6523 North Galena Rd.
Peoria, IL 61632
Phone: (309) 689-3850
Web site: www.springhill
nursery.com/brecks.html

Brent & Becky's Bulbs
7463 Heath Trail
Gloucester, VA 23061
Phone: (804) 693-3966
Fax: (804) 693-9436
E-mail: BBHeath@aol.com
Web site: www.brentand
beckysbulbs.com

Dutch Gardens
P.O. Box 200
Adelphia, NJ 07710-0200
Phone: (800) 775-2852
Fax: (732) 780-7720
E-mail: cs@dutchgardens.nl
Web site: www.dutchgardens.nl

McClure & Zimmerman
P.O. Box 368
108 W. Winnebago
Friesland, WI 53935-0368
Phone: (920) 326-4220
Fax: (800) 692-5864
Web site: www.mzbulb.com

Van Bourgondien Bros.
P.O. Box 1000
Babylon, NY 11702-9004
Phone: (800) 622-9959
Fax: (516) 669-1228
E-mail: blooms@dutch
    bulbs.com
Web site: www.dutchbulbs.com

FLOWERS AND ORNAMENTAL GRASSES

Abundant Life Seed Foundation
P.O. Box 772
Port Townsend, WA 98368
Phone: (360) 385-5660
Fax: (360) 385-7455
E-mail: abundant@olypen.com
Web site: http://csf.Colorado
    .edu/perma/abundant

Kurt Bluemel, Inc.
2740 Greene Lane
Baldwin, MD 21013-9523
Phone: (410) 557-7229
Fax: (410) 557-9785
E-mail: kbi@bluemel.com
Web site: www.blue
    mel.com/kbi

Bountiful Gardens
18001 Shafer Ranch Rd.
Willits, CA 95490-9626
Phone/fax: (707) 459-6410

Burns Water Gardens
R.R. #2
Baltimore, Ontario
K0K 1C0 Canada
Phone: (905) 372-2737
Fax: (905) 372-8625
E-mail: wtrgdn@eagle.ca
Web site: www.eagle.ca
    /~wtrgdn

W. Atlee Burpee & Co.
300 Park Ave.
Warminster, PA 18991-0001
Phone: (800) 888-1447
Fax: (800) 487-5530
Web site: www.burpee.com

Busse Gardens
5873 Oliver Ave., SW
Cokato, MN 55321-4229
Phone: (800) 544-3192
Fax: (320) 286-6601
E-mail: bussegardens@
    cmgate.com

California Carnivores
7020 Trenton-Healdsburg Rd.
Forestville, CA 95436
Phone: (707) 838-1630
Fax: (707) 838-9899
E-mail: califcarn@aol.com
Web site: www.california
    carnivores.com
*Commercially propagated
    pitcher plants* (Sarracenia*)*

Carroll Gardens
444 E. Main St.
Westminster, MD 21157
Phone: (800) 638-6334
Fax: (410) 857-4112

Collector's Nursery
16804 N.E. 102nd Ave.
Battle Ground, WA 98604
Phone: (360) 574-3832
Fax: (360) 571-8540
E-mail: dianar@collectors
    nursery.com
Web site: www.collectors
    nursery.com
*Pulmonarias by Terra Nova
    Nurseries*

Daydreamer Aquatic
& Perennial Gardens
Route 1, Box 438
Belpre, OH 45714
Phone: (800) 741-3867
Fax: (740) 423-4355
E-mail: trishatdpg@aol.com
Web site: www.daydreamer
    gardens.com

Daylily Discounters
1 Daylily Plaza
Alachua, FL 32615
Phone: (904) 462-1539
Fax: (904) 462-5111
E-mail: daylily@earthlink.com
Web site: www.daylily
    discounters.com

Ferry-Morse Seed Co.
P.O. Box 488
Fulton, KY 42041-0488
Phone: (800) 283-3400
Fax: (800) 283-2700
Web site: www.gardennet.com/
    FerryMorse

Forestfarm
990 Tetherow Rd.
Williams, OR 97544-9599
Phone: (541) 846-7269
Fax: (541) 846-6963
E-mail: forestfarm@aone
    pro.net
Web site: www.forestfarm.com

Fragrant Farms, Inc.
413 Woods Lane
New Harmony, IN 47631
Phone: (888) 814-4665
Fax: (812) 682-4577
E-mail: mark@fragrant
    farms.com
Peony plants and cut flowers

The Fragrant Path
P.O. Box 328
Fort Calhoun, NE 68023
*Seeds of fragrant, old-
    fashioned, and rare plants*

Goodness Grows, Inc.
Highway 77 N
P.O. Box 311
Lexington, GA 30648
Phone: (706) 743-5055
Fax: (706) 743-5112

Goodwin Creek Gardens
P.O. Box 83
Williams, OR 97544
Phone: (541) 846-7357

Greer Gardens
1280 Goodpasture Island Rd.
Eugene, OR 97401-1794
Phone: (541) 686-8266
Fax: (541) 686-0910

Heronswood Nursery
7530 N.E. 288th St.
Kingston, WA 98346
Phone: (360) 297-4172
Fax: (360) 297-8321
Web site: www.herons
   wood.com
*Pulmonarias by Terra Nova
Nurseries*

Jackson & Perkins
P.O. Box 1028
Medford, OR 97501
Phone: (800) 292-4769
Fax: (800) 242-0329
Web site: www.jacksonand
   perkins.com

Johnny's Selected Seeds
Foss Hill Rd.
Albion, ME 04910-9731
Phone: (207) 437-4357
Fax: (800) 437-4290
E-mail: customerservice@
   johnnyseeds.com
Web site: www.johnny
   seeds.com

J. W. Jung Seed Co.
335 S. High St.
Randolph, WI 53957-0001
Phone: (800) 297-3123
Fax: (800) 692-5864

Limerock Ornamental
Grasses, Inc.
70 Sawmill Rd.
Port Matilda, PA 16870
Phone: (814) 692-2272
Fax: (814) 692-9848

Logee's Greenhouses, Ltd.
141 North St.
Danielson, CT 06239-1939
Phone: (860) 774-8038
Fax: (888) 774-9932
E-mail: logee-info@logees.com
Web site: http://logees.com/www

Louisiana Nursery
5833 Highway 182
Opelousas, LA 70570
Phone: (318) 948-3696
Fax: (318) 942-6404

Dan Majeski Nurseries
P.O. Box 674
117 French Rd.
West Seneca, NY 14224-0674
Phone: (716) 825-6410
Fax: (716) 827-8537
E-mail: danjr@majeski
   nursery.com
Web site: www.majeski
   nursery.com
*Pulmonarias by Terra Nova
Nurseries*

Milaeger's Gardens
4838 Douglas Ave.
Racine, WI 53402-2498
Phone: (800) 669-9956
Fax: (414) 639-1855

The Natural Garden
38W443 Highway 64
St. Charles, IL 60175
Phone: (630) 584-0150
Fax: (630) 584-0185

Niche Gardens
1111 Dawson Rd.
Chapel Hill, NC 27516
Phone: (919) 967-0078
Fax: (919) 967-4026
E-mail: orders@nichegdn.com
Web site: www.nichegdn.com

Nichols Garden Nursery
1190 N. Pacific Highway
Albany, OR 97321-4580
Phone: (541) 928-9280
Fax: (541) 967-8406
E-mail: info@gardennursery.com
Web site: www.garden
   nursery.com

Park Seed
1 Parkton Ave.
Greenwood, SC 29647-0001
Phone: (800) 845-3369
Fax: (800) 275-9941
E-mail: orders@parkseed.com
Web site: http://parkseed.com

Pinetree Garden Seeds
Box 300
616A Lewiston Rd.
New Gloucester, ME 04260
Phone: (207) 926-3400
Fax: (888) 527-3337
E-mail: superseeds@world
   net.att.net
Web site: www.superseeds.com

Plant Delights Nursery, Inc.
9241 Sauls Rd.
Raleigh, NC 27603
Phone: (919) 772-4794
Fax: (919) 662-0370
E-mail: office@plantdel.com
Web site: www.plantdel.com
*Nursery propagated pitcher
plants (Sarracenia)*

Prairie Moon Nursery
Route 3, Box 163
Winona, MN 55987
Phone: (507) 452-1362
Fax: (507) 454-5238

Prairie Nursery
P.O. Box 306
Westfield, WI 53964
Phone: (608) 296-3679
Fax: (608) 296-2741
Web site: www.prairie
   nursery.com

Roslyn Nursery
211 Burrs Lane
Dix Hills, NY 11746
Phone: (516) 643-9347
Fax: (516) 427-0894
E-mail: roslyn@concentric.net
Web site: www.cris.com/
~Roslyn
Pulmonarias by Terra Nova Nurseries

Seeds Blüm
HC 33, Box 2057
Boise, ID 83706
Phone: (800) 742-1423
Fax: (208) 338-5658
E-mail: 103374.167@compu
serve.com
Web site: www.seedsblum.com

Seeds of Change
P.O. Box 15700
Sante Fe, NM 87506-5700
Phone: (888) 762-7333
Fax: (888) 329-4762
E-mail: service@seedsof
change.com
Web site: www.seedsof
change.com

Shepherd's Garden Seeds
30 Irene St.
Torrington, CT 06790-6658
Phone: (860) 482-3638
Web site: www.shepherd
seeds.com

Southern Perennials & Herbs
98 Bridges Rd.
Tylertown, MS 39667-9338
Phone: (800) 774-0079
Fax: (601) 684-3729
E-mail: sph@neosoft.com
Web site: www.s-p-h.com

Stokes Seeds Inc.
P.O. Box 548
Buffalo, NY 14240-0548
Phone: (716) 695-6980
Fax: (888) 834-3334
E-mail: Stokes@stokeseeds.com
Web site: www.stokeseeds.com

Territorial Seed Co.
P.O. Box 157
Cottage Grove, OR 97424-0061
Phone: (541) 942-9547
Fax: (888) 657-3131
E-mail: tertrl@srv1.vsite.com
Web site: www.territorial
-seed.com

Thompson & Morgan, Inc.
P.O. Box 1308
Jackson, NJ 08527-0308
Phone: (800) 274-7333
Fax: (888) 466-4769
E-mail: c-svcs@thompson
-morgan.com
Web site: http://thompson
-morgan.com

Van Ness Water Gardens
2460 North Euclid Ave.
Upland, CA 91784-1199
Phone: (909) 982-2425
Fax: (909) 949-7217
E-mail: vnwg@vnwg.com
Web site: www.vnwg.com

Wayside Gardens
1 Garden Lane
Hodges, SC 29695-0001
Phone: (800) 845-1124
Fax: (800) 457-9712
E-mail: orders@wayside
gardens.com
Web site: www.wayside
gardens.com

We-Du Nurseries
Route 5, Box 724
Marion, NC 28752
Phone: (704) 738-8300
Fax: (704) 738-8131

White Flower Farm
P.O. Box 50
Litchfield, CT 06759-0050
Phone: (800) 411-6159
Fax: (860) 496-1418
Web site: www.whiteflower
farm.com

Wildseed Farms
P.O. Box 3000
425 Wildflower Hills
Fredericksburg, TX 78624-3000
Phone: (800) 848-0078
Fax: (830) 990-8090
Web site: www.wildseed
farms.com

Woodlanders, Inc.
1128 Colleton Ave.
Aiken, SC 29801
Phone/fax: (803) 648-7522

FRUITS AND BERRIES

Adams County Nursery, Inc.
26 Nursery Rd.
P.O. Box 108
Aspers, PA 17304
Phone: (717) 677-8105
Fax: (717) 677-4124
E-mail: acn@cvn.net
Web site: www.acnursery.com

Applesource
1716 Apples Rd.
Chapin, IL 62628
Phone: (800) 588-3854
Fax: (217) 245-7844
E-mail: vorbeck@csj.net
Web site: www.apple
source.com
Apples only, not apple trees

Bear Creek Nursery
P.O. Box 411
Northport, WA 99157
Phone: (509) 732-6219
Fax: (509) 732-4417
E-mail: BearCreek@plix.com
Web site: http://BearCreek
Nursery.com

Country Carriage
Nurseries & Seed, Inc.
P.O. Box 548
Hartford, MI 49057
Phone: (616) 621-2491

Cummins Nursery
18 Glass Factory Bay Rd.
Geneva, NY 14456
Phone: (315) 789-7083
E-mail: jmc1@epix.net
Web site: www.dabney.com/
   cumminsnursery

Edible Landscaping
361 Spirit Ridge Lane
P.O. Box 77
Afton, VA 22920-0077
Phone: (804) 361-9134
Fax: (804) 361-1916
E-mail: el@cstone.net
Web site: www.eat-it.com

Hidden Springs Nursery
170 Hidden Springs Lane
Cookeville, TN 38501
Phone: (931) 268-2592
Grafted bareroot fruit trees

Indiana Berry & Plant Co.
5218 West 500 South
Huntingburg, IN 47542
Phone: (812) 683-3055
Fax: (812) 683-2004
E-mail: inberry@psci.net

Raintree Nursery
391 Butts Rd.
Morton, WA 98356
Phone: (360) 496-6400
Fax: (888) 770-8358
E-mail: leonard@rain
   treenursery.com
Web site: www.rain
   treenursery.com

Rocky Meadow
Orchard & Nursery
360 Rocky Meadow Rd. NW
New Salisbury, IN 47161
Phone: (812) 347-2213
Fax: (812) 347-2488
E-mail: rockymdw@net
   pointe.com

St. Lawrence Nurseries
325 S. H. 345
Potsdam, NY 13676
Phone: (315) 265-6739
E-mail: trees@sln.pots
   dam.ny.us
Web site: www.sln.pots
   dam.ny.us

Southmeadow Fruit Gardens
P.O. Box 211
10603 Cleveland Ave.
Baroda, MI 49101
Phone: (616) 422-2411
Fax: (616) 422-1464
E-mail: smfruit@aol.com

Stark Bro's Nurseries
& Orchards Co.
P.O. Box 10
Louisiana, MO 63353
Phone: (800) 478-2759
Fax: (573) 754-5290
E-mail: service@starkbros.com
Web site: www.starkbros.com

GARDENING SUPPLIES AND TOOLS

Alsto's Handy Helpers
Route 150 East
P.O. Box 1267
Galesburg, IL 61402-1267
Phone: (800) 447-0048
Fax: (800) 522-5786

Bountiful Gardens
18001 Shafer Ranch Rd.
Willits, CA 95490-9626
Phone/fax: (707) 459-6410

W. Atlee Burpee & Co.
300 Park Ave.
Warminster, PA 18991-0001
Phone: (800) 888-1447
Fax: (800) 487-5530
Web site: www.burpee.com

Delgard Aluminum
Ornamental Fencing
Delair Group, Inc.
8600 River Rd.
Delair, NJ 08110
Phone: (800) 235-0185
Fax: (609) 663-1297
Web site: www.delair
   group.com/delgard
*Manufacturers of decorative
fencing, including aluminum
picket-style fencing*

Dripworks
231 E. San Francisco St.
Willits, CA 95490
Phone: (800) 616-8321
Fax: (707) 459-9645
E-mail: dripwrks@pacific.net
Web site: www.dripworks
   usa.com
Drip irrigation products

Gardener's Supply Co.
128 Intervale Rd.
Burlington, VT 05401-2850
Phone: (800) 863-1700
Fax: (800) 551-6712
E-mail: info@gardeners.com
Web site: www.gardeners.com

Gardens Alive!
5100 Schenley Pl.
Lawrenceburg, IN 47025
Phone: (812) 537-8650
Fax: (812) 537-5108

Harmony Farm
Supply & Nursery
P.O. Box 460
Graton, CA 95444
Phone: (707) 823-9125
Fax: (707) 823-1734
E-mail: info@harmonyfarm.com
Web site: www.harmony
   farm.com

The Horchow Collection
P.O. Box 620048
Dallas, TX 75262-0048
Phone: (800) 456-7000
Web site: www.nmdirect.com
   /hc.html
Two-tiered topiary system

Ideal Concrete Block Co.
55 Power Rd.
Westford, MA 01886
Phone: (978) 692-3076
Fax: (978) 692-0817
Concrete wall systems

Jim Jeansonne
Baton Enterprises
8867 Highland Rd.
Suite 160
Baton Rouge, LA 70806
Phone: (225) 766-1268
Fax: (225) 757-8161
E-mail: info@spira-stake.com
Web site: www.spira-stake.com
Spira-stake

Jerith Manufacturing Co., Inc.
3901 G St.
Philadelphia, PA 19124
Phone: (800) 344-2242
Fax: (215) 739-4844
E-mail: sales@jerith.com
Web site: www.jerith.com
*Manufacturers of decorative
fencing, including aluminum
picket-style fencing*

Johnny's Selected Seeds
Foss Hill Rd.
Albion, ME 04910-9731
Phone: (207) 437-4357
Fax: (800) 437-4290
E-mail: customerservice@
johnnyseeds.com
Web site: www.johnny
seeds.com

Keystone Retaining Walls, Inc.
4444 W. 78th St.
Bloomington, MN 55435
Phone: (800) 747-8971
Fax: (612) 897-3858
Web site: http://psld.ipr.com
/keystone
Concrete wall systems

Kinsman Co., Inc.
P.O. Box 357
River Rd.
Point Pleasant, PA 18950
Phone: (800) 733-4146
Fax: (215) 297-0450
E-mail: contact@kinsman
garden.com
Web site: www.kinsman
garden.com

A. M. Leonard, Inc.
241 Fox Drive
Piqua, OH 45356
Phone: (800) 543-8955
Fax: (800) 433-0633
E-mail: info@amleo.com
Web site: www.amleo.com

The Natural Gardening Co.
217 San Anselmo Ave.
San Anselmo, CA 94960
Phone: (707) 766-9303
Fax: (707) 766-9747
E-mail: info@natural
gardening.com
Web site: www.natural
gardening.com

Ohio Earth Food, Inc.
5488 Swamp St., NE
Hartville, OH 44632
Phone: (330) 877-9356
Fax: (330) 877-4237

Peaceful Valley Farm Supply
P.O. Box 2209
Grass Valley, CA 95945
Phone: (530) 272-4769
Fax: (530) 272-4794
Web site: www.grow
organic.com

Pinetree Garden Seeds
Box 300
616A Lewiston Rd.
New Gloucester, ME 04260
Phone: (207) 926-3400
Fax: (888) 527-3337
E-mail: superseeds@world
net.att.net
Web site: www.superseeds.com

Plow & Hearth
P.O. Box 5000
Madison, VA 22727-1500
Phone: (800) 627-1712
Fax: (800) 843-2509

Risi Stone Systems
Le Parc Office Tower
8500 Leslie St., Suite 390
Thornhill, Ontario
L3T 7P1 Canada
Phone: (905) 882-5898 *or*
(800) 626-WALL
Fax: (905) 882-4556
E-mail: info@risistone.com
Web site: www.risistone.com
Concrete wall systems

Ruibal's Topiary Systems
1118 S. Central Expressway
Dallas, TX 75201
Phone: (214) 744-3434
Two-tiered topiary system

Saratoga Rail Fence & Supply Co.
P.O. Box 13864
Albany, NY 12212-9600
Phone: (800) 869-8703
Fax: (518) 869-8755
PVC post and rail fencing

Seeds of Change
P.O. Box 15700
Sante Fe, NM 87506-5700
Phone: (888) 762-7333
Fax: (888) 329-4762
E-mail: service@seedsof
change.com
Web site: www.seedsof
change.com

Smith & Hawken
Two Arbor Lane
Box 6900
Florence, KY 41022-6900
Phone: (800) 981-9888 *catalog
requests only*
Fax: (606) 727-1166
Web site: www.smith
-hawken.com

Sto-Cote Products, Inc.
P.O. Box 310
Richmond, IL, 60071
Phone: (800) 435-2621
Fabrene

Territorial Seed Co.
P.O. Box 157
Cottage Grove, OR 97424-0061
Phone: (541) 942-9547
Fax: (888) 657-3131
E-mail: tertrl@srv1.vsite.com
Web site: www.territorial
-seed.com

Unilock New York, Inc.
51 International Blvd.
Brewster, NY 10509
Phone: (914) 278-6700
Fax: (914) 278-6788
E-mail: newyork@unilock.com
Web site: www.unilock.com
*Paving stones, retaining walls,
and curbing*

Whatever Works
Earth Science Bldg.
74 20th St.
Brooklyn, NY 11232
Phone: (800) 499-6757
Fax: (718) 499-1005
Web site: www.whatever
works.com
Garden-Lite rock planters

Worm's Way
7850 N. Highway 37
Bloomington, IN 47404
Phone: (800) 274-9676
Fax: (800) 316-1264
e-mail: info@wormsway.com
Web site: http://wormsway.com

HERBS

Fox Hollow Seed Co.
P.O. Box 148
McGrann, PA 16236
Phone: (412) 548-7333
Fax: (412) 543-5751

The Fragrant Garden
Katherine Glynn
P.O. Box 281
Port Perry, Ontario
L9L 1A3 Canada
Phone: (905) 985-0079
Fax: (905) 985-4788
E-mail: kglynn@sprint.ca
*Potpourri, essentials oils, and
other fragrance products*

Gaia Garden Herbal
Dispensary
Chanchal Cabrera
2672 West Broadway
Vancouver, B.C.
V6K 2G3 Canada
Phone: (604) 734-4372
Fax: (604) 734-4376
E-mail: GAIA
GARDEN@bc.sympatico.ca
*Classically trained English
herbalist who teaches interna-
tionally*

Goodwin Creek Gardens
P.O. Box 83
Williams, OR 97544
Phone: (541) 846-7357

Horizon Herbs
P.O. Box 69
Williams, OR 97544
Phone: (541) 846-6704
E-mail: herbseed@chatlink.com
Web site: www.budget.net
/~herbseed
*Seed, rootstock, and live plants
of medicinal herbs*

Johnny's Selected Seeds
Foss Hill Rd.
Albion, ME 04910-9731
Phone: (207) 437-4357
Fax: (800) 437-4290
E-mail: customerservice@
johnnyseeds.com
Web site: www.johnny
seeds.com

Long Creek Herbs
Route 4, Box 730
Oak Grove, AR 72660
Phone: (417) 779-5450
Fax: (417) 779-5450
E-mail: LCHerbs@tri-lakes.net
Web site: www.longcreek
herbs.com
*Herb products and books;
demonstration gardens open
to public*

Lunar Farms Herbals
3 Highland-Greenhills
Gilmer, TX 75644
Phone: (800) 687-1052
E-mail: spritsong1@aol.com
Web site: www.herbworld.com
/lunarfarms
*Herbal salves, oils, and
personal care products*

Nichols Garden Nursery
1190 N. Pacific Highway
Albany, OR 97321-4580
Phone: (541) 928-9280
Fax: (541) 967-8406
E-mail: info@garden
nursery.com
Web site: www.garden
nursery.com

Richters Herb Catalogue
357 Hwy. 47
Goodwood, Ontario
L0C 1A0 Canada
Phone: (905) 640-6677
Fax: (905) 640-6641
E-mail: inquiry@richters.com
Web site: www.richters.com

Sage Mountain Herbs
Rosemary Gladstar
P.O. Box 420
E. Barre, VT 05649
Phone: (802) 479-9825
Fax: (802) 476-3722
*Ongoing classes, apprenticeship
program, and correspondence
course*

The Sandy Mush Herb Nursery
316 Surrett Cove Rd.
Leicester, NC 28748
Phone: (704) 683-2014

Shepherd's Garden Seeds
30 Irene St.
Torrington, CT 06790-6658
Phone: (860) 482-3638
Web site: www.shepherd
seeds.com

Well-Sweep Herb Farm
205 Mt. Bethel Rd.
Port Murray, NJ 07865
Phone: (908) 852-5390

SOIL TESTING

Cook's Consulting
R.D. 2, Box 13
Lowville, NY 13367
Phone: (315) 376-3002
*Organic recommendations,
free soil testing kit*

Peaceful Valley Farm Supply
P.O. Box 2209
Grass Valley, CA 95945
Phone: (530) 272-4769
Fax: (530) 272-4794
Web site: www.grow
   organic.com
*Basic soil test as well as one for
micronutrients; organic
recommendations provided*

Timberleaf Soil Testing Services
39648 Old Spring Rd.
Murrieta, CA 92563
Phone: (909) 677-7510
*Basic and trace mineral soil
tests; organic recommendations provided*

Wallace Laboratories
365 Coral Circle
El Segundo, CA 90245
Phone: (310) 615-0116
Fax: (310) 640-6863
*Analyses for essential nutrients
along with nonessential poten-
tially toxic heavy metals;
analyses of water, plant tissues,
composts, fertilizers, and
building materials; recommendations provided*

Woods End Research Laboratory
P.O. Box 297
Mt. Vernon, ME 04352
Phone: (207) 293-2457
Fax: (207) 293-2488
*Soil testing for homeowners
and soil life testing; compost
testing kit*

TREES, SHRUBS, AND VINES

Carroll Gardens
444 E. Main St.
Westminster, MD 21157
Phone: (800) 638-6334
Fax: (410) 857-4112

Forestfarm
990 Tetherow Rd.
Williams, OR 97544-9599
Phone: (541) 846-7269
Fax: (541) 846-6963
E-mail: forestfarm@aonepro.net
Web site: www.forestfarm.com

Greer Gardens
1280 Goodpasture Island Rd.
Eugene, OR 97401-1794
Phone: (541) 686-8266
Fax: (541) 686-0910

Gurney's Seed & Nursery Co.
110 Capital St.
Yankton, SD 57079
Phone: (605) 665-1930
Fax: (605) 665-9718

Pickering Nurseries, Inc.
670 Kingston Rd.
Pickering, Ontario
L1V 1A6 Canada
Phone: (905) 839-2111
Fax: (905) 839-4807
Roses

The Roseraie at Bayfields
P.O. Box R
Waldoboro, ME 04572-0919
Phone: (207) 832-6330
Fax: (800) 933-4508
E-mail: zapus@roseraie.com
Web site: www.roseraie.com
*Roses and lobster-trap metal
climbing rose supports*

Roslyn Nursery
211 Burrs Lane
Dix Hills, NY 11746
Phone: (516) 643-9347
Fax: (516) 427-0894
E-mail: roslyn@concentric.net
Web site: www.cris.com
   /~Roslyn

Wayside Gardens
1 Garden Lane
Hodges, SC 29695-0001
Phone: (800) 845-1124
Fax: (800) 457-9712
E-mail: orders@wayside
   gardens.com
Web site: www.wayside
   gardens.com

White Flower Farm
P.O. Box 50
Litchfield, CT 06759-0050
Phone: (800) 411-6159
Fax: (860) 496-1418
Web site: www.whiteflower
   farm.com

Woodlanders, Inc.
1128 Colleton Ave.
Aiken, SC 29801
Phone/fax: (803) 648-7522

VEGETABLES

Abundant Life Seed Foundation
P.O. Box 772
Port Townsend, WA 98368
Phone: (360) 385-5660
Fax: (360) 385-7455
E-mail: abundant@olypen.com
Web site: http://csf.Colorado
   .edu/perma/abundant

W. Atlee Burpee & Co.
300 Park Ave.
Warminster, PA 18991-0001
Phone: (800) 888-1447
Fax: (800) 487-5530
Web site: www.burpee.com

The Cook's Garden
P.O. Box 535
Londonderry, VT 05148
Phone: (800) 457-9703
Fax: (800) 457-9705
Web site: www.cooks
   garden.com

Johnny's Selected Seeds
Foss Hill Rd.
Albion, ME 04910-9731
Phone: (207) 437-4357
Fax: (800) 437-4290
E-mail: customerservice@
johnnyseeds.com
Web site: www.johnny
seeds.com

Ferry-Morse Seed Co.
P.O. Box 488
Fulton, KY 42041-0488
Phone: (800) 283-3400
Fax: (800) 283-2700
Web site: www.gardennet.com
/FerryMorse

Fox Hollow Seed Co.
P.O. Box 148
McGrann, PA 16236
Phone: (412) 548-7333
Fax: (412) 543-5751

Gurney's Seed & Nursery Co.
110 Capital St.
Yankton, SD 57079
Phone: (605) 665-1930
Fax: (605) 665-9718

Native Seeds/Search
2509 N. Campbell Ave., #325
Tucson, AZ 85719
Phone: (520) 327-9123
no orders
Fax: (520) 327-5821
orders welcome
Web site: http://desert.net/seeds

Park Seed
1 Parkton Ave.
Greenwood, SC 29647-0001
Phone: (800) 845-3369
Fax: (800) 275-9941
E-mail: orders@parkseed.com
Web site: http://parkseed.com

Pinetree Garden Seeds
Box 300
616A Lewiston Rd.
New Gloucester, ME 04260
Phone: (207) 926-3400
Fax: (888) 527-3337
E-mail: superseeds@world
net.att.net
Web site: www.superseeds.com

Ronniger's Seed & Potato Co.
P.O. Box 307
Ellensburg, WA 98926
Phone: (800) 846-6178

Seeds Blüm
HC 33, Box 2057
Boise, ID 83706
Phone: (800) 742-1423
Fax: (208) 338-5658
E-mail: 103374.167@compu
serve.com
Web site: www.seedsblum.com

Seeds of Change
P.O. Box 15700
Sante Fe, NM 87506-5700
Phone: (888) 762-7333
Fax: (888) 329-4762
E-mail: service@seedsof
change.com
Web site: www.seedsof
change.com

Shepherd's Garden Seeds
30 Irene St.
Torrington, CT 06790-6658
Phone: (860) 482-3638
Web site: www.shepherd
seeds.com

R. H. Shumway, Seedsman
P.O. Box 1
Graniteville, SC 29829-0001
Phone: (803) 663-9771
Fax: (803) 663-9772

Southern Exposure
Seed Exchange
P.O. Box 170
Earlysville, VA 22936
Phone: (804) 973-4703
Fax: (804) 973-8717
E-mail: gardens@southern
exposure.com
Web site: www.southern
exposure.com

WILDFLOWERS

Abundant Life Seed Foundation
P.O. Box 772
Port Townsend, WA 98368
Phone: (360) 385-5660
Fax: (360) 385-7455
E-mail: abundant@olypen.com
Web site: http://csf.Colorado
.edu/perma/abundant

Clyde Robin Seed Co.
P.O. Box 2366
Castro Valley, CA 94546
Phone: (510) 785-0425
Fax: (510) 785-6463
Web site: www.clyderobin.com

Native Seeds/Search
2509 N. Campbell Ave., #325
Tucson, AZ 85719
Phone: (520) 327-9123
no orders
Fax: (520) 327-5821
orders welcome
Web site: http://desert.net/seeds

The Natural Garden
38W443 Highway 64
St. Charles, IL 60175
Phone: (630) 584-0150
Fax: (630) 584-0185

Plants of the Southwest
Agua Fria Rd.
Route 6, Box 11A
Santa Fe, NM 87501
Phone: (505) 471-2212
Fax: (505) 438-8800
E-mail: contact@plantsofthe
southwest.com
Web site: www.plantsofthe
southwest.com

Prairie Moon Nursery
Route 3, Box 163
Winona, MN 55987
Phone: (507) 452-1362
Fax: (507) 454-5238

Prairie Nursery
P.O. Box 306
Westfield, WI 53964
Phone: (608) 296-3679
Fax: (608) 296-2741
Web site: www.prairie
nursery.com

Wildseed Farms
P.O. Box 3000
425 Wildflower Hills
Fredericksburg, TX
78624-3000
Phone: (800) 848-0078
Fax: (830) 990-8090
Web site: www.wildseed
farms.com

Recommended Reading

BIRD AND BUTTERFLY GARDENS

Adams, George. *Birdscaping Your Garden.* Emmaus, PA: Rodale Press, 1994.

Roth, Sally. *Attracting Birds to Your Backyard.* Emmaus, PA: Rodale Press, 1998.

———. *Natural Landscaping.* Emmaus, PA: Rodale Press, 1997.

Schneck, Marcus. *Butterflies.* Emmaus, PA: Rodale Press, 1990.

———. *Your Backyard Wildlife Year.* Emmaus, PA: Rodale Press, 1996.

COMPOSTING AND SOIL

Appelhof, Mary. *Worms Eat My Garbage.* Kalamazoo, MI: Flower Press, 1982.

Greshuny, Grace. *Start with the Soil.* Emmaus, PA: Rodale Press, 1993.

Hynes, Erin. *Rodale's Successful Organic Gardening: Improving the Soil.* Emmaus, PA: Rodale Press, 1994.

Martin, Deborah, and Grace Gershuny, eds. *The Rodale Book of Composting.* Emmaus, PA: Rodale Press, 1992.

GENERAL GARDENING

Benjamin, Joan, ed. *Great Garden Shortcuts.* Emmaus, PA: Rodale Press, 1996.

Bradley, Fern Marshall, and Barbara Ellis, eds. *Rodale's All-New Encyclopedia of Organic Gardening.* Emmaus, PA: Rodale Press, 1992.

Coleman, Eliot. *The New Organic Grower.* White River Junction, VT: Chelsea Green Publishing Co., 1995.

Costenbader, Carol W. *The Big Book of Preserving the Harvest.* Pownal, VT: Storey Communications, 1997.

Cunningham, Sally Jean. *Great Garden Companions.* Emmaus, PA: Rodale Press, 1998.

Lanza, Patricia. *Lasagna Gardening.* Emmaus, PA: Rodale Press, 1998.

Logsdon, Gene. *The Contrary Farmer's Invitation to Gardening.* White River Junction, VT: Chelsea Green Publishing Co., 1997.

Stone, Pat. *Easy Gardening 101.* Pownal, VT: Storey Communications, 1998.

Swain, Roger. *The Practical Gardener.* Boston: Little, Brown and Company, 1989. Reprint, New York: Galahad Books, 1998.

FRUITS AND BERRIES

McClure, Susan. *Rodale's Successful Organic Gardening: Fruits and Berries.* Emmaus, PA: Rodale Press, 1996.

Nick, Jean, and Fern Marshall Bradley. *Growing Fruits and Vegetables Organically.* Emmaus, PA: Rodale Press, 1994.

Reich, Lee. *Uncommon Fruits Worthy of Attention.* Reading, MA: Addison-Wesley Publishing Co., 1991.

HERBS AND CRAFTS

Bethman, Laura Donnelly. *Nature Printing with Herbs, Fruits, and Flowers.* Pownal, VT: Storey Communications, 1996.

Duke, James A. *The Green Pharmacy.* Emmaus, PA: Rodale Press, 1997.

Gladstar, Rosemary. *Herbal Healing for Women.* New York: Simon & Schuster, 1993.

Hart, Rhonda. *Easter Eggs—By the Dozens!: Fun and Creative Egg Decorating Projects for All Ages!* Pownal, VT: Storey Communications, 1993.

James, Tina. *The Salad Bar in Your Own Backyard.* Reisterstown, MD: Gardening from the Heart, 1996.

Kowalchik, Claire, and William H. Hylton. *Rodale's Illustrated Encyclopedia of Herbs*. Emmaus, PA: Rodale Press, 1987.

Long, Jim. *Herbs, Just For Fun: A Beginner's Guide to Starting an Herb Garden*. Oak Grove, AR: Long Creek Herbs, 1996.

———. *Classic Herb Blends*. Oak Grove, AR: Long Creek Herbs, 1996.

McClure, Susan. *The Herb Gardener: A Guide for All Seasons*. Pownal, VT: Storey Communication, 1995.

Oster, Maggie. *Herbal Vinegar*. Pownal, VT: Storey Communication, 1994.

Oster, Maggie, and Sal Gilbertie. *The Herbal Palate Cookbook*. Pownal, VT: Storey Communications, 1996.

Smith, Miranda. *Your Backyard Herb Garden*. Emmaus, PA: Rodale Press, 1997.

Sombke, Laurence. *Beautiful Easy Herbs*. Emmaus, PA: Rodale Press, 1997.

Tourles, Stephanie. *The Herbal Body Book*. Pownal, VT: Storey Communications, 1994.

———. *Natural Foot Care*. Pownal, VT: Storey Communications, 1998.

Weed, Susun. *Healing Wise*. Woodstock, NY: Ash Tree Publishing, 1989.

———. *Menopausal Years: The Wise Woman Way*. Woodstock, NY: Ash Tree Publishing, 1992.

LANDSCAPE AND FLOWER GARDENING

Bender, Steve, and Felder Rushing. *Passalong Plants*. Chapel Hill, NC: The University of North Carolina Press, 1993.

Bradley, Fern Marshall, ed. *Gardening with Perennials*. Emmaus, PA: Rodale Press, 1996.

Byczynski, Lynn. *The Flower Farmer: An Organic Grower's Guide to Raising and Selling Cut Flowers*. White River Junction, VT: Chelsea Green Publishing Co., 1997.

Cox, Jeff. *Perennial All-Stars: The 150 Best Perennials for Great-Looking, Trouble-Free Gardens*. Emmaus, PA: Rodale Press, 1998.

D'Amato, Peter. *The Savage Garden: Cultivating Carnivorous Plants*. Berkeley, CA: Ten Speed Press, 1998.

DiSabato-Aust, Tracy. *The Well-Tended Perennial Garden: Planting and Pruning Techniques*. Portland, OR: Timber Press, 1998.

Ellis, Barbara. *Taylor's Guide to Growing North America's Favorite Plants*. Boston: Houghton Mifflin, 1998.

Harper, Pamela, and Frederick McGourty. *Perennials: How to Select, Grow and Enjoy*. Los Angeles: Price Stern Sloan, Inc., 1985.

McKeon, Judy. *The Encyclopedia of Roses*. Emmaus, PA: Rodale Press, 1995.

Phillips, Ellen, and C. Colston Burrell. *Rodale's Illustrated Encyclopedia of Perennials*. Emmaus, PA: Rodale Press, 1993.

Sombke, Laurence. *Beautiful Easy Flower Gardens*. Emmaus, PA: Rodale Press, 1995.

Taylor, Norman. *Taylor's Guide to Annuals*. Rev. ed. Boston: Houghton Mifflin Co., 1986.

PEST MANAGEMENT

Ellis, Barbara W., and Fern Marshall Bradley. *The Organic Gardener's Handbook of Natural Insect and Disease Control*. Emmaus, PA: Rodale Press, 1992.

Gilkeson, Linda, et al. *Rodale's Pest and Disease Problem Solver*. Emmaus, PA: Rodale Press, 1996.

Hart, Rhonda. *Bugs, Slugs, and Other Thugs*. Pownal, VT: Storey Communications, 1991.

SEASON EXTENSION

Colebrook, Binda. *Winter Gardening in the Maritime Northwest*. Seattle, WA: Sasquatch Books, 1989.

Coleman, Eliot. *Four-Season Harvest: How to Harvest Fresh, Organic Vegetables from Your Home Garden All Year Long.* White River Junction, VT: Chelsea Green Publishing Co., 1992.

SEED STARTING

Bubel, Nancy. *The New Seed-Starter's Handbook.* Emmaus, PA: Rodale Press, 1988.

Ondra, Nancy, and Barbara Ellis. *Easy Plant Propagation.* (Taylor's Weekend Gardening Guides.) Boston: Houghton Mifflin Co., 1998.

Powell, Eileen. *From Seed to Bloom.* Pownal, VT: Storey Communications, 1995.

WEEDS

Hynes, Erin. *Rodale's Successful Organic Gardening: Controlling Weeds.* Emmaus, PA: Rodale Press, 1995.

Pleasant, Barbara. *The Gardener's Weed Book.* Pownal, VT: Storey Communications, 1996.

MAGAZINES AND NEWSLETTERS

Avant Gardener, The, P.O. Box 489, New York, NY 10028

Common Sense Pest Control Quarterly, Bio-Integral Resource Center (BIRC), P.O. Box 7414, Berkeley, CA 94707-0414

Country Living Gardener, 224 W. 57th St., New York, NY 10019

Growing for Market, P.O. Box 3747, Lawrence, KS 66046

Homesteader's Connection, P.O. Box 5186, Cookeville, TN 38505

HortIdeas, 750 Black Lick Road, Gravel Switch, KY 40328

Organic Gardening, Rodale Press Inc., 33 E. Minor St., Emmaus, PA 18098

Index

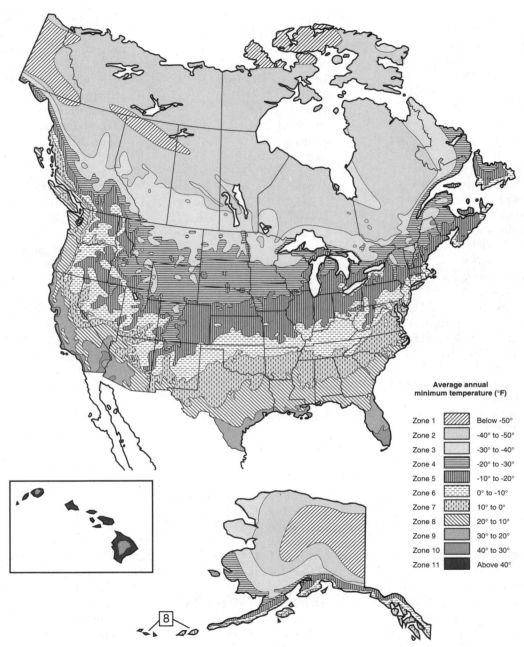

Average annual minimum temperature (°F)

Zone 1		Below -50°
Zone 2		-40° to -50°
Zone 3		-30° to -40°
Zone 4		-20° to -30°
Zone 5		-10° to -20°
Zone 6		0° to -10°
Zone 7		10° to 0°
Zone 8		20° to 10°
Zone 9		30° to 20°
Zone 10		40° to 30°
Zone 11		Above 40°

This map was revised in 1990 to reflect the original USDA map, done in 1965. It is now recognized as the best indicator of minimum temperatures available. Look at the map to find your area, then match its pattern to the key at the right. When you've found your pattern, the key will tell you what hardiness zone you live in. Remember that the map is a general guide; your particular conditions may vary.